Trading Barriers

Trading Barriers

IMMIGRATION AND THE REMAKING OF GLOBALIZATION

Margaret E. Peters

PRINCETON UNIVERSITY PRESS

Princeton and Oxford

Copyright ©2017 by Princeton University Press

Published by Princeton University Press, 41 William Street,
Princeton, New Jersey 08540
In the United Kingdom: Princeton University Press, 6 Oxford Street,
Woodstock, Oxfordshire OX20 1TR

press.princeton.edu

Cover art courtesy of Free Vector Maps

Library of Congress Cataloging-in-Publication Data

Names: Peters, Margaret E., 1980– author.
Title: Trading barriers : immigration and the remaking of globalization /
    Margaret E. Peters.
Description: Princeton : Princeton University Press, [2017] | Includes
    bibliographical references and index.
Identifiers: LCCN 2016020679 | ISBN 9780691174471 (hardcover : acid-free
    paper) | ISBN 9780691174488 (pbk. : acid-free paper)
Subjects: LCSH: Emigration and immigration—Economic aspects. | Emigration
    and immigration—Government policy. | Emigration and immigration—Public
    opinion. | International trade—Social aspects. | Labor and globalization.
Classification: LCC JV6217 .P48 2017 | DDC 325/.1—dc23 LC record
    available at https://lccn.loc.gov/2016020679

British Library Cataloging-in-Publication Data is available

This book has been composed in Sabon Next LT Pro

Printed on acid-free paper. ∞

Typeset by Nova Techset Pvt Ltd, Bangalore, India
Printed in the United States of America

1 3 5 7 9 10 8 6 4 2

To Matthew and Callie

Contents

List of Figures

List of Tables

Acknowledgments

THIS BOOK STARTED LONG AGO as a second-year paper for my PhD at Stanford University. It then turned into a dissertation and now a book. Along the way, my adviser, Judy Goldstein, has been an invaluable mentor, providing resources to hire undergraduate research assistants; commenting on countless drafts of the project; and helping me respond to the feedback I have gotten along the way. I could not have undertaken this research without her help.

I have also been lucky to have the support of many other scholars. Michael Tomz first ignited my interested in international political economy in addition to serving on my dissertation committee. He always came prepared with more questions than I could possibly answer, making the research much stronger. The other members of my dissertation committee also provided important feedback: David Laitin challenged me to dig further on the issue of undocumented immigration; Douglas Rivers provided advice on methodological issues; and Kyle Bagwell provided excellent feedback as my outside chair. David Leblang has been an incredible cheerleader since I was a lowly graduate student from another institution. He met with me at conferences, provided feedback on my work, shared data, and answered methodological questions. Lawrence Broz, Jeff Frieden, Eddy Malesky, Helen Milner, and David Singer, along with Judy Goldstein and David Leblang, attended my book conference at Yale and pushed me to create a much better book.

I also want to thank the many scholars and colleagues who have given me terrific feedback over the years: Lisa Blaydes, Mark Copelovitch, Kathy Cramer, Christina Davis, Alex Debs, Jim Fearon, Gary Freeman, Scott Gehlbach, Steve Haber, Marc Helbling, Yoi Herrera, Greg Huber, Susan Hyde, Simon Jackman, Karen Jusko, Steve Krasner, Andy Kydd, Lisa Martin, Ken Mayer, Nuno Monteiro, Jon Pevehouse, Frances Rosenbluth, Ken Scheve, and the anonymous reviewers at Princeton University Press. Ian Shapiro, through the MacMillan Center for International and Area Studies, provided funding for my book conference and for my research. My book conference was also funded by Jacob Hacker at the Institute for Social and Policy Studies at Yale and the Leitner Program in Political Economy at Yale. This research was also made possible thanks to research support from the University of Wisconsin–Madison, Stanford University, and a Congressional Research Award from the Dirksen Congressional Center.

I had the opportunity to present the book project in its various stages throughout the years and want to thank the audiences at APSA, MPSA, IPES, and ISA as well as at New York University, University of Maryland, University of Pennsylvania, Notre Dame, George Washington University, Princeton University, University of Wisconsin–Madison, Yale University, University of Texas at Austin, University of Michigan (Go Blue!), Harvard Business School, University of Wisconsin–Rock County, UCSD Project on International Affairs, National University Singapore, WZB (Social Science Research Center Berlin), Stanford University, Washington University in St. Louis, and UCLA for all their feedback.

In addition to meeting with me one-on-one, Judy Goldstein also ran an almost weekly adviser meeting in which I presented my work. My fellow advisees, Andrea Abel van Es, Ashley Conner Jester, Moonhawk Kim, and James Morrison, have probably commented on and read more versions of this project than almost anyone. It was through these meetings that I really developed my ideas. After graduating, James Morrison suggested we continue our discussions and created an online political economy roundtable. I could always count on my friends Jeff Colgan, Andrew Kerner, David Steinberg, and Felicity Vabulas, along with James and Ashley, to read my work closely, even when they were reading it for the fourth or fifth time. Through this forum came some of the most helpful, most detailed feedback that I have received.

Several friends helped me along the way. Rikhil Bhavnani, in addition to being a great friend, has let me spitball ideas with him for the past eleven years. Erica Simmons provided critical emotional support and advice. Ellie Powell provided much-needed advice, especially about issues on Congress, and dinners while we were both at Yale. Laurel Harbridge answered every question I had about Congress and congressional voting. Alex Tahk has been my go-to person when I have had methods questions. I also want to thank Claire Adida, John Ahlquist, Kate Baldwin, Deborah Beim, Sarah Bermeo, John Bullock, Dara Cohen, Luke Condra, Ana De La O, Bobby Gulotty, Daniel Kapust, Alex Kuo, Bethany Lacina, Adria Lawrence, Avital Livny, Aila Matanock, Sonia Mittal, Kelly Rader, Molly Roberts, Thania Sanchez, Luke Stein, Rachel Stein, Jed Stiglitz, Julia Tobias, Jeremy Wallace, Jessica Weeks, and Jessica Chen Weiss for all their support and advice over the years.

I could not have finished this project without an army of research assistants. Hans Luders was an amazing jack-of-all-trades RA. He managed my undergraduate coders while I was on maternity leave, allowing me to enjoy my time at home knowing that my research was progressing. He worked on additional coding projects and put in extra time at the end of the project. He read many drafts of the chapters, both providing critical feedback and checking for typos. While I might have been able to finish the project without Hans, his work made it so much better. Lauren Pinson helped me develop the coding scheme for the congressional testimony data and did additional coding work to help me finish the project. She is an incredibly careful researcher and made the project better for her attention to detail. Torey McMurdo, Stephen Moncrief, and Molly Offer-Westort all provided great research assistance late in the project as well. Charlotte Hulme, Elizabeth McGuire, Gautam Nair, and Beth Wellman provided feedback on the penultimate draft, helping shorten the manuscript tremendously. Seth Kolker, Gloria Mejia-Cuellar, Federico Rinco, Radu Simion, and Samone Wheeler coded the trade press documents. At University of Wisconsin–Madison, Dominic DeSapio, Richard Loeza, Vikram Ramesh, Jack van Thomme helped collect all the documents on the National Textile Association and the American Institute of Steel and Iron. At Stanford, Lucia Hennelly, Karine Hoffman, Vinnie Intersimone, Roxana Moussavian, and Minh Dan Vuong helped me collect and code the low-skill immigration policy dataset. My freelance editor, Madeleine Adams, made me sound like me but better.

I have to thank the Western Growers Association, and especially its president, Tom Nassif, and Cory Lunde, who provided me access to their archives, let me use their copier, and even gave me lunch. Soo Yeon Kim provided me an office and introductions to complete my fieldwork in Singapore. I would also like to thank all those in Singapore and the Netherlands who took the time to talk with me.

I also have to thank the amazing folks at Princeton University Press. Eric Crahan has been a wonderful editor, providing helpful feedback on the reviewers' comments. Lauren Lepow is a fantastic copyeditor. The rest of the staff at PUP have been terrific to work with.

My family supported me along the way. My sister Mary let me stay with her to do research at the National Archives. My sister Liz and her husband, Jon, let me live with them on and off in Palo Alto during graduate school. My dad and step-mom, Kat, provided me with moral and financial assistance through graduate school, and my mom, in addition to everything else, has provided feedback on and copyedited several versions of this project.

Last, but not least, I want to dedicate this book to my husband, Matthew, and my daughter, Callie. This book would never have been completed without Matthew's love and support. He helped me keep perspective throughout the process and is the best cheerleader one could have. Callie came at the end of the book-writing process, but her birth spurred me on to finish the book and made me more productive than ever. I hope one day when she is old enough, she'll read this book (OK, the introduction) and think I have made a contribution to the understanding of immigration in the world.

A Note to the Reader on the Online Appendixes

THE ONLINE APPENDIXES are available at http://press.princeton.edu/titles/ 11040.html. Appendix B lists all the sources used to compile the low-skill immigration policy dataset. Appendix C presents additional statistical tests. Appendixes D, E, and F are the codebooks for the congressional testimony, lobbying, and trade association articles data, respectively.

Trading Barriers

CHAPTER 1

Immigration and the Shape of Globalization

MIGRATION WAS ONCE A WAY FOR THE POOR to escape crushing poverty and even an early death. In 1840s and 1850s, more than a million people died in the Great Famine in Ireland, but another million escaped that fate by emigrating to the United States. Thousands more escaped to Great Britain and the British dominions.[1] These migrants also sent money to remaining family members (support known as *remittances*), saving them from starvation as well. Famine struck again in the mid-1980s, this time in Ethiopia and East Africa, killing about a million people. But there were no great waves of Ethiopian immigrants to the United States. Immigration from the whole of Africa to the United States for the entire decade was only about 140,000, or one-tenth what Irish migration had been.[2] Comparatively, it had a much smaller impact as well: Irish immigration increased US population by about 5 percent whereas African migration increased it by less than one-tenth of 1 percent. Instead of getting a chance to escape famine and poverty, these famine victims got a pop song ("We Are the World").

The situation for those escaping conflict, persecution, and poverty has only worsened since the 1980s. In the West, countries have made it much more difficult to claim asylum, contributing to three refugee crises in the first half of the 2010s alone: the Central American child refugee crisis in the United States, the Rohingya refugee crisis in Southeast Asia and Australia, and the Syrian refugee crisis in Europe. Instead of providing a safe haven for those fleeing conflict, persecution, and violence, in all three cases, wealthy countries—including the United States, Australia, and the European Union (EU)—have prevented entry to those seeking a better life. They have foisted the problem on developing countries, essentially paying developing countries (through development aid and other benefits) to host migrants and prevent their entry into developed states. These developing states, however, often have worse human rights records and give migrants fewer rights, leading to additional abuse of an already vulnerable population. Yet the West has not always been so ungenerous to those fleeing conflict. In the 1970s, Western countries resettled 2.5 million of the 3 million people fleeing the Viet Cong. The Syrian Civil War, which had produced

[1] Ferenczi and Willcox (1929).
[2] Office of Immigration Statistics (2006).

almost 5 million refugees by spring 2016, has seen much lower rates of resettlement.[3]

Immigration policy has become more restrictive not only for those fleeing conflict or natural disasters, but also for those seeking a better life for themselves and their families. Today, few developed states open their borders to immigrants, especially low-skill immigrants. Comprehensive immigration reform has stalled yet again in the US Congress over the issue of whether undocumented immigrants, who are almost always low-skill, should have the right to stay in the United States. Old EU member states like Great Britain and the Netherlands are seeking ways to stop low-skill immigration from the new member states—in the case of Great Britain going so far as to vote to leave the EU (what is known as the *Brexit*)— as well as from outside the EU, while pressuring these same new member states into taking more refugees, so they don't have to. Even states like those in the Persian Gulf or Singapore that had recently been relatively open to immigration are seeking to slow the flow of low-skill immigrants.

It was not always this way. The nineteenth century did not have migration crises like those we have seen in the twentieth and twenty-first centuries—with refugees crowded into camps or migrants desperately running across borders hoping not to be caught—because migrants, regardless of their reasons for migrating, were allowed entry to most countries. Immigration to the New World and within Europe, Africa, and Asia was largely unrestricted. Instead of trying to outdo one another in their anti-immigration stance, statesmen argued that "to govern is to populate"[4] and invited the world to send them "your tired, your poor, / Your huddled masses yearning to breathe free."[5] In fact, King George III's unwillingness to allow immigration into the American colonies was the third complaint listed in the Declaration of Independence, far above taxation without representation. Migrants, especially those from Europe, but also from the Middle East and Asia, could legally move to almost any country they wished as long as they had the money. The demand for immigrant labor was so high that even those without the means to relocate often received subsidies from foreign governments or businesses to help them move. This brings us to the first puzzle that this book seeks to answer: Why is immigration, especially for those with fewer skills (what I term *low-skill immigration*), much more restricted today than it was in the nineteenth century or even, for that matter, in the immediate post–World War II period?

---

[3] Eurostat (2016); UNHCR (2016).

[4] "Gobernar es poblar." Attributed to Juan Bautista Alberdi, Argentine political theorist and diplomat. Alberdi (1952).

[5] Lazarus (1883), lines 10–11.

Restrictions on low-skill immigration are even more puzzling when we compare them to policies governing trade and foreign direct investment. The same wealthy countries that have put immigration restrictions in place have greatly lowered trade barriers, including on low-skill-labor-intensive goods such as clothing, toys, and electronics. They have also tolerated, and at times encouraged, businesses making these goods (what we refer to as *firms*) to move production to countries with cheap, low-skill labor (what I term *firm mobility*). As has been much decried even by pro–free trade politicians, this openness to trade and offshoring production has increased competition with foreign workers and led to the loss of "good middle-class" manufacturing jobs. This brings us to a second puzzle about the shape that globalization has taken: Why are politicians today willing to let their constituents compete with foreign labor overseas but not at home?

LOW-SKILL IMMIGRATION AND THE POLITICAL DILEMMA OF GLOBALIZATION

In this book, I argue that the two questions posed in the previous section are related through a political dilemma: wealthy states, those that are likely to receive low-skill immigrants, can either import the labor they need to produce low-skill-intensive goods or import those goods from countries that have low-skill labor in abundance. Similarly, firms can either bring low-skill labor to their factories or move their factories to countries with low-skill labor. What states cannot do, for political reasons, is open low-skill immigration, trade, and firm mobility simultaneously.

I argue that the political behavior of firms creates the political dilemma. Opposition to immigration is omnipresent, even if it is not always organized; thus open low-skill immigration is always a difficult choice for policymakers, one for which they will need support from a powerful interest group. Although there are other pro-immigration groups—immigrants themselves, humanitarians, and cosmopolitans—firms were once the pro-immigration interest group without equal. Given that firms are powerful forces in both democracies and autocracies, they often got what they wanted: an open low-skill immigration policy. Restrictions on low-skill immigration, I argue, are not the product of declining (relative) power of firms—most political analysts still believe that firms have outsized power in the political system—but are due to changing incentives for firms to push for open low-skill immigration. It is trade and firm mobility, along with technology, that have changed these incentives.

As I show in this book, trade and firm mobility affect the number of firms that use low-skill labor, and thus affect the level of support for low-skill immigration. Trade barriers in wealthy countries allow

low-skill-labor-intensive domestic production to expand by sheltering the goods produced domestically from competition with comparable goods produced overseas; with expanded production comes increased demand by firms for immigrant labor. Because firms are a powerful interest group, low-skill immigration policy opens, all else equal. Trade openness—whether due to policy change or to transportation advances that decrease the costs of trade—leads many low-skill-labor-intensive firms to close, taking their support with them. This allows anti-immigration groups, such as nativist organizations or organized labor, or the anti-immigration mass public to have more of a voice in deciding immigration policy, leading to restrictions. Firm mobility—again, whether it is due to policy changes or to technological advances—has a similar effect: the easier it is for a firm to move its factory to another country, the less likely it is to support open immigration at home. Finally, technological development affects low-skill immigration policy: technology allows firms to do more with less labor, reducing their incentive to lobby for immigration.

These changes in the international economy, which were often the result of exogenous policy choices or technological developments, sapped the support of low-skill-intensive firms for immigration at home. It is not the case that the remaining firms do not want more immigration, only that they are unwilling to pay the political costs to get it. My argument, thus, boils down to the options firms have: if firms have other options—the ability to move overseas, or a new technology that will reduce their need for labor—or simply have closed owing to trade, anti-immigration groups have the loudest voice, leading to greater restrictions on immigration. The difference between earlier eras of immigration and today is that the anti-immigration forces are winning because businesses have left the playing field.

My argument on the cause of this political dilemma helps to answer both questions about immigration and globalization. It helps explain the temporal change in low-skill immigration. In the nineteenth and early twentieth centuries, trade was more costly owing to both technological impediments and, in the last quarter of the nineteenth century and the interwar period, relatively high tariffs. Moving production overseas was all but impossible until the early twentieth century, as firms simply did not have the communications technology or managerial know-how to operate production far from headquarters. Even then, only a handful of the largest firms could operate in other countries. The only choice most firms had was to bring labor to their capital.

After World War II, trade barriers fell and shipping costs dropped dramatically with the rise of container ships, allowing trade to flourish. Growing trade, especially with the developing world, led to the closure of many low-skill-labor-intensive manufacturing firms (what is termed *deindustrialization*). For other firms, increased international competition prompted them to increase their use of laborsaving technology or switch product lines to ones that employ less labor. The reduction of capital controls and restrictions on foreign direct investment (FDI) after the end of the Bretton Woods agreement in the early 1970s, along with improvements in communications technology, made offshoring possible. The ability to move overseas gave these firms another option in the face of international competition: if they could not beat the competition, they could join them.

Declining trade barriers and increasing opportunities to offshore production thus explain the over-time variation in low-skill immigration policy: trade forced many firms that produced low-skill-intensive goods in wealthy countries out of business; firm mobility convinced them to join the competition overseas; and technology allowed them to do more with less. Once these firms exited the marketplace, either by closing or by moving overseas, or moved up the value chain, they no longer lobbied for open immigration. Furthermore, when firms closed, moved overseas, or moved up the value chain, they laid off workers, who could now be employed in other industries, especially in the service sector. As these sectors had more native workers, their need for low-skill immigrant labor declined and, with it, their willingness to lobby for low-skill immigration. With less political support for open immigration from firms, policymakers enacted restrictions.

My argument also explains why politicians let their constituents compete with foreign labor overseas but not at home. To some extent policymakers have not really had a choice in the matter; technological developments have, in large part, driven increases in trade and firm mobility. But policymakers have also made decisions not to counteract these technological developments by increasing trade barriers and barriers to moving capital overseas (what are known as *capital controls*). Instead, in the past fifty years, policymakers have decreased both trade barriers and controls on capital. By opening up their economies to foreign goods and by allowing home-country firms to invest in foreign countries, policymakers have shrunk the coalition for open low-skill immigration.

EXISTING ANSWERS TO THE IMMIGRATION PUZZLE

The existing scholarly literature on immigration policy has largely focused on only the first question, trying to explain immigration restrictions. There are three major explanations in the literature, all focused on the opposition to open immigration by either organized interest groups or the mass public. Immigration scholars have focused on anti-immigration groups because they have assumed that firms' willingness to act on immigration is constant. In contrast, I argue that although firms still want open immigration—firms want any and all policies that will increase their profits—their willingness to fight for immigration has changed.[6]

The first explanation focuses on the role of native labor and labor unions as opposition to immigration. Native labor is thought to dislike low-skill immigration owing to its effects on wages. With increased power due to expansions of the franchise after 1900[7] and/or increases in the size and power of unions,[8] labor has increasingly won immigration restrictions. The second major explanation examines the fiscal effects of immigrants and the rise of the welfare state after World War II as the source of restrictions on immigration (what is known as the *fiscal burden argument*).[9] Low-skill immigrants are hypothesized to use the social welfare state more than natives and thus to place a burden on the state. Wealthy natives have to contribute more taxes to pay for these benefits, and poor natives may see their benefits decline as they have to share resources with immigrants. With the rise of the social welfare system, then, both wealthy and poor natives had reasons to oppose low-skill immigration, leading to the increased restrictions in the post–World War II period.

The final explanation, and the one that often appears in the media, is that restrictions are due to culturally based anti-immigrant sentiment (what is known as *nativism*). Theories on the role of nativism suggest that high levels of immigration in the past led to a backlash and closure, as natives and immigrants increasingly came into conflict with each other over jobs, social welfare benefits, neighborhoods, and culture.[10] Alternatively, proponents of this explanation argue that states have identities that make them more or less receptive to immigrants.[11] For nativism to explain restrictions, it must be the case that nativism has increased in the late twentieth and early twenty-first centuries. Yet every era has its own anti-immigration political parties and associations: the 1840s had the Know-Nothing Party in the United States; the mid-1800s had anti-Asian immigration groups in Australia, Canada, New Zealand, and the United States; the 1920s saw the rise of anti–Southern and Eastern European immigration groups throughout the New World; and today we have the Far Right exemplified

---

[6] The conventional wisdom is that firms prefer a system of undocumented immigration in which they can easily exploit immigrant workers. As I argue in chapter 2 in greater detail, firms prefer a stable workforce and so prefer legal immigration to illegal immigration.

[7] For example, see Foreman-Peck (1992) and Hatton and Williamson (2008).

[8] For example, see Briggs (2001).

[9] For example, see Hanson, Scheve, and Slaughter (2007), Hatton and Williamson (2005*a*, *b*), and Money (1999).

[10] Zolberg (1989).

[11] Freeman (1995).

by the National Front in France, the Danish People's Party, the Swiss People's Party, and Donald Trump in the United States. If anything, nativism may have declined some or, at least, it has become socially unacceptable in many circles.[12]

Further, although arguments based on immigration's negative effects on labor market outcomes, the welfare state, and nativism may help explain some of the immigration restrictions, they do not help us solve the other puzzle. As explained by the Stolper-Samuelson theorem, opening trade and allowing capital to move overseas should have had the same negative effect on wages as open immigration, as all expose native workers to competition from labor overseas. Arguments based on the power of labor, then, cannot explain the second puzzle—why states are open to trade and allow firms to move—because they fail to explain why labor has "lost" on trade and firm mobility but has "won" on immigration. The fiscal burden explanation is also incomplete; trade openness and offshoring have led to large-scale layoffs, putting increased pressure on the welfare state. So why do natives worry (or worry more) about immigrants' increased use of the welfare system but not natives'? Finally, if nativism is about preserving the national culture, then foreign influences from trade should also be problematic.

DEFINING LOW-SKILL IMMIGRATION

In the study of migration, migrants are often placed into several different categories: low-skill or high-skill migrants; temporary, circular, long-term, or permanent migrants; the legal or undocumented (irregular); and refugees (or forced migrants), family migrants, or economic migrants. The first categorization, low-skill versus high-skill migrants, focuses on the skills that the migrants have in comparison to populations either in their home country or in the receiving country. The second categorization is based on the length of time the migrant plans to spend away from home. The third categorization examines whether the migrant is legally allowed to be in the receiving state. The final categorization focuses on the reasons migrants leave their homes: they are fleeing violence or persecution; they want to reconnect with family overseas; or they want to improve their economic position. Migrants often fit in many of these categories, and the categorizations themselves are fluid—someone with a high level of skills at home may nonetheless end up in a low-skill job in the receiving country;

---

[12] Freeman (1995). Moreover, Peters and Tahk (2010) find that opposition to immigration in the United States has been relatively stable since 1980, when survey data first began tracking opinions on immigration, ranging between 45 percent and 55 percent; if anything, it has decreased since the early 1990s.

migrants often plan to be away for only a few years but end up staying longer or going back and forth between home and the receiving country; those who enter legally can overstay a visa, and those who enter illegally can gain legal status; those who are persecuted may seek asylum in a country where they can maximize their income; and so on.

The important characteristics for this book are the ones that affect how businesses perceive the usefulness of migrants as workers and the ones that affect whether or not migrants engender anti-immigrant sentiment. In this study, I include all migrants regardless of the duration of their stay in the receiving country. From a business perspective, in most positions, firms would prefer legal, permanent or long-term, potentially circular, migrants over temporary workers, as firms want a stable workforce, so they spend less time and money training new workers. That said, firms would prefer temporary migrants over no migrants, and in many countries temporary migrants become long-term temporary or circular migrants, working for the same employer for years. From the political perspective, temporary migration is usually more politically palatable for some groups, as the migrants can make fewer claims on the state, but often engenders increased hostility from labor organizations, as temporary migrants often are easier to exploit. Thus the length of time migrants are allowed to stay in the country will be part of the political process: business interests will often want permanent or long-term immigration, whereas anti-immigrant groups will fight for shorter stays for migrants.

I also focus less on the motivations for migration—for example, economic migrants vs. refugees—as policy toward noneconomic migrants follows a similar logic. While the politics of noneconomic migration may differ in some respects—countries tend to be more generous to those they label as noneconomic migrants for either humanitarian or geostrategic reasons[13]—overall, the refugee and asylum process follows the same logic as policy toward low-skill economic migrants. Firms, the major actors in this study, are indifferent as to why someone migrated; their concern is only whether or not that person is qualified and willing to take a position, and they are therefore willing to support openness to refugees as a way to get labor. As most noneconomic migrants are low-skill or, at least, tend to be poor, often for the same reasons that made them refugees, they are often lumped in with other low-skill immigrants. Further, those designated as refugees often gain special access to the state and the benefits of membership. Anti-immigrant groups thus try to limit who is designated as a refugee, leading to the discourse about who counts as a "real refugee"

---

[13] For example, during the Cold War, the United States allowed in many more refugees from communist countries than from right-wing dictatorships, even if those dictatorships committed more human rights violations. Rosenblum and Salehyan (2004).

and who is a "bogus refugee." The rules that determine who qualifies for refugee status become part of the political bargain, with firms often lobbying for a more expansive definition, and nativists, labor, and other anti-immigration groups lobbying for a more restrictive one.

The Displaced Persons Act in the United States, signed in 1948, serves as an example of how firms affect the entry of ostensibly noneconomic migrants. In the aftermath of World War II, millions of people were displaced throughout Europe and Asia, causing a humanitarian and political crisis. President Truman sought to resettle many of them in the United States but faced great opposition as members of Congress and their constituents feared the effects of millions of destitute, generally low-skill migrants entering the country. Accordingly, Truman and his allies sought the support of the business community to pass the Displaced Persons Act. By prioritizing the resettlement of those with experience in agriculture and planning to work in agriculture (Section 6(a)) and "persons who are household, construction, clothing, and garment workers, and other workers" (Section 6(b)), the bill garnered support from the American Farm Bureau, according to archival Senate lobbying records, and likely from other business groups as well. In line with the argument of this book, three of the five industries mentioned were nonmobile at the time, and the other two had low productivity. Geostrategic concerns also played a role—the act included those fleeing the communist takeover of Czechoslovakia—as did humanitarian concerns. Yet the fingerprints of anti-immigration sentiment that had militated for restrictions on economic immigration prior to the war can be seen on this legislation as well: the act did not pertain to people displaced by the conflict in Asia nor to those fleeing the communist takeover of China or, later, Korea.

While policies on refugees and asylum seekers have become more humanitarian since the 1940s and 1950s, with less weight placed on the skills refugees possess, they have become more restrictive in most countries over time, especially since the end of the Cold War. Both the more humanitarian nature and the greater restrictions on refugees and asylum seekers may be due to decreased business interest in immigration in general—most refugee and asylum policies were crafted in the 1970s and 1980s, when business interest in low-skill immigration had already greatly decreased. Business thus has less incentive to get involved in refugee and asylum policy, which gave anti-immigrant forces more weight. Without the strong backing of either strategic interests or business groups, refugee and asylum policies become more restrictive. Thus I argue, and show with evidence, that refugee and asylum policy process follows the same logic that policy toward low-skill economic migrants follows, albeit with an additional push for openness from humanitarian and geostrategic interests.

I also include illegal (irregular/undocumented) immigration in this study where possible. Defining what forms of immigration are illegal is also part of the political process. In the nineteenth century, there were few restrictions and thus little illegal immigration; it was only with the advent of greater restrictions that illegal immigration proliferated. Moreover, because undocumented immigrants often work, they can be an important source of labor for firms. To guard against the possibility that a preference by firms for undocumented labor has driven the increased restrictions on immigrant admission, I include enforcement of immigration laws in this study.[14]

While I do not exclude migrants by length of stay or reasons for migrating, I do exclude high-skill migrants from this study. While I was researching migration for this book, it became clear to me that the politics of high-skill migration are quite different from the politics of low-skill migration. Although there are some people who oppose both high- and low-skill immigration, most natives are much more supportive of high-skill immigration.[15] This preference for high-skill immigrants is not a new feature of politics, either. In the United States, for example, most of the nativist sentiment has been targeted at low-skill migrants: in the 1840s, the target was Irish immigrants; in the 1860s–1880s, it was Chinese immigrants; in the early 1900s, it was Southern and Eastern European immigrants; and today it is Hispanic immigrants, all of whom were the least-educated immigrant group on average. Politically, it has always been easier for a politician to support a more open policy toward high-skill than toward low-skill immigration.

Policymakers often treat these flows differently when they craft policies, as well. Policymakers approach high-skill immigration as a global competition for talent. This has become increasingly true since World War II, as many states have enacted immigration policies, such as points systems, special visas like H-1B visas in the United States or Blue Cards in Europe, and investor visas, that grant much easier access to high-skill migrants in hopes of enticing them to move. The politics of high-skill immigration, then, may be a very different beast from the politics of low-skill immigration.

Although I exclude high-skill immigrants, this exclusion does not affect the majority of those who would like to migrate. The vast majority of actual migrants and *potential migrants*, those who would like to migrate if they were legally allowed to do so, have been low-skill.[16] Only 23.5 percent

---

[14] Ideally, I would directly measure undocumented immigration, but, as it is an illegal act, data on this are scarce.

[15] Goldstein and Peters (2014) and Hainmueller and Hiscox (2007, 2010).

[16] Hatton and Williamson (2005*b*).

of migrants have a high level of education; even this relatively high level of skilled migration is endogenous to the policies in this study—without immigration barriers, the share of low-skill migrants would increase greatly.[17]

Moreover, my argument generates empirical implications for high-skill immigration. Just as trade, firm mobility, and technology adoption have greatly decreased the size of the low-skill-intensive sector in wealthy countries, these same factors have led to an increase in the size of the high-skill-intensive sector. We might expect, then, that there should be an increase in support for *high-skill* immigration from *high-skill*-intensive firms. I examine this hypothesis with lobbying data from the United States in chapter 4. Yet we have reason to believe that this hypothesis may not hold true for long. Since the expansion of the Internet, many high-skill jobs do not need to be geographically located in any one country.[18] Companies that rely on high-skill labor therefore may have less need for high-skill immigrant labor over time, leading to decreased support for high-skill immigration and restrictions. As the politics of high-skill immigration differs from that of low-skill immigration, I leave this hypothesis to scholars as an area for future research.

THE IMPORTANCE OF IMMIGRATION POLICY AS AN ECONOMIC FOREIGN POLICY

My argument differs from most theories of immigration policy because it brings political economy back into immigration. I treat immigration policy as an economic foreign policy, affected by trade barriers and firm mobility. Immigration scholars have assumed firms' willingness to act on immigration to be constant and have focused, instead, on the factions in the polity that oppose immigration. In contrast, I argue that although firms still want open immigration—firms want any and all policies that will increase their profits—their willingness to fight for immigration has changed. This explanation provides a more complete picture of the politics of immigration.

For the broader literature on international political economy (IPE), this book brings *firms* back into the picture. Although firms and interest groups had a central place in the early days of IPE, more recently scholars have turned to examining individual preferences. In part, they did this because it is relatively easy to conduct survey experiments, which allow the researcher

---

[17] United Nations Development Program (2009).

[18] For example, ten of the top fifteen offshorable jobs on Blinder's offshorability index are high-skill positions. Blinder (2007).

to show that their treatment changed opinion. But by examining individual attitudes, we have missed a critical driver of policy: firms. In many areas of IPE, scholars have, like immigration scholars, treated firm preferences and willingness to lobby as relatively static. Recent scholarship has begun to examine firm preferences again, often using the insights of "new" new trade theory, which examines how firms may develop different preferences based on their productivity.[19] I, too, rely on theories of heterogeneous firms from "new" new trade theory to understand the preferences of firms, but I argue that firms' preferences for immigration vary based on their ability to move overseas, which is in part driven by productivity but also by the nature of their product and changes in their environment.

My argument challenges the way scholars have examined international political economy through open economy politics (OEP). OEP derives individuals' preferences over economic policy based on their position in the international economy, examines how domestic institutions aggregate these preferences, and then integrates international bargaining over policy when necessary.[20] Yet this manner of examining economic policy formation relies little on whether the economy is open or not because it often fails to account for how different foreign economic policies interact.[21] Many scholars have examined trade *or* capital *or* (much more rarely) migration; few examine how these areas affect one another.[22] I argue that, as trade, capital, and migration policies can serve as substitutes or complements, we need to examine their interactions in order to gain a better understanding of how foreign economic policy is formed.

My analytical framework has implications beyond immigration policy as well. It clarifies how globalization may affect a range of domestic policies. Some argue that trade and firm mobility have led to a race to the bottom on tax, social, and environmental policy, as states lower tax burdens and weaken regulatory standards so that firms can compete. But the evidence is mixed. It may well be the case that trade openness and firm mobility affect firm lobbying on these issue areas as well. In the realm of environmental policy, trade openness and firm mobility allow developed nations to outsource environmentally destructive production to the developing world. Once "dirty" firms close or move to the developing world, it may be the case that the remaining firms are relatively "green" and

---

[19] Melitz (2003).

[20] Lake (2009, 225).

[21] This critique is similar to Oatley (2011) in that we both argue that scholars need to take more seriously the international situation in which policy is made; however, I am concerned about how one policy affects another, whereas Oatley is more concerned about whether states can be examined apart from consideration of the international system.

[22] Notable exceptions are Copelovitch and Pevehouse (2013), Leblang (2010), and Singer (2010).

environmental standards can be raised without hurting the bottom line of the remaining firms.

In addition to its theoretical contribution, this book brings a trove of new data to bear on the question of immigration policy. Existing scholarship has focused on the post–World War II period and has thus been unable to explain the long-run trends of the two centuries of globalization. In contrast, I examine original data on sectors' preferences on immigration, sectors' lobbying, policymakers' decision making, and immigration policy, with much of the data spanning the two centuries of globalization. Moreover, the existing literature has focused on a handful of cases, mostly those in Europe or the United States, Canada, and Australia. I expand this sample to the Persian Gulf and East Asia, allowing us to gain a more comprehensive view of immigration today.

Finally, for policymakers and those who care about increasing the ability of people to migrate from the developing to the developed world for normative or familial reasons, this book suggests that they need to forge new coalitions on immigration. Policymakers and activists used to be able to count on low-skill-intensive firms to act as allies when they wanted to open immigration. But now, the economic rationale for open low-skill immigration has greatly decreased; those allied firms no longer care about immigration at home or they no longer exist. This may mean that it will be very difficult, although not impossible, to secure greater openness on low-skill immigration. Moreover, as more middle-income countries develop, they too will see the loss of their low-skill-intensive firms as they open to trade or offshore to countries with even lower labor costs. These countries are also likely to close their doors to low-skill immigration. At a time when open borders would do much to decrease poverty[23] and provide a safe haven for those fleeing conflict, closed borders will likely be the default.

THE PLAN OF THE BOOK

My argument proceeds in three steps: first, trade, firm mobility, and productivity change firms' preferences over immigration and their willingness to support low-skill immigration, which, second, makes it harder for policymakers to support low-skill immigration, which, third, leads to restrictions on low-skill immigration. In chapter 2, I further elucidate the argument as well as the alternative explanations from the literature. At the end of the chapter, I discuss the empirical implications of my argument—what we expect to see if my argument is correct—for firms and sectors, policymakers, and immigration policy.

[23] Clemens (2009).

In chapter 3, I test the implications of my argument at the most macro level: low-skill immigration policy across countries. I argue that increases in trade openness and firm mobility should lead to increased restrictions on immigration.[24] To test my argument, I use an original dataset on low-skill immigration policy from the nineteenth century through the twenty-first and find that the data strongly support the implications of my argument.[25]

As, in chapter 3, the hypothesized relationship among trade, firm mobility, and low-skill immigration is shown to hold over very different states and many time periods, chapters 4 and 5 dig deeper into the causal chain of my argument. They show how trade, firm mobility, and productivity change firms' preferences and willingness to lobby on low-skill immigration, and how policymakers react to these changes in the United States. Having established that the entire sequence of my argument holds for the United States, in chapter 6 I show that each component of my theory fits the data for two very different countries, Singapore and the Netherlands. Chapter 7 returns to the cross-national data to test the empirical observations of the alternative explanations; it shows that the data support my argument even when we account for these alternatives. The concluding chapter considers the implications of my argument for other areas of international relations.

[24] I cannot test the implications about productivity or the intermediate steps of my argument at this level because the data do not exist.

[25] Appendix A provides information on the collection and coding of these data.

CHAPTER 2

Immigration, Trade, and Firm Mobility: A Political Dilemma

IN THE NINETEENTH CENTURY, countries in the New World had few restrictions on immigration; today these countries tightly regulate the entry of low-skill migrants and police their borders. In the 1950s and 1960s, millions of Southern Europeans, Turks, and North Africans moved to Northern Europe as guest workers (temporary, low-skill labor migrants); today a migrant without high-level skills who is not a citizen of the European Union has little possibility of entering Northern European states.[1] Even in the Persian Gulf, where low-skill immigrants were welcomed historically, restrictions on low-skill immigration have increased in recent years.

Yet while restrictions on immigration have increased, these same countries have opened their borders to foreign goods and have allowed their firms to move production overseas. I argue that these flows of people, goods, and capital are connected. Modern globalization—the increased ability to trade and produce goods in any country in the world—and laborsaving technology have changed firms' willingness to lobby for low-skill immigration. In the developed world trade openness has led to the closure of firms that use low-skill labor, especially smaller, less productive firms. The ability to produce goods in almost any country in the world, what I call *firm mobility*, has led firms—especially larger, more productive firms—to move overseas when production is no longer profitable at home. When firms close or move, they take their support for immigration with them. Laborsaving technology has allowed firms to do more with less labor, reducing their support for open immigration. Furthermore, when firms adopt laborsaving technology, move overseas, or close, they lay off native workers, pushing down wages throughout the economy. All other firms, including firms in the nontradable sector, can use these laid-off workers, decreasing their incentive to push for open immigration.

Immigration policy, then, is in something of a political dilemma with free trade and firm mobility. Political support for open immigration for low-skill immigrants relies on restrictions on the movement of goods and firms. Policymakers can choose to open their doors to low-skill immigrants

---

[1] The exception to some extent has been Syrians fleeing civil war, yet as of 2015 only half of those who had applied for asylum had been granted refugee status or temporary protected status. Eurostat (2016).

but keep trade relatively restricted and keep firms at home, or they can choose to open trade and/or firm mobility and restrict immigration. There may be moments when all three policies are open, as the effects of trade and firm mobility may take a few years to affect firms. Yet, as I show in chapters 3–6, these moments do not last long; open trade and firm mobility quickly undermine support for open immigration.

In this chapter, I develop the theoretical framework to understand this dilemma, building the foundations of the argument from both classic Ricardian trade theory, in which countries trade goods in different industries (interindustry trade) based on the country's comparative advantage, and "new" new trade theory, in which countries trade different varieties of goods in the same industry (intraindustry trade) based on the productivity level of the firm. I then discuss alternative explanations. The chapter concludes with the observable implications of my argument, along with the implications of the alternative theories, which are tested in the empirical chapters that follow.

IMMIGRATION AND THE DILEMMA OF GLOBALIZATION

I argue that trade openness and firm mobility decrease political support for low-skill immigration in wealthy countries. Although almost all countries experience some immigration, my argument applies especially to states to which many immigrants want to move—states that are wealthy relative to other states in their region or the world. These states must decide whether and how to control their borders.

Low-skill immigration and trade are *political* substitutes owing to their similar effects on low-skill-intensive sectors of the economy. In classic trade theory, states trade based on their comparative advantage. Wealthy states are abundant in capital and high-skill labor; they export goods that depend on those factors in their production (*capital-intensive* and *high-skill-intensive goods*). By contrast, developing countries are abundant in low-skill labor and export goods that are produced with low-skill labor (*low-skill-intensive goods*). When states open their borders to trade, the export sector, in which they have a comparative advantage, will expand as there is greater demand for these goods from overseas, and the import sector, in which they are at a comparative disadvantage, will contract as there is more competition for these goods from overseas. For wealthy countries, this means that the low-skill-intensive sectors of the economy will contract. These are the same sectors that employ low-skill immigrants. When firms in these sectors close, they take their support for low-skill immigration with them. Without businesses' support for immigration, anti-immigration supporters gain relatively more power, and policymakers restrict immigration to appeal to these forces.

The contraction of the low-skill tradable sector (e.g., manufacturing and agriculture) also has secondary effects on the low-skill nontradable sector (e.g., construction and services). When firms in the tradable sector close, they lay off both their native and their immigrant workers. The native workers can now be employed in the nontradable sectors. These firms too lose their need for low-skill immigrant labor—they might still like additional immigrant labor, but it becomes a lower priority for them—and they become less likely to support low-skill immigration. Policymakers can thus restrict immigration to make others in the polity, including native labor and those who oppose immigration, better off without making nontradable firms worse off.

The converse also holds: greater trade restrictions should lead to more support for low-skill immigration. With the increase in restrictions, more firms will enter the low-skill-intensive sector, and/or existing firms will expand to fill the demand that was once covered by imports. As these sectors expand, wages for low-skill workers increase. Wages for low-skill labor in nontradable sectors will also increase, assuming that labor can easily move between sectors. Together the wage increases lead firms in both tradable and nontradable low-skill-intensive sectors to increase their support for low-skill immigration. Assuming that firms are an important group in any polity, regardless of its government structure, low-skill immigration should become more open. Thus trade and low-skill immigration are substitutes: if trade is restricted, immigration for low-skill immigrants should open, whereas if trade opens, immigration policy for these migrants should be restricted.

In contrast, if immigration policy is driving trade policy, we would expect to see trade and immigration as complements rather than substitutes. Immigration lowers wage costs for firms, making them more competitive. As their costs drop, these firms can remain in business even given a lower price. Low-skill-intensive firms, then, do not oppose more open trade to the same degree they would if immigration were restricted. In contrast, if immigration is closed, import-competing firms are less competitive and favor more restrictive trade. If trade opens first, immigration and trade should be substitutes, but if immigration opens first, they should be complements.

Even if immigration is open, it may be challenging for *both* trade and immigration to remain open. As trade opens further, low-skill-intensive firms face greater foreign competition. In the extreme case of no trade barriers, low-skill-intensive firms in wealthy countries would need immigration open enough that wages of low-skill workers at home fell to the level of wages in developing countries.[2] This level of open immigration is

---

[2] Assuming firms in wealthy states have higher levels of productivity, the wages may not need to fall all the way to the developing country wage, but they would still need to fall.

probably impossible to maintain politically. Once the reduction in trade barriers subjected domestic firms to competition that they could not meet, firms would begin to close, reducing support for immigration and leading to restrictions. Thus it is very difficult for policymakers to maintain political support for both open trade and open immigration.

Firm mobility also acts as a substitute for low-skill immigration. But while policymakers have significant control over trade, they have much less control over many aspects of firm mobility—for example, the technical ability to move production or other states' willingness to allow investments. There are, however, some factors affecting firm mobility that the policymaker can control. For example, policymakers can reduce their currency's convertibility, which makes moving money from the parent company to the subsidiary more difficult, thereby making it less attractive for home-country firms to establish plants overseas; or they might sign a bilateral investment treaty with another country, which would give firms greater legal protections in the face of potential expropriation, smoothing the path for home-country firms to invest in overseas production.

With firm mobility, firms can either bring low-skill workers to their factories in wealthy countries or take their factories to the low-skill workers in developing countries. Which option they choose will depend on the relative ease of moving the factory versus bringing in immigrant labor. If the industry is immobile, firms will support open immigration. For example, when the Central Pacific Railroad built its section of the transcontinental railroad in the United States, it had to bring labor (much of it from China) to the building site. Today, many industries are mobile across international borders, and firms in these sectors take their factories to China rather than bringing Chinese immigrants to their home countries. As with trade, greater firm mobility has spillover effects to nonmobile sectors. When mobile firms move overseas, they lay off native workers who can work in nonmobile sectors, leading these sectors to decrease their support for low-skill immigration, as well. As it becomes easier for firms to move overseas, firms' support for low-skill immigration at home declines. In contrast, if it becomes more difficult for firms to move overseas, they will be more likely to spend political capital, which includes actual capital but also time, goodwill, and other nonfinancial resources, on immigration, and immigration should become more open, all else being equal.

Unlike immigration and trade, immigration policy and firm mobility always act as substitutes. Open immigration should make firms more competitive, which would make them less likely to move overseas. More restrictions on immigration, in contrast, raise the costs of producing at home and make firms more likely to move overseas.

It is likely that trade openness will have a greater effect than firm mobility on immigration policy. Moving a factory overseas is a

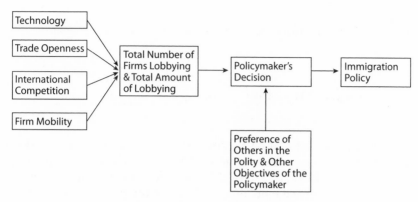

Figure 2.1: Overview of the Argument.

capital-intensive venture. As we know from "new" new trade theory, only the most productive firms, which also tend to be the largest, will be able to afford the costs of moving. Firm mobility, then, has a direct effect on a relatively small number of large firms, but their exit, and concomitant layoffs, reverberate throughout the home economy. Policymakers, then, are left with a choice: to open immigration for low-skill immigrants but keep trade and firm mobility restricted, or to allow open trade and/or firm mobility but restrict immigration of low-skill workers.

FIRMS AND LOBBYING: THE FOUNDATION OF IMMIGRATION POLICY

Firms' willingness to lobby for immigration is the foundation of the political dilemma that policymakers face. Figure 2.1 provides an overview of my argument. Policymakers determine immigration policy based on the total amount of lobbying on immigration by firms, as well as other groups' preferences and the policymakers' own objectives. I assume that any firm that wants to lobby can lobby either on its own or as part of a larger organization.[3] Firms base their lobbying strategy on the benefit they receive from a policy, the probability they can get that policy passed, and the costs, in terms of both money and time, of obtaining that policy.

Firms have heterogenous preferences on low-skill immigration, and these preferences are affected by what other options they have for production besides using low-skill labor. Table 2.1 shows this heterogeneity.

---

[3] I abstract away from the collective action costs. We can think of collective action costs as part of the costs of lobbying: if collective action costs are high, the cost of lobbying will increase.

TABLE 2.1
Sources of Firms' Heterogeneity of Preferences on Low-Skill Immigration.

		Mobility	
		Low	High
Skill	Low-skill	Supports immigration	Indifferent
intensity	High-skill	Indifferent	Indifferent

The first cleavage is based on the low-skill labor intensity of production: firms that use much low-skill labor will favor open low-skill immigration, whereas firms that use little low-skill labor will be indifferent. As technology advances, more and more firms will move from the low-skill-intensive sector to the high-skill-intensive sector. The second cleavage is mobility across international borders: sectors that are relatively immobile are more likely to support open immigration than are sectors that can move overseas. As firm mobility increases, more firms move from the immobile category to the mobile category.

Trade acts on these preferences by changing the number of firms in the low-skill-intensive, low-mobility sector. Trade restrictions increase the number of firms in this category and allow these firms to grow in size. Trade openness both decreases the number of firms in this category and shrinks the size of existing firms.

The total amount of lobbying on immigration by firms—both the total number of firms lobbying and how much each firm lobbies—will be based on the number of firms that use low-skill labor. When low-skill-intensive firms close owing to trade competition, when they move overseas, or when they adopt laborsaving technology, support for open immigration will drop. This, in turn, allows anti-immigrant forces to have more influence over immigration policy and leads to more immigration restrictions.

Policymakers and Firms in a World without Trade or Firm Mobility

Imagine a country in a world with no international trade and where firms are unable to move production overseas. In this country there is a rational policymaker, either an elected official in a democracy or an autocratic leader, who wishes to stay in office. To do so, she needs the support both of firms and other interest groups but must balance what interest groups want with the interests of the unorganized mass public. By lobbying (or, alternatively, spending *political capital*), firms are expressing their likelihood of supporting the policymaker given the choice of immigration policy, with, for example, campaign contributions, votes from their employees, or bribes for the policymaker or key members of her government.[4] The closer the policy is to the firm's ideal policy, the more support the policymaker will receive from that firm.[5]

I model firms' interactions with policymakers on the American style of lobbying. Lobbying may look different in other countries. In other democracies, businesses are often tied to political parties or have official channels through which to influence policy. For example, in the Netherlands, firms and labor advise the government on policy through the Social and Economic Council (SER). In autocracies, policymakers often rely on powerful firms to stay in power or take bribes in return for policies that organized interests want. Thus although in this discussion we can imagine firms paying lobbyists to stalk the halls of Congress, the results generalize to a more inclusive definition of lobbying that encompasses all the activities that firms and other organized interests undertake in hopes of influencing policy.

The Policymaker's Decision-Making Process

The policymaker chooses an immigration policy based on the lobbying by firms and other actors, the mass public's opinion, and the economic effects of the policy. The policymaker sets an immigration policy with a target number of immigrants in mind, and she can, more or less, effectively implement this target.[6] A policymaker will receive political capital, including money, time, and effort, from firms and other interest groups based on the immigration policy she implements—capital that can be used to run a reelection campaign or to reward supporters. Immigration policy also affects the amount of tax revenue she receives and can redistribute to ensure her reelection: greater immigration will lead to greater production and more tax revenue, and lower immigration will lead to less production and less tax revenue. Immigration policy affects mass attitudes toward

---

[4] For simplicity, I assume that organized interests cannot use their lobbying dollars to support a political rival if the policymaker enacts a policy they don't like. The results hold if interest groups can contribute to a rival; the policymaker would take into account the probability that the rival would win in the next election or would be able to overthrow her with this support given the policy choice.

[5] To make sure that the policymaker enacts the policy she says she will, I assume that firms give political capital at the same time as the policy is enacted and that firms could always withdraw support if the policymaker reneged. Similarly, the policymaker can always change the policy if the firms and other organized interests renege.

[6] Historically, policymakers have been able to pass very restrictive policies, including deporting large numbers of people to reduce the number of immigrants, and have been able to pass very open policies, including recruiting immigrants, and paying for their transportation to increase the number of immigrants. Additionally, given differential in incomes in the world, policymakers have been able to attract migrants as long as the economic incentives are right, something that is likely to continue.

the policymaker as well: immigrants are thought to lower wages, use social services more than natives, engage in crime, and harm the national culture. More immigration leads to increased anti-immigrant sentiment and decreased support for the policymaker. Essentially then, when deciding an immigration policy, the policymaker is trading off political support and tax revenue from firms for support from a generally anti-immigrant public.

Firms' Decision-Making Process

When firms decide whether and how much to lobby, they take into account the policymaker's need to balance political support from firms with support from the mass public and other interest groups. In their ideal world, immigration would be completely open, so that labor costs would be as low as possible.[7] But firms know that they do not live in their ideal world; instead, they must react to the society they live in.

Unlike what is seen in models of trade, immigration affects firms through the costs of making their product rather than the price they receive for it. Scholars disagree about whether immigrants are substitutes for low-skill natives, leading to lower wages for natives, or complements for low-skill natives, leading to higher wages for natives but overall lower labor costs for businesses.[8] If immigrants substitute for native labor, increased immigration directly lowers costs by lowering wages. If immigrants complement native labor, low-skill immigrant labor can be used to perform the least-skilled tasks, and low-skill native labor can perform tasks demanding more skill. The native labor, then, is used more productively instead of being "wasted" on very low-skill tasks. Overall, firms' wage bills decrease as labor is used more productively. For simplicity, I assume that immigration lowers the wage that the firm pays for low-skill labor and thereby lowers the firm's costs.

I assume that firms operate in a perfectly competitive market. Firms are price takers—they have no power to set their price and instead must price their goods at the same price as the rest of the firms in the market—and at the equilibrium level of production the marginal cost to produce must be equal to the price. Firms will lobby for immigration as long as the cost of lobbying for an additional immigrant is less than or equal to the cost savings they will receive for an additional worker in the economy.[9]

---

[7] I assume that firms do not have noneconomic preferences over the immigration policy.

[8] See Borjas, Grogger, and Hanson (2008) and Longhi, Nijkamp, and Poot (2005) on the debate.

[9] For ease of understanding, firms lobby individually; in the real world some firms lobby individually, some firms lobby as part of an industry association, and some firms do both. If firms need to join an industry association to lobby, we can include the collective action

Firms that need more low-skill workers, then, will lobby more for low-skill immigration, as they will receive a greater benefit for it.[10]

Immigration Policy in the World without Trade or Firm Mobility

The level of immigration policy in this case will depend on two quantities: the total economy-wide need for low-skill labor, which affects how much firms are willing to lobby for immigration, and the level of anti-immigrant sentiment in the rest of the polity. From the policymaker's side, if political support from firms increases, all else equal, she will open immigration; analogously, if firms want a more open policy, they have to provide more support. If the total amount of political capital the policymaker receives stays the same, but the level of anti-immigrant sentiment increases (decreases), the policy will become more (less) restrictive. In a similar fashion, if anti-immigrant sentiment increases (decreases), firms will have to lobby more (less) to get the same policy. At low levels of anti-immigrant sentiment, the benefit of immigration still outweighs the costs, and firms increase their total lobbying effort to keep the same policy. As anti-immigrant sentiment increases, there comes a point where the cost of lobbying outweighs the benefits. At this point, there will be a more restrictive immigration policy. In contrast, if anti-immigrant sentiment recedes, or if pro-immigrant sentiment increases, marginal firms will be more likely to lobby on immigration, and immigration should become more open.[11]

In short, policymakers balance firm support for immigration with the preferences of the rest of the polity. If firm support increases, the policymaker opens immigration; if firm support declines, she restricts immigration. If there is more anti-immigrant sentiment, policymakers are likely to restrict immigration—which, if anti-immigrant sentiment is high enough, leads the marginal firm to choose not to lobby and either to spend that money on its business or to close.[12] Conversely, if

---

costs in their total lobbying costs; each lobbying dollar will be less effective because some percentage of it must go to the industry association rather than the policymaker. Nonetheless, all the comparative statics results still hold.

[10] In a "new" new trade theory approach, firms have different levels of productivity. Firms that are very productive need much less labor and tend to need high-skill labor (Helpman, Itskhoki, and Redding, 2009), making them less likely to lobby for low-skill immigration. Firms with lower levels of productivity use more low-skill labor and will be more likely to lobby.

[11] If anti-immigrant sentiment is below the point where the costs of lobbying are lower than the benefits, a decrease in anti-immigrant sentiment will allow firms to spend less to get the same policy.

[12] If we allowed for a multidimensional policy space, firms could also choose to lobby on another issue like tax policy that would reduce their costs.

anti-immigrant sentiment recedes or pro-immigration sentiment increases, the policymaker will be more likely to open immigration, knowing that this time marginal firms will lobby.

The Effect of Technology on Firms' Willingness to Lobby

If laborsaving technology is available, firms could choose to adopt it rather than lobby for increased immigration. In this case, firms will compare the cost and benefits of technology adoption to the cost and benefits of lobbying, choosing the one that provides greater cost savings. As the price of laborsaving technology decreases, technology becomes a better deal and firms will be less likely to lobby. Analogously, if anti-immigrant sentiment is high (low), firms will be more (less) likely to adopt technology because it will be relatively cheaper (more expensive) compared to lobbying.[13] Alternatively, firms may adopt (and, in some cases, develop) technology in response to a chosen policy if that policy did not provide enough immigrants to keep the firm in business, which will make them less likely to lobby for low-skill immigration in the future.

Technology adoption will also affect whether firms lobby in the future. Firms that are high-skill-intensive or are very productive—that is, those that need few workers—get little benefit from an additional low-skill immigrant; therefore, the costs of lobbying are likely to outweigh the benefits, making these firms less likely to lobby. As more and more firms adopt technology, the total demand for low-skill workers decreases—reducing the wage for these workers—which makes other firms less willing to lobby for low-skill immigration. Because wages will decline with the adoption of technology, the policymaker can reduce immigration to the point where wages will return to their level prior to the adoption of technology. This makes the firms that did not adopt the technology as well-off as before, while reducing the harm the technology did to natives' wages and making anti-immigrant elements of society happier. All else being equal, then, as the proportion of high-skill-intensive firms in the state increases, immigration will become more restrictive.[14] An additional observable implication from the technology-adoption effect

---

[13] Lewis (2011) finds that firms substitute technology for expensive native labor in areas of low immigration, and in areas with greater immigration firms substitute immigrant labor for native labor, illustrating the trade-off between immigration and technology adoption.

[14] If we allow for oligopoly, increasing immigration conveys an advantage to firms using more labor. Low-skill-intensive firms can lower their price and collect a greater share of the market, reducing the profitability of the high-skill-intensive firms. High-skill-intensive firms may want to keep their competitive edge by limiting the availability of cheap labor and give political contributions for immigration restrictions.

tested in chapter 4 is that with a greater proportion of high-skill-intensive firms, there should be increased lobbying for *high-skill* immigration.

Firms' Willingness to Lobby, Trade Openness, and International Competition

Trade openness and international competition have two countervailing effects: they increase firms' influence over immigration, but also increase the proportion of firms in the country that are more productive and capital/high-skill intensive. Which of these effects prevails in the short run depends on the policymaker's choices; in the long run, the changing composition of the economy will dominate, leading to a more restrictive immigration policy. Trade openness and international competition affect firms in two ways depending on whether trade is opened to countries with different endowments of capital and labor (explained by the Ricardo-Viner model) or to those with the same endowments (explained by the "new" new trade theory model). I begin by examining what happens to firms' support for immigration when trade opens under the Ricardo-Viner model.

Assume that there is some shock that increases trade openness or international competition. Under the Ricardo-Viner model, trade openness in developed countries leads to an increase in prices for the tradable goods produced by high-skill-intensive firms and a decrease in prices for the tradable goods produced by low-skill-intensive firms. The high-skill-intensive firms will increase production, taking advantage of the higher prices, while the low-skill-intensive firms are threatened with closure owing to the lower prices. As prices for low-skill-intensive goods decrease, these firms have to decrease their costs or close (I refer to these firms as *threatened firms*).

Threatened firms are unable to be profitable using the same technology given the cost of labor after the trade shock and have three choices as to how to respond: adopt technology that makes them high-skill-intensive; lobby for more immigration; or close, paying out what capital they can to the firms' owners and creditors. Adopting laborsaving technology will allow the firm to produce profitably at the new price.[15] As earlier, firms will choose between adopting technology and lobbying based on the relative cost of each action. The trade shock then should induce some firms to adopt laborsaving technology. As more firms adopt technology, they will be less likely to lobby for open immigration, and the policymaker can restrict immigration.

If firms in low-skill intensive tradable firms close, this decreases support for open immigration from the *nontradable* sector as well. When firms

---

[15] The firm could also adopt technology that allows it to produce a new product that uses less low-skill labor and the effects would be the same.

in the low-skill-intensive tradable sector close, they lay off their workers. This leads to a lower wage for low-skill workers. The policymaker then can restrict immigration, decreasing the supply of labor so that the wage remains the same as it was before the change in trade openness, and the same number of *native* workers are employed as before, without making these sectors worse off. We expect, nonetheless, that firms and industry associations in these sectors may still lobby for open immigration in the near term, since more immigration would lower their costs, regardless of the level of trade.[16] As we will see in chapter 4, that nontradable firms and industry associations are the major supporters of open immigration today is a result of less lobbying by the tradable sector as firms in these industries have closed.

Assuming there is no laborsaving technology that the firm can use to cut costs, the firm can either lobby for immigration, in hopes of lowering its wage bill, or close. Realizing that the firm will close unless immigration is opened, the policymaker may be more willing to open immigration than she was prior to the trade shock. If the firm closes, the policymaker loses any political capital that firm was paying before the shock, as well as its tax revenue. But the policymaker could restrict immigration without making any other firms worse off—the other firms could use the native laid-off workers[17]—while making native labor and other anti-immigration groups happier.[18] Policymakers, then, have to balance their desire for political capital and tax revenue with their desire to please anti-immigration constituencies.

Although the policymaker may be willing to increase immigration when trade is only slightly or moderately open, she may realize that it's not in her interest to continue to subsidize firms at higher levels of openness. Imagine that, given the new level of trade openness, all low-skill-intensive industries would close, or, alternatively, new communications and transportation technologies have meant that sectors that used to be nontradable are now tradable. The policymaker now has to try to support an even larger set of firms, increasing immigration so that the wage decreases to the world wage, which would greatly increase anti-immigration sentiment. At this point, it's not worthwhile for the policymaker to continue to support these firms with

[16] If we assume perfect competition and that firms in nontradable industries all use the same technology, nontradable firms should not care about immigration. Immigration lowers the wage bill for all firms equally; therefore, none gain an advantage from it.

[17] I assume that all immigrant workers would return to their home country.

[18] I assume that even though high-skill-intensive firms are likely to increase production owing to the greater openness of trade, they are unlikely to utilize all the laid-off labor. Empirically, rising wage inequality due to increases in productivity and trade seem to bear this out. See, for example, Feenstra and Hanson (1996) or Kremer (2006).

increased immigration, and the firms will close, allowing her to restrict immigration.[19]

Larger increases to trade openness, then, lead to greater immigration restrictions as the amount of political capital for open immigration declines through three channels. First, some firms close their doors and no longer lobby for open immigration. Second, some firms increase their productivity (or change product lines from low-skill-intensive to high-skill-intensive ones) and spend less political capital on immigration. Finally, nontradable firms and high-skill-intensive firms can use the native labor laid off by the firms that close, reducing their need for immigration as well. All of these channels reduce the amount of political capital the policymaker will receive for immigration, which means she will restrict immigration to make other groups in society happier, all else being equal. If trade is restricted or if international competition decreases, the opposite occurs: firms in the low-skill-intensive sector expand and new firms enter the market, taking labor from the nontradable and high-skill-intensive sectors, increasing the demand for low-skill immigration and the resulting policy.

These results do not depend on the Ricardo-Viner model's assumptions; most important, they do not depend on comparative advantage and interindustry trade. Instead, the results are similar if I examine the effects of intraindustry trade under "new" new trade theory, such as the Melitz model.[20] Examining the effects of intraindustry trade is important because a large proportion of trade is intraindustry rather than interindustry.

Under "new" new trade theory, countries with similar endowments open trade. Instead of producing a single good, firms within industries each produce their own variety of the good, and each firm is a monopolist in that variety. Each firm then captures part of the market for that good. For example, in the automobile market, Ford is a monopolist in the production of Fords, and Toyota monopolizes the production of Toyotas; each firm captures part of the automobile market. Firms have different levels of productivity; some are more productive than others. Exporting is not costless; firms have to pay some fixed costs that do not vary with the amount exported. Because of this fixed cost, only the most productive firms can export, as they can cover the costs of exporting; moderately productive

[19] Policymakers can also use subsidies to keep firms in business, in which case the immigration policy could remain constant in the face of trade openness. These subsidies would be difficult to maintain at higher levels of openness because they'd become more expensive and also are often targets of trade agreements.

[20] The Melitz (2003) model without costs to trade can also be thought to model increased immigration under autarky. Increased immigration increases the country size; however, increased country size has no effect on firm-level outcomes—the same number of firms produce the same output and earn the same profits (Melitz, 2003, 1706).

firms can produce for the domestic market; and the least productive firms have to close.

Trade openness is modeled as a reduction in trade costs. Lower trade costs mean that firms with lower levels of productivity are able to cover the costs of exporting. Trade liberalization, then, allows domestic producers with lower levels of productivity to export, but it subjects all the firms— foreign firms, domestic exporters, and domestic-only suppliers alike—to increased competition in the domestic market. The least productive firms, which prior to the change in trade were producing for only the domestic market, lose market share to the new foreign competition and close. After trade liberalization, there is a higher average level of productivity than before.[21]

Trade openness under "new" new trade theory has an effect on immigration policy similar to that of trade opened under a Ricardo-Viner model. When trade is opened, the least productive firms close. These firms would have been the major supporters of immigration policy prior to the liberalization of trade because they benefited the most from lower labor costs. When they close, they take their support for more open immigration with them and release their labor. The more productive firms expand to serve both the domestic market and the export market. Not only do these firms need less labor to produce, they also are likely to need high-skill labor, making them less likely to lobby for low-skill immigration.[22]

Policymakers thus face the same trade-off of whether to increase immigration to keep these less productive firms from closing or to allow them to close and restrict immigration. Moreover, under the "new" new trade theory model, without the assumption of perfect competition, more productive firms may want to spend political capital to reduce immigration. These firms can capture more market share if their less productive competition closes. They may want to hasten the less productive firms' demise by ensuring that less productive firms are not kept in business with open immigration. Thus the results all carry through if we assume that trade follows a "new" new trade theory model instead of the Ricardo-Viner model.

[21] New firms that enter the market will be more productive, since only those more productive firms can compete with foreign firms. For a formal discussion, see Helpman (2006, 596).

[22] These results, however, implicitly assume that production by either the more capital-intensive and high-skill-intensive firms under the Ricardo-Viner model or the more productive firms under the Melitz (2003) model does not increase so much as to increase the economy-wide demand for low-skill labor. Empirically, rising wage inequality due to increases in productivity and trade seems to bear this out. Rising wage inequality occurs precisely because low-skill jobs have not been replaced at a high enough rate to keep low-skill wages at the same level.

Firm Mobility and Firms' Willingness to Lobby

Firm mobility is affected by many factors. Country-level factors include the following: the legal ability to move capital out of the home state, the legal ability to invest in the host state, the likelihood that the investment will be expropriated, difference in tax regimes, difference in regulations, and difference in labor costs. There are also industry-level factors. Some types of production are relatively immobile:

- owing to their inputs (e.g., although it is possible to sell farmland and move grape plants, it's impossible to move the soil and climate conditions of Napa Valley);
- owing to the costs or feasibility of transporting the outputs (e.g., it's impossible to transport wet concrete long distances); or
- because the activity cannot take place overseas (e.g., it's impossible to cut hair in New York from China).

Moving production overseas can occur in two ways: the firm could move its "factory" overseas through foreign direct investment, or it could outsource part of its production process to a firm overseas. I assume that all firms produce for the home market regardless of production location; therefore, all firms receive the same price for their goods.[23]

Firm mobility gives firms one more option when they decide whether to lobby. They may also choose to move after the immigration policy is chosen, which changes their preference for low-skill immigration in the future. As moving production becomes less expensive, firms will be more likely to move rather than lobby for open immigration.

Firm mobility decreases the incentives to lobby both for firms that move and for firms that do not. Once firms move overseas, they have no incentive to lobby for immigration at home. They may, in fact, oppose immigration because immigration at home will give the firm's competition that still produces at home an advantage, or because workers from their production location may move to the home country. For example, firms that produce in Mexico may oppose a more open immigration policy in the United States because they would lose Mexican workers. Firms that do not move can always move overseas if the policy environment is not to their liking, and therefore they will become less willing to pay for additional immigration. Finally, as in the case of trade shocks, firms that cannot move may also be affected by other firms' mobility. As these firms move, they lay off their workers, who can now be used by the nonmobile firms. These firms,

---

[23] The model does not change if firms are producing for a third-country market. Instead, the price they receive is based on that third market and the tariffs they have to pay to ship goods there. The trade costs can be thought of as the difference in shipping costs and tariffs between producing the good in the home country and doing so in the host country.

too, will be less willing to pay for immigration, and political capital for immigration should decline.

There is a debate among political scientists and economists about whether having an exit option gives firms relatively more leverage over policy. On the one hand, if firms leave, they take their tax revenue and jobs with them, and their exit serves as a sign of dissatisfaction with the government. Governments react by anticipating firms' policy preferences and change policy to keep firms at home. This can lead to a race to the bottom as governments cut corporate taxes and the social welfare state rather than have firms leave.[24] On the other hand, policymakers have to appeal to other constituencies and are unwilling to change policy to keep firms if that policy is politically important.[25] Empirically, the fact that firms do move production abroad suggests that governments don't capitulate to every business's demands in order to keep them.

In my model, the policymaker has to balance her need for tax revenue against the prospect of losing support from anti-immigration constituencies. If firms exit the state, the policymaker will lose the tax revenue that the firm provides, but she can restrict immigration, so that wages return to their earlier level, which would make the other firms *and* native labor as well off as before.[26] To the policymaker, then, firms moving overseas are the same as firms closing their doors; however, moving is much better for the firm owners.

When only a small number of firms can move, the policymaker may increase immigration to keep them at home. However, if firm mobility makes production overseas vastly less expensive, many firms will move unless costs at home are extremely low. This could be done with very high levels of immigration, but politically it is unlikely that the policymaker would open immigration this far.[27] Therefore, some firms will leave, and immigration can be restricted without making other firms worse off.

How Costly Is Lobbying? Alternative Explanations of Immigration Policy

Thus far, I have assumed that policymakers have to balance firms' demands for immigration with anti-immigration sentiment from the rest of the

[24] Garrett (1995) and Strange (1996).

[25] Basinger and Hallerberg (2004) and Mosley (2000).

[26] I assume that states cannot tax overseas production. This is not always the case, but states almost always tax overseas earnings at a lower rate.

[27] This is similar to Mosley's (2000) argument that policymakers have some issues on which they will not compromise for bond markets.

polity. I now examine what affects the opposition to (and support for) immigration from the mass public and other interest groups, relying on the existing literature.

Power of Labor Argument. A first set of arguments is based on the labor market effects of immigrants. Although there has been a debate over whether immigration leads to higher or lower wages for them, natives often believe that wages decrease with immigration.[28] What matters for the policymaker is not whether immigrants actually affect wages, but whether the mass public *thinks* that they affect wages and will punish the policymaker based on this perception.

Fiscal Burden Argument. Other scholars have focused on the fiscal implications of immigrants.[29] Rich taxpayers oppose immigration because of the increased tax burden they assume it entails, and poor taxpayers—those likely to be the welfare state's recipients—oppose immigration because they believe that immigrants crowd them out of welfare benefits.[30] Again, there is not clear evidence that immigrants are a fiscal burden: some studies show that immigrants are a net fiscal gain, and others show them to be a net fiscal loss.[31] As in the case of the labor market effects of immigration, what may matter more for the policymaker is the mass public's perception rather than actual effects. There is some evidence in the survey literature that the *perceived* fiscal effects of immigrants lead to less support for immigration.[32]

Nativism Argument. As some recent survey data have not confirmed the labor market or fiscal arguments, a third set of scholars have examined the role that nativism plays in public opinion and policymaking on immigration.[33] One effect of immigration is that it changes the national culture, and this change is threatening to some members of society. There have been waves of nativism throughout modern history. For example, there were nativist waves against Asian immigration in the United States, Canada, Australia, and New Zealand in the last half of the nineteenth century, against Southern and Eastern Europeans throughout the New World in the early twentieth century, and against Muslim immigrants in

[28] For example, Goldstein and Peters (2014) found that high-skill natives opposed high-skill immigration more during the Great Recession, when they felt that their economic situation was threatened, and Gerber et al. (2014) find that both high-skill and low-skill survey respondents believe that immigration leads to increased chances of job or wage loss.

[29] Hanson, Scheve, and Slaughter (2007), Hatton and Williamson (2005a), Hatton and Williamson (2005b), and Money (1999).

[30] On the other hand, a generous welfare program may lead to increased support for immigration because social welfare programs redistribute the overall gains from immigration to "losers," e.g., Ha and Tsebelis (2010) and Ruggie (1982).

[31] Smith and Edmonston (1997) and Dustmann, Frattini, and Halls (2010).

[32] See Hanson, Scheve, and Slaughter (2007) and Gerber et al. (2014), but see also Goldstein and Peters (2014).

[33] See Hainmueller and Hiscox (2007, 2010).

Europe and elsewhere today, all of whom tended to be, on average, the least skilled immigrant groups. Although we know that the public has opposed immigration for cultural reasons and that this dislike is targeted at low-skill immigrants, it's not clear when nativism becomes more salient and when it can affect immigration policy. Thus nativism remains a residual category for explaining anti-immigrant sentiment.

Immigrants as an Interest Group/Electoral Motive Argument. Although there are many reasons why the mass public may oppose low-skill immigration, there are reasons the mass public may favor low-skill immigration. Open immigration allows foreign-born citizens to bring family members or friends into the state, surrounding themselves with their culture and improving their family's economic position.[34] Immigrants have been able to influence immigration policy, it is argued, because left-wing parties consider immigrants to be a likely base of support.[35] Some natives may favor more open low-skill immigration because they like the cultural changes brought by immigrants or they believe that immigration is a human right. These cosmopolitans and humanitarians will push for more open immigration, especially low-skill immigration.

Macropolitical and Macroeconomic Explanations. Scholars have also offered explanations for immigration policy based on systemic factors, security concerns, state identity, and regime type. Systemic effects include global recessions. An economic shock might lead to greater concern about fiscal transfers or a large decrease in wages, which would lead to immigration restrictions, all else being equal. Similarly, conflict is likely to affect immigration policy. If policymakers need more labor to fight a war, immigration policy should open. On the other hand, if policymakers are worried about the security externalities of immigrants, they may restrict immigration.[36] Policymakers may also want to open immigration if they want to take in refugees from an ally, making immigration policy more open, all else being equal.

States' identities may also play a role. Settler states were built by immigrants and therefore are more open to immigrants because the immigrant experience is part of their national identity.[37] Alternatively, homogenous states may be wary of accepting immigrants who will change the national culture, whereas heterogeneous states have a longer tradition

---

[34] Foreman-Peck (1992) and Tichenor (1994, 2002).

[35] Faist (1994), Glaeser and Shleifer (2005), Messina (2008), and Money (1999). Nonetheless, most left parties face a trade-off between getting the immigrant vote and keeping their traditional working-class base of support. Dancygier (2013).

[36] Mirilovic (2010). See Salehyan and Gleditsch (2006) and Salehyan (2008) on security externalities.

[37] Freeman (1995).

of integrating minorities without too much disruption.[38] Finally, some states have special relationships with their former colonies that may lead to more liberal immigration policies.[39]

Additionally, immigration policy is affected by the weight politicians place on the interests of business vis-à-vis other groups in the polity. Democratization or an increase in the franchise may change these weights.[40] As states democratize or increase the franchise, the skill level of the median voter decreases, making the (perceived) effect of immigration on wages a more important issue for the policymaker.

Firms' Preference for Undocumented Immigrants. My argument is based on the increasing indifference of firms toward immigration; but the conventional wisdom argues that firms prefer relatively restricted immigrant admissions policy that fosters illegal immigration, providing an easily exploitable workforce. Firms can pay these workers less than the minimum wage, refuse to pay their employment taxes and the employers' share of the social welfare payments, and subject them to dangerous working conditions. Because undocumented immigrants fear deportation, they are unwilling to go to the authorities to report such problems, allowing firms that use illegal labor to make greater profits. Immigration policy, then, may be more restrictive not because firms' lobbying for open immigration has *decreased* but because their lobbying for immigration restrictions has *increased*.

Although it is clear that some firms exploit undocumented immigrants, other firms exhibit behavior that is puzzling in light of this explanation. For example, industries such as agriculture and hospitality that use a largely undocumented immigrant workforce spend money lobbying for more open immigration. At times, firms even lobby for greater enforcement of immigration regulations. Although there may be several reasons for the difference in firm preferences over enforcement, I focus on two: first, the need for a stable workforce makes firms prefer legal immigration to illegal immigration, and, second, the cleavage between large and small firms can lead to increased enforcement of immigration laws.

One factor that can divide firms' preferences over the use of undocumented immigrants is the need for a stable workforce. In industries with time-sensitive operations, using undocumented immigrants or illegal workers can make the firm vulnerable to hold-up by the government. The clearest example of this is agriculture, which in places like California relies almost exclusively on undocumented immigrants.[41] The Immigration and

---

[38] Zolberg (1989).
[39] Hansen (2002).
[40] Hatton and Williamson (2008).
[41] Caldwell (2011).

Customs Enforcement (ICE) Agency has the right to search farmers' fields and is likely to check the status of immigrants during key moments in the production process, such as harvesttime. If the workers are found to be in the country illegally, ICE can detain them, leaving farmers without a workforce at a critical juncture. For industries where hold-up is a problem, using an illegal workforce can place them at the government's mercy. To prevent these problems, as I show in chapter 4, farmers in the United States have lobbied for a legal agricultural workers program.

Large and small firms also differ in their ability to use undocumented workers. Small firms can fly under the radar, so to speak, attracting less attention to their operations. Large firms, in contrast, are often subject to more scrutiny. Owing to this greater scrutiny—from government, unions, and consumers—larger firms often face greater liability for using undocumented workers.

Since large firms cannot use undocumented immigrant workers, they are at a disadvantage when competing with smaller firms that can. Owing to their competitive disadvantage, large firms may lobby the government for increased enforcement of immigration laws. Increased enforcement makes it more difficult for smaller firms to use undocumented labor, raising their labor costs to that of the large firm. We know that large firms typically have more influence over politics; thus it is possible that large firms support greater enforcement, leading to more enforcement in general, to take this advantage away from small firms. Chapter 6 explores this mechanism further.

CONCLUSION AND EMPIRICAL STRATEGY

Whereas the research literature has mostly focused on the changing fortunes of anti-immigration groups to explain low-skill immigration policy, my argument focuses on how changes in the international economy—through their effects on firms' willingness to support low-skill immigration—have affected the politics of immigration. Trade openness leads to the closure of low-skill-intensive firms that use immigrant labor. Increased firm mobility allows these same low-skill-intensive firms to move overseas. In both cases, the exit of the firm from the home market leads to fewer firms supporting low-skill immigration. Finally, laborsaving technology allows firms to do more with less labor, also decreasing firms' support for low-skill immigration.

My argument and those from the literature have observable implications—what we would need to observe in the world if a theory is correct—at the cross-national level, the subnational level, and the firm/sector level. Table 2.2 summarizes these implications. In chapters 3

TABLE 2.2
Observable Implications.

	Increase in	Macro-level Cross-national	Micro-level Firm/sector (chapter 4)	Micro-level Sub-national (chapters 5 & 6)
My argument	Trade openness	Restrictions in immigration policy (chapter 3)	Less lobbying in sectors with less trade protection	Less support for immigration from areas with more trade-exposed sectors
	Firm mobility	Restrictions in immigration policy (chapter 3)	Less lobbying in sectors that are more mobile	Less support for immigration from areas with more mobile sectors
	Productivity	Not able to test owing to data availability (NA)	Less lobbying in sectors with greater productivity	Less support for immigration from areas with more high-skill sectors
Power of labor argument	Democracy/franchise	Restrictions in immigration policy (chapter 7)	NA	Less support for immigration from areas with a larger franchise
	Union strength	Restrictions in immigration policy (chapter 7)	Increased union lobbying correlated with restrictions	Less support for immigration from areas with greater unionization rates
Fiscal burden	Size of welfare state	Restrictions in immigration policy (chapter 7)	NA	Less support for immigration from areas with larger welfare states

TABLE 2.2
Continued

| | | Macro-level | Micro-level | |
	Increase in	Cross-national	Firm/ sector (chapter 4)	Sub-national (chapters 5 & 6)
Nativism	Rise of the (radical) Right	Restrictions in immigration policy (chapter 7)	NA	Less support for immigration from areas with right parties
	Immigrant flows (conflict theory)	Restrictions in immigration policy (chapter 7)	Increased lobbying by nativists correlated with restrictions	Less support for immigration from areas with larger immigrant inflows
Immigrants as an interest group/electoral motives	Immigrant flows	Greater openness in immigration policy (chapter 7)	Increased lobbying by immigrant groups correlated with fewer restrictions	More support for immigration from areas with larger immigrant inflows
Cosmopolitans	Immigrant flows (contact theory)	Greater openness in immigration policy (chapter 7)	Increased lobbying by cosmopolitan groups correlated with fewer restrictions	More support for immigration from areas with larger immigrant inflows
Macropolitical/ macroeconomic factors	Global recessions	Restrictions in immigration policy (chapter 7)	Less lobbying by firms	Less support for immigration from areas in economic downturn

TABLE 2.2
Continued

Increase in	Macro-level Cross-national	Micro-level Firm/sector (chapter 4)	Micro-level Sub-national (chapters 5 & 6)
War (increased demand for labor)	Greater openness in immigration policy (chapter 7)	NA	More support for immigration during wartime
War (immigrants as fifth column)	Restrictions in immigration policy (chapter 7)	NA	Less support for immigration during wartime
State identity as country of immigrants	Greater openness in immigration policy (chapter 7)	NA	NA
State identity as ethnic country	Restrictions in immigration policy (chapter 7)	NA	NA
Firms' preference for undocumented immigrants Increase in entry restrictions	Decrease in enforcement (chapter 7)	No support for more open immigration	Support for decreasing enforcement from all sectors
Increase in entry restrictions	Increase in deportation (chapter 7)	Support for decreasing enforcement	Support for increasing deportation from all sectors

through 6, I use data at each of these three levels over long periods, at least fifty years and in many cases two centuries, to test these implications. My goal is not to show that my argument is the *only* one that empirically explains low-skill immigration policy, but that it does a better job of explaining it than the existing arguments. Along the way, I also provide much more rigorous evidence for the alternative explanations than has been provided thus far.

In chapter 3, I test my argument at the most macro level: immigration policy across nineteen countries over two centuries. Although other scholars have created measures of immigration policy, thus far no one has created measures that span the nineteenth, twentieth, and twenty-first centuries.[42] In this chapter, I show how immigration policy has changed, using a new measure I developed on low-skill immigration policy,[43] and compare it to the evolution of trade openness and firm mobility across those two centuries. Through this long time period, there is great variation in trade openness and firm mobility both in individual countries and across the world economy. There are also differences in the structure of the international system, the number and nature of democracies, the power of labor both between countries and within countries over time, and a whole host of other confounding variables. If we find that the observable implications hold over all these different countries and different time periods, we should have great confidence in my argument.

In chapters 4 through 6, I use different types of evidence to examine the micro foundations of my argument. Even though chapter 3 finds that the observable implications on the cross-national level hold in the nineteen countries studied and through different time periods, it does not fully substantiate my argument. There are two threats to the empirical results in chapter 3. First, it is possible that something else besides firm lobbying is causing the relationship (what is known as the *omitted variables problem*), and, second, it may be that changes in immigration policy are causing the changes in trade and firm mobility (what is known as *reverse causality*). The following chapters address these two potential problems and provide evidence for the relationship between productivity and immigration policy, something that is impossible to test across countries, as data on productivity are sparse at this level.

Chapter 4 examines evidence at the sector level using three different types of data to eliminate the first threat to causal identification of the relationship found in chapter 3, the omitted variables problem, by showing that preferences and lobbying on low-skill immigration by different sectors follow the patterns that we expect. I use data on which sectors testify before

---

[42] See Bjerre et al. (2014) for a review.

[43] See appendix A for details on the creation of this measure.

the US Congress on immigration and data on their lobbying behavior in the United States to show that industries that have been more vulnerable to trade, that are more mobile, and that are more productive lobby less on immigration, even as they continue to lobby on other issues. Next, I focus on the preferences of three different industries more closely by examining their trade associations in the United States: one in textiles, one in steel, and one in agriculture. Each of these industries has, at one point in its history, used a great deal of low-skill labor, and so we might expect them to support open immigration, but these industries have varied in their exposure to trade competition and their ability to move production overseas. For each group, I use content analysis of their annual meeting minutes and other publications to understand how their willingness to lobby on low-skill immigration has changed with trade openness, firm mobility, and technology adoption.

In chapter 5, I move from sectors to policymakers through an examination of US Senate votes on immigration. This chapter helps to exclude the second threat to causal identification of the results, the reverse causation problem, by examining two time periods when senators did not have control over the most important policies that affected trade and firm mobility. In the first period, from the founding of the republic to World War II, I examine how the creation of a national market affected voting on immigration. Technological innovations during this time period transformed the US economy from several regional markets protected by distance into one national market. Increased trade openness between US states, increased ability to relocate to areas with lower costs of production (namely, the South), and increased use of laborsaving technology should have had the same effect on immigration policy as do international trade openness, firm mobility, and productivity gains. In the post–World War II era, the competitive pressures on firms and their ability to move production overseas fluctuated with changes in other countries' willingness to allow foreign direct investment, technological innovation, and US trade protection, which was moved out of the hands of senators with the Reciprocal Trade Agreements Act (RTAA). The data show that increased "Americanization" and globalization of the economy led senators increasingly to vote for immigration restrictions, as predicted by my argument.

Chapter 6 uses process tracing of immigration policy in two small countries—Singapore and the Netherlands—to answer both the omitted variables and reverse causality questions outside the US context. Firms in both countries largely produce for export markets; the expansion of low-skill firms crucially depends on competition within those markets and not necessarily within the domestic market. But, as rulers of small countries, policymakers in Singapore and the Netherlands have little leverage over the policies of these export markets. Firms in these countries thus have been affected by changes that policymakers have had little control over, such as the rise of China and the entrance of Eastern European states into the European Union. I demonstrate that these changes have led to decreasing support for open immigration. These cases bolster the case that my argument is a general one, not just one specific to the United States.

In chapters 4 through 6, I examine many of the alternative explanations (discussed earlier in this chapter) and find mixed support for them in the case studies. Chapter 7 completes our study of these alternatives by examining their observable implications across countries. Again, I find decidedly mixed support for most of them; I also do not find that policymakers pass immigration restrictions coupled with lax enforcement to allow firms to exploit undocumented workers. Instead, business support for enforcement is much more complicated, with some firms supporting greater enforcement, some firms supporting more legal immigration and less enforcement, and a small number of firms wanting to exploit undocumented immigrants.

Altogether, the data presented in this book provide broad support for my argument. From the nineteenth century to today and across many different countries, firms have been the major supporter of open low-skill immigration; prior policy choices to open the border to goods and to allow capital to move overseas have led to a decrease in firms' support for open low-skill immigration and, with it, a decrease in open borders for low-skill immigrants. Although anti-immigration forces have always been a feature of the political landscape, their power has grown as firms have ceded the issue to them.

CHAPTER 3

Immigration Policy and Two Eras of Globalization

IN RECENT YEARS, ANTI-IMMIGRATION FORCES HAVE GAINED large victories in many developed countries. In 2006, 2007, and 2014, the US Congress failed to pass a comprehensive immigration bill that would have decreased overall low-skill immigration but legalized undocumented immigrants. At the same time, far-right, anti-immigration parties gained seats in the 2014 European parliamentary elections and the 2015 UK elections; in Singapore, anti-immigrant sentiment led to the worst electoral performance by the regime in fifty years. As I show in this chapter, these recent victories by anti-immigrant sentiment are part of a larger trend: in the post–World War II era, low-skill immigration has been increasingly restricted around the world.

Ideally, we would test the full causal chain of my argument, starting with changes in trade, firm mobility, and technology adoption through their effects on firms' support for low-skill immigration to policymakers' decisions and finally to low-skill immigration policy in a broad range of countries. Unfortunately, as often happens when we examine political phenomena at the cross-national level, data do not exist for many of the variables we would want in order to test the causal chain: importantly, there is no good record of firms' support for immigration policy in most countries. We are also missing data on technology adoption across countries, so this implication cannot be tested cross-nationally either.

Owing to this lack of data, in this chapter I test two of the implications of my argument by focusing on the political dilemma that policymakers face with greater globalization, without testing the role firms play in this dilemma (what is known in political science and economics as testing the *reduced form*). The first implication is that the increasing ability to trade should lead to greater restrictions on immigration. Increasing openness of borders to foreign goods from the developing world leads to the closure of low-skill-intensive firms, and increasing openness to intraindustry trade from other developed countries leads to the closure of the least productive firms, which need more labor. Either form of trade openness, then, decreases the business community's support for low-skill immigration.

Second, the increased ability of firms to move production overseas should also lead to increased restrictions on low-skill immigration. Firm mobility—owing to lowered restrictions on capital outflows in the developed world, lowered restrictions on foreign direct investment (FDI) in the developing world, and an increased technological ability to control production over long distances—allows the most productive firms in many, but not all, sectors to move their production overseas. With the move, these firms no longer support open immigration at home, giving anti-immigration forces a louder voice.

To test these two implications, I develop a new dataset on de jure immigration policies of nineteen countries over two centuries. The dataset is the first to include the nineteenth, twentieth, and twenty-first centuries and is one of the few datasets that include not only Organization for Economic Cooperation and Development (OECD) countries but also wealthy autocracies from the Persian Gulf and East Asia. I use these data to test whether trade openness and firm mobility have a negative effect on the openness of low-skill immigration policy. The empirical analysis shows a robust relationship among trade, firm mobility, and low-skill immigration policy across many time periods and many countries, strongly supporting my argument that policymakers are constrained in their choice between these policies.

TRADE AND IMMIGRATION POLICY

In chapter 2, I argued that trade openness affects immigration policy through its effects on firms. Policymakers have many tools they can use to regulate trade: tariffs, which are a tax on foreign-produced goods; quotas, which limit the amount of foreign goods that can enter the country; other nontariff barriers, such as regulations on food safety, which increase costs for foreign firms; and the exchange rate, which affects the prices of domestic goods in comparison to foreign goods.[1] In addition to these tools, firms can face more or less trade competition owing to transportation costs; when transportation costs fall, foreign goods become cheaper.

Together, trade policy in all its forms and transportation costs affect whether firms can profitably produce their goods in the home country. Higher prices for low-skill-intensive goods, whether caused by trade barriers, an undervalued exchange rate, or high transportation costs, allow more production to occur at home, increasing the demand for low-skill labor and, with that, increasing firms' support for open immigration. Conversely,

---

[1] When a country's exchange rate is undervalued (overvalued), its products are cheaper (more expensive) than those produced in other countries, putting domestic firms at an advantage (disadvantage) against goods made elsewhere.

lower prices, whether caused by reductions in trade barriers, an overvalued exchange rate, or lower transportation costs, lead to less production at home, lower demand for low-skill labor, and less support from firms for open immigration. This discussion leads to three hypotheses: first, a decrease (increase) in trade barriers should lead to more (fewer) restrictions on low-skill immigration. Second, decreases (increases) in transportation costs should lead to more (fewer) restrictions on low-skill immigration. Third, an increasing (decreasing) value of the currency should lead to more (fewer) restrictions on low-skill immigration.

The effects of trade barriers, transportation costs, exchange rates, and international competition may be felt differently depending on the structure of the economy. Trade barriers will likely have a larger effect in states with large economies—the United States, the United Kingdom, France, Germany, and Japan and to some extent Argentina, Australia, Brazil, and Canada. Firms in these states produce mostly for the domestic market; policymakers, therefore, are better able to shield them from international competition. Similarly, falling transportation costs, because they act like a tariff, should have a large, negative effect on firms in large economies since they expose these firms to more competition. The value of the exchange rate will likely have less effect on firms in these states than it would in small, open economies where more of the economy engages in the international market.

Trade barriers should have smaller effects in the states with small, open economies: New Zealand, the Netherlands, Switzerland, Hong Kong, Singapore, South Korea, and Taiwan. Firms in these states produce mostly for export markets. Policymakers are less able to shield these firms from international competition because they can adopt few policies that affect prices in their main export markets. The one exception is the value of the currency. If the country adopts an undervalued exchange rate, domestic firms get an advantage on the world market. Falling transportation costs may also have a smaller effect on these states: on the one hand, they make it less costly to export goods; on the other hand, they make it less costly for all other countries to export goods as well.

Natural-resource-rich states, Saudi Arabia, Kuwait, South Africa, and, to some extent, the Netherlands, face yet another set of competitiveness issues. Immigration policy will be driven in part by the need for labor in the commodities industry. The manufacturing sector in these states will often be at a competitive disadvantage arising from so-called Dutch disease—commodities booms often lead to an overvalued exchange rate and increased wages. Trade barriers may have a larger effect in these states because they offer a source of protection from international competition in the face of Dutch disease.

Immigration Policy across Three Centuries

To test these hypotheses, we need a way to measure low-skill immigration. Other scholars have created measures of immigration policy, but these measures have covered only one time period and often only wealthy, OECD states.[2] Because my argument has implications for time periods when trade was relatively restricted and when it was open, and for time periods when firms could easily move and when they could not, we need data that bridge the nineteenth century through today.

In addition to examining a longer time period, we also want data that cover a more representative sample of states. Although the states of the OECD are important immigration destinations, examining only these states might bias the conclusions we can draw. There are many important immigration destinations in the Persian Gulf and East Asia in which politics are very different from those in the OECD democracies, which might change how immigration policy is crafted.

To address these issues, I collected and coded data on low-skill immigration policy for nineteen countries from the nineteenth (and occasionally the late eighteenth) century to the twenty-first century (appendix A provides more detailed information on the data collection and coding process). As discussed in chapter 2, my argument applies to wealthy countries, which attract immigrants. I define a wealthy country as any country that had twice the world average of GDP per capita for at least ten years, or that had twice the GDP per capita of countries in its continent. From this list, I selected nineteen countries for analysis that have a range of values of important variables both for my argument and for the arguments from the literature.

Table 3.1 shows the states I chose and the dates included in the dataset. For ease of comparison, states are listed geographically, with Australia, New Zealand, and South Africa listed with the Americas as settler states. In addition to the great variation in countries, I also chose to examine several time periods—preglobalization, nineteenth-century globalization, the interwar period, the Bretton Woods era, and today—to test whether my argument held over very different structures of the global economy. If the data support my argument in all these countries and time periods, we should have greater confidence in the empirical support for my argument.

I collected data on the low-skill immigration policies of these countries, including policies that governed who could enter the state, policies on the rights immigrants received once in the state, and policies on deportation and enforcement. I include refugee and asylum policy as well as family immigration policy, as firms care little about why an immigrant enters the state, only that she is given entry. From these different policy dimensions,

---

[2] See Bjerre et al. (2014) for a review.

TABLE 3.1
Countries Included in the Dataset and the Dates of Inclusion.

Region	Country
Settler states/New World	US (1790–2010) Australia (1787–2010) Canada (1783–2010) New Zealand (1840–2010) South Africa (1806–2010) Argentina (1810–2010) Brazil (1808–2010)
Europe	UK (1792–2010) France (1793–2010) Germany (1871–2010) Netherlands (1815–2010) Switzerland (1848–2010)
East Asia	Japan (1868–2010) Hong Kong (1843–2010) Singapore (1955–2010) South Korea (1948–2010) Taiwan (1949–2010)
Persian Gulf	Saudi Arabia (1950–2010) Kuwait (1961–2010)

Originally published in Peters (2015) and reprinted with permission.

I, with the help of research assistants, categorized the data on low-skill immigration policies into twelve subdimensions and coded each of the subdimensions separately. I then aggregated these codings, using principal component analysis to create a single immigration policy variable.

Trade Barriers and Immigration Policy

Economists have long debated how best to measure barriers to trade. The tariff rate, calculated as total duties over imports, is a useful measure because it is available over a very long period of time. Tariffs are by no means the only trade barrier; in the last quarter century or so, tariffs have become less important as negotiations have led to internationally binding decreases in their rates. Nonetheless, tariffs were long an important and effective tool for trade policy, and their decline has created greater trade between states.

Figures 3.1–3.3 plot how trade openness, as measured by the percent of goods not duted or 1 minus the tariff rate, and immigration policy have

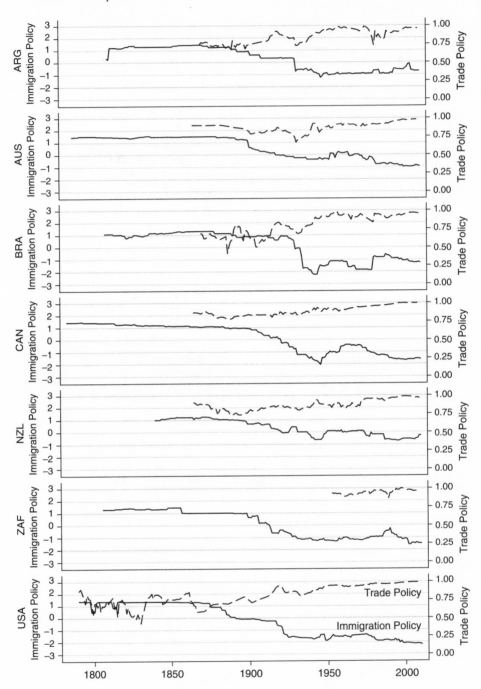

Figure 3.1: For caption see next page.

changed over the past 225 years for the nineteen countries in the dataset, grouped as follows: the settler states of the New World, European states, East Asian states, and Persian Gulf states.[3] For both, more open policies take higher values.

The immigration data confirm the conventional wisdom on the restrictiveness of immigration policy over time. Even though states have used different policy instruments, immigration policy has become generally more restrictive.[4] Nonetheless, the data challenge the conventional wisdom on the different level of openness between countries, especially during the nineteenth century. Most important, it has been argued that European countries were not as open to immigration as the settler states were in the nineteenth century.[5] Yet we see that immigration policy was quite open for many of these states during the nineteenth century, which led to large flows of immigrants.[6]

Even though states in East Asia and the Persian Gulf have used different tools to control immigration, their policies look remarkably similar to the post–World War II policies of the settler states and Europe as well. Hong Kong and Japan, the two states for which we have data on low-skill immigration policy going back to the nineteenth century, have similar trends of being more open to low-skill immigration in the nineteenth century than they are today. In the East Asian countries there was some increasing openness in the 1980s and/or 1990s, but restrictions have increased since the Asian Financial Crisis of 1997. One interesting variation is that the autocracies in this set of countries, Saudi Arabia, Kuwait, and Singapore, combine relatively open borders with draconian enforcement measures that limit undocumented immigration, in contrast to democracies that have limited entry but do not engage in as much enforcement, leading to

---

Figure 3.1: Immigration Policy and Trade Policy for the Settler States.
    Note: Higher values of trade and immigration policy signal greater openness. Trade policy is calculated as 1 minus the tariff rate. Data are from Clemens and Williamson (2004) and updated by the author. Originally published in Peters (2015) and reprinted with permission.

---

[3] Tariff data are from Clemens and Williamson (2004) and were updated by the author.

[4] E.g., Hatton and Williamson (2005b, 2008).

[5] Freeman (1995, 889).

[6] Moch (1995, 128). According to Ferenczi and Willcox, more than 700,000 migrants (excluding transmigrants) from Europe arrived in Great Britain between 1891 and 1905; there were more than 200,000 foreign workers each year in France between 1920 and 1924; almost 3.6 million alien workers entered Germany between 1910 and 1924; and more than a million immigrants entered the Netherlands between 1865 and 1924, not including immigrants from the colonies. Ferenczi and Willcox (1929).

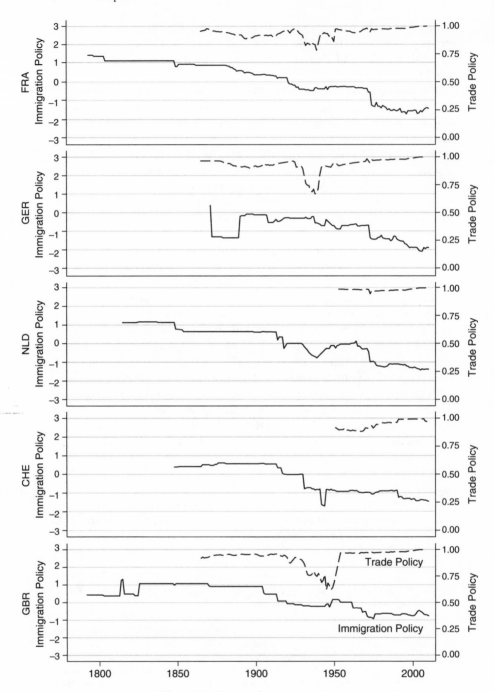

Figure 3.2: For caption see next page.

higher flows of undocumented immigrants. Together, then, we see that although these states have used different tools to control immigration, the overall trends have been remarkably similar, with increasing restriction of low-skill immigration over time.

Turning to the relationship between trade and immigration, we find a clear negative relationship between trade policy and immigration policy for the settler states of the New World. In the nineteenth century, these states had relatively high tariff rates and very open immigration policies. In the interwar period, especially during the Great Depression, these states continued to have high tariff rates but restricted immigration. Even though there were high tariffs, the slowdown of these states' economies starting in the mid-1920s—except for the US economy, which remained relatively healthy until 1929—meant that labor was relatively cheap in these states, which likely decreased firms' willingness to lobby for immigration.

After World War II, many of the settler states opened their economies to trade while also opening somewhat to immigration. Others, like Argentina, South Africa, and the United States, maintained the interwar-period policies of closure. However, none reopened their doors as far as they had prior to World War I. As the postwar period continued, trade barriers were increasingly lifted, often through the General Agreement on Tariffs and Trade/World Trade Organization (GATT/WTO) or other international agreements, while immigration was increasingly restricted, especially after the end of the Bretton Woods exchange rate regime. By the 2000s, low-skill immigration was highly restricted in most of these states, whereas trade was very open.

The European countries show similar, but less extreme, trends in trade and immigration policy. In the nineteenth century, France, Germany, and the United Kingdom had much more open borders for goods than did the settler states, but they also tended to have more restrictive immigration policies during this period. During the interwar period and especially after the start of the Great Depression, these three states enacted relatively high trade barriers while also restricting immigration.

While I argue that higher tariffs should lead to more open immigration policy, we have reason to think this might not occur during recessions, but instead may be delayed until the economic recovery. During recessions, especially large contractions of the economy, many firms, especially the

Figure 3.2: Immigration Policy and Trade Policy for the European States.
   Note: Higher values of trade and immigration policy signal greater openness. Trade policy is calculated as 1 minus the tariff rate. Data are from Clemens and Williamson (2004) and updated by the author. Originally published in Peters (2015) and reprinted with permission.

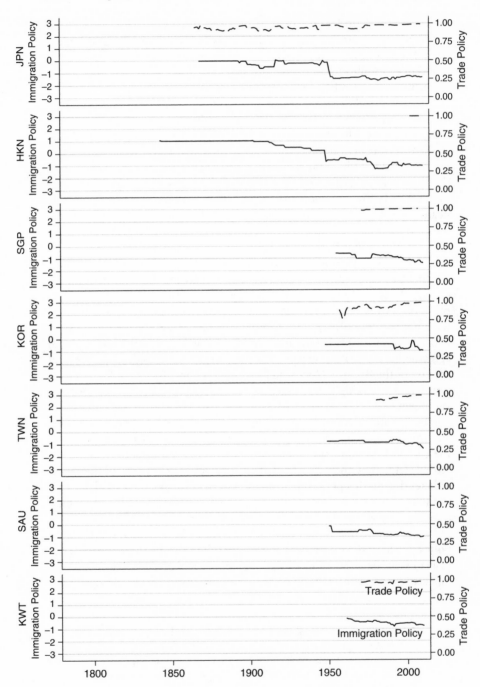

Figure 3.3: For caption see next page.

least productive, go out of business, decreasing the economy-wide need for labor. Even with increased trade barriers (either through tariffs or through devaluations), the economy may not return to full capacity for several years. Until it does so, wages will remain relatively low, decreasing the need for immigration. As there is less demand for low-skill immigrant labor, it is less likely that trade restrictions will lead to open immigration during recessions.

Once the recession ends, higher trade barriers should lead to increased openness. This is what we see happening at the end of World War II. While the European countries began dismantling their interwar-period tariff barriers, some of these barriers remained. With their economies protected (in part owing to low values of their currencies in comparison to the US dollar), low-skill-intensive sectors expanded in these states and with them the demand for more open immigration. In all five countries except for Great Britain, this demand was met with guest worker programs (in Great Britain it was met with immigration from the [former] colonies). Nonetheless, none of these countries opened as far as they did prior to World War I. When European states opened trade through decreased tariffs and by revaluing their exchange rates at the end of Bretton Woods, immigration became much more restrictive.

The countries of East Asia and Kuwait, like the European countries, have had much lower tariff barriers throughout their histories as independent states.[7] For all but Kuwait this is in part because of their development strategy to target export markets. Given that most of their firms produce for export markets and that, except for Japan, these are small, open economies, their tariff levels have been low to allow the import of inputs as well as goods they do not produce domestically. We expect, then, less of a relationship between trade, measured as tariffs, and immigration policy in these states. Yet there does seem to be a negative correlation between trade openness and immigration. Tariff barriers also seem to have less of an effect on immigration in Kuwait. This may be due to the structure of Kuwait's economy. Given that Kuwait imports most goods and produces

Figure 3.3: Immigration Policy and Trade Policy for the East Asian and Persian Gulf States.
Note: Higher values of trade and immigration policy signal greater openness. Trade policy is calculated as 1 minus the tariff rate. Tariff data are not available for Saudi Arabia. Data are from Clemens and Williamson (2004) and updated by the author. Originally published in Peters (2015) and reprinted with permission.

[7] There are no tariff data for Saudi Arabia and almost no data for Hong Kong; these countries are not included in this part of the analysis.

little besides petroleum products, it has few low-skill-intensive tradable firms, and thus trade barriers may have little effect because there are few firms to protect.

Table 3.2 examines the relationship between trade and immigration more rigorously by regressing immigration on trade using an ordinary least squares (OLS) model. Each model contains country and year fixed effects to capture unchanging country characteristics and yearly shocks to the international system, and a linear time trend to ensure that the relationship is not spurious.[8] Polity as a measure of regime type, GDP growth, and an indicator variable for war are also included.[9] Model 1 examines all years of the data, while the next six models examine each historical era from preglobalization through the post–Bretton Woods era.

Over all years, we see a negative and statistically significant relationship between trade and immigration. A change in trade openness from the 25th to the 75th percentile, or from 17 percent average tariff level to a 4 percent average tariff level, leads to a –0.39 change in immigration policy or about half a standard deviation. We also see a negative and statistically significant relationship between trade and immigration if we examine each era.[10] Argentina is an outlier in the post–Bretton Woods period and is excluded from the regression in model 7.[11]

The statistical significance of trade in each era should give us greater confidence that we are discovering a true relationship between trade and immigration and not one caused by an omitted variable. Importantly, eras vary on dimensions that affect the entire world system and economy. The relationship holds in the cases of multiple great powers during the nineteenth century, two great powers during the Cold War, and one great power in the post–Cold War era, and it holds through periods when an economic hegemon was rising and declining, making it less likely that the structure of the international system or the existence of an economic hegemon is causing the changes in both trade and immigration policy. These different eras also had different exchange rate regimes and different systemic levels of capital openness, again making it less likely that either of these variables is the cause of changes in both policies.[12] It also

---

[8] The results are robust to excluding the linear time trend and including a five-year moving average of lagged immigration policy instead. See Peters (2015).

[9] Maddison (2011), Marshall, Gurr, and Jaggers (2011), and Sarkees and Wayman (2010). See chapter 7 for more on the results for these variables.

[10] The preglobalization era is all years before and including 1879, when most states adopted the gold standard; the nineteenth-century era of globalization is 1880–1913; the interwar period is 1914–45; Bretton Woods is 1946–72; and post-Bretton Woods is 1973 onward.

[11] The results in table 3.2 are robust to estimation techniques that reduce the weight of outliers. See Peters (2015).

[12] See Rajan and Zingales (2003) for a similar estimation strategy.

TABLE 3.2
Immigration Policy Regressed on Trade Policy by Era.

DV: immigration policy	All years	Preglobalization	19th-century globalization	Interwar	Bretton Woods	Post–Bretton Woods	Post–Bretton Woods, no Argentina
Trade openness	−3.04**	−1.81*	−1.68*	−3.27+	−1.25*	−1.33	−3.61**
	(0.89)	(0.67)	(0.58)	(1.66)	(0.55)	(1.21)	(1.13)
Linear time trend	−0.02***	−0.00	−0.02***	−0.03**	0.01	−0.01***	−0.01**
	(0.00)	(0.01)	(0.00)	(0.01)	(0.01)	(0.00)	(0.00)
Polity	0.01	0.06*	0.15	0.02	0.02+	0.01+	0.01
	(0.01)	(0.02)	(0.09)	(0.02)	(0.01)	(0.00)	(0.01)
GDP growth	0.17	0.18	0.19	−0.15	0.05	0.16	0.01
	(0.16)	(0.16)	(0.12)	(0.33)	(0.34)	(0.18)	(0.16)
War	0.17	0.96	0.00	0.20	−0.00	−0.03	−0.03
	(0.12)	(0.52)	(0.05)	(0.21)	(0.10)	(0.04)	(0.04)
Constant	4.32***	2.07*	2.79***	6.04*	−1.98	1.78	3.75***
	(0.89)	(0.81)	(0.52)	(1.95)	(1.45)	(1.21)	(0.92)
Observations	1577	77	297	298	325	580	548
R^2	0.77	0.64	0.53	0.56	0.30	0.36	0.48

Notes: Also included: country and year fixed effects. Robust standard errors in parentheses. $^+$ $p < 0.10$, * $p < 0.05$, ** $p < 0.01$, *** $p < 0.001$. Trade openness is 1 minus the tariff rate from Clemens and Williamson (2004) and updated by the author. GDP growth is from Maddison (2011). Polity is the measure of regime type from Marshall, Gurr, and Jaggers (2011). War is an indicator variable for war from Sarkees and Wayman (2010). Linear time trend is a time trend for each country. Originally published in Peters (2015) and reprinted with permission.

holds through different waves of emigration from Europe, Asia, and Latin America, through wars and peacetime, and through good economic times and bad, again indicating that trade is likely responsible for the change in immigration policy rather than another variable causing changes in *both* policies.

We can also have confidence that the relationship is driven by trade affecting immigration rather than immigration affecting trade. As chapter 2 discusses, if immigration were the driver of trade policy, we would expect there to be a positive relationship between immigration and trade policy, not a negative one. More open immigration policy lowers low-skill-intensive firms' total wage bill—either directly, by lowering wages for low-skill workers, or indirectly, by allowing firms to use immigrant labor for the least-skilled positions and native labor for more skilled positions, increasing productivity—which should make them more competitive. As such, they should be less likely to oppose the removal of trade barriers. Moreover, countries' trade policy was often driven by reasons far removed from immigration policy, including to serve as revenue for the government and for national security reasons, further suggesting that immigration policy was not changed specifically to affect trade policy.

In table 3.2, I examined trade and immigration policy in the same year; however, we might think that it would take some time for the effect of trade policy to be felt. Firms may be able to stay in business for a while after trade protection is reduced, and so we expect that immigration policy may not change in the same year. To examine this, I regressed immigration policy on the trade policy measure lagged one year and lagged five years (table 3.3), including the same control variables and fixed effects I mentioned earlier. I find that in all years of the data, there continues to be a negative, statistically significant relationship between trade and immigration policy, and that the relationship continues to hold through most of the different eras. These results should give us additional confidence that the relationship predicted by the argument exists. Further, although lagging does not solve the problem of reverse causality, it should give us greater confidence that trade policy is driving immigration policy rather than the other way around.

Trade barriers should have a larger effect on the immigration policy of large economies than on small economies or the resource-rich economies. Because many firms in small economies produce for the export market, trade barriers at home cannot protect them in their main markets, whereas since firms in larger economies produce for only the domestic market or for both the domestic and export markets, trade barriers at home can protect or increase their share of the domestic market. To test this argument, I coded countries by their economy type. Argentina, Australia, Canada, Brazil, France, Germany, Japan, the United Kingdom, and the United States are coded as large

TABLE 3.3
Effect of Trade Policy Lagged on Immigration Policy by Era.

DV: immigration policy	All years	Preglobalization	19th-century globalization	Interwar	Bretton Woods	Post–Bretton Woods	Post–Bretton Woods, no Argentina
One-year lag	−3.09**	−1.39	−1.73*	−3.41+	−1.65**	−1.77	−3.81**
	(0.88)	(0.82)	(0.63)	(1.61)	(0.48)	(1.16)	(1.03)
Five-year lag	−3.04***	−1.05	−0.98	−3.40*	−1.82**	−0.46	−1.62+
	(0.73)	(0.80)	(0.62)	(1.16)	(0.57)	(0.78)	(0.84)

Notes: Coefficients from separate regression of immigration policy on a one-year and five-year lag of trade policy. *One-year lag* is 1 minus the tariff rate lagged one year and *five-year lag* is 1 minus the tariff rate lagged five years, both from Clemens and Williamson (2004) and updated by the author. Included but not shown: country and year fixed effects, a linear time trend for each state, Polity, GDP growth, war. Robust standard errors in parentheses. + $p < 0.10$, * $p < 0.05$, ** $p < 0.01$, *** $p < 0.001$.

economies. Hong Kong, the Netherlands, New Zealand, Singapore, South Korea, Switzerland, and Taiwan are coded as small, open economies, and Kuwait, Saudi Arabia, and South Africa are coded as resource economies. I regress immigration policy on the measure of trade barriers and an interaction between trade barriers and economy type, with large economies as the excluded group.[13] I included the same control variables and fixed effects as I did earlier.

Table 3.4 shows the effect of trade policy in the three different types of economies. If we consider the entire time span, there is a negative and statistically significant relationship between trade policy and immigration policy for the large economies, but trade policy has little effect on immigration policy in the small and the resource economies. This negative relationship between trade and immigration policy in the large economies remains if we disaggregate by time periods, with the exception of Argentina in the post–Bretton Woods period. There is little effect of trade policy in the small economies, as predicted, except in the interwar period and the Bretton Woods period.[14]

In the resource economies, Kuwait and South Africa, there is a negative effect of decreasing trade barriers on immigration policy in the Bretton Woods and post–Bretton Woods periods.[15] The effect of changing trade barriers is larger than it is in the large economies. This result may be caused, in part, by the effect of resource wealth on the rest of the economy. Because labor is often attracted into the resource sector, wages are higher than they would be in countries without natural resources. Additionally, the currency has a higher value than it would without the resources. Given these two factors, there may be little that policymakers can do to make low-skill-labor-intensive firms competitive, except for trade protection. The absence of protection, then, may have a large effect, as other tools are ineffective.

I argued in chapter 1 that *refugee* and *asylum* policy should follow a logic similar to that of the rest of low-skill immigration—firms do not care about why an immigrant is allowed entry—but there may be greater openness in these issue areas owing to humanitarian and strategic concerns. To test this, I regress the standardized average of refugee and asylum policy on trade

[13] The indicator variables for the economy types are excluded from the regression because they are collinear with the country fixed effects.

[14] The result in the interwar period is driven by the changes in New Zealand. Unlike many countries that restricted both trade and immigration during the Great Depression, New Zealand greatly restricted immigration in 1931 but continued to lower tariffs. As it was a small, pastoral economy, most industrial goods were imported, rather than produced domestically; since there were few firms that tariffs could help, higher tariff rates only hurt consumers. Wright (2009, 48, 54).

[15] Saudi Arabia is not included in this analysis owing to a lack of tariff data.

TABLE 3.4
Effect of Trade Policy on Immigration Policy by Era and Economy Type.

DV: immigration policy	All years	Preglobalization	19th-century globalization	Interwar	Bretton Woods	Post-Bretton Woods	Post-Bretton Woods, no Argentina
Large economies	-3.34**	-1.71*	-1.85*	-3.22+	-1.60**	-0.70	-4.12*
	(0.85)	(0.71)	(0.63)	(1.69)	(0.43)	(1.35)	(1.47)
Small economies	0.06	-2.27	-0.44	-6.86***	0.93*	-1.94	-1.98
	(0.84)	(1.38)	(0.76)	(1.27)	(0.35)	(1.23)	(1.34)
Resource economies	2.24				-3.59***	-5.48***	-5.34***
	(1.60)				(0.88)	(0.81)	(0.76)

Notes: Coefficients from regression of immigration policy on trade policy interacted with economy type. *Small economies* is the sum of the coefficient on trade openness for large economies (the excluded category) and the interaction term of small economies with trade openness. *Resource economies* is the sum of the coefficient on trade openness for large economies (the excluded category) and the interaction term of resource economies with trade openness. Trade openness is 1 minus the tariff rate from Clemens and Williamson (2004) and updated by the author. Indicators of small and resource economies are dropped owing to perfect collinearity with the country fixed effects. Included but not shown: country and year fixed effects, a linear time trend for each state, Polity, GDP growth, war. Robust standard errors in parentheses.
+ $p < 0.10$, * $p < 0.05$, ** $p < 0.01$, *** $p < 0.001$.

openness, as measured by tariffs, after 1945, as most states did not have a refugee or asylum policy until after World War II. I include an indicator for the Cold War, as geostrategic considerations were particularly salient during this time period, and the same covariates as before. I find that trade had a limited effect on refugee and asylum policy during the Cold War; the coefficient on trade openness is negative but not significant at conventional levels $(-1.27, p = 0.36)$.[16] After the Cold War, trade policy has a much greater effect on refugee and asylum policy; increasing trade openness from the 25th to the 75th percentile leads to a decrease of 0.46 $(p < 0.01)$, more than half a standard deviation on this measure. Thus when geostrategic concerns became less salient after the end of the Cold War, declining business support for immigration had an effect on refugee and asylum policy similar to that which it has on the rest of immigration policy.

As seen in the results above, Argentina is an outlier in the post–Bretton Woods period. During this time Argentina lowered its tariffs and opened immigration. Argentina's immigration policy is even more puzzling given its choice to peg to the dollar in 1991, which led to an overvalued peso in comparison to its main trading partners in Europe and its major competitor economy, Brazil. These two factors—decreasing trade protection through tariffs and an overvalued currency—should have led to a more restrictive immigration policy. Instead, immigration opened during this time period as the new democratic regime replaced the draconian laws of the dictatorship, giving immigrants more rights and an easier path to citizenship; granting amnesty for undocumented immigrants; and reforming deportation proceedings. Thus it is possible for humanitarian concerns to have a strong positive effect on immigration policy, but these periods are few and far between.

In sum, the relationship between trade barriers, measured using the tariff rate, and immigration policy is as predicted by my argument. When states have lower trade barriers, immigration policy is more restrictive than when states have greater barriers. The effect of trade barriers is larger for large economies and for resource economies, as expected. Trade barriers have less effect on small economies because most firms in these states produce for the international export market rather than the domestic market.

Transportation Costs and Immigration Policy

Transportation costs act as a trade barrier: the higher the transportation cost, the more expensive imports will be, giving domestic producers a greater advantage. Because transportation costs have an effect similar to

[16] See online appendix C for full table.

that of tariffs, they should have a larger effect in large economies, which have more firms that produce for the domestic market than do small economies. Because firms in small economies are often export-oriented, a decrease in transportation costs may act like a decrease in other countries' trade barriers and help exporters, while at the same time hurting import-competing firms in the home market. Together, they may have no effect on net in small economies. It is unclear how transportation costs will affect resource economies.

To gauge transportation costs, I use two measures. The first is the number of rail miles in the country, available from 1825 for Europe and from the 1830s for the United States and Canada until 2001.[17] Greater rail networks open up more of the country to trade, leading to a convergence in prices to the world price. The effect of railroads, however, may not move solely through their effects on prices but may also move through rail companies' support for immigration, especially in the nineteenth century. Rail companies often needed low-skill immigrants to build the railroads. Further, many settler states offered rail companies large tracts of land to sell to settlers, many of whom were immigrants, to pay for the development of rail networks. Finally, immigrants were major customers of the railroads during their move. Rail companies, therefore, had an incentive to lobby for more open immigration. Increasing rail networks, then, may have led to less lobbying for immigration from tradable industries, as the railroads led to greater competition for tradable goods, but more lobbying by railroads for a workforce and customers. Which effect dominates is an empirical question.

The second measure of transportation costs is a measure of containerization. Bernhofen and colleagues find that the container revolution greatly increased trade by reducing the cost of shipping goods from a producer to a customer.[18] Containers meant that the goods did not have to be loaded and unloaded every time they were moved from one mode of transportation (say, a truck) to another (say, a railroad or ship), saving much time and expense. Locked containers reduced the amount of goods that would be stolen in transit, reducing insurance costs.

To be most effective, both the exporting country and the importing country need to have ports for container ships (such countries are said to have *containerized*). I use Bernhofen and colleagues' indicator for whether each state has containerized along with an interaction with the total number of countries in the world that have containerized to capture the effect of containerization. Following Bernhofen and colleagues, I begin the analysis in 1960, six years before the first states adopted container

---

[17] The rail data are from Comin and Hobijn (2009).
[18] Bernhofen, El-Sahli, and Kneller (2013).

TABLE 3.5
Immigration Policy Regressed on Shipping Technology.

DV: immigration policy	(1) Railroads	(2) Railroads, 19th century	(3) Containerization
Rail (10,000 km)	−0.05***	−0.04***	
	(0.01)	(0.01)	
Containerized			0.40*
			(0.14)
# of containerized countries in world			0.00
			(0.00)
Containerized * # of containerized countries			−0.01[+]
			(0.00)
Linear time trend	−0.01***	−0.01**	−0.00
	(0.00)	(0.00)	(0.01)
GDP growth	0.00	0.07	−0.22
	(0.24)	(0.13)	(0.26)
Polity	0.01	0.01	0.02
	(0.01)	(0.03)	(0.01)
War	0.20[+]	0.16	0.06
	(0.11)	(0.11)	(0.07)
Constant	1.17***	1.20***	−0.52
	(0.06)	(0.09)	(1.24)
N	1715	582	516
R^2	0.78	0.46	0.26

Notes: Also included: country and year fixed effects. Robust standard errors in parentheses. $+$ $p < 0.10$, * $p < 0.05$, ** $p < 0.01$, *** $p < 0.001$. *Rail (10,000 km)* is the total number of rail miles in the country from Comin and Hobijn (2009). *Containerized* is an indicator as to whether the state has ports that can take container ships and *# of containerized countries in world* is the total number of countries that have adopted container ship ports; both are from Bernhofen, El-Sahli, and Kneller (2013). *GDP growth* is from Maddison (2011). *Polity* is the measure of regime type from Marshall, Gurr, and Jaggers (2011). *War* is an indicator variable for war from Sarkees and Wayman (2010). *Linear time trend* is a time trend for each country.

technology, and end in 1990, seven years after the last states containerized, when the authors argue that air freight prices likely had a greater effect on shipping prices.[19] This test more plausibly can be considered causal because containerization should have very little effect on immigration policy except through its effect on trade.[20]

In table 3.5, I regress the low-skill immigration policy variable on the measure of railroads and containerization using OLS. Included in the

[19] Bernhofen, El-Sahli, and Kneller (2013).
[20] In a very few cases, undocumented immigrants entered countries in a container.

regression are country and year fixed effects, a linear time trend, GDP growth, Polity, and an indicator for war, as before. The first two models examine the relationship between rail lines and immigration policy, and the last measures the effect of containerization on immigration policy. Rail lines have the hypothesized effect: a greater rail network is associated with a more restrictive immigration policy. This is also true in the nineteenth century, defined as all years prior to 1914, even though rail companies had an incentive to lobby for immigration during this time period. The effect of railroads is also greater on the large economies than on small economies, as predicted. If we reestimate model 1 with interactions with the economy types, the coefficient on railroads for large economies is -0.05 ($p < 0.01$), while the linear combination of the coefficient on railroads and the interaction for small economies is statistically indistinguishable from zero (-0.1, $p = 0.86$), and the linear combination for resource economies is positive (2.3, $p = 0.001$).[21]

As with trade policy, it may be the case that some time elapses between when rail networks are built and when their effect on immigration policy is felt. To examine whether this is the case, I also regressed immigration policy on the measure of rail networks lagged one year and five years, including all the same controls and fixed effects. The results are very similar to the unlagged regressions: the coefficient on the one-year lag was -0.051 ($p < 0.001$), and that on the five-year lag was -0.047 ($p < 0.001$) for all years of the data; when only the nineteenth century was examined, the coefficient on the one-year lag was -0.042 ($p < 0.001$), and that on the five-year lag was -0.040 ($p < 0.001$). Thus again we find that increasing trade—this time by examining increases through lower shipping costs—leads to more immigration restrictions in the near future.[22]

Greater containerization also leads to more immigration restrictions. While the indicator for containerization is positive, the interaction with the total number of states that have containerized is negative. Together, this means that once about eighty-seven states have containerized, which happened only twelve years after the first states containerized, the effect of greater containerization is more immigration restrictions. This suggests that there was a "first mover" advantage: exporters in states that containerized early were able to take advantage of lower shipping costs, while import-competing firms found some protection from the fact that many states, especially developing states with lower labor costs, had not yet containerized. As more countries containerized, this first-mover advantage disappeared, and the increase in trade resulting from containerization led to more immigration restrictions. The effect of containers varies by economy

[21] See online appendix C for the full regression table.
[22] See online appendix C for the full regression table.

type as well. The effect on small and large economies is substantially the same: given the large number of countries that containerized in 1978, first movers in both types of states lost their advantage in that year. For the resource economies, containerization again had positive effects on immigration policy throughout the period.[23]

In sum, shipping technology also has the predicted effect on immigration policy: as transportation costs declined, reducing a barrier to trade, immigration policy became more restrictive. The effect of shipping technology was large and negative in the large economies, but had a smaller effect in small economies and a positive effect in resource economies.

Exchange Rates and Immigration Policy

The level of the exchange rate acts as trade policy by changing the price of domestically produced goods in comparison to foreign goods. The value of China's currency, the yuan renminbi, provides an example. When China first opened its economy, its currency was undervalued against the US dollar. This made Chinese goods cheaper in both China and the United States and made American goods more expensive in China. Chinese companies were more competitive in the US market, receiving an implicit *export subsidy*, and American goods were more expensive in China, receiving an implicit tariff. In comparison, Argentina has often had an overvalued currency in comparison to the dollar. This has meant that American goods are cheaper in Argentina than similar Argentinian goods, receiving an *import subsidy*, and that Argentinian goods have been more expensive in the United States. When a wealthy state's currency is undervalued, low-skill-intensive production will increase, as these firms are protected at home and are at an advantage abroad. When the currency is overvalued, low-skill-intensive production will decrease, as firms are at a disadvantage at home and abroad.

The exchange rate should have the greatest effect in states that interact the most with the international economy. Firms in small, open economies produce mostly for the export market. An undervalued currency provides protection for these firms on the international market, while an overvalued currency will place these firms at a competitive disadvantage. There will be less of an effect in large economies, since many firms produce, at least to some extent, for the domestic market, where the value of the currency does not matter.

To test the effects of the value of the exchange rate, I regressed immigration policy on the level of over/undervaluation and an interaction with economy type, along with the same controls and fixed effects as have been

---

[23] See online appendix C for the regression table.

used thus far.[24] The data on over/undervaluation are available from 1973 to 2006 from Steinberg and Malhotra.[25] For large economies, the coefficient on overvaluation is negative but not statistically significant (-0.13, $p = 0.56$). There is no statistically significant effect of the exchange rate for the resource economies, either (linear combination of the overvaluation coefficient and interaction with resource economies is -0.11, $p = 0.4$). As predicted, for small economies, the effect of overvaluation is negative, -0.41, and statistically significant at the 10 percent level ($p = 0.08$). The effect of overvaluation (or at least less undervaluation) in these states is substantially significant as well; a one-standard-deviation increase in the level of the exchange rate leads to a -0.16 change in the immigration policy score, or about half of a standard deviation for the small economy states during this time.

The effect of a change in the exchange rate might also take some time to affect immigration policy. I reran the regressions of immigration policy on the exchange rate lagged one and five years.[26] The results are similar: the coefficient on the one-year lag for small economies is -0.41 ($p = 0.06$), and that for the five-year lag for small economies is -0.39 ($p < 0.05$). There is no effect of a lagged change in the exchange rate for either large or resource economies, as predicted. Thus again we find a negative relationship between trade openness and immigration policy when we examine this third measure of openness.

FIRM MOBILITY AND IMMIGRATION POLICY

As chapter 2 explores, firm mobility can affect immigration policy by allowing threatened firms—those most likely to be harmed by open trade—to move production overseas, where they can be more competitive. Firm mobility was relatively low until after World War II. Although few states in the nineteenth century had restrictions on capital moving in or out, it was technically infeasible in most industries to move production, as communications and transportation technology made controlling overseas agents very difficult and made overseas investment more risky. While firm mobility rose during the interwar period, many goods still had to be produced relatively close to the final market.[27] Since World War II,

---

[24] See online appendix C for the regression table.

[25] Steinberg and Malhotra (2014) calculate a predicted level of the currency based on GDP per capita and year fixed effects, and then examine the difference between the actual real exchange rate and the predicted real exchange rate.

[26] See online appendix C for the regression table.

[27] Nicholas (1983), Stopford (1974), and Wilkins (1970).

it has become ever easier to move production. Technology has facilitated the control of agents overseas and the production of more goods far from their final markets. States have opened up their economies to FDI as well, increasing the number of potential host markets in which to produce.

To examine the effects of firm mobility on immigration policy, we do well to examine the post–World War II period. While firm mobility is affected by many factors—whether production can be moved, whether overseas agents can be controlled, how easy it is to get capital out of the home country, and how easy it is to invest in desirable foreign countries—I examine two aspects that are more readily measured, capital openness in the home country and the ease of investment in potential host countries. Both measures are available only after 1970, so these tests focus on the post–Bretton Woods period.

Capital openness allows firms to move their capital out of the country. Whereas capital restrictions affect portfolio investments—investments that do not entail active management of a company—to a greater extent than FDI capital, the use of multiple exchange rates and restrictions on the capital account make it more difficult and costly for firms to move capital out of the home country to set up their factories abroad and to repatriate profits. To capture capital openness, I use the Chinn-Ito measure of capital openness.[28]

The ease of investment in potential host countries also affects how costly moving overseas will be. I use Pandya's entry restriction measure to assess this.[29] Pandya has found that greater entry restrictions lead to less FDI because they force multinationals to share profits and technology with local partners, making overseas production less profitable and more risky.[30] Because it is unlikely that a company would consider investing in any and every country in the world, I use a country's language group as the possible destinations for FDI and take the average of entry restrictions for the group. A shared language makes doing business easier, which would make firms more likely to invest in those countries.[31] To make interpretation of the coefficients easier, I have recoded the variable as the percentage of industries that do not have restrictions on entry.[32]

Table 3.6 examines the effect of firm mobility on immigration policy. I regress immigration policy on capital openness, the average of nonrestricted entry in the language group, and their interaction—firms have to

[28] Chinn and Ito (2008).

[29] Pandya (2014). Entry restrictions measure the percentage of all manufacturing and service industries in which FDI is restricted in a state in a given year.

[30] Pandya (2014).

[31] Results are similar but not statistically significant with states in the same colonial system or all the states in Pandya's dataset as the potential host states.

[32] I also recoded Hong Kong to share the same language group as Taiwan.

TABLE 3.6
Immigration Policy Regressed on Trade and Firm Mobility.

DV: immigration policy	(1) All states	(2) Always open states	(3) States that change capital policy	(4) Without Asian Financial Crisis and Argentina
Trade openness	−4.69*	−5.39	−1.63[+]	−3.22
	(2.36)	(4.59)	(0.91)	(1.82)
Capital openness	0.26		0.13[+]	0.29**
	(0.16)		(0.07)	(0.09)
Nonrestricted entry	−0.62	−1.09	0.16	0.60
	(0.46)	(0.46)	(0.15)	(0.40)
Capital openness* nonrestricted entry	−0.38* (0.18)		−0.14 (0.08)	−0.35** (0.10)
Linear time trend	−0.00[+]	−0.03*	−0.02*	−0.02
	(0.00)	(0.01)	(0.01)	(0.01)
Polity	0.02		0.01*	0.01
	(0.02)		(0.01)	(0.01)
GDP growth	−0.07	0.51	0.01	0.01
	(0.26)	(1.13)	(0.07)	(0.07)
War	−0.13	−0.24*	0.04	0.02
	(0.14)	(0.04)	(0.07)	(0.10)
Constant	4.52[+]	10.46[+]	3.59*	3.99[+]
	(2.57)	(3.34)	(1.38)	(1.97)
Observations	347	93	347	292
R^2	0.37	0.90	0.43	0.45
Country FE	No	Yes	Yes	Yes
Standard errors	Clustered	Robust	Robust	Robust

Notes: Also included: year fixed effects. Standard errors in parentheses. [+] $p < 0.10$, * $p < 0.05$, ** $p < 0.01$, *** $p < 0.001$. *Trade openness* is 1 minus the tariff rate from Clemens and Williamson (2004) and updated by the author. *Capital openness* measures how freely capital can flow in and out of a country, from Chinn and Ito (2008). *Nonrestricted entry* is the average percent of all manufacturing and service industries that foreigners can invest in directly in developing states that share the same language from Pandya (2014). *GDP growth* is from Maddison (2011). *Polity* is the measure of regime type from Marshall, Gurr, and Jaggers (2011). *War* is an indicator variable for war from Sarkees and Wayman (2010). *Linear time trend* is a time trend for each country.

get their money both out of the home country and into the host country—using ordinary least squares (OLS). For several states in the dataset, the measure of capital openness does not change throughout this time period because these states always allow free capital. The inclusion of country fixed effects drops these states from the regression. In model 1, the standard errors are clustered by country so that these states are included in the analysis. In model 2, I examine the effect of the average openness to FDI in the language group only for those states that always have open capital policy. In model 3, I include fixed effects, dropping the states that always have open capital, and in model 4, I repeat that analysis but drop the Asian Financial Crisis years as well as Argentina, which I will discuss shortly. Also included in the regressions are trade openness, measured as 1 minus the tariff rate, a linear time trend, year fixed effects, Polity, GDP growth, and an indicator for war.

From models 1 and 4, we see that firm mobility has the predicted effect on immigration policy when capital is open and there is nonrestricted entry in many target states. To interpret the interaction of capital openness and FDI restrictions, figure 3.4 plots the effect of nonrestricted FDI policies in the language group when capital openness is at the 25th and 75th percentile, respectively, for models 1 and 4.[33] When we cluster the standard errors by country (model 1), we see that there is a negative effect of nonrestricted entry for both open and restricted capital, but that the effect is stronger when capital is open. When we include fixed effects and drop the Asian Financial Crisis and Argentina, we see that there is a positive effect of nonrestricted entry of FDI when capital is restricted but a negative effect when it is open.

In models 2 and 3, we see a similar pattern but one that is not statistically significant at the same level. In model 2, there is a negative coefficient on nonrestricted entry in the language group for these states. While the coefficient is not statistically significant, this may be due in part to the relatively small sample size (93 observations) and the inclusion of country and year fixed effects (a total of 34 variables), which leave little variation to explain. In model 3, the effects are the same as in model 4 but not as large; nonrestricted entry is associated with more immigration restrictions in states with open capital, while it is associated with more open immigration policy in states that have restricted capital.

In model 4, I excluded the years of the Asian Financial Crisis and again excluded Argentina. In response to the Asian Financial Crisis and the subsequent recession, East Asian states, including Japan, South Korea, and Singapore, restricted capital in hopes of stopping the crisis. They also restricted immigration following the economic downturn. As in the case of the Great Depression, we might think that capital restrictions would not lead to more open immigration during an economic crisis because firms do not need additional labor and likely have other policies that they would prefer to spend their lobbying dollars on.

---

[33] The 75th percentile of capital openness is completely free capital movement. War is held at the median, 0, and all other variables are held at their means.

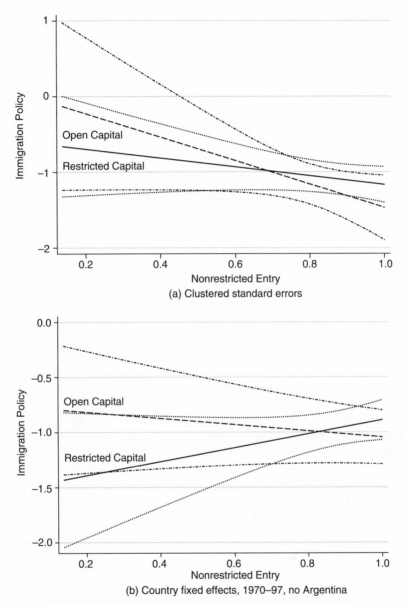

Figure 3.4: Predicted Effects of Capital Openness and Nonrestricted Entry of FDI
for the Language Group.
Note: All other variables except war are held at their means; war held at
median value, 0. Dotted lines are the confidence intervals for restricted
capital and dash-dotted lines are the confidence intervals for open
capital.

Argentina is again an outlier. As in the case of trade policy, Argentina opened capital when it abandoned import-substitution industrialization for open markets in the late 1980s and early 1990s. At the same time, it liberalized the more draconian features of its immigration policy. The change in both policies had more to do with the changing political regime than with firm activity.

CONCLUSION

I argue that policymakers are constrained in their choice of policies to open their state to the international economy: either they can choose openness to low-skill immigrants but restrict trade and firm mobility, or they can choose openness to goods and allow firms to move but restrict low-skill immigration. Policymakers may face additional constraints as well; shipping technologies, like the railroad or the rise of container ships, may so vastly reduce trade costs that trade opens whether policymakers like it or not, and developing countries may open to FDI, enticing firms to move. When these exogenous shocks to trade and firm mobility happen, the policymaker has little room to move on low-skill immigration policy.

The data in this chapter confirm these expectations. Even though the nineteen states examined have used very different regulations to control low-skill immigration, increases in trade openness and firm mobility have led to increased immigration restrictions. These relationships hold whether we examine all the data or examine different time periods. Furthermore, the argument is widely applicable to states that have different types of economies, different regime types, different histories of immigration, and so on. Now that we have established the political dilemma as a general phenomenon, we can examine whether the mechanism I propose to explain this phenomenon holds—that is, whether changes in trade openness, firm mobility, and technology adoption affect firms' willingness to lobby on immigration. In the subsequent chapters, I focus first on the sector level and then on the subnational level to show that it does.

CHAPTER 4

Changing Industry Preferences in the United States

I BEGIN THE INVESTIGATION OF THE MICRO FOUNDATIONS OF MY THEORY at the start of the causal chain. To review, the causal chain linking trade, firm mobility, and productivity to low-skill immigration policy proceeds in four steps. I argue that (1) increase in trade openness, firm mobility, and technology adoption should (2) decrease firms' support for open immigration, which then (3) reduces the support that policymakers receive for open low-skill immigration, which (4) leads them to restrict low-skill immigration. The previous chapter showed that step 1, increased trade openness and firm mobility, leads to step 4, restrictions on low-skill immigration, with data from nineteen very different countries across two centuries of globalization. This chapter examines the link between step 1 and step 2, firms' willingness to support low-skill immigration.

I begin by looking at the more macro-level data—data on lobbying activity by sector for all industries—and then examine in more detail three cases of representative trade associations. My argument has three observable implications at the sector level. First, sectors that have less trade protection or that lose their trade protection should be less supportive of low-skill immigration and less likely to lobby for it. Second, sectors that are more mobile or that become more mobile should be less supportive of and less likely to lobby for low-skill immigration. Third, sectors that are more productive or that increase their productivity should also be less supportive of and less likely to lobby for low-skill immigration. There is also a fourth observable implication that we can test with these data: sectors that use more high-skill labor or become more dependent on high-skill labor should be more likely to lobby for *high-skill* immigration.

The alternative explanations based on the power of labor, nativists, immigrants' groups, and cosmopolitans have implications at this level as well. If the power of labor or nativism arguments are correct, then we should see increased lobbying by unions and nativist groups over this time period, as immigration restrictions have increased. If arguments based on the power of immigrants themselves or cosmopolitans are correct, then we should see less lobbying by these groups over time.

We can also examine the alternative explanation that firms prefer lax enforcement of rules that prevent immigrants from entering the United States legally. If this is the case, then we should see sectors that often hire undocumented immigrants support restrictions on entry *and* support lax enforcement. We should also find that these sectors are relatively unconcerned about enforcement because the government is doing little of it.

SETTING THE STAGE: LOW-SKILL IMMIGRATION POLICY IN THE UNITED STATES

We can split US low-skill immigration policy into four eras. From the founding of the republic until 1875, Congress passed few laws on immigration, and low-skill immigration was very open. From 1875 until the 1920s, immigration was increasingly restricted but still very open. The 1920s ended open immigration and began the era of national origins quotas, when Congress enacted first the Quota Act of 1921 and then a more restrictive Quota Act in 1924. These restrictions remained more or less in place until the 1965 Immigration and Nationality Act (INA) did away with preferential quotas for Northern and Western Europeans. Since then, Congress has tweaked the system but not overhauled it. Over the full span of US history, we see increasing restrictions against low-skill immigrants.

Congress was instrumental in the introduction and passage of almost all these laws, at times over the president's veto. Congress had been the initiator of action on immigration policy—including the Literacy Act in 1917, the two Quota Acts in 1921 and 1924, the McCarren-Walter Act in 1952, the INA in 1965, the Immigration Reform and Control Act in 1986, and the Illegal Immigration Reform and Immigrant Responsibility Act of 1996—until President George W. Bush proposed comprehensive immigration reform.[1]

FIRMS VERSUS SECTORS

In this chapter, I use data on the preferences and activities of different trade associations and industries rather than examining firms. A major issue when one studies firms is the record keeping, or lack thereof, of many firms. Although US corporations, even those not publicly traded, must keep records of their board meetings, little else needs to be recorded. Larger firms are more likely to have kept more detailed records; using firm-level data, then, would bias us toward examining primarily larger firms. Furthermore, the argument is based, in part, on the effects of firms closing; an examination of firms would likely be based on the more successful firms

---

[1] Hutchinson (1981).

that have not closed, as the records of firms no longer in operation are often destroyed. In contrast, trade associations often persist long after some firms have closed, moved overseas, or become more productive, but their preferences are likely to have shifted along the lines of the argument.

Examining the industry as a whole or even representative trade organizations is not without its problems. There is much heterogeneity within industries. Large and small firms often have different preferences, and this may lead to disagreements. Within industries, some product lines may be given trade protection while others are not; some may be able to move production; and some may be able to mechanize, which again may lead to disagreements over policy. Trade associations have to make judgments based on what the leadership thinks will be best for the association and its members, but these judgments will often reflect the domination of larger firms. Even with these caveats, the data provided shed much light on how industry preferences, and by extension firms, change with shifts in the global economy.

INDUSTRY LOBBYING ON IMMIGRATION

I begin by examining which groups lobby Congress on immigration through an examination of data on which groups testify before Congress for 1946–2010 and which groups file lobbying disclosure forms with Congress for 1998–2011. These data show which industries and other interest groups have tried to influence immigration policy, and how this has changed over time. If my argument is correct, I expect that we should see less lobbying by industries as their trade protection declines, they move their factories overseas, and their labor productivity increases. In this sense, we are as interested in the dogs that didn't bark—the firms that do not lobby—as in those that did.

Selection Process in the Lobbying and Testimony Data

As we are interested in which firms do and *do not* lobby on immigration, we must understand the other reasons individual firms, sectors, and interest groups choose not to lobby. One reason interest groups may not lobby is that lobbying is an expensive activity that only the well-organized and well-financed can afford. These costs, known as *collective action costs*, are likely to have a large effect on those groups that do not benefit from or are not hurt greatly by a policy.[2]

---

[2] Olson (1965).

Collective action costs may affect the distribution of firms that lobby. Firms often have two choices when they want to lobby: lobby on their own or as part of a larger trade association. Only very large firms are likely to have the resources to be able to lobby on their own: in Baumgartner and colleagues' seminal research on lobbying, corporations that lobbied on their own spent on average over $1 million on lobbying.[3] Even the much less well-funded citizen groups spent on average a combined total of over $300,000 on lobbying and contributions to political action committees. The average US firm—with sales of $4.4 million and a payroll of about $800,000[4]—cannot afford theses costs.

Instead, the majority of firms lobby through industry trade associations. Still, small firms have less voice and may free ride on the actions of larger firms in these organizations. In more specialized trade associations, large firms in the industry often dominate the association with small firms paying a nominal fee.[5] Even the US Chamber of Commerce, which represents all types of businesses and is one of largest lobbying organizations in the United States, has a board of directors composed mostly of members from large corporations.[6] Trade associations are the site of intraindustry battles about a given issue, but they often take the position of their larger members or a "lowest common denominator" position that appeals to the broad range of members, at the expense of small firms.[7]

Critically for this study, small firms are the ones that are most likely to close when trade openness increases. From "new" new trade theory, we know that smaller firms are likely to be among the least productive firms, making them the most likely to close as international competition increases with trade. But small firms generally have less lobbying voice in Washington, which should delay the effect of trade on lobbying.

In addition to the deterrent of collective action costs, firms and other interest groups may not lobby because they are happy with the status quo. For many reasons—agenda setting and gatekeeping, institutional veto players, and lack of salience—it is more difficult to change the status quo than to defend it.[8] Those who benefit from the status quo, then, may not bother lobbying until it becomes clear that there is a relatively high probability that a new piece of legislation will pass.[9] Nonetheless, when it appears that change might occur, we should expect firms that benefit from the status quo to lobby to defend it. In the analysis below, I will pay special attention to the years leading up to a major change in immigration law.

---

[3] Baumgartner et al. (2009, 199).
[4] Census Bureau (2011).
[5] Walker (1983, 401).
[6] US Chamber of Commerce (2015).
[7] Drutman (2015, 19).
[8] Baumgartner et al. (2009, 41–44).
[9] Baumgartner et al. (2009, 150).

A final reason that firms may not lobby is a belief that they will be unable to sway the will of Congress. While I hypothesize that firms and sectors will lobby less when they care less about immigration, firms and sectors may anticipate that their lobbying will be ineffective, and choose not to lobby. If anti-immigration forces are strong, lobbying by business interests will likely be ineffective, and firms may lobby on another issue or spend their lobbying dollars elsewhere.

When we use congressional testimony data as a measure of lobbying, we add another layer of selection. In both the House and the Senate, those who testify must be invited either by the committee chair or by members of the minority party.[10] Submissions likewise are placed into the record by the committee. Committee members thus play the role of the gatekeeper: groups that have more resources and have established relationships with key committee members and their staff are more likely to be invited, as the committee's staff know that the group exists and, importantly, know the viewpoint of the group and whether it aligns with the goals of the hearing.[11] Thus the best-organized groups are the ones that are invited to testify; as smaller firms are not as well represented in Washington, we again expect that testimony will be biased toward larger firms. Because larger firms are more productive, they are less likely to bear the brunt of trade openness, which may mean its effects also take longer to appear in the testimony data.

Who Testifies before Congress?

Congressional hearings play an important role in policymaking. Members of Congress hold both legislative and nonlegislative hearings: legislative hearings help shape current legislative efforts, and nonlegislative hearings often establish new turf for future legislative battles.[12] Moreover, committees, especially in the House of Representatives, exert significant gatekeeping and agenda-setting power.[13] Who testifies, then, tells us which voices get represented when legislation is crafted or when the status quo is defended.

To find data on which groups testify before Congress on immigration, I used the Policy Agendas Project's list of congressional hearings from 1946 to 2010 to identify the relevant hearings in the House and Senate.[14] One concern we might have is that committees tend to have close ties to interest

[10] Carr (2006) and Sachs (2003).
[11] Leyden (1995, 434).
[12] Talbert, Jones, and Baumgartner (1995)
[13] Kollman (1997).
[14] Baumgartner and Jones's (2013). See online appendix D for more on the coding of the hearings.

groups that care deeply about an issue—for example, the Agriculture Committee may have close ties to farm groups, and the committees on labor have close ties to unions—and we may, therefore, not get a representative sample of organizations that care about immigration.[15] Yet almost every committee in both the House and the Senate has held hearings on immigration policy during this time period, making it likely that the testimony data will include the broad swath of groups that are interested in immigration.

There are a total of 783 hearings on immigration.[16] On average, Congress held 12 hearings on immigration per year (median of 11). The number of hearings increases in years in which major pieces of legislation were being debated (fig. 4.1). There have also been more hearings over time, reflecting the greater activity in Congress in general.

The organizations and individuals who testified were classified as industries or nonbusiness groups to match with existing data on tariffs, trade, foreign direct investment, and productivity, and to match existing explanations on immigration from the literature.[17] In these 783 hearings, there were a total of 7,362 witnesses and 4,093 submissions. The number of witnesses per hearing range from 0 to 103, with 9.3 witnesses on average (median of 7), and the number of submissions per hearing range from 0 to 104, with 5.2 on average (median of 2). Public sector officials, including members of Congress, the executive branch, and state and local government, are the most common witnesses. This is not surprising, as hearings are often used by Congress as oversight of the executive branch. After public sector officials, left-leaning organizations testified most often (768 witnesses), but agriculture and high-skill professional services (IT, finance, and consulting, but not including health care or chemicals) were not far behind, with 618 and 635, respectively. Submissions follow the same pattern: public sector groups have the most submissions (1,131), followed by left-leaning organizations (579), and among businesses, agriculture submits most often (380), followed by high-skill professional services (291).

---

[15] Kollman (1997).

[16] Baumgartner and Jones's (2013) database originally had 827 hearings listed, but we found that 30 of them were duplicates and that 14 were on the immigration status of a single individual.

[17] Individuals representing an organization or submissions from an organization were coded as belonging to that organization. Citizen witnesses are classified based on their profession, as they are often used as representatives of others who are in a situation similar to their own. Van Der Slik and Stenger (1977, 471). The most limiting factor is data on tariffs; for tariff data early in the period, the Statistical Abstract of the United States categorized data into 15 categories. Census Bureau (Various Years*c*). Nontradable industries were classified based on the categorization of firms by the Bureau of Economic Analysis (to be matched to data on FDI); these groupings, more or less, conform to two-digit Standard Industry Classification (SIC) codes. See the codebook in online appendix D for more details.

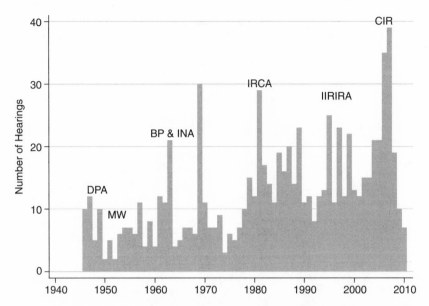

Figure 4.1: Number of Hearings in the US House of Representatives and Senate on Immigration and Migrant and Seasonal Workers.

Note: Data from Baumgartner and Jones's (2013) and includes all hearings except those for individual cases. *DPA* is the Displaced Persons Act; *MW* is the McCarren-Walter Act; *BP & INA* is the end of the Bracero Program and the 1965 Immigration and Nationality Act; *IRCA* is the Immigration Reform and Control Act; *IIRIRA* is the Illegal Immigration Reform and Immigrant Responsibility Act; and *CIR* is comprehensive immigration reform.

Witnesses and submissions from businesses were on average 20 percent of all witnesses and 22 percent of all submissions.

If the argument of this book is correct, we should expect that businesses should testify and submit less often over time. Businesses are powerful interests in US politics and thus could get on the agenda if they wanted to. It is likely that if they *do not* appear on the agenda, it is because they do not care to testify, not because they cannot testify. As we saw in chapter 3, during this time period tariff barriers have fallen, on average, from a high of almost 10 percent in 1946 to about 1.2 percent in 2009; it has become much easier for firms to move overseas as other states have removed their barriers to foreign direct investment; and the use of laborsaving technology has increased, leading to increased productivity. The reduction in trade barriers should have led to the closure of firms, especially small firms, that use much low-skill labor. The reduction in barriers to FDI should have allowed firms,

(a) Total Witnesses/Submissions

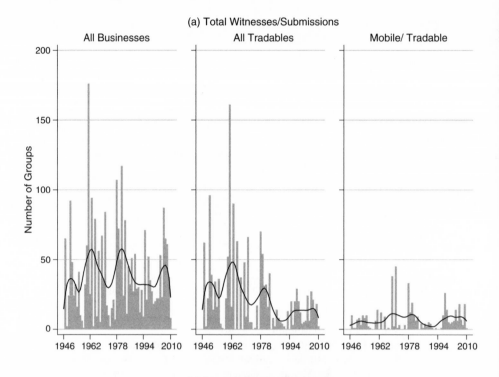

(b) Average Number Per Hearing

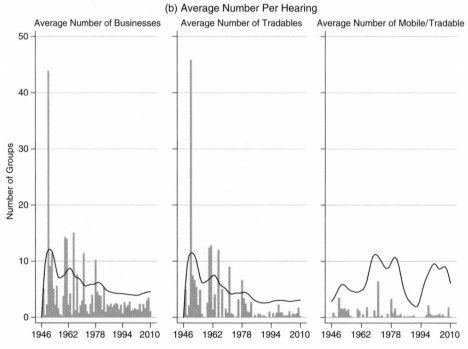

Figure 4.2: For caption see next page.

especially large firms, to move their low-skill-labor-intensive production overseas. Technology would have allowed many of the remaining firms to do more with less labor. Finally, even the nontradable/immobile sectors may have decreased their support for open immigration because they could use native, laid-off labor.

The data provide support for these hypotheses (fig. 4.2). The top panel, figure 4.2a, shows the total number of times that a representative testified or put a submission into the record in a given year for all business groups, including both trade associations and individual businesses; for all tradable industries, which include all manufacturing, mining, and agriculture; and for all mobile and tradable industries, which include all manufacturing but exclude mining and agriculture. Overall, we see that the number of businesses has remained fairly constant over the sixty-four years. However, this result is driven by the increasing number of hearings. In the bottom panel, figure 4.2b, we see that the average number of businesses appearing before Congress or submitting a document per hearing has dropped from a high of 8.76 on average per hearing during the 1950s to 2.07 on average per hearing in the 2000s. The picture is even more stark if we examine all tradable industries; the number of times that tradable industries testified or placed submissions into the record drops in both total numbers and per hearing. When we exclude tradable industries that are relatively immobile—agriculture and mining—we see a similar pattern to that for all tradable industries, but it is not as stark. The drop in the number of times tradable and mobile firms testified or submitted to the record holds even during periods in which immigration policy was reformed: smaller numbers of firms from all tradable and mobile sectors testified around IRCA in the early 1980s than around the changes to the INA in the mid-1960s; even smaller numbers testified during the debates around CIR in 2006 and 2007. Thus even during times when the status quo was under threat, fewer tradable and mobile firms were interested in influencing immigration policy than previously.

Figure 4.2: Number of Times That a Representative from Business Served as a Witness or Placed a Submission in the Record.
Note: Bars show the total and average number of times groups served as a witness or placed a submission in the record, respectively. Line is the loess-smoothed trend line (bandwidth of 0.25). Data on which groups testified were collected and coded by the author. Tradable industries include all manufacturing, mining, and agriculture. Mobile/Tradable includes all manufacturing but excludes mining and agriculture.

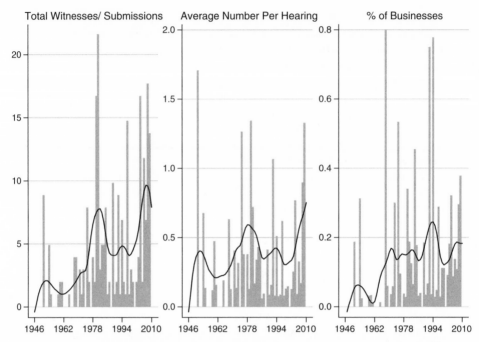

Figure 4.3: Number of Times That a Representative from the Low-Skill
Nontradable Sector Served as a Witness or Placed a Submission in the
Record.

Note: Bars show the total and average number of times groups served
as a witness or placed a submission in the record, respectively. Line
is the loess-smoothed trend line (bandwidth of 0.25). Data on which
groups testified were collected and coded by the author. The low-skill
nontradable sector includes construction, hospitality, recreation, retail,
low-skill services, travel, utilities, and wholesale.

In contrast to the tradable and mobile sector, the low-skill nontradable
sector has continued to testify on immigration and tends to be more active
in periods when changes to the status quo are likely (fig. 4.3).[18] While
these firms have been more active in congressional hearings since the mid-
1960s, they have not greatly increased their numbers since then either in
total or per hearing. Nonetheless, they have become a larger proportion of
the business lobby on immigration. This is consistent with the argument;
because these firms can use the native labor that has been laid off and
have had their own increases in productivity, they do not need much

---

[18] The low-skill nontradable sector includes firms and trade associations in construction,
hospitality, recreation, retail, low-skill services, travel, utilities, and wholesale.

more immigrant labor. Instead, these firms can use their influence on other issues.

To examine this more rigorously, I regressed the activity of the different industries on their level of trade openness and productivity in table 4.1. To measure trade openness, I use Bernard and colleagues' measure of import penetration—which captures the effect of tariffs, nontariff barriers, and other trade costs—from low-wage countries and from all countries.[19] The authors find that increased trade in an industry from low-wage countries led to more plant closures, lower output, and lower employment in that industry.[20] Further, surviving plants were more likely to switch their product line to one that was more capital intensive.[21] Increased low-wage trade in an industry, and increased import penetration in general, should lead to less support for open immigration from that industry as plants close or change to a more capital-intensive product line. To measure productivity, I include the real value added per worker.[22] Both measures are lagged three years as the effect of changes in trade and productivity might not be immediately felt. I also include industry fixed effects to capture any unchanging aspects of the industry that might affect their lobbying and access to Congress.

In table 4.1, we find results consistent with the argument. Industries with greater import penetration, in general or from low-wage countries, testify or place submissions into the record less often, regardless of whether we look at the total number of appearances per year or per hearing. The results on productivity are in the hypothesized direction (negative) but are not statistically significant. That may be because trade openness often leads to productivity increases, and so the effect of productivity may be included in the trade variables. As in the cross-national data presented in chapter 5, trade has a larger effect on firms' willingness to lobby on immigration than does firm mobility; there is no statistically significant effect of outward foreign direct investment.[23] On the one hand, industries with more outward FDI are larger and thus may be more likely to testify or place submissions into the record, leading to a positive correlation between the two. On the other hand, more FDI may lead to less support for immigration at home. These two effects together may be leading to the null result. Nonetheless, prior choices to open an industry to trade have led to greater import penetration and less support for open immigration.

---

[19] Data are from Bernard, Jensen, and Schott (2006). Results are similar with import penetration from China but not statistically significant.

[20] Bernard, Jensen, and Schott (2006).

[21] Bernard, Jensen, and Schott (2006).

[22] Data are from Bartelsman and Gray (2013).

[23] See online appendix C for the regression table.

TABLE 4.1

Effect of the Trade Openness and Productivity on Groups' Participation in Congressional Hearings.

Dependent variable:	Total times serving as a witness or placing a submission		Average per hearing	
Low-wage import penetration	−3.05*		−0.15*	
(3-year lag)	(1.24)		(0.06)	
Import penetration		−0.59***		−0.03***
(3-year lag)		(0.09)		(0.00)
Value added	−0.30	−0.29	−0.04	−0.04
(3-year lag)	(0.32)	(0.32)	(0.04)	(0.04)
Constant	2.55	2.53	0.28	0.28
	(1.50)	(1.52)	(0.19)	(0.19)
Observations	360	360	360	360
R^2	0.025	0.032	0.035	0.038

Notes: All models include industry fixed effects. Robust standard errors in parentheses. + p < 0.10, * p < 0.05, ** p < 0.01, *** p < 0.001. *Low-wage import penetration (3-year lag)* is import penetration in each industry from low-wage countries, and *import penetration (3-year lag)* is total import penetration; both are lagged 3-years, and are from Bernard, Jensen, and Schott (2006). *Value added (3-year lag)* is the real value added per worker (logged), lagged 3 years, from Bartelsman and Gray (2013).

With the congressional testimony data, we can also examine some of the other hypotheses from the literature. Arguments based on the relative power of labor unions hypothesize that as unions become more powerful, there should be increasing restrictions. What we find in the testimony data is that the power of organized labor has greatly decreased over the past half century, consistent with the conventional wisdom about organized labor in the United States (fig. 4.4). As discussed above, this pattern is not likely to have occurred because organized labor is happy with the status quo; instead, at times of major reform, such as around IRCA in 1986 or around CIR in 2006 and 2007, labor should have been involved. Instead, we see the decline of US labor at the same time restrictions have increased; suggesting that, at least in the United States, this argument has less explanatory power.

Another hypothesis from the literature is that as nativism increases, immigration policy should become more restrictive. One way to measure nativism is the number of times that right-leaning groups, those that are explicitly anti-immigration, testify or place submissions into the record. Right-leaning organizations do not necessarily testify before Congress or place submissions into the record every year, but they are active in years when major changes to immigration are being debated (fig. 4.5). While it is clear from these data that nativist groups have important access to

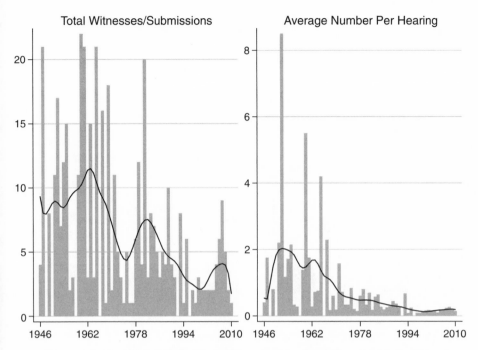

Figure 4.4: Number of Times That a Representative from Organized Labor Served as a Witness or Placed a Submission in the Record.
Note: Bars show the total and average number of times groups served as a witness or placed a submission in the record, respectively. Line is the loess-smoothed trend line (bandwidth of 0.25). Data on which groups testified were collected and coded by the author. Organized labor includes all private sector labor unions.

Congress, there is not clear evidence that nativism has increased. While the total number of witnesses and submissions from right-leaning groups has increased, this is largely an artifact of the increased number of hearings; the average number of right-leaning groups testifying per hearing has remained constant at about one per hearing since the late 1970s.

A final hypothesis from the literature that we can examine is that when organizations representing immigrants or cosmopolitans (generally left-leaning, pro-immigration groups) have relatively more power, immigration policy should be more open. Left-leaning groups are more active around the major immigration debates (fig. 4.6). However, the average number of these groups testifying per hearing has dropped over time, with the exception of the debate on comprehensive immigration reform in the late 2000s. This all suggests that the nonbusiness pro-immigration groups have

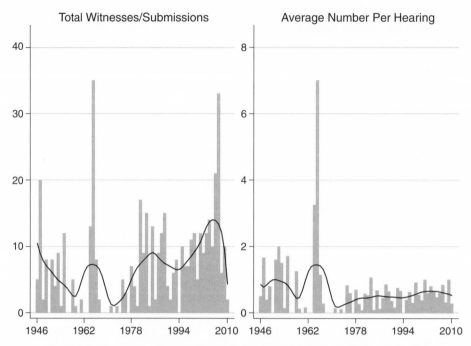

Figure 4.5: Number of Times That a Representative from Right-Leaning Groups
Served as a Witness or Placed a Submission in the Record.
Note: Bars show the total and average number of times groups served as
a witness or placed a submission in the record, respectively. Line is the
loess-smoothed trend line (bandwidth of 0.25). Data on which groups
testified were collected and coded by the author. Right-leaning includes
all explicitly anti-immigration and single-issue nativist groups.

become less influential over time as well, which also likely explains the
increase in restrictions.

One observable implication of this book's argument is that while
support for low-skill immigration may have declined, the expansion of the
high-skill sector should have led high-skill firms to increase their lobbying.
In the testimony data, we see exactly that (fig. 4.7). Starting in the 1980s,
the number of high-skill firms in sectors like consulting, information
technology, and finance testifying or placing submissions in the record
increased in both total numbers and on average per hearing. That said,
in the 2000s these firms still make up only about 13 percent of the groups
testifying or placing a submission in the record. The relatively low level of
access given to these groups may explain why the United States still had not
passed a large-scale high-skill immigration program as of 2015.

Who Lobbies?

I now turn to examining data on which groups lobby Congress on immigration.[24] Consistent record keeping of lobbying activity has occurred only since the passage of the Lobbying Disclosure Act (LDA) in 1995, and records are available starting in 1998. Under the LDA, lobbyists are required to file if they have made more than one contact with a covered individual, which includes members of Congress and their staff and some members of the executive branch, including the secretary of homeland security, the commissioner of customs and border protection, and the director of the Bureau of Citizenship and Immigration Services. Groups can do a small amount of lobbying without having to register. The threshold for registration biases the data toward observing only lobbying by medium and large firms and trade associations. The filings include data on what issues the firms or organizations lobbied on, but not whether they lobbied for or against a specific bill, and the total amount they spent on all lobbying, but not how much was spent on any given issue.

In contrast to the testimony data, the lobbying data show more activity by business organizations than by nonbusiness groups. On average about 561 firms or trade associations and about 269 nonbusiness groups lobbied on immigration each year.[25] This discrepancy may be driven by who has to report their lobbying; many of the nonbusiness groups that testify are nonprofits and religious organizations that likely do not meet the threshold for registration.

My argument about the effects of trade, firm mobility, and productivity on support for immigration has three observable implications that we can examine with these data. First, in chapter 2, I had assumed that firms may have other issues besides immigration that they care about. Given these other issues, if immigration is not as useful for the industry or if there is a high level of anti-immigrant sentiment, firms may choose to lobby on other issues that would increase their profits. Consistent with this hypothesis, immigration is not the only issue that firms lobby on; on average firms and trade associations that lobby on immigration also lobby on 7.15 other issues in a given year. Even firms and trade associations lobbying on agricultural or seasonal low-skill immigration lobby on average on 7.38 other issues a year.

The second implication is that, as the lobbying data are available only since 1998, when tariffs were already quite low and firm mobility and

---

[24] Data on firm lobbying are available for 1998–2011 from the Center for Responsive Politics (CRP). Center for Responsive Politics (N.d.). For more details on the coding of the data see online appendix E.

[25] I categorized the firms, trade associations, and other interest groups into the same groups as in the congressional testimony data.

(a) Total Witnesses/Submissions

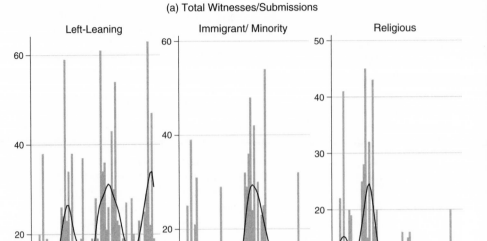

(b) Average Number Per Hearing

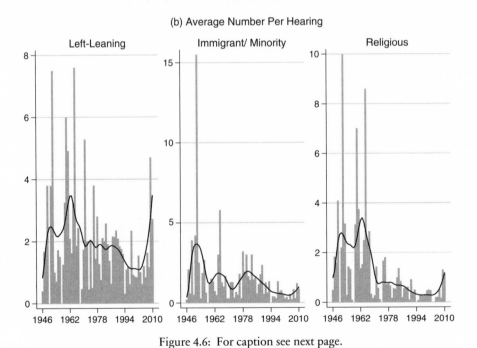

Figure 4.6: For caption see next page.

productivity were quite high, we should expect that firms in tradable industries and in industries that are more mobile or more productive should lobby on immigration less than firms in services or immobile or less productive sectors. One measure of intensity of lobbying on immigration examines the percent of issues that firms/organizations in an industry lobby on that are about low-skill immigration. If we examine a difference of means, immigration makes up 15 percent of the issues that nontradable/nonmobile firms lobbied on compared to only 4 percent of the issues lobbied on by tradable/mobile firms ($p < 0.001$ in a two-tailed test).[26] It might be the case that tradable firms show up to lobby only if they think that there may be a change in the status quo. Yet if we examine only 2006 and 2007, when comprehensive immigration reform was a real possibility, the difference in lobbying between tradable and nontradable sectors stands; immigration comprised 12 percentage points more of the issues that nontradable firms lobbied on (15 percent of issues) than was the case for tradable (3 percent) firms ($p < 0.001$ in a two-tailed test). Thus tradable sectors were much less likely to lobby on immigration than were nontradable sectors.

There is also an effect of increased trade openness among the tradable sectors. As tariffs decrease, firms and trade associations in those tradable industries are less likely to lobby on immigration. To examine this hypothesis, I used a simple regression of immigration as a percent of issues lobbied upon on the tariff level for the industry with robust standard errors, which allows us to examine whether there is a statistically significant relationship

Figure 4.6: Number of Times That a Representative from Left-Leaning, Immigrant/Minority, and Religious Groups Served as a Witness or Placed a Submission in the Record.
Note: Bars show the total and average number of times groups served as a witness or placed a submission in the record, respectively. Line is the loess-smoothed trend line (bandwidth of 0.25). Data on which groups testified were collected and coded by the author. Left-leaning includes human rights groups, children's rights, refugee single-issue groups, pro-immigration single-issue groups, civil rights groups that are not explicitly tied to an immigrant or minority group, aid and relief groups, and pacifist groups. Immigrant and minority groups include all groups representing a single ethnic or minority group; if groups represent both an issue or religion and an ethnic group, they were coded as an immigrant/minority group. Religious groups are those that are explicitly religious, but do not include health-care systems tied to religions.

[26] All services, construction, transportation, government, utility, wholesale, retail, hospitality, amusement, and health care are categorized as nontradable/nonmobile.

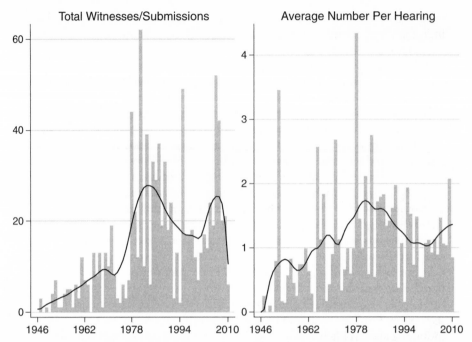

Figure 4.7: Number of Witnesses and Submissions from High-Tech Professional Services Firms.
Note: Bars show the total and average number of times groups served as a witness or placed a submission in the record, respectively. Line is the loess-smoothed trend line (bandwidth of 0.25). Data on which groups testified were collected and coded by the author. High-tech professional services include consulting, information technology, finance, insurance, real estate, telecom, and law, among other high-skill professions.

between tariffs and lobbying. The coefficient on tariff lagged five years is 0.47 and is statistically significant at conventional levels ($p < 0.01$).[27] I lag the tariff level five years because, as argued above, it may take time for the effect of a tariff change to be felt in trade associations or by firms. Substantively, the effect of an increase from no tariff (the minimum tariff at this time) to an 11.2 percent tariff (the maximum tariff) would mean that immigration makes up 5 percentage points more of the issues the firms and trade associations lobby on; for comparison, immigration makes up 8 percent of the issues that the median firm lobbies on, making the effect of tariffs quite substantial.

---

[27] Tariff data are from Schott (2010). See online appendix C for the regression table.

Import penetration also has an effect on lobbying by tradable sectors, but the effect is felt faster than that of tariff barriers. In the similar regression model of the percent of issues on low-skill immigration with robust standard errors, the regression coefficient on import penetration from low-wage countries lagged two years is -0.02 and statistically significant at conventional levels ($p < 0.05$).[28] If import penetration increases from its minimum of about 0 to the maximum of 78 percent, the proportion of issues that are on low-skill immigration drops almost 2 percentage points. Given that for the median firm immigration makes up 8 percent of the issues firms lobby on, low-wage trade has an important effect on firm lobbying, even if the effect is smaller than that of tariffs. Thus as trade openness increases—whether owing to decreased tariffs or to increased import penetration—firms lobby less on low-skill immigration.

As in the cross-national data and in the data on congressional testimony, trade has a larger effect on firms' willingness to lobby on immigration than does firm mobility; there is no statistically significant effect of outward foreign direct investment.[29] Industries with more outward FDI are larger, and larger industries tend to lobby more in general, which could lead to a positive correlation between the two, but more FDI may lead to less support for immigration at home. These two effects together may be leading to the null result.

Sectors that have greater productivity are also less likely to lobby on low-skill immigration. Much as I did with the trade and foreign direct investment variables, I regress the percent of issues on low-skill immigration on an index of productivity for the sector lagged three years with robust standard errors.[30] Consistent with my argument, the coefficient on the productivity index is -0.08 ($p < 0.01$). If productivity increases from the 25th percentile to the 75th percentile, the percent of issues on low-skill immigration drops from about 4 percentage points to about 3 percentage points, a smaller but still substantively important change for the median firm. Thus the data confirm the argument: sectors with lower

[28] The results are substantively the same if we use import penetration from China as the explanatory variable or in general, and if we lag any of these variables one to four years. Data are from Bernard, Jensen, and Schott (2006). Low-wage import penetration is highly correlated with tariffs and so cannot be included in the same regression. See online appendix C for the regression table.

[29] See online appendix C for the regression table.

[30] Data are from Bartelsman and Gray (2013). Productivity, FDI, tariffs, and import penetration are highly correlated—as we might expect—and so cannot be included in a single regression. Here I use the five-factor index; results are similar with a different lag of the five-factor productivity index, as well as the four-factor index and logged value added per worker. See online appendix C for the regression table.

tariffs, more import penetration, and/or higher productivity are less likely to lobby on immigration.[31]

With these data, we can also examine arguments from the literature as well as other observable implications of the argument. Unions, which generally oppose immigration, have increased lobbying on immigration, especially since comprehensive immigration reform became a major issue in 2006. On average 28 unions and affiliated organizations lobbied on immigration each year prior to 2006, whereas 83 did so after 2006 (the difference is statistically significant in a two-tailed test at $p < 0.001$). Immigration also has increased in comparative importance among the issues with which unions are concerned; on average before 2006 immigration made up 8.5 percent of the issues that unions lobbied on, but after 2006 it made up 10.5 percent. The lobbying data for unions contradicts the congressional testimony data; it thus appears that unions have increased their lobbying on immigration but that they have had less influence, as measured by testimony, over the issue. The increasing restrictions on immigration, then, are unlikely to have been the result of union activity.

Lobbying by right-leaning—nativist and anti-tax—groups on immigration has changed little since 1998. There has been a small uptick in the number of these groups around comprehensive immigration reform (difference of means between before 2006 and after is 13.75, $p < 0.05$), but the percent of issues that immigration makes up has not changed much over the time period (difference of less than 5 percent, $p = 0.3$). As with to the data from congressional testimony, this suggests that nativism has remained fairly constant over time.

A third argument from the literature focuses on left-leaning groups—cosmopolitan/human rights groups, ethnic groups, and religious groups that often are pro-immigration—as agents of openness (fig. 4.8). As was the case with labor unions, lobbying by these left-leaning groups, especially the cosmopolitan and religious groups, has increased since comprehensive immigration reform was proposed, but their access to Congress, as measured by their testimony, has decreased. Thus it appears that the organized public has not become more nativist; if anything, it may have become more left-leaning on immigration over these thirteen years, but the influence of left-leaning groups has waned over time even when Democrats have controlled Congress.

A final observable implication of my argument is that as the high-skill sector has expanded, it should have increased lobbying on immigration.[32]

---

[31] Firms' lobbying behavior is also affected by the lobbying of other sectors; see online appendix C.

[32] The high-skill sector includes consulting, information technology, finance, insurance, real estate, telecommunications, and law, among other high-skill professions.

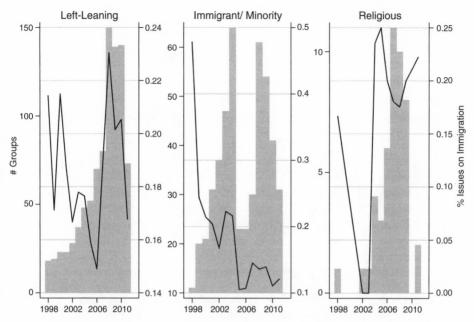

Figure 4.8: Number of Left-Leaning Groups That Lobby on Immigration and Immigration as a Percent of Issues That They Lobby On.
Note: Data on which groups lobby are from Center for Responsive Politics (N.d.) and were coded by the author.

Since 1998, the number of firms and trade associations that represent the high-skill professional services sector has increased greatly, especially since comprehensive immigration reform first came up for a vote in Congress in 2006 (fig. 4.9). Prior to 2006, on average 150 firms and trade associations from this sector lobbied on immigration, whereas after 2006 the average number has more than doubled to 359 (the difference is statistically significant in a two-tailed test at $p < 0.001$). Immigration now makes up a somewhat larger percentage of issues that these firms lobby on as well, increasing from 11.7 percent pre-2006 to 13.9 percent thereafter ($p < 0.01$ in a two-tailed test).

In sum, the data on sectoral lobbying—both the data on congressional testimony and those on lobbying as defined by the Lobbying Disclosure Act—support the argument of this book. Firms and trade associations in sectors with lower tariffs or more import penetration are less likely to lobby or testify; they are also less likely to lobby if they have higher firm mobility, and/or if they have higher productivity. There is less evidence for the existing arguments from the literature: nativism does not seem to have increased—if anything, cosmopolitanism has increased among the

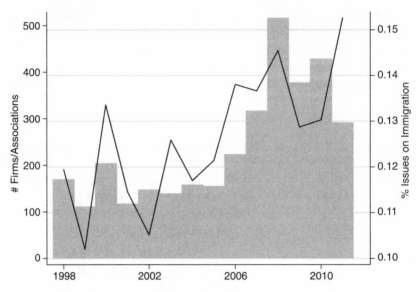

Figure 4.9: Number of High-Tech Professional Services Groups That Lobby on Immigration and Immigration as a Percent of Issues That They Lobby On.
Note: Data on which groups lobby are from Center for Responsive Politics (N.d.) and were coded by the author. High-tech professional services include consulting, information technology, finance, insurance, real estate, telecommunications, and law, among other high-skill professions.

organized public. Labor unions, left-leaning groups, immigrant groups, and religious groups have all increased their lobbying on immigration since 1998, but this has not led to increased access at congressional hearings, regardless of which party controls Congress. The data, then, suggest that less support for open low-skill immigration from firms and their trade associations has resulted in nativist groups having comparably, but not absolutely, more influence over immigration policy, leading to more restrictions.

CHANGES IN INDUSTRY GROUP PREFERENCES

Congressional testimony and lobbying data provide evidence about how different sectors' willingness to lobby has changed with trade openness, firm mobility, and productivity. Yet these data do not cover all firm and trade association activity that we might call lobbying, such as grassroots campaigning or contacts with noncovered members of the executive branch. Additionally, there is the selection issue when we examine lobbying data: firms and trade associations first have to decide whether it is worth their time to lobby. They may not lobby because they are not interested in the issue; because they are satisfied with the status quo; or because they think their lobbying will be ineffective. To overcome these limitations, I examine the words of the industry associations directly to understand their changing preferences on immigration; the data give us some ability to distinguish between cases where firms do not care about immigration and cases where they are satisfied with the status quo or think that there is too much opposition to overcome.

When trade first begins to open, the trade association may be more or less supportive of immigration or may be split on the issue. Some firms in the industry may take advantage of technology, if possible, to become more productive; some may move overseas; some may choose to close and take what capital they can out of the business; and some may have no other option but to push for more open immigration to stay in business. The firms that adopt technology or move overseas may want to lobby on other issues, as immigration will not lower their costs (much). Depending on industry characteristics—whether there is technology firms can adopt or whether they can move production—the trade association may stop supporting low-skill immigration immediately or may continue to support it, deeming that low-skill immigration is the only option left to enable them to stay in business. However, over time we should see a decrease in support for immigration from the trade association as greater trade openness leads more firms to close, adopt technology, or move overseas.

To test these hypotheses, I examine three trade associations: in textiles (the National Textile Association, NTA), in steel (the American Iron and Steel Institute, AISI), and in labor-intensive, specialty crop agriculture (the Western Growers Association, WGA). While lobbying data do not exist prior to the mid-1990s, we have reason to think that these industries supported low-skill immigration at some point during their history; in the early twentieth century, textiles and metals, including steel, were the third- and fourth-largest employers of immigrants by share of the workforce, respectively, and agriculture joined them in the top ten by the 1980s.[33]

While all three of these industries have been major employers of low-skill labor at some point in their history, they differ in their tradability, mobility, and ability to use technology. Increasing trade openness and international competition have hit these industries at different times. Textiles have always been very tradable; they were some of the early goods that were imported in bulk from Great Britain to the United States. When the textile industry was first developed in the United States, it was protected, first, by

[33] Ruggles et al. (2010).

an undervalued currency, as the country remained on a bimetallic standard until 1879, and then by relatively high tariffs.[34] In the early twentieth century, however, textiles began to face increased competition from new producers in places with lower labor costs like Japan, South America, and the American South. The NTA was an organization primarily based in the North during this time period; while tariffs provided protection from *foreign* producers, they could provide no relief from *Southern* producers. Thus textiles had to react to this increased competition and had a few options to choose from: they could have moved production to the American South; they could have adopted new technologies to enhance productivity; they could have lobbied for increased immigration; or they could have closed.

Steel didn't face much trade pressure or international competition until the mid-twentieth century. American steel companies were the most technologically advanced in the early twentieth century and could compete on price against European steel. In the mid-twentieth century, with the dollar overvalued and increased competition from Europe and Japan, the steel industry faced a set of choices similar to those the textile industry had faced fifty years earlier: move production overseas (instead of to the South); change technology to become more productive; lobby for increased immigration; or close.

It wasn't until the late twentieth and early twenty-first centuries that labor-intensive agriculture felt much trade pressure or international competition. In part, this was due to technology; it was very difficult to ship perishable goods long distances. Many of these labor-intensive crops were also subject to tariffs and nontariff barriers that made foreign production more difficult. A major change in trade protection for these goods occurred with the passage of the North American Free Trade Agreement (NAFTA). The agreement gave Mexican producers—who were competitive with the United States—greater access to US markets. Free trade agreements with other Latin American countries have also increased competition, as has China's entry into the World Trade Organization. Labor-intensive agriculture has not had the same choices as textiles and steel when faced with this increase in competition: many of their crops are not yet mechanized and mobility is limited, although it has increased in recent years. Farmers, then, are mostly faced with either lobbying on immigration or going out of business.

Given the timing of the trade shocks and the different options available to firms in these industries, I expect that the NTA would be the first of the three groups to cease to care about open low-skill immigration, followed by steel, and then, perhaps, by agriculture. When the trade shocks first begin to hit these different organizations, textiles and steel may increase their

[34] Frieden (2014).

interest in immigration or may increase their interest in one of the other options, such as increasing productivity or moving. Because these options are more limited for agriculture, I expect that the trade shocks should lead to increased support for open immigration.

To measure how each group perceived and reacted to these changes in competition and trade openness, I examined each group's trade publication. In the case of the NTA and the AISI, I reviewed the minutes of their biannual or annual meetings. The WGA publishes a monthly magazine about issues affecting the farmers, which includes both a report from the annual meetings and additional articles, and a random sample of articles from this magazine were coded. In total, there were 186 articles coded from the NTA, 147 articles from the AISI, and 660 articles (out of a total of 998 articles on trade, immigration, FDI, and technology) from the WGA. Meeting minutes were available for the NTA for 1906–41, for the AISA for 1910–71, and for the WGA for 1931–2012. Each article was coded to reveal how the group perceived the changes in the national and global economy, and how they reacted to these changes. Variables included trade openness, general trade, imports, exports, international competition, and domestic competition; firm mobility both within the United States and internationally; productivity enhancement through both human capital and technology; and immigration, including general, low-skill, and high-skill immigration, and enforcement.[35]

The National Textile Association

The National Textile Association, now part of the National Council of Textile Organizations, is the oldest textile organization still in existence. The NTA was founded in 1854 in Massachusetts and was primarily an organization for textile manufacturers in the Northeast. Beginning in the early 1900s, it recruited a few members from the South as well; however, most Southern manufacturers were members of the American Cotton Manufacturers Association at the time.

Throughout its history, the NTA has faced competition from trade, even with the relatively high tariffs placed on textiles. By the late 1800s, the NTA faced increased international competition from European, Japanese, and South American producers. This increased competition is reflected in their meeting minutes. The first two graphs in figure 4.10 show how the NTA perceived international competition, in terms of imports and

---

[35] Occasionally, authors discussed trade between two other countries, and this was not coded. Also not coded were articles on productivity (technology or human capital) that were not tied to issues of trade, competition, immigration, or firm mobility. For more details on the coding process, see the codebook in online appendix F.

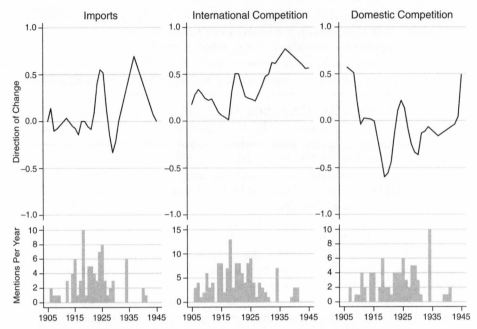

Figure 4.10: The NTA's Perceptions of Imports, International Competition, and Domestic Competition.
Note: Top graph is the loess-smoothed trend line (bandwidth of 0.25) of the average perceived change in the variable. Scores greater than zero mean that on average the variable is increasing; less than zero, decreasing; and at zero, there is no change, the positive changes equal the negative changes, or the variable simply was mentioned. The bottom graph is the number of articles mentioning the variable per year. Data coded by the author; see the codebook in online appendix F.

other fractures. The top part of the graph shows the average perceived change in imports and international competition each year, respectively, and the bottom graph shows the number of mentions per year. In the top graph, scores above zero mean that the NTA thinks imports or international competition is increasing; less than zero, decreasing; and at zero, they think there has not been a change, the positive changes equal the negative changes, or the variable simply was mentioned. Both imports and international competition are mentioned in many articles until the Great Depression, and in most years, international competition is perceived to be increasing, as are imports, although to a lesser degree.

The NTA also had to contend with increased competition from domestic producers in the US South. Textile mills began to be developed in the US South after the Civil War, but the major expansion began after the

International Cotton Exposition in Atlanta in 1881.[36] The Southern mills had several advantages over the Northern mills. Wages in the South were much lower than in the North. In 1900 in South Carolina, wages were about one-third to one-half of those in the textile industry in Massachusetts, where many of the NTA's members were located.[37] While the wage differential decreased over time, wages in the South were still 75 to 80 percent what they were in Massachusetts in 1920, and the wage differential began widening again after 1920 to 50 to 60 percent in 1924–26.[38] The South also had lower labor costs owing to fewer labor regulations. While Northern firms were contending with increased restrictions on the use of child labor and night work, many states in the South had no restrictions on child labor, or the laws that they did have were not enforced, and had few restrictions on night work.[39] Not only did the South have lower wage costs, but it also tended to have greater productivity. Southern mills were newer, and thus many of them installed the latest technology.[40] For example, many Southern mills were among the first to install the Northrop loom, an automatic loom that saved on labor.[41]

Southern textile mills began by threatening the most low-skill-intensive firms first. Textile mills in the South initially produced the lowest-quality yarn and cloth, which demanded the least skill to produce, and then moved into producing higher-quality yarn and cloth, which demanded greater skill.[42] Thus their effect would have hit the most low-skill-intensive members of the NTA first, followed by the more skill-intensive firms.

The firms represented by the NTA were right to be worried about competition from these Southern mills. As seen in figure 4.10, the NTA perceived domestic competition to be increasing before World War I. During the war, domestic competition decreased as the federal government stepped in to ensure supplies for the war effort. Domestic competition again increased after the war. It became less of an issue after the start of the Great Depression, when again the federal government stepped in to regulate production, including the implementing of national labor regulations and a minimum wage.[43]

The NTA discussed three potential strategies to remain competitive (fig. 4.11): move production to the South or overseas, increase productivity through technology or human capital, or increase immigration. The top

---

[36] Andrews (1987, 11).
[37] Smith (1944, 89).
[38] Smith (1944, 89).
[39] Friedman (2000), Smith (1944), and Wright (1981).
[40] Feller (1974, 576) and Galenson (1985, 39–42).
[41] Smith (1944, 102).
[42] Galenson (1985, 4).
[43] Smith (1944, 150).

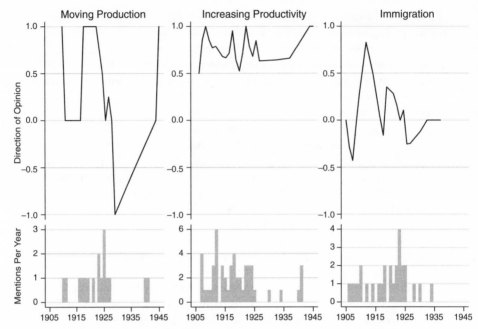

Figure 4.11: The NTA's Perceptions on Moving Production, Increasing Productivity, and Immigration.
Note: Top graph is the loess-smoothed trend line (bandwidth of 0.25) of the average opinion of the variable. Scores greater than zero mean that on average the NTA has a positive opinion; less than zero, indicate a negative opinion; and at zero, there is no opinion or the positive opinions equal the negative opinions. The bottom graph is the number of articles mentioning the variable per year. Data coded by the author; see the codebook in online appendix F.

part of the graphs shows the direction of the opinion of these strategies: scores greater than zero indicate that on average articles were positive about the issue; scores less than zero indicate that they were negative; zero indicates equal positive and negative opinions or no opinion.[44] The bottom half of the graph shows the number of mentions of each potential strategy.

[44] To code the average opinion, I first multiplied the direction of change in each variable by the opinion in each individual article. If an increase (decrease) in the variable is desirable (undesirable), then this opinion variable gets a score of 1; if an increase (decrease) is undesirable (desirable), it gets a score of −1. If the article does not mention a direction but is viewed positively (negatively), the variable also takes the score of 1 (−1). In cases where no opinion was discussed, the variable takes the value of 0. The scores for the articles were then averaged for the year.

Increasing productivity is most often mentioned in response to trade and was always viewed positively. In almost 19 percent of the articles that mention imports, international competition, or domestic competition, productivity is also mentioned. For example, in response to increasing domestic competition from the South, Mayor Quincy of Boston argued in his address to the New England Cotton Manufacturers' Association in 1896 that

> as other sections, nearer to the sources of the supply of fuel, enabled to command cheaper labor in some respects, coming to the market and taking up manufacturing industries as the South is largely doing, it seems to me that those who are engaged in similar industries in New England must recognize the fact that in order to hold their supremacy they must put more brains, more skill and more education in the carrying on of the manufacturing business in this part of the country.[45]

The increase in skilled labor would decrease the total cost of labor for these firms by increasing productivity.[46] According to a speaker at the annual meeting, increasing skill, however, often meant hiring more native and less foreign-born labor: "One fact which I have noted repeatedly is, that however countrified a family may be when they first appear for work at the mill, it takes from one-fourth to one-half less time to make good hands of them, than it does to train farm hands of foreign extraction."[47]

Moving production elsewhere was also mentioned as a possible solution, but much less often than increasing productivity. In part this may have been because, as a regionally based organization, the NTA was worried about losing members should firms move overseas or to the South. In the 1920s, and to some degree before then as well, significant numbers of New England firms were moving their production to the South to take advantage of the lower labor costs.[48] For example, in 1924, the Borden company announced that it was closing two plants in Fall River, Massachusetts—a major center of textile activity, which in total contained over 100,000 spindles and 2,000 looms and employed 1,000 people—and moving it to Kingsport, Tennessee. Similarly, after suffering heavy losses owing to the stock market crash in 1929, the United Merchants Company moved its printing machines in 1933 from its textile mill in Fall River to its plant in South Carolina and to a new operation in Argentina in 1934.[49]

[45] Quincy (1896, 66).
[46] Atkinson (1891, 109).
[47] Wilbur (1898, 160).
[48] Galenson (1985, 3).
[49] Smith (1944, 124, 145).

The NTA also discussed the possibility of increasing immigration in response. In general, the NTA was more positive than negative on immigration (average opinion of 0.3) but tended to be somewhat divided on immigration. As the above quotation makes clear, in 1898 immigrants were deemed to be inferior workers. But in 1904, immigrants were a necessity to the development of the country: "The last thing to be tolerated is the wasting of resources of rich lands through the lack of native labor ... it would appear, from what we are told, that the relief may come though immigration from Southern Europe."[50] In 1908, after the recession of 1907, immigrants were again less desired: "Immigration is, however, no longer as necessary to this country as it was in pioneer times."[51]

There is little mention of immigration after 1925. This may be a product of the environment that the NTA was facing. Given the restrictions on immigration—first with the Literacy Act in 1917 and then with the 1921 and 1924 Quota Acts—the NTA may have felt that lobbying on immigration would be ineffective. For example, in 1922, a speaker at the National Textile Associations' October meeting tied his concern about foreign competition to productivity and immigration: "How is [the textile manufacturer] to meet foreign competition?"[52] His answer was that "for the North, the operation of the immigration restrictions seems likely to handicap the textile mills in recruiting their working forces in the same manner as during the last half century. This means keen competition with other industries for labor and the necessity of using labor-saving methods even more generally than heretofore."[53] In this case, given that anti-immigration forces had already won a decisive victory with the Quota Act of 1921, it was argued that textile firms in the North had to turn to technology instead.

Thus it appears that when dealing with increased competition, the NTA advocated increasing productivity, followed by support for immigration, and then moving production. Interestingly, the data reveal a drop-off in the discussion of any of these responses after 1925. This may have occurred because the textile industry in the North was in great decline, with many firms choosing to close. By the late 1920s, the South housed more spindles than the North[54] and had expanded into more specialized goods, producing 89 percent of print cloth in 1929.[55] Employment in the North fell: between 1923 and 1924, average cotton mill employment in Fall River, Massachusetts, declined by a third, and over the next fifteen years

[50] Walmsley (1904, 105).
[51] Clews (1908, 257).
[52] Copeland (1922, 68).
[53] Copeland (1922, 71).
[54] Morris (1953, 66).
[55] Smith (1944, 86).

73 more mills in Fall River were liquidated.[56] As a result of the North's less competitive position, by 1952, 81 percent of the active cotton spindles were in the South, in comparison to only 5 percent in 1880.[57]

The closure of some plants was a clear strategy by the management in some cases. Feller notes that among textile mill managers in the North, "to continue to operate with outdated equipment until forced to shut down was a recognized alternative" rather than further mechanizing production.[58] For example, in 1925 the management of the Amoskeag mill in Manchester, New Hampshire, chose not to reinvest profits into the plant and in 1927 began purposefully neglecting the physical plant in hopes of hastening its demise.[59] It was finally liquidated in 1936.[60] Another example comes from Smith, who in the early 1940s interviewed managers of many of the plants at Fall River. He argues that

> it seems likely that a decision may have been made in these and other corporations to run the mills as long as possible without substantial renovation, pay large dividends, and then either change over or liquidate. When the time came liquidation was generally the only possible alternative. It is, of course, impossible to demonstrate this motivation in actual operation without more detailed material on the inner workings of the corporations than is available in Fall River. However, there is widespread opinion among Fall River business men today that such was the practice. Then, too, such motivations are known to have operated in other textile mills in New England.[61]

Many mill managers appear to have decided not to fight to stay in business by increasing productivity or lobbying for immigration—although it does appear that some mills lobbied for and received a tax break[62]—but instead chose to take what capital they could out of the mills while they were still turning a profit.

The result of the closures in the North meant that the textile industry was very different after the interwar period from what it had been before. Most of the production of textiles had moved from the North to the South, and both the Southern and the surviving Northern mills had invested in new, laborsaving technology.[63] Yet these newly productive firms were unable to maintain their edge for long. As early as the 1940s, the US textile industries' positive trade balance began to decline, turning into a

---

[56] Smith (1944, 124).
[57] Morris (1953, 66).
[58] Feller (1974, 580).
[59] Sweezy (1938, 501).
[60] Feller (1974, 580).
[61] Smith (1944, 133–134).
[62] Smith (1944, 158).
[63] Morris (1953, 77) and Smith (1944, 149).

deficit by 1968.[64] In response the US government negotiated quotas on textiles in bilateral agreements and the Multi-Fiber Arrangement (MFA) in 1974, which was phased out in 2005.[65] The MFA proved to be only a stopgap measure. Even before its end, textiles faced increased international competition: the US textile industry lost about 30 percent of its workforce between 1970 and 1995[66] in comparison to an 8 percent decline in all manufacturing.[67] With the end of the Multi-Fiber Arrangement, US-made apparel dropped from a high of 56.2 percent of market share to 2.5 percent.[68] In response, some textile firms moved overseas, just as they had moved to the South 70 years before;[69] others became more productive, in some cases producing as much with less than a tenth of the workforce needed in 1980;[70] and still others closed.[71]

Owing to these changes, the US textile industry needs many fewer workers than it did even thirty years ago, let alone a century ago.[72] This has translated into less lobbying and less testifying on immigration (fig. 4.12). Textile firms and trade associations testified on immigration much more in the 1950s and 1960s than they have since, consistent with the argument. Groups from the textile sector have acted as a witness or placed a submission in the record only six times since the passage of NAFTA and only once, in 2006, after quotas were withdrawn in 2005. Data on lobbying on immigration from 1998 to 2011 shows a similar pattern; only four textile organizations lobbied on immigration, spending a total of only $260,000 on all their lobbying activity in those years.[73]

The history of the textile industry highlights many aspects of the argument. Northeastern textile firms in the early twentieth century faced increased competition from both home (the South) and abroad. In response to this competition, they increased their skill intensity of production; moved South or overseas; or in many cases closed their doors. All three strategies decreased their need for low-skill labor and their demand for immigration; it is not surprising, then, that the textile industry has done little testifying before Congress or lobbying on immigration in the last fifteen years.

[64] Feller (1974, 591).
[65] Kenney and Florida (2004, 31, 33) and Mittelhauser (1997).
[66] Minchin (2009, 288).
[67] Mittelhauser (1997, 24).
[68] Clifford (2013).
[69] Bureau of Economic Analysis (2012).
[70] Clifford (2013).
[71] Mittelhauser (1997, 24, 27).
[72] Clifford (2013).
[73] Center for Responsive Politics (N.d.).

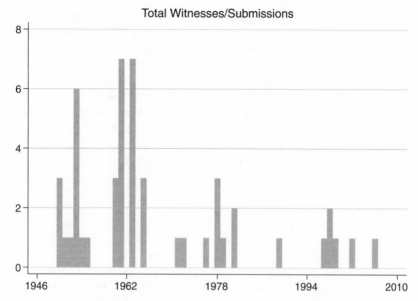

Figure 4.12: Number of Witnesses and Submissions from Textile Firms and Trade Associations.
Note: Data coded by the author.

The American Iron and Steel Institute

The AISI was organized in 1855 to "advance the interest" of iron producers, mostly in the Northeast and Mid-Atlantic.[74] The AISI now has grown to represent about 22 member companies, including major steel corporations such as AK Steel (formerly Armco) and US Steel Corporation, and 125 associate members including suppliers or customers of the steel industry.[75] Together, the firms represented by AISI control about 80 percent of the steel capacity throughout North America.[76] I examined the yearbooks of the American Iron and Steel Institute from 1910 to 1971 to understand how changes in the international economy have affected its stance on immigration.[77] Altogether there were 147 articles that mentioned at least one of the following: trade, international competition, domestic competition, foreign direct investment, immigration, and/or technological or human capital changes in light of the other variables.

[74] American Iron and Steel Institute (2014*a*).
[75] American Iron and Steel Institute (2014*b*).
[76] American Iron and Steel Institute (2014*b*).
[77] The year range was chosen based on availability of yearbooks.

The steel industry did not face the same degree of international competition and trade pressure as did textiles until after World War II. In the earliest days of the steel industry, steel products generally were not traded internationally, which protected US plants from international competition. In the 1880s, the American steel industry gained an advantage over its competitors thanks to the development of the Iron Range in Minnesota, which produced high-quality iron ore. In combination with the new open-hearth production technology introduced from England in 1875, American steel plants could use this ore to produce high-quality steel products on a relatively cheap basis.[78] Throughout the pre–World War II period, American plants were the most productive and produced the cheapest steel on the international market, leading the United States to become a net exporter of steel in 1893.[79]

Unlike the textile industry, the American steel industry created less domestic competition and more cooperation too, driven in part by mergers in the industry. US Steel, one of the largest steel producers, was formed when Carnegie Steel Company (itself a product of mergers), Federal Steel Company, and National Steel Company merged in 1901. In 1907, it bought its largest competitor, the Tennessee Coal, Iron, and Railroad Company, which was the major producer in the US South, based in Birmingham, Alabama. Steel companies also consolidated vertically by either buying the companies that supplied the coal and ore or by buying the firms that made steel products.[80] Thus, through its early history, American steel faced few competitive pressures.

The dominance of American steel ended in the late 1950s and early 1960s. The change in competitiveness was driven by a few factors. After World War II, Europe and Japan built new steel mills to replace those destroyed in the war; these new mills were more efficient than US mills, even the ones that had been upgraded.[81] The US dollar was overvalued relative to the Japanese yen and many European currencies, making American steel more expensive. Finally, transportation costs were dropping, allowing increased trade openness.[82] As imports increased, the ASIS lobbied for tariffs in 1966; however, the Johnson administration was unwilling to grant them, in part because they went against the agreements the United States had under the GATT.[83] Instead, the United States was able to convince

---

[78] Rogers (2009, 20).
[79] Rogers (2009, 51–52) and Hall (1997, 179).
[80] Rogers (2009, 27–28).
[81] Rogers (2009, 51–52).
[82] Rogers (2009, 51–52).
[83] Hall (1997, 51–53).

Japanese and European producers to agree to voluntary export restraints (VERs) in 1969.[84]

The steel industry continued to face increased international competition through the 1970s and 1980s. The VERs expired in 1974 but were reinstated in 1984 until 1992. From 1977 to 1981, trigger-price mechanisms were used to threaten antidumping duties if imports were sold below the set price. This policy, however, backfired as foreign firms were attracted by the higher prices.[85] Even with the VERs and other nontariff barriers, import penetration in the steel industry has increased, from 5 percent in 1963 to 30 percent in 2002.[86]

Concern about imports and international competition can clearly be seen when we examine what the AISI said at its (bi)annual meetings. The first two graphs in figure 4.13 show how the AISI perceived imports and international competition, coded as in the textile case. There is a large increase in the mentions of imports after World War II, and especially during the late 1950s through the early 1970s. Imports were also thought to be increasing during this time period. Similarly there is an uptick in the mentions of international competition, and it too was thought to be increasing during this time period. There was less discussion of domestic competition; until the early 1960s, when it *was* discussed the AISI most often perceived that it was decreasing. Yet with the increase in international competition, the AISI also perceived that domestic competition was increasing among US producers as well.

Figure 4.14 shows the AISI's discussion of three potential strategies to remain competitive and its opinion of these changes: move production overseas; increase productivity through technology or human capital; or increase immigration, coded as before. Increasing productivity was the most frequently mentioned strategy to meet the challenge of increased international and trade competition. As can be seen in figure 4.14, the AISI rarely mentioned moving production, but it did mention it more in the 1960s and had a generally positive view. While the AISI may have viewed foreign direct investment positively, the US steel industry did not engage in much of it. In the 1960s, there were some moves into Mexico and Latin America, as well as Italy and Spain, but many US firms pulled back from these investments when the industry floundered in the 1970s and 1980s.[87] Instead, there has been a fair amount of inward FDI since the 1970s and

[84] Hall (1997, 51–53).
[85] Hall (1997, 113–114).
[86] Collard-Wexler and De Loecker (2013, 18).
[87] Hall (1997, 181–182).

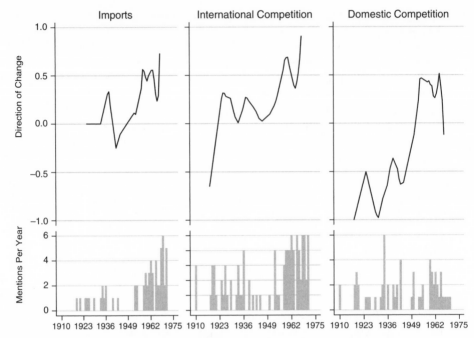

Figure 4.13: The AISI's Perceptions on Imports, International Competition, and Domestic Competition

Note: Top graph is the loess-smoothed trend line (bandwidth of 0.25) of the average perceived change in the variable. Scores greater than zero mean that on average the variable is increasing; less than zero, decreasing; and at zero, there is no change, the positive changes equal the negative changes, or the variable simply was mentioned. The bottom graph is the number of articles mentioning the variable per year. Data coded by the author; see the codebook in online appendix F.

1980s as European, Canadian, and Asian firms have bought US firms.[88] More recently, the American steel industry has increased outward FDI from $662 million in 1982 to almost $7 billion in 2013.[89]

Similarly, the AISI did not discuss immigration much once international competition was fierce; there is only one mention of it after 1945. Instead, as the industry was expanding in the early twentieth century, immigration was of greater importance. Prior to the passage of the 1921 Quota Act, most of what the AISI discussed on immigration was about how to "Americanize" the large foreign workforce. Several speakers brought up the

---

[88] Hall (1997, 202, 206).
[89] Bureau of Economic Analysis (2012).

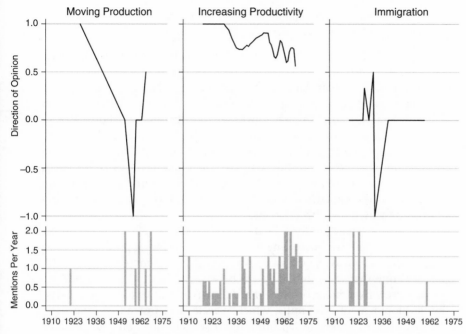

Figure 4.14: The AISI's Perceptions on Moving Production, Increasing Productivity, and Immigration.

Note: Top graph is the loess-smoothed trend line (bandwidth of 0.25) of the average opinion of increasing productivity and the average opinion for moving production and immigration, given the few mentions of these two issues. Scores greater than zero mean that on average the AISI has a positive opinion; less than zero, a negative opinion; and at zero, there is no opinion or the positive opinions equal the negative opinions. The bottom graph is the number of articles mentioning the variable per year. Data coded by the author; see the codebook in online appendix F.

importance of educating foreign-born workers so that they could become better workers. After the 1921 Quota Act was passed, there was some concern on the part of the AISI about how the law affected their ability to produce. For example, in 1923, Elbert Gary, the president of the AISI argued:

> The responsibility for the numbers of employe[e]s is partly with the American Congress because [it is] affected by immigration. There should not be permitted too much immigration, and certainly there should be none of dangerous or injurious quality; but there ought to be enough to keep our production of foodstuffs, of metals and of manufactures up to the necessities

of the consuming public; and sufficient to meet the demands of the national welfare, which embraces the export trade.[90]

Yet by 1927 the decrease in immigration did not seem to be as much of a problem for the AISI in part because the steel mills could take advantage of "the excess labor force released from the older industries."[91] To some extent, the AISI filled the unskilled positions that had been held by Southern and Eastern European immigrants with both African Americans and whites who migrated from the US South, and also with Mexican immigrants who were not covered by the 1921 or 1924 Quota Act.[92] Thus when the steel industry was expanding in the early twentieth century, it was supportive of immigration; when it came under pressure from increased competition, rather than push for more open immigration it instead focused on other strategies.

The main strategy put forth by the AISI in the wake of increased competition in the 1960s was increasing productivity. Increasing productivity was almost always seen as a good thing by the AISI, as evidenced by figure 4.14, and was one that was often adopted: between 1962 and 2005 output per worker grew by a factor of five.[93] Productivity increases have been driven by development of mini-mills, which recycle steel instead of processing the iron ore to make steel. Mini-mills first were used only to produce relatively low-quality products, but over time they were able to produce increasingly high-quality products.[94] The development of mini-mills led to increased competition in some sectors of the steel market, which forced the least productive traditional, integrated steel mills out of business.[95] The remaining integrated steel mills increased their productivity as well.[96] The large increase in productivity has meant that steel shipments have returned to their early 1960s level,[97] while employment has dropped precipitously from over 5 million people in 1970 to 1.5 million in 2010.[98]

Given the increases in import penetration, foreign direct investment, and productivity, it may not be surprising in light of the argument of this book that steel firms have not lobbied much on immigration over the last sixty years. No steel firms have testified before Congress or entered submissions into the record since 1946.[99] Steel firms did not do much

[90] Gary (1923, 14).
[91] Jordan (1927, 509).
[92] Rogers (2009, 48, 65).
[93] Collard-Wexler and De Loecker (2013, 2).
[94] Collard-Wexler and De Loecker (2013, 17).
[95] Collard-Wexler and De Loecker (2013, 17).
[96] Collard-Wexler and De Loecker (2013, 17).
[97] Collard-Wexler and De Loecker (2013, 2).
[98] Census data are from Ruggles et al. (2010).
[99] One iron worker testified in 1978.

lobbying on immigration either. From 1998 to 2011, only thirty-one firms or associations in this industry mentioned immigration on their disclosure form; immigration accounted for less than 20 percent of the issues they listed; and these firms and associations spent less than $700,000 on all lobbying.[100] In contrast, steel has continued to be active in other areas; the industry spent at least $5 million in total lobbying each year from 1998 to 2014.[101]

In sum, when the steel industry was growing in the early twentieth century, it generally favored low-skill immigration, as immigrants took many of the unskilled positions in the industry. When steel became threatened by international competition in the 1960s through today, most firms chose to focus on increasing productivity or closed. These increases in productivity and closures have meant that the industry is no longer an active supporter of low-skill immigration.

The Western Growers Association

When we think of business support for low-skill immigration, we often think about agriculture. Agriculture tends to be low-skill-labor-intensive and historically has been a draw for immigrant workers. Yet not all agricultural producers need as much labor as they once did. The production of grains was mechanized relatively early, in the mid-nineteenth century, allowing farmers to produce large yields with relatively little labor. Similarly, the production of cotton was fully mechanized in the 1950s and 1960s. However, there are many agricultural products, especially fresh fruits and vegetables, that have not been mechanized. In this case study, I focus on this last group, easily perishable fruits and vegetables, which are known collectively as *specialty crops*.

The Western Growers Association (WGA) is the main trade organization of growers of specialty crops in California and Arizona, representing over half of California's agricultural production in dollar terms, a $37.5 billion industry in 2010. California and Arizona farmers have faced great changes over the last eighty years in the ability to trade their product and the ability to move production overseas. When the WGA was founded in 1926, transporting fresh fruits and vegetables over long distances was still relatively difficult. Early articles in the monthly trade publication of the WGA, *Western Grower and Shipper* (*WGS*), discussed the best ways to ice down vegetables for transport to markets in the eastern United States and Canada. There was no discussion of shipping goods to Europe or Asia yet. As technology has advanced, so has the ability to ship goods and produce

---

[100] Center for Responsive Politics (N.d.).
[101] Center for Responsive Politics (N.d.).

overseas. Now, the top ten destinations for California agricultural exports include far-flung locations like the EU, China, Japan, the UAE, India, and Australia.[102] Similarly, the top ten places from which the United States imports agricultural goods now include China, Brazil, Indonesia, Chile, and Thailand.[103]

To examine how the WGA has experienced and responded to trade openness and international competition, I examined the archives of *WGS*. The first two graphs in figure 4.15 show how the WGA perceived imports and international competition, and the third panel examines domestic competition, coded as in the textile case. Domestic competition was a larger issue in the 1930s when the farmers of the WGA were still competing for market share against producers in the East, but it has been rarely mentioned since. In contrast, imports and international competition became an increasingly important issue starting in the 1980s. Both were thought to be increasing during this time period until the Great Recession in 2008 and were thought to have a large effect on the industry, including decimating the domestic garlic industry.[104]

The WGA has focused on two major sources of competition: Mexico and China. Since the 1960s and 1970s, Mexico has been discussed as a source of competition, but concern over Mexican agriculture really came to a head in the early 1990s with the North American Free Trade Agreement (NAFTA). The WGA was concerned, rightly, that increased openness to Mexico would lead to a decrease in their US and Canadian market share. While Mexico has remained a source of competition, concern over Mexican imports has receded as concern over China has increased since the introduction of economic reforms in 1978. Even though Chinese goods compete with goods produced by the WGA on a limited basis, China is "coming at [WGA Members] like a freight train. [WGA Members] can't compete with them. They've got 3 percent of [US] labor costs."[105]

One strategy to respond to increased foreign competition would be for farmers to join their competitors overseas. Interest in moving production first appeared in the early 1960s when the Bracero Program—the bilateral agricultural guest workers program with Mexico—ended (fig. 4.16). At that time, it was difficult for farmers to move because many countries, including Mexico, did not allow foreigners to own farmland. In 1992, that changed when Mexico's land reform allowed foreign corporations to own and lease land and increased the amount of land they could hold.[106] Since then,

---

[102] California Department of Food and Agriculture (2012).

[103] US Census Bureau (2012). While not all these states export fresh fruits and vegetables, many of them do.

[104] Nassif (2006*a*).

[105] *Nassif Takes on Dobbs, transcript* (2005).

[106] Key and Runsten (1999).

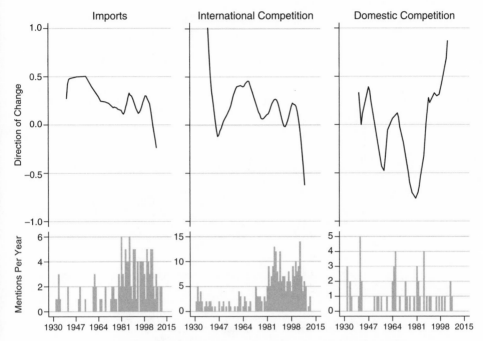

Figure 4.15: The WGA's Perceptions on Imports, International Competition, and Domestic Competition.

Note: Top graph is the loess-smoothed trend line (bandwidth of 0.25) of the average perceived change in the variable. Scores greater than zero mean that on average the variable is increasing; less than zero, decreasing; and at zero, there is no change, the positive changes equal the negative changes, or the variable simply was mentioned. The bottom graph is the number of articles mentioning the variable per year. Data coded by the author; see the codebook in online appendix F.

some members of the WGA have moved at least part of their production to another country, many to Mexico.[107] While WGA members have begun to believe that they need to relocate their operations overseas "or face extinction,"[108] moving production overseas is still the least-mentioned potential strategy owing to the difficulty in doing so.

The WGA has often mentioned increasing productivity through technology as a potential solution to labor shortages and increased competition (fig. 4.16), especially when the Bracero Program was slated to end in

---

[107] Nassif (2006*a*).
[108] Nassif (2006*a*).

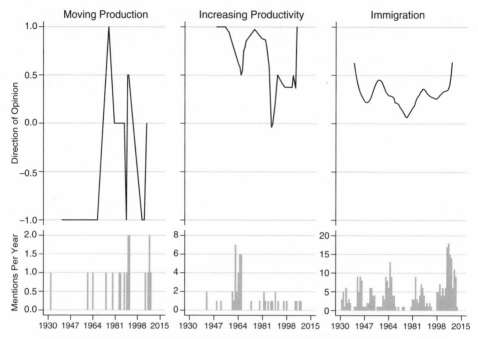

Figure 4.16: The WGA's Perceptions on Moving Production, Increasing
Productivity, and Immigration.
Note: Top graph is the loess-smoothed trend line (bandwidth of 0.25)
of the average opinion of the variable. Scores greater than zero mean
that on average the AISI has a positive opinion; less than zero, a
negative opinion; and at zero, there is no opinion or the positive
opinions equal the negative opinions. The bottom graph is the
number of articles mentioning the variable per year. Data coded by
the author; see the codebook in online appendix F.

the early 1960s. But mentions of productivity enhancements have fallen
off since then. This is likely a product of increased disillusionment with
technology: "for most fruit and vegetable growers, mechanization is not
yet a comprehensive or readily adaptable solution."[109]

Since moving overseas and adopting technology are not feasible yet
for most of their members, the WGA has focused mostly on increased
immigration as the tool to enable them to remain competitive in an
increasingly globalized sector (fig. 4.16). Immigration has always been a
major issue for the WGA, and it is an issue that has almost always been

[109] Resnick (2006).

viewed positively. Nonetheless, there have been waves of increased focus on immigration by the WGA: in the early 1930s around conflicts between the immigrant workers from Mexico and the Philippines and new migrants from the Dust Bowl states; during World War II when the Bracero Program began; in the late 1950s through the mid-1960s as the Bracero Program ended; and around IRCA in the 1980s. Since the late 1990s, however, immigration has become an increasingly important issue.

The WGA's greatly increased focus on immigration has been a product of the increase in international competition in this sector. The leadership of the WGA clearly understands how trade openness and international competition interact with immigration. For example, in 2004, the WGA lobbied for the Specialty Crops Competitiveness Act to help put US agriculture on "a level playing field to compete fairly on even ground with other countries."[110] Included in this bill was an "effective guest worker program."[111] This bill did not pass. Similarly, the WGA has argued that

> politicians and policy-makers don't understand the fragile ground that our industry stands upon. The immigration debate, lack of proportionate government financial support, unfavorable trade practices, continuing regulation, urban encroachment, water rights and other issues seem to conspire to dare anyone [to] continue doing business in California and Arizona.[112]

Further, the leadership of the WGA understands that mechanization would be an effective solution to lower labor costs instead of immigration; WGA president Tom Nassif argues, "It is time for those anti-immigration reform legislators in Washington D.C. to realize that the higher the use of technology and innovation, the lower the need for foreign labor."[113]

With the increase in competitive pressures from overseas and the inability to mechanize production, the WGA has increased lobbying for low-skill immigration. The WGA has lobbied Congress since the late 1990s to pass legislation that would create an agricultural guest workers program in order to better compete with foreign agriculture. Congress, however, has not responded to this lobbying, in part because agriculture has not had much help from other industries.[114]

Given the increased globalization of the food supply, the inability to mechanize production, and the inability to get an agricultural immigrant workers program through Congress, it is likely that the United States will lose more of its specialty crop industry to foreign countries. As noted above,

[110] *Legislative Report* (2004).
[111] *Legislative Report* (2004).
[112] Nassif (2006*a*).
[113] Nassif (2006*b*).
[114] Nassif (2005).

many domestic garlic producers have been forced out of business.[115] The WGA argues that the trade-off for policymakers, then, is that much of the foodstuff Americans eat will be produced by foreign labor; "they will either be doing it within our borders with our domestic food supply or they will be doing it outside our borders and shipping us a foreign-grown food supply."[116]

Finally, the WGA can help us examine the conventional wisdom that increased restrictions on low-skill immigration are driven by firms that want to exploit undocumented workers, as almost 80 percent of their members' workforce is undocumented.[117] If the conventional wisdom is correct, the WGA should be unconcerned about enforcement because little enforcement is taking place, and the enforcement actions that are taking place should not be particularly harmful for farmers. However, as seen in figure 4.17, enforcement has been an increasing concern for the WGA. There were a few mentions of it during the Bracero Program in the 1940s through the 1960s. Mentions became much more frequent after the passage of the Immigration Control and Reform Act, which first criminalized the hiring of undocumented workers, and have substantially proliferated since the late 1990s when, at least in the opinion of the WGA, enforcement greatly escalated.

Second, if the conventional wisdom is correct and farmers are happy with the status quo of border restrictions and enforcement, we would not expect that they would support a legal immigration program. Yet, for almost twenty years now, these same farmers have been pushing for immigration reform to get access to a legal workforce.

These farmers have lobbied for a legal agricultural workers program because they face two risks using an undocumented workforce. First, farmers face potential legal sanctions for employing undocumented workers, resulting in hefty fines. This requirement leads to extra paperwork and legal work for the farmer. For example, to protect themselves, the WGA recommends to their farmers: "Have a good I-9 policy. Audit your current I-9 records and clean up your act before the INS does ... Police your crew leaders and make sure no one is selling slots on your workforce. That is the quickest [way] to trouble."[118] Thus even if farmers are rarely fined for their use of illegal labor, they must pay higher costs to ensure that they are at least complying with the letter, if not the spirit, of the law.

Second, farmers face the *hold-up problem* when they use undocumented immigrants. The Immigration and Customs Enforcement (ICE) Agency

[115] Simonds (2007).
[116] Linden (2006).
[117] Caldwell (2011).
[118] Linden (1997).

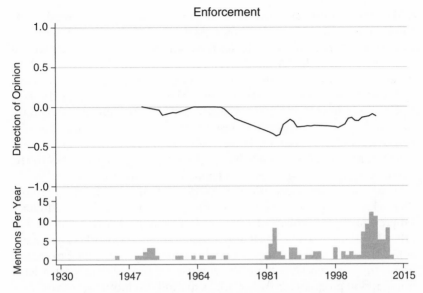

Figure 4.17: The WGA's Perceptions on Enforcement of Immigration Laws.
Note: Top graph is the loess-smoothed trend line (bandwidth of 0.25) of the average opinion of the variable. Scores greater than zero mean that on average the WGA has a positive opinion; less than zero, a negative opinion; and at zero, there is no opinion or the positive opinions equal the negative opinions. The bottom graph is the number of articles mentioning the variable per year. Data coded by the author; see the codebook in online appendix F.

has the right to search farmers' fields and is likely to check the status of immigrants during key moments in the production process, such as at harvesttime. If the workers are found to be in the country illegally, ICE can detain them, leaving farmers without a workforce at a critical juncture. For example, in 1999, the INS raided fruit-packing plants in Washington State. Farmers began to worry that they too would be raided: "We don't like having this threat hanging over our heads ... There is the possibility of losing a sizable portion of acres during critical work on a perishable crop."[119] Even if farms are not raided, farmers worry that their employees will be arrested or detained outside of work, leading to the loss of their workforce. Using an illegal workforce, then, can place the farmers at the mercy of the government.

[119] Linden (1999).

The hold-up problem was recognized as a reason to seek a legal work-force as early as 1983 when employer sanctions were being discussed in Congress. The need for a stable, legal workforce was tied to international competition as well. "A sudden cutoff of Mexican workers would be devastating to the citrus industry. Citrus suffers from growing overseas competition and could lose some of its foreign markets if a labor shortage interrupted harvesting."[120] It was argued that the citrus growers should try to "stabilize" their workforce as farmers in Ventura County did after the end of the Bracero Program. There "ex-braceros became legal 'green card' immigrants, and growers encouraged them to bring their families to the US by offering the workers pensions and health insurance benefits."[121]

Thus, by using undocumented workers, farmers potentially expose themselves to fines, additional legal costs, and hold-up by the government. To prevent these problems, farmers in California and Arizona, as well as other US states, have lobbied for a legal agricultural workers program. While there are likely some farmers who would like to continue to exploit undocumented workers, there are enough farmers who support a legal immigration program for farm workers to fund this lobbying activity.

The WGA and the farmers it represents in many ways are the exception that proves the rule. When the sector was expanding and labor was scarce in the 1940s through the 1960s, immigration was mentioned as an important way to keep labor costs competitive. As international competition and trade have increased, the WGA did focus on three possible strategies to maintain competitiveness: moving overseas, mechanizing production, or increasing immigration. As the first two options have proven difficult, the WGA has focused on the third, immigration. This focus on immigration is not, however, driven by a desire to exploit undocumented immigrants, even though the majority of their workers are likely undocumented immigrants. Quite the opposite: instead, the WGA has worried about the legal costs for farmers of enforcement, and, more important, the hold-up problem, and has lobbied for a legal immigrant workers program.

CONCLUSION

In this chapter, I examined how changes in trade openness, international competition, firm mobility, and productivity affected firms' willingness to lobby on immigration, the first step in the causal chain I described in chapter 2. Through data on which organizations have testified before Congress on immigration since World War II and which organizations

---

[120] Mines and Martin (1983, 36).
[121] Mines and Martin (1983, 36).

have lobbied on immigration since 1998, this chapter showed that, consistent with my argument, sectors that have greater exposure to trade, that have seen greater gains in productivity, and that have engaged in more foreign direct investment have been less likely to engage in either of these lobbying activities. The low-skill-intensive nontradable sector has not made up for the decreased support for immigration from these groups.

Through the case studies on the textile industry, the steel industry, and labor-intensive agriculture, the chapter showed how these industries have responded to increases in competition. The textiles industry mostly either moved production to an area with lower labor costs—in this case, first to the American South and later overseas—or closed; some firms increased their productivity. Consistent with my argument, regardless of the option these firms choose, they no longer support low-skill immigration. The steel industry focused on increasing productivity to the detriment of supporting immigration, as predicted in chapter 2. Finally, agriculture has faced difficulties moving or mechanizing production. As it has faced increased trade openness and international competition only recently, it has continued to lobby for open immigration.

Moreover, the data presented in this chapter provide less support for the existing explanations from the literature. Although organized labor has lobbied on immigration more in recent years, its influence has waned, as have its numbers, making it less likely that labor's opposition to immigration can explain the restrictions. Similarly, lobbying by cosmopolitan and immigrants' groups has also increased recently, but their influence has remained low, even during periods of Democratic control of Congress. Nativist groups do seem to be an important counterweight to firms, but I find no evidence that their numbers have increased over time. Instead, it appears that they have gained more influence because of the decrease in overall business support for immigration. Finally, the agriculture case study showed that even an industry that uses much undocumented labor wants a legal immigration program because it faces a hold-up problem when it employs undocumented immigrants.

CHAPTER 5

Policymakers' Responses to Firms in the United States

THE CONVENTIONAL WISDOM IS THAT THE UNITED STATES has long been open to immigration, but its history suggests otherwise. When the United States was founded, it adopted few restrictions on immigration, and immigration remained relatively unrestricted until the end of the Civil War (fig. 5.1). Then, between 1875 and 1924, the United States passed a series of laws that closed the door to immigrants. The United States then reversed policy in a series of laws between 1965 and 1990 that reopened the door to immigration to a limited degree. Most recently, the United States has again embarked on a program of closure. In this chapter, I examine these shifts through the lens of Senate voting, which I argue allows us to test the causal argument, namely, that increased trade openness, firm mobility, and productivity—and not some other factor—led to decreased support for low-skill immigration and increased restrictions.

I examine the three observable implications of my argument at the subnational level. Senators should be more likely to vote in the restrictionist direction—either for restrictions or against openness—as industries in their states become more exposed to trade, more mobile, and more productive. In this chapter, I do not measure firm lobbying directly but instead infer it from senators' voting behavior. I also examine the support for the alternative explanations: the power of labor hypothesis through both the change to direct elections and the size of unions in the state; the fiscal burden hypothesis through growth of state welfare programs; and the nativism and immigrant interest group hypotheses through the size of the foreign-born population. Throughout the main analysis, I include senator fixed effects to control for ideology. At the end of the analysis, I show that my argument can help explain the partisan shift on immigration—Republicans becoming more anti-immigration and Democrats more pro-immigration—after World War II.

I examine these implications in two different eras, 1865–1945 and 1945–2008, in which the changes that affected firms were outside the control of US senators. This strategy allows me to ensure that changes in the way senators felt about immigration were not causing them to vote differently on bills about trade, firm mobility, or technology, which then affected how firms lobby on immigration. In the first era, immigration policy was affected not by globalization but by the "Americanization" of the US economy, something that senators could do little to change. At

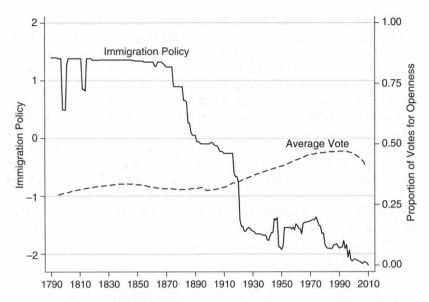

Figure 5.1: US Immigration Policy and Senate Voting on Immigration, 1790–2010. *Note*: Immigration policy data coded by the author; see chapter 3. Voting is the loess-smoothed line (bandwidth of 0.5) of all votes in the US Senate in a given year; see below for coding. Voting data are from Poole (2009), Poole and Lewis (2009), and Poole and McCarty (2009). Originally published in Peters (2014*b*) and reprinted with permission.

the end of the Civil War, the US economy was still a set of regional economies. Firms had "trade protection" from other regions in the US economy and were relatively immobile across regions. As transportation and communications technology improved, it became easier for firms to "trade" between regions of the United States and for firms to locate their factories far from their headquarters. The increased trade across regions subjected firms in the Northeast and Midwest, the primary employers of immigrant labor, to increased competition from other regions in the United States, especially the South, which had lower labor costs. Some firms could not compete and closed their doors; others moved to the South to take advantage of cheap native labor; and still others increased productivity by adopting laborsaving technology. Together these changes led to less support for open immigration.

In the modern era, it was globalization leading to changing firm preferences that resulted in more restricted immigration policy. Some aspects of globalization were outside the control of US senators. With the Reciprocal Trade Agreements Act (RTAA), Congress tied its own hands on tariff policy. Trade was also opened through international institutions such as the General Agreement on Tariffs and Trade/World Trade Organization (GATT/WTO), which helped perpetuate trade openness far removed from the influence of US senators. The ability to move production overseas during this time period was largely driven by other countries' decisions to open their markets to foreign direct investment (FDI). Furthermore, technological developments allowed some firms to do more with less labor.

Altogether, the evidence supports my argument. I find that trade openness, firm mobility, and increased productivity have a substantial effect on how senators vote. I also find that the adoption of direct election of senators, which should have increased the power of native labor, leads to less support for open immigration. I find some support for the alternative explanations: there is evidence that nativism, the power of the foreign-born, and the rise of the welfare state have affected the way senators vote on immigration as well.

ROLL CALL VOTES

Senate roll call votes allow us to understand how senators' support for immigration changed with changes in support for immigration in their constituencies. When voting, senators balance their own ideological stance on the issue, the preferences of their constituency, and the desires of their party's leadership. In aggregate, though, a senator's voting behavior should be generally consistent with the preferences of her state as senators need to take the preferences of their constituents into account to stay in office.[1]

While senators in general will vote in a way that would reflect the preferences of their constituency, on any single vote a senator's vote may not reflect her constituency. Because of the idiosyncrasies of any given vote, I aggregate all the votes on immigration in a given year and use the proportion of votes for open immigration as my dependent variable. This would be problematic if there were non-constituency-based factors that affected the way senators voted on all votes. One potential factor might be political party. As Lee argues, parties not only want to enact their preferred policies, but they also want to make political gains for their party.[2] As such, parties use whatever institutional powers they have to control the agenda, giving roll call votes only to those propositions that will create divisions between, rather than within, the parties. This process results in

---

[1] Canes-Wrone, Brady, and Cogan (2002), Clinton (2006), and Levitt (1996).
[2] Lee (2009).

roll call votes that are more partisan than standard theories of ideology would predict. This problem of agenda control and its effects on the pattern of roll call voting is less pronounced in the Senate than in the House: there are fewer restrictions on senators' ability to offer amendments, and there are procedural votes—such as the filibuster—that give the minority party greater control over the agenda. Because of the limits on agenda control in the Senate, the effect of party will be overestimated in an analysis of House votes to a greater degree than in Senate votes.[3] As the effect of partisanship is smaller in the Senate, it is a better place to study the effects of changing firm preferences on support for immigration.

Examining Senate voting also allows us to study an observable implication of the power of labor argument owing to the change to direct election of senators, instead of appointment by the state legislature. Direct election was thought to make senators more responsive to voters than to the business interests or party machines.[4] When states moved from appointment to direct election of senators, we would expect that senators would have become more anti-immigrant as the anti-immigration public gained relatively more power.

I include all votes on immigration from 1795, when the first vote on immigration was cast, to 2008.[5] As in the cross-national data, I include votes on provisions for entry, enforcement, rights of immigrants, naturalization, and refugees; on average there were 6.13 votes on 1.86 bills per year. While the Supreme Court decided that immigration control was strictly the purview of the federal government in the *Passenger Cases* decision in 1849, Congress did not do much to regulate immigration until the 1870s (fig. 5.2). From 1870 to 1930, in contrast, the Senate voted on immigration almost every year. Surprisingly Congress did not focus much on immigration during the Great Depression or during the Second World War, perhaps because immigration was already relatively restricted. Starting in the 1950s, Congress again began to consider immigration bills almost every year. The last vote in 2008 was on increased border security and enforcement procedures.

I coded the substance of each vote—what the senators were actually voting on, whether amendment, procedural, cloture, or final passage—as

[3] Hartog and Monroe (2011), Irwin and Kroszner (1996), and Lee (2009).

[4] Bernhard and Sala (2008), Crook and Hibbing (1997), Gailmard and Jenkins (2006), Lapinski (2004), and Meinke (2008).

[5] Data on votes are from Vote View. Poole (2009), Poole and Lewis (2009), and Poole and McCarty (2009). To ensure that each vote was captured, I relied on Hutchinson's seminal work on voting on immigration for 1789 to 1965. Hutchinson (1981). For years after 1965, I relied on Baumgartner and Jones (2009) and Congressional Quarterly (2003, 2005, 2006a, b).

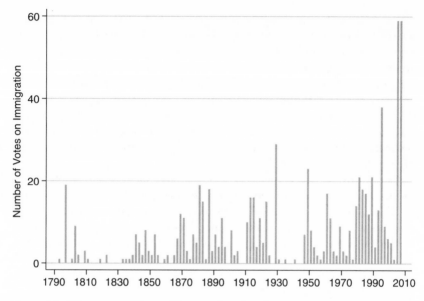

Figure 5.2: Histogram of Senate Votes on Immigration.
   Note: Voting data from Poole (2009), Poole and Lewis (2009), and Poole and McCarty (2009).

restrictive or expansive.[6] After coding the substance of each vote, I gave the vote of each senator a score of 0 or 1. A zero indicates that the senator voted in the restrictive direction—either by voting for a restrictive bill or voting against an expansive bill. A one indicates that the senator voted in the expansive direction—either by voting for an expansive bill or against a restrictive bill.[7]

THE "AMERICANIZATION" OF THE US ECONOMY AND IMMIGRATION, 1790–1945

I examine the "Americanization" of the US economy to gain empirical traction, as the changes in the economy were largely outside the control

---

[6] Procedural and cloture votes were included because they were often used to kill amendments or bills on the floor of the Senate. Votes that sought to restrict immigration were given a score of 0, and votes that sought to open immigration were given a score of 1. For more on the coding of the votes see Peters (2014*b*).

[7] Abstaining (or simply not voting) and votes of "present" were excluded, as it is unclear what they signal in this context.

of senators. The main threat to the analysis would be if senators had control over the amount of intra-US trade, firm mobility, or changes in productivity. If this is the case, senators could be reacting to increased immigration restrictions by increasing intra-US trade and firm mobility instead of the other way around, or some other variable could be causing senators to vote to increase immigration restrictions, intra-US trade, and firm mobility. As I discuss in further detail below, the changes to intra-US trade and firm mobility were largely driven by technological change and thus help us identify a causal effect of trade openness, firm mobility, and technology development on low-skill immigration policy.

One of the major changes in the US economy during this time period concerned the ability to transport goods cheaply among the different regions of the United States. While turnpikes and canals were important transportation improvements, the most important transportation advancement of the nineteenth century was the railroad. Railroads in the United States grew from nothing in 1830 to over 400,000 kilometers of rail by 1920. Starting in 1860, the miles of rail increased sharply and rail lines adopted a standard gauge.[8] Once the railroad connected an area to the rail network, it had much greater market access: Donaldson and Hornbeck argue that without railroads, GNP would have been about 3.40 percent lower in 1890.[9] Transportation costs continued to drop in the early twentieth century as locomotives became faster and increased the tonnage they could haul.[10]

Greater market access allowed for a convergence in goods prices.[11] Small firms, which once had a local monopoly, were often pushed out of the market once railroads were expanded into their region.[12] For example, the completion of the transcontinental railroad led to mass manufacturing layoffs in California, as Californian producers could not compete with their Eastern rivals.[13] Railroads had a similar effect on the meatpacking industry, an industry that historically employed a large number of immigrant workers. With the development of refrigerated railcars, Swift & Company cut costs by moving meatpacking closer to where the cattle were raised in the Midwest and shipping the final product, rather than shipping the

---

[8] Kim (1995, 885).

[9] The lower GNP is due to lower values for agricultural land. Without rail networks, some areas would have paid much higher prices to get their goods to market; in other areas, agriculture would have simply been unprofitable. Donaldson and Hornbeck (2013, 24). Their estimate is in line with Fogel's estimate of a loss of 3 percent of GNP without railroads owing to the social savings of the railroads. Fogel (1994).

[10] Kim (1995).

[11] Kim (1995, 886).

[12] Engerman and Sokoloff (2000).

[13] Saxton (1971).

live cattle to the East or West Coast and then slaughtering them.[14] Swift & Company's use of the railroad to centralize meatpacking led to the closure of hundreds of smaller meatpackers that could not compete on price.[15] Thus increased intra-US trade led to the closure of small, less productive firms and should have led to less support from firms for open immigration.

While the US federal government provided some support for the completion of rail networks, the size of the rail network was outside the control of any given senator. Many railroads were privately financed during this time period.[16] Others turned to international financing, especially from Great Britain, to fund construction, using as collateral land grants from the US federal government.[17] While the Senate as a whole voted for or against these land grants, few US senators, beyond those on influential committees or in the leadership, could have stopped or started a rail project on their own. Further, many individual states also built out their own networks, something that was very difficult for a senator from another state to stop. Thus the rail network, and states' connection to it, were largely exogenous to US senators.

In addition to the increase in intra-US trade during the nineteenth century, intra-US firm mobility increased owing to technological advances. The telegraph and later the telephone allowed for quick transmission of information between geographically separated parts of the firm. Inventions like the typewriter allowed for increased written communication, giving managers greater control over workers as well as more information about the production process.[18] These technological and managerial changes allowed firms both to grow in size and to move the plant far from the headquarters.

Changes in the US banking and financial sector also affected firm mobility during this era. Prior to the Civil War most firms had to self-finance capital improvements, including new plants.[19] After the Civil War, changes in the structure of the banking sector as well as the development of the commercial paper market and stock markets allowed firms to expand both in size and geographically.[20] Legal restrictions that prevented bank capital from moving were lowered and circumvented as well, leading to increased competition in the banking sector.[21] Banks in areas with little

---

[14] Lamoreaux (2000, 422–23).

[15] Lamoreaux (2000, 423).

[16] Eichengreen (1995, 79).

[17] Eichengreen (1995, 87).

[18] Yates (1993).

[19] Engerman and Sokoloff (2000).

[20] Davis (1965, 372) and Engerman and Sokoloff (2000).

[21] James (1976).

capital began offering certificates of deposits across the country to solicit funds from the relatively capital-abundant East, which they could then lend to firms.[22] All in all, it became easier for capital to move throughout the United States, for businesses to gain short-term capital wherever they were located, and to produce goods in one market for another market.

A final feature of the US economy that changed firm support for immigration was increasing productivity based on technological advancements. Increases in productivity were especially pronounced in agriculture. Starting in the 1850s, plows, seed drills, and threshers led to large productivity increases in wheat and other grains.[23] For example, the work needed per acre of corn fell from 109.25 hours of hand labor in 1855 to 17.9 hours of machine labor in 1894; per acre of wheat, it fell from 53.75 hours of hand labor in 1829 to 2.45 hours of machine labor in 1894.[24] Productivity increased further with the introduction of the gas-powered tractor; in 1925 (the first year the Census of Agriculture collected data on tractors) there were on average about 10,325 tractors in each state; by 1950 that number had increased to almost 71,000.[25] While not all agriculture was mechanized to the same degree as grains—the mechanical cotton picker and mechanical tree shaker would not be developed until the middle of the twentieth century, and there are still many specialty crops that primarily use hand labor—mechanization released large amounts of labor. Farmers as a percent of US population declined from a high of 16 percent in 1870 to less than 10 percent in 1925, and less than 6 percent in 1950.[26] Farmers producing grains were less likely to hire labor, reducing their demand for immigrant labor, and farmers' children were more likely to leave the farm for the factory, reducing demand from industry for immigrant labor as well.

Technological development affected labor productivity and the need for skilled labor in manufacturing as well. The first shift in industry from artisanal shops to factories and assembly lines in the 1830s to the 1880s led to an increased need for relatively unskilled labor, including labor from women, immigrants, and children, which may have led to an increase in support for open immigration. The next shift from factories to continuous and batch-processing methods beginning in the 1890s led to

---

[22] Davis (1965, 370).

[23] Mechanical reapers and plows were available starting in the 1830s and 1840s but were not adopted until their price declined in the 1850s and the price of wheat increased. David (1975) and Atack, Bateman, and Parker (2000).

[24] Calculated from US Commissioner of Labor (1899), as cited in Atack, Bateman, and Parker (2000, 269).

[25] Data from Haines, Fishback, and Rhode (2014).

[26] Calculated from Ruggles et al. (2010).

an increased need for skilled labor at the expense of unskilled labor.[27] Even within industries that continued to produce using assembly lines, increased automation and changes in managerial techniques led to increased labor productivity: the average value produced in manufacturing per worker increased in constant dollars from $199.83 in 1850 to $614.96 in 1939.[28]

Testing the Effect of "Americanization"

Table 5.1 examines how the "Americanization" of regional markets, increases in productivity, and changes in the election of senators affected the way senators voted on immigration. The dependent variable is the proportion of votes for open immigration in a given year. This variable captures how supportive the senator is in general on immigration in a given year. Given the shifting ideologies of the parties during this time period, as well as the strange bedfellows of Southern conservatives and Northern labor in the Democratic Party, I use senator fixed effects rather than political party to control for a senator's ideology. The use of senator fixed effects also means that the results estimate how changes that occur during a senator's term affect her voting on immigration rather than estimating how differences between senators affect their voting behavior, leading to a harder test of the argument. I include year fixed effects to control for yearly shocks that affect the entire United States as well as a linear time trend to control for time trends. I use an ordinary least squares regression (OLS), as most of the observations lay within the interval [0, 1].

As argued in chapter 3, the effects of changes in trade openness, firm mobility, and productivity may not be instantaneous; instead, it may take some time for their effects to be felt. In chapter 3, I addressed this by testing the effects of the variables lagged as well. In this chapter, many of the variables are available only in census years. I use data from the last census year, in some sense building time lags into the regressions.[29]

THE EFFECT OF INTRA-US TRADE ON SUPPORT FOR IMMIGRATION

I argue that increasing trade between the regions in the United States should have acted like international trade, leading low-skill-intensive firms to close, taking their support for open immigration with them. To measure the ability to trade, I examine the size of the US rail network interacted

---

[27] Goldin and Katz (1998).

[28] Data on value produced and number of wage earners are from Census Bureau (Various Years*b*), and CPI data are from Officer and Williamson (2015).

[29] Because of the amount of missing data, I do not use multiple imputation, as it produces estimates with very large standard errors.

TABLE 5.1
Effect of Intrastate Trade and Firm Mobility on Senators' Preference for Immigration.

DV: proportion of votes for open Immigration	(1) 1850–1936	(2) 1850–1936	(3) 1870–1914	(4) 1882–1914	(5) 1882–1936	(6) 1882–1936	(7) 1882–1914	(8) 1882–1936	(9) 1882–1936
US rail	-0.01*	-0.01+		-0.02	-0.00	-0.00	-0.02	-0.01	-0.01
	(0.01)	(0.01)		(0.02)	(0.01)	(0.01)	(0.02)	(0.01)	(0.01)
State rail	-0.60	-0.43		0.91	1.70	1.72	0.27	1.14	1.16
	(1.71)	(1.63)		(3.56)	(2.34)	(2.28)	(3.50)	(2.50)	(2.45)
US rail*state rail	0.02	0.02		-0.01	0.01	0.01	-0.01	0.00	0.00
	(0.03)	(0.03)		(0.03)	(0.03)	(0.03)	(0.03)	(0.03)	(0.03)
South*US rail	0.00	0.01		0.00	-0.00	-0.00	0.00	-0.01	-0.01
	(0.01)	(0.01)		(0.02)	(0.02)	(0.02)	(0.02)	(0.02)	(0.02)
Mt West*US rail	0.03***	0.03***		0.03*	0.04***	0.04***	0.03*	0.04***	0.04***
	(0.00)	(0.00)		(0.01)	(0.01)	(0.01)	(0.01)	(0.01)	(0.01)
West*US rail	-0.00	0.00		-0.01	-0.00	-0.00	-0.01	-0.00	-0.00
	(0.01)	(0.01)		(0.03)	(0.01)	(0.01)	(0.03)	(0.02)	(0.02)
South*state rail	-7.06	-6.84		-7.44	-13.53*	-13.53*	-6.63	-12.76*	-12.76*
	(4.79)	(4.93)		(5.78)	(5.96)	(5.93)	(5.30)	(5.81)	(5.78)
Mt West*state rail	51.83***	51.91***		53.30*	83.83**	86.14**	54.31**	84.49**	86.80**
	(12.12)	(11.87)		(19.82)	(26.08)	(24.38)	(19.09)	(26.44)	(24.73)
West*state rail	-47.06**	-44.95**		-139.93***	-127.65***	-127.33***	-140.90***	-125.66***	-125.37***
	(14.13)	(14.38)		(35.46)	(29.21)	(29.61)	(36.46)	(28.61)	(29.01)
South*US rail*state rail	0.06	0.04		0.03	0.19	0.19	0.03	0.20	0.20
	(0.11)	(0.12)		(0.04)	(0.16)	(0.16)	(0.05)	(0.16)	(0.16)
Mt West*US rail*state rail	-1.62***	-1.62***		-1.90***	-2.47***	-2.48***	-1.89***	-2.49***	-2.50***
	(0.20)	(0.19)		(0.33)	(0.42)	(0.40)	(0.32)	(0.45)	(0.43)

TABLE 5.1
Continued

DV: proportion of votes for open Immigration	(1) 1850–1936	(2) 1850–1936	(3) 1870–1914	(4) 1882–1914	(5) 1882–1936	(6) 1882–1936	(7) 1882–1914	(8) 1882–1936	(9) 1882–1936
West*US rail*state rail	0.76* (0.34)	0.65+ (0.36)		2.34*** (0.48)	2.07** (0.59)	2.06** (0.59)	2.35*** (0.49)	2.05** (0.57)	2.04** (0.56)
Direct elections		−0.08** (0.03)		−0.07*** (0.01)	−0.09*** (0.02)	−0.09*** (0.01)	−0.07*** (0.01)	−0.09*** (0.02)	−0.08*** (0.02)
Financial integration			0.10 (0.19)						
South*financial integration			−0.32 (0.26)	−0.10 (0.23)			−0.10 (0.23)		
Mt West*financial integration			0.41** (0.11)	0.88*** (0.13)			0.89*** (0.13)		
West*financial integration			0.11 (0.27)	0.06 (0.33)			0.06 (0.33)		
South*financial integration (est)						−0.11 (0.23)			−0.12 (0.22)
Mt West*financial integration (est)						0.84*** (0.15)			0.84*** (0.15)
West*financial integration (est)						0.03 (0.31)			0.03 (0.31)
Agricultural tech (horses and mules)				−0.16 (0.18)	−0.16+ (0.08)	−0.16+ (0.08)			
% Grains							−0.95 (1.15)	−1.89* (0.69)	−1.91* (0.69)

TABLE 5.1
Continued

DV: proportion of votes for open Immigration	(1) 1850–1936	(2) 1850–1936	(3) 1870–1914	(4) 1882–1914	(5) 1882–1936	(6) 1882–1936	(7) 1882–1914	(8) 1882–1936	(9) 1882–1936
Value added				−0.38	−4.60*	−4.57*	−0.35	−4.13+	−4.10+
				(2.63)	(1.97)	(1.92)	(3.04)	(2.42)	(2.33)
Weighted tariff				3.06	4.68**	4.71**	3.08	4.55**	4.58**
				(2.09)	(1.65)	(1.61)	(1.99)	(1.39)	(1.35)
% Foreign-born				−3.39+	0.90	0.83	−1.82	1.20	1.13
				(1.88)	(1.19)	(1.20)	(3.26)	(1.03)	(1.03)
% Foreign-born^2				6.50*	−1.27	−1.11	3.96	−1.55	−1.39
				(3.04)	(2.62)	(2.66)	(5.15)	(2.16)	(2.17)
Observations	3866	3866	2362	1564	3168	3168	1564	3168	3168
R^2	0.121	0.122	0.006	0.148	0.124	0.126	0.148	0.124	0.126

Notes: Included but not shown: linear time trend, constant. All models include senator fixed effects and, except for (3), year fixed effects. Robust standard errors clustered by Congress in parentheses. $^+$ $p < 0.10$, * $p < 0.05$, ** $p < 0.01$, *** $p < 0.001$. US rail is the total rail in the United States (10,000km), from Comin and Hobijn (2009). State rail is the number of rail miles in the state (from Census Bureau (Various Years)) divided by the state size (from Carter et al. (2006)). Direct elections is an indicator for direct elections from Davis (1965) and financial integration (est) uses the five-year average from 1910–14 for 1915–36. Agricultural tech (horses and mules) is the number of horses and mules (in millions) and % grains is the percent of grains produced in the state, both from Haines, Fishback, and Rhode (2014). Value added is the real value added per worker (logged) from Census Bureau (Various Years b). Weighted tariff is the tariff rate weighted by employment; tariff data from Census Bureau (Various Years a) and employment data from Ruggles et al. (2010). % foreign-born and % foreign-born^2 is the percentage of foreign-born in the state and its square from Ruggles et al. (2010). South is defined as in the US Census; Mt. West and West are defined as by ICPSR. State size, horses and mules, % grains, value added, state employment by industry, and foreign-born are from the last census year.

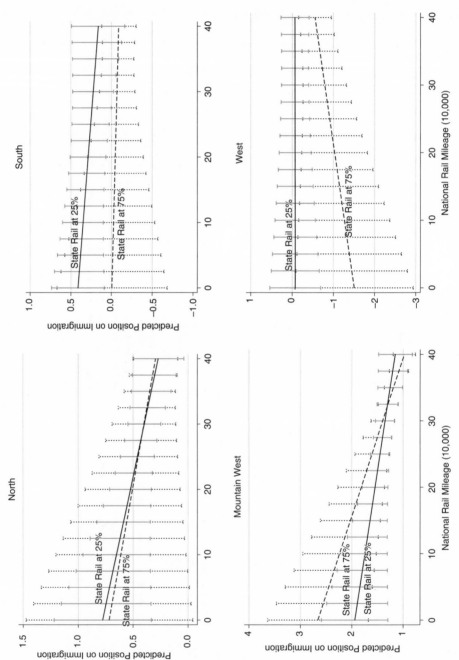

Figure 5.3: For caption see next page.

with the size of the rail network in the state. A larger US rail network means that more parts of the country are connected to each other, making trade easier.[30] Of course, for a state to be affected by this increase in trade, it must be connected to the rail network. To measure how connected a state is to the rail network, I divide the total miles of rail in a state by the state's size.[31] I then interact the size of the US rail network with the size of the state's rail network. Additionally, analysis showed that the effects of the rail network in the North differed from those in the South, the Mountain West, and the West, and so interaction terms are included with these regions.[32]

The increase in the rail network had the predicted effect on the way that US senators voted on immigration. Because interpreting a triple interaction term is difficult, figure 5.3 shows how the changing size of the US rail network affects senators' voting on immigration in the different regions in model 1. The effects are similar across all nine models, even with the inclusion of other variables. For the North, we see that there was a greater negative effect of the building of US rail networks than of state rail networks. This may be because the North was an early builder of rail, and thus, to be connected to other regions, it had to wait for the rest of the regions to build out their rail network. For the South, we find that the building of the state rail systems had a greater negative effect on support for immigration, as states in the 75th percentile of rail had a much lower likelihood of voting for open immigration. The South was a relative latecomer to the building of railroads, with much of the network built after 1885, when over half the US network had been built, making a

---

Figure 5.3: Effect of US and State Rail Networks on Support for Immigration.
Note: Estimated support from model 1. Solid lines are the effect when state rail is at the 25th percentile for the region and dashed lines are for the 75th percentile. Bars represent 95 percent confidence intervals with dashed bars for the 75th percentile. The year variable is set at 1912, which had a fixed effect close to 0, and the time trend variable is set at the median for the region. Estimates do not all lie within 0 and 1 owing to the constraints on the year fixed effect.

[30] Total US rail is from Comin and Hobijn (2009).

[31] State rail data are from Census Bureau (Various Yearsd), and state size is from Carter et al. (2006). I use the size of the state as of the last census year; a majority of states during this time period already had their borders fixed.

[32] The South is defined as in the US Census as DE, MD, VA, WV, KY, NC, SC, TN, GA, FL, AL, MS, AR, LA, TX, and OK; the Mountain West is defined as by ICPSR as AZ, CO, ID, MT, NV, NM, UT, and WY; and the West is defined as by ICPSR as CA, OR, and WA (AK and HI were not yet states.)

state connection to the network more important than the size of the overall network. For the Mountain West, also a relative latecomer to the building of rail, connection to the US national network had a stronger effect when the state also had a larger rail network for similar reasons. Finally, for the West, like the South, larger state rail networks had a larger effect on the support for open immigration, but that effect was attenuated as the US rail network increased. This effect may be driven in part by California. As I will discuss in greater detail below, when the transcontinental railroad was completed relatively early in 1869, this had a large, negative effect on the support for open immigration as many firms in San Francisco closed. Rail networks in the West were very small during this time, and this may be driving the effect.

THE EFFECT OF INCREASING THE POWER OF THE AVERAGE VOTER ON SUPPORT FOR IMMIGRATION

Next, I examine whether the direct election of senators had an effect on support for open immigration in model 2. The direct election of senators should have taken away power from business interest and given it to the average voter. As the average voter tends to be anti-immigration, this change in election law should lead senators to vote for restrictions more often. To measure this, I created an indicator variable coded as 1 for the year in which the state adopts a popular control mechanism and all subsequent years.[33] For states that did not adopt a popular control mechanism prior to the ratification of the Seventeenth Amendment in 1913, the indicator was coded as 1 starting in 1913. All previous years were coded as 0. The majority of these measures were adopted in the West, Midwest, and South in the first decade of the twentieth century. Most of the Northeast adopted these measures only when forced to do so by the Seventeenth Amendment.

I find that the move to direct elections tends to make senators vote for more restrictive immigration policies, but that this electoral change did not alter the effect of rail networks (the coefficients are largely unchanged in size or significance). The move to direct elections was made possible, in part, through the efforts of the Progressive movement, which was anti-immigration. The relationship between direct elections and voting on immigration, therefore, may be spurious—simply a sign of the strength of the Progressive movement. To examine this, I run the same regressions only in the states that changed to direct elections with the Seventeenth Amendment. If the effect of direct elections simply shows the strength of the Progressive movement, we should expect to see a positive relationship

---

[33] This is similar to Lapinski (2004).

between direct elections and immigration in these states, as the Progressives were not strong enough to change the elections in these states. I find, however, a negative relationship between direct elections and voting on immigration in these states as well; in a regression specified as in model 9 but with this coding of direct election, the coefficient on the indicator is -0.10, $p < 0.1$.[34] These results show that increasing the power of voters through direct election led senators to vote for immigration restrictions more often.

THE EFFECT OF INCREASING INTRA-US FIRM MOBILITY ON SUPPORT FOR IMMIGRATION

Third, I examine whether increased firm mobility led senators to vote for restrictions on immigration more often (model 3). Ideally, we would have a measure similar to the measure of FDI restrictions in other countries used in chapter 3; however, states are not legally allowed to restrict intra-US movement of firms. Nor do we have good measures of the technological ability to move production. Instead, I use financial market integration as a proxy. When integration was higher, it would have been easier for firms to move money between factories and headquarters across state lines, and easier to finance plants in different locations.

To measure financial market integration, I used the coefficient of variation of profits for banks to measure how integrated regional capital markets are.[35] The coefficient of variation is the standard deviation of profits made by banks over the mean profits. If capital is fully mobile across the United States, all banks should make the same profits, as capital would move from less profitable areas to more profitable areas.[36] Capital, therefore, is more mobile at lower levels of the coefficient of variation and less mobile at higher levels; to ease interpretation, I rescale the variable as 1 minus the coefficient of variation so that higher values denote greater integration.[37] Because the coefficient of variation is the same for the entire

---

[34] See online appendix C for the regression table.

[35] As the coefficient of variation can be measured only at the national level, the variation in this variable is across time and not across states.

[36] This empirical strategy is similar to that used in Hiscox (2002) to measure whether capital is mobile across industries.

[37] To create the variable, I use the weighted net nonreserve city bank regional profit data on banking. Data are from Davis (1965). The data are weighted by the earning assets of the banks in each region, which decreases the importance of large city banks in the region. Profits in the large cities converged more quickly than in the entire United States, as capital was more likely to flow to these cities. Davis (1965, 367). Similarly, reserve bank cities' profits converged more quickly than did those of nonreserve bank cities. Finally I use net profits rather than gross profits, which controls for differing levels of risk across the regions.

United States, in model 3 I do not include year fixed effects (which are collinear with the variable). The data on bank capital are available only from 1870 to 1914; to get a longer time span in models 6 and 9, I use the five-year average for 1910–14 as the value for each subsequent year. I assume that once one national financial market was created, it did not become (much) less integrated during the rest of the interwar period.

I find that financial market integration has different effects by region, and they are similar to the estimated version of financial integration as well. There is little effect on the North; the North had the most active financial markets and therefore was the standard by which other markets were judged, leading to a null result. For the South, the effect was negative (the sum of the coefficient on bank capital and the interaction is -0.21, $p < 0.05$); as capital became more integrated, Southern senators opposed immigration more. The effect of firm mobility on the South is somewhat counterintuitive given that many low-skill-intensive firms were using their newfound mobility to move to the South because of its lower wage costs. I argue that Southern politicians were voting increasingly for restrictions to protect their low-wage advantage. As we saw in the example of textile firms in chapter 4, increasing immigration would have lowered costs for Northern firms but would likely have had little effect on Southern firms, since few immigrants moved to the South.[38]

For the Mountain West, the effect was positive (0.51, $p < 0.05$). The number of manufacturing establishments in the Mountain West increased with greater financial integration,[39] as did the number of immigrants.[40] In contrast to the South, senators from the Mountain West had an incentive to support immigration as more low-skill-intensive firms moved to their states, to give firms in their states a competitive advantage. Finally, there was no effect of integration on the West. Similar to what we saw in chapters 3 and 4, then, there seems to be less effect of firm mobility than of trade openness. This may be because this measure is somewhat far removed from actual firm mobility, or because trade openness affects all firms, while usually only large firms can move production.

THE EFFECT OF INCREASING PRODUCTIVITY ON SUPPORT FOR IMMIGRATION

I argue that technology adoption and increasing productivity should also decrease support for immigration. I use two different measures of productivity in agriculture and one in manufacturing. The first measure in agriculture is the number of horses and mules (in millions) in the state

[38] Ruggles et al. (2010).
[39] Census Bureau (Various Years*b*).
[40] Ruggles et al. (2010).

(models 4, 5, and 6).[41] Throughout much of this time period, most farmers relied on farm machinery pulled by horses and/or mules, including plows, mowers, and reapers.[42] The first commercial gasoline tractors were not sold until 1902 (and the Census of Agriculture did not begin counting tractors until 1925).[43] Horses and mules, then, provided much of the (literal) horsepower that took the place of hand labor. Greater numbers of horses and mules should be associated with a higher level of productivity and less demand for human labor. The second measure is the amount of grains produced in the state as a percentage of all grains produced in the United States (models 7, 8, and 9).[44] Grains were the first major commodity to be largely mechanized. States that produce a lot of grains, then, should have needed much less labor than states that produced more labor-intensive crops.

For manufacturing, I use a much more straightforward measure of productivity, the log real value added per worker.[45] Data on productivity changes are available from the mid-1880s onward, allowing us to test the effect of the change from factories to continuous and batch-processing methods, which should have decreased support from industrial firms for open low-skill immigration.

Productivity had a negative effect on voting on immigration. In agriculture, increasing the number of horses and mules from the 25th percentile (about 100,000) to the 75th percentile (almost 600,000) in model 5 would lead to a change in support for open immigration by -0.08 ($p < 0.1$), and increasing the percentage of grains from the 25th percentile (0.4 percent) to the 75th percentile (3.3 percent) in model 8 leads to a change of -0.06 ($p < 0.05$). In industry, a one-standard-deviation change in the value added per worker (about $1,000 in 1982–84 dollars) in model 5 leads to a change of -0.02 ($p < 0.05$) in support for immigration. Productivity attenuates the effect of trade openness for the Northern states. As firms in the Northeast and Midwest were often among the first to adopt new technology, these results suggest that Northern firms responded to increases in competition from other regions by increasing productivity.

[41] The data are from Haines, Fishback, and Rhode (2014).

[42] White (2008).

[43] White (2008).

[44] The data are from Haines, Fishback, and Rhode (2014). Grains include all grass-like commodities, as well as corn, that can easily be harvested with a mechanical reaper and so include all the varieties of wheat, corn, oats, rye, wild grasses, alfalfa, and clover, but exclude rice. Percent grains is highly collinear with the number of horses and mules, since draft animals were used heavily in their production and so are not included in the same model.

[45] Data on value added are from the Census of Manufacturers, Census Bureau (Various Years*b*), and CPI data are from Officer and Williamson (2015). Data from the last census year are used.

THE EFFECT OF INCREASED OPENNESS TO INTERNATIONAL TRADE

The process of "Americanization" was not the only process of integration going on during this time period; there was a large amount of international trade as well. Increased openness to international trade should have had an effect similar to that of increased intra-US trade: it led firms to close, taking their support for open immigration with them. To measure the amount of trade protection that firms and agriculture had in each state, I created a weighted tariff variable, weighting the tariff data by industry by the amount of employment in that industry in the state.[46] If we include the later years of the time period—when the Americanization of the US market was almost complete and international factors likely had a greater effect—I find that senators from states that had higher tariffs were more likely to support open immigration than were senators from states with less trade protection, consistent with my argument.

SUPPORT FOR ALTERNATIVE EXPLANATIONS

Finally, I examine support for two alternative explanations for immigration policy: the nativism argument and the immigrants as an interest group argument. I use the proportion of immigrants in the state to test these arguments. On the one hand, it was very easy for European immigrants to become citizens during this time. Thus even if not all the foreign-born in a senator's state were citizens, she should have considered them as potential voters. A greater proportion of immigrants, then, should have made the senator more supportive of immigration. On the other hand, greater immigration would likely cause a nativist backlash, which should have made the senator less supportive of immigration. Which effect dominates is an empirical question. I include both the percent of foreign-born and its square to account for nonlinearities that appear in the data.[47] In model 4, foreign-born has a statistically significant effect. Overall, greater numbers of foreign-born have a negative effect on voting, consistent with arguments based on nativism. At higher levels, the marginal effect of increasing immigration declines; if the number of foreign-born reached about 50 percent of the population (outside the range of the data), the effect of the foreign-born would be positive. This smaller marginal effect is consistent with the argument that immigrants themselves can help push for greater openness, but only when they are a large part of the population. With other

[46] Data for tariffs are from Census Bureau (Various Yearse), and employment data are from Ruggles et al. (2010) and calculated by the author.

[47] The data are from Ruggles et al. (2010). There are not enough data to do multiple imputation, and so the last census year is used. The 1890 census is not available; for 1890, the average of 1880 and 1900 is used, and for 1891–99, the 1900 figure is used.

specifications, the percent of foreign-born has the same signs but is not statistically significant. This suggests that nativists and immigrants affect the way senators vote.

WHY DIDN'T THE SOUTH ANTICIPATE THE GREAT MIGRATION?

Increased firm mobility allowed firms to take advantage of the low labor costs in the South. I argued that, paradoxically, this led the South to decrease support for open immigration to deny Northern firms access to cheaper labor, thereby protecting Southern firms from Northern competition. However, one consequence of the strict immigration restrictions enacted in 1917 through 1924 was the eventual migration of workers from the South to the North during and after World War II, which eroded some of the South's low-wage advantage. Yet Southern politicians in the early twentieth century did not seem worried that greater restrictions on immigration would lead to internal migration from the South to the North.

While migration out of the South began during World War I when immigration decreased owing to the war, Southern politicians may not have anticipated that so large a share of their workforce would eventually move North. Importantly, African Americans faced discrimination and low wages in Northern factories in the early twentieth century, reducing the incentive to move.[48] In contrast to farm families in the Midwest during this time period, children of African American farm families were still needed on the farm; there was no mechanization of cotton, the main cash crop of the South, similar to what occurred in grains, and discrimination in capital markets made it difficult for African American farmers to invest in the laborsaving technology that did exist. It wasn't until after World War II— when agricultural policy during the Great Depression and the development of the mechanical cotton harvester had displaced sharecroppers,[49] and antidiscrimination laws made it easier to get a job in the North[50]—that the bulk of the migration of African Americans out of the South occurred. As these factors were caused by events largely exogenous to Southern politicians, the Southern politician in the 1910s and 1920s was probably justified in believing that a large out-migration of workers was improbable. Thus the anti-immigration votes of Southern senators were rational: they denied the North immigrant labor, protecting Southern firms' low-wage advantage.

Overall, then, the creation of a national market in the United States had an effect on US senators' voting on immigration similar to that which

---

[48] Collins (2003).
[49] Whatley (1983).
[50] Collins (2003).

globalization has had on countries' low-skill immigration policy. As the US market became more integrated—especially as intra-US trade increased owing to the building of railroads—senators from states exposed to this trade and firm mobility became less supportive of open immigration. Changes in productivity, something that is hard to measure on a cross-national basis, also made senators less supportive of open immigration. Senators from states with greater protection from international competition supported open immigration to a larger extent. Finally, there is some support for the view that nativism and immigrant lobbies played a role: senators from states with more immigrants opposed open immigration more than did senators from states with fewer immigrants, but this effect was attenuated with more immigration.

Chinese Exclusion and the Transcontinental Railroad

While the data support my argument that the integration of US regional markets led to restrictions on low-skill immigration, there were pieces of legislation that clearly show the role that nativism played. One such piece of legislation was the Chinese Exclusion Act. Explanations for the passage of this bill have focused on the rising anti-Chinese sentiment of native workers.[51] Yet anti-Chinese nativism materialized in periods long prior to the passage of the Exclusion Act: in 1852–54 miners rioted against Chinese immigrants working the gold fields; in 1867–69 white miners again attacked Chinese miners; and in 1876–82 white workers and small business owners joined forces in the Democratic Party to craft the Exclusion Act.[52] Why didn't the earlier waves of xenophobia lead to legislation while the final wave did?

In 1869, the transcontinental railroad was completed, linking the industrial East and Midwest to the the West. The completion of the railroad had two major effects on the economy of California. First, the completion of the railroad led to massive layoffs of both Chinese and white workers, pushing down wages.[53] Second, it led to a recession as California producers had to compete with Eastern producers, who were often more productive and had lower labor costs. To compare, Chinese workers in California were paid only slightly less than white workers in the East, and white workers in California often made twice as much as those in the East.[54] This competition forced manufacturers in California to increase productivity, which some firms did through mechanization, or to close.[55] The closure of

---

[51] See for example, Boswell (1986) and Saxton (1971).
[52] Boswell (1986, 356).
[53] Boswell (1986) and Saxton (1971).
[54] Boswell (1986, 363).
[55] Boswell (1986) and Saxton (1971).

these firms led to even lower wages. I argue that after the completion of the transcontinental railroad there were fewer firms to push for Chinese immigration, and for the remaining firms, there was less need for new immigration as the firms could use the laid-off white and Chinese labor.

To examine this hypothesis, I regressed senators' voting behavior on the percent of Chinese immigrants in the state, an indicator denoting the time period, and the interaction between the percent of Chinese immigrants and the indicator. As Chinese immigrants were welcomed (or at least not prohibited) at first, the goal of this exercise was to see when a large Chinese population in a state transformed from a benefit into a liability. As above, I used an OLS regression; senator and year fixed effects and a linear time trend are included; and the standard errors are clustered by Congress. I broke the time period as before and after the completion of the transcontinental railroad (as either 1869 or 1870, since the railroad did not reach Oakland until November 1869) and several placebo periods, including a few years before and after the completion of the railroad; 1881, the year before the Chinese Exclusion Act was first passed; 1897, a randomly chosen year; and 1914, the start of World War I. All regressions included all years of data for this time period, not just the years around the break.[56] If my argument is correct, we should find a structural break in the relationship between support for immigration based on the percentage of Chinese foreign-born at the time of the completion of the railroad but not at the placebo periods. Prior to the completion of the railroad, the coefficient on Chinese foreign-born should be positive, as Chinese immigration would have been supported by the firms who used the labor. Afterward, the relationship should become negative, as firms in the West, where most Chinese immigrants were located, could use laid-off labor, decreasing the need for open immigration.

Figure 5.4 shows the coefficient on the percent of Chinese immigrants in each state and the interaction term. Prior to the completion of the railroad (for breaks at both 1869 and 1870), the effect of Chinese immigration is positive and statistically significant; states with more Chinese immigration— states in the West—were much more supportive of immigration in general, including on bills on immigration from China. After 1869 or 1870, the percent of Chinese has no effect or a slight negative effect on voting behavior (when a squared term is included). As can be seen in figure 5.4, this break occurs only in the year of the completion of the railroad and the following year. The same difference is not found if we split the time period before the completion of the railroad or long after it. A Chow test further shows that only the structural breaks at 1869 and 1870 are statistically significant.

---

[56] See online appendix C for regression table.

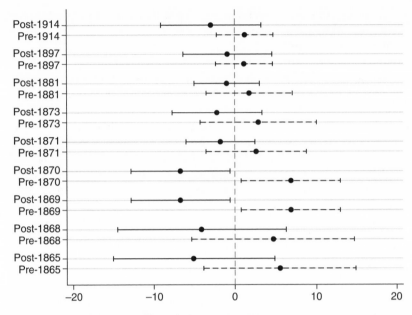

Figure 5.4: Change in the Effect of Chinese Foreign-Born on Senators' Voting.
Note: Coefficients and 95 percent confidence intervals from OLS regression of proportion of votes for open immigration on the percent Chinese foreign-born interacted with indicator for time period. *Pre-*time period is the coefficient on percent Chinese foreign-born (dashed 95 percent confidence interval) and *Post-* time period is the coefficient on percent Chinese foreign-born interacted with time period indicator (solid 95 percent confidence interval). All years of the data are used in the regression. Regressions also include senator and year fixed effects and linear time trend.

Thus something happened in 1869 or 1870 that led to a change in the way the number of Chinese immigrants affected voting. Consistent with my argument, prior to the completion of the railroad, Western firms were protected by high transportation costs. Production expanded, leading to an increased need for labor and increased demands for immigration. After the completion of the railroad, firms lost this protection and faced increased competition, leading to the closure of some firms. Larger firms were able to mechanize production, which, in contrast to the post-1890 period, meant that they often replaced more skilled craft labor with less skilled immigrant, child, or female labor. Smaller firms often did not have the capital to mechanize; these firms were forced to produce with old technology that necessitated more expensive white male craft labor.[57] Smaller firm owners believed that they could regain competitiveness if they could eliminate the perceived advantage that larger firms had from using immigrant labor.[58] Larger firm owners did not need to bring in even more immigrant labor—labor costs were down owing to the layoff by the railroads and the closure of other firms—and likely chose to lobby on other issues or to not lobby at all, allowing anti-Chinese immigration legislation to be passed.

MODERN GLOBALIZATION AND IMMIGRATION, 1950–2008

Senate voting provides us with empirical tractability in the modern era as well. The post-1950 period in the United States has been a time of increasing trade openness, firm mobility, and immigration restrictions. The main threat to identification of a causal effect is, as it was in the previous section, whether senators are responding to increased immigration restrictions with increasing trade openness or firm mobility, or some other variable is causing senators to choose a policy bundle of trade openness, firm mobility, and immigration restrictions. I argue that trade openness and firm mobility were largely out of the hands of senators during this time period as well, allowing us to identify a causal effect.

With the passage of the Reciprocal Trade Agreements Act (RTAA) in 1934, Congress effectively tied its own hands on tariff policy. The RTAA and its successor, known as Trade Promotion Authority, or Fast Track, allows the president to negotiate reciprocal trade agreements with other countries that lower tariffs and, after 1974, nontariff barriers (NTBs) as well, which Congress can only vote up or down; they cannot amend the treaty. The RTAA and Fast Track have meant that, on tariffs and later NTBs, the choice for senators when approving negotiating authority or a treaty was the status quo tariff rate and NTBs or a new lower tariff rate and fewer NTBs. Throughout this time period, a senator could not vote to increase tariffs, which is the outcome we would expect if senators were responding to firm lobbying in the face of increasing immigration restrictions.

Moreover, choosing the status quo was, in fact, a choice for openness in many cases because specific tariffs were inflated away. Irwin estimates that only about 29 percent of the drop in tariffs from 1932 to 1954 was due to tariff cuts; the rest was due to inflation.[59] Congress could have corrected

[57] Boswell (1986).
[58] Boswell (1986).
[59] Irwin (1998, 347).

the tariffs to adjust for inflation, but this would have violated the reciprocal agreements that the United States had signed.[60]

Finally, it is telling that Congress has not set tariff rates, as it did prior to the RTAA, in large omnibus tariff bills. Bailey, Goldstein, and Weingast argue that the durability of the RTAA is due to its endogenous effects on the composition of exporters and import-competing firms, which are the effects that my argument is built upon.[61] Tariff levels and NTBs, therefore, were largely outside the control of senators after the passage of the RTAA.

The change in trade policy was not driven by concerns over immigration policy. The Democrats passed tariff reductions in 1934 in the form of the RTAA because they did not think they could pass unilateral tariff cuts; they were concerned that the tariff reductions would have little effect given other countries' trade barriers; and they wanted a durable tariff reduction.[62] In contrast, Congress passed only two minor immigration laws from the beginning of Roosevelt's first term in 1933 to the start of World War II.[63] Trade continued to open after World War II because leaders in the United States believed that the trade wars of the Great Depression helped foment the conflicts that led to World War II; they wanted to integrate the West; and they wanted to provide economic growth as a bulwark against communism.[64] By examining trade openness during this time period as the reduction in tariffs, measured as percent nondutied imports or 1 minus the ad valorem tariff rate[65] then, we use a measure that senators could not directly control, and we can have more confidence that increasing immigration restrictions did not cause increasingly lower tariffs.

For the 1970s onward, I also use Bernard and colleagues' measure of low-wage trade penetration by industry weighted by employment in that industry in each state.[66] Increased trade in an industry from low-wage

[60] Congress increased nontariff barriers in some cases to protect industries, but the ad valorem tariff rates do not include these measures. Further, Congress abdicated their authority on NTBs to the president in 1974.

[61] Bailey, Goldstein, and Weingast (1997).

[62] Bailey, Goldstein, and Weingast (1997) and Irwin (1998).

[63] In 1935, Congress repealed a law automatically giving citizenship to those serving on US vessels, and in 1937, Congress voted to deport those who had migrated to marry but had not yet married, and to allow the government to deport people to a country other than their country of citizenship.

[64] Barton et al. (2006), Hull (1948), Ikenberry (2001), and Irwin (1998).

[65] Clemens and Williamson (2004). This measure uses the national rate, as the Census Bureau stopped publishing data on tariffs by industry in 1959 until 1989.

[66] Bernard, Jensen, and Schott (2006). Employment data are from Ruggles et al. (2010). Similar to the weighted tariff variable used in the previous section, I use employment data from the last census or American Community Survey. I then standardized the variable by dividing by the total percent of people working in all tradable industries in the state. The

countries led more firms to close or to change their product line to one that was more capital intensive[67] and should lead to less support for open immigration. Import penetration by low-wage states is also largely out of the hands of senators, as it was affected by tariffs and NTBs, which were out of the control of senators in 1934 and 1974, respectively, and by low-wage countries' own decisions to open their markets rather than continuing import-substitution industrialization. While the increase in trade from low-wage countries is likely exogenous to US senators, the level of employment in these industries (which is used to weight the data) reflects the size of the industry and potentially its power. Larger industries that are facing increased competition from low-wage countries may lobby more for open immigration until they either close or change their product mix. To control for this potential source of endogeneity, I lag this measure by one year.[68]

As argued in chapter 2, it is possible that increasing immigration restrictions lead firms to lobby for policies that would increase firm mobility. Firms that are hurt by immigration restrictions can increase their profits by moving production overseas. Yet for most US firms the obstacle to successful offshoring was not the US government but foreign governments. The United States has had few capital controls; therefore, to produce overseas, firms need locations where they could legally invest.[69] To measure the ability to invest overseas, I use two measures: Pandya's measure of entry restrictions in foreign direct investment (FDI) in English-speaking states and the Chinn-Ito measure of average of capital openness for the rest of the world.[70] As in chapter 3, I rescale the FDI restrictions measure so that a higher number means fewer restrictions. Fewer restrictions make FDI easier, leading to increased flows of FDI out of the United States and into these countries.[71] Similarly, firms need to be able to move capital into a state, and lower barriers on average to capital mobility make that easier. The average world level of capital openness may also capture the expropriation risk; von Stein has argued that states sign IMF Article VIII,

---

variable can increase in size if there is an increase in the low-wage import penetration or if sectors are larger. Larger tradable sectors should lead to more support for open immigration. By dividing by the size of the tradable sector, we control for this possibility.

[67] Bernard, Jensen, and Schott (2006).

[68] Results are similar if I lag the measure by two, three, four, or five years, or if I use the weighted import penetration from all countries or from just China, the weighted trade deficit, or the weighted tariff (which is available only from 1989 to 2008). See online appendix C for the regression table.

[69] The United States did impose capital controls for a few years in the late 1960s and early 1970s, but these controls did not greatly restrict the flow of capital.

[70] Chinn and Ito (2008) and Pandya (2014).

[71] Pandya (2014).

which encourages the openness that these variables measure, as a signal of their friendliness to foreign investment.[72]

Both average world capital controls and FDI restrictions in other countries are also exogenous to US senators. In 1947, the United States pushed Great Britain to reduce its capital controls, leading to the Sterling Crisis.[73] After this experience, the United States did not push other states to liberalize their capital markets. Since the end of Bretton Woods, there has been a push for removal of capital controls through IMF conditionality agreements. While the United States has influence over these agreements, individual senators and the Senate as a whole do not. For FDI restrictions, Pandya shows that the decrease in restrictions on FDI since the 1970s has been driven by the large number of states that have democratized during this time period.[74] While US foreign policy likely played some role, the majority of the forces that led to democratization in these states were exogenous to US senators, and hence we can have confidence that senators could not control firm mobility during this time.

Finally, the immediate post–World War II politics suggest that trade and capital policy were set first and then had path-dependent effects on immigration policy. Even before the war ended, US policymakers began making plans for the peace. These plans included opening trade, through what eventually became the GATT/WTO, and re-creating the liberal international order in finance through the IMF. These policies, along with the Marshall Plan and the United States' liberal capital policies, which allowed firms to invest overseas, were implemented in hopes of rebuilding Europe and Japan; preventing communism from spreading further; and binding European countries together to prevent another war.[75]

On immigration, however, the focus was on how to maintain the status quo while dealing with the problems that war refugees posed. Roosevelt recognized that refugees, "surplus" population in Europe and Asia, and "geopolitical problem children," minorities who were traditionally exploited for political gain, were a potential threat to the stability of the world system.[76] He proposed to resettle these populations in less developed areas in North Africa and Latin America, but not in the United States, as he had little congressional or popular support for resettlement in this country.[77]

---

[72] von Stein (2005).

[73] Obstfeld and Taylor (2004).

[74] Pandya (2014). Leaders in developing democracies want to increase the flow of capital in hopes of increasing employment, which will help them (or their party) stay in office, whereas autocratic leaders need to keep the support of the elite, who often own businesses that would have to compete with foreign capital, and thus are more likely to restrict FDI. Pandya (2014, 89).

[75] E.g., Barton et al. (2006), Hull (1948), Ikenberry (2001), and Irwin (1998).

[76] Holborn (1965, 347).

[77] Holborn (1965, 347).

Instead of creating a GATT of migration, the United States and other European and New World states created the Intergovernmental Committee for European Migration, which helped move migrants from Europe to the New World, but not to the United States. Thus at the end of World War II the United States decided to open trade and allow firms to move, while maintaining its immigration policy. Although these policies helped exporters and firms that wanted to invest overseas, the United States chose these policies because of national security concerns, not primarily because of firm lobbying.[78]

In addition to changes in the global economy, there were large productivity gains. In agriculture, the major expansion of the use of tractors in the 1950s and 1960s and the development of the cotton picker increased productivity. For example, as late as World War II, it still took about 100 man-hours of work per acre of cotton.[79] Even with the slow adoption of the mechanical cotton picker in the South—in the early 1960s only about half the cotton was harvested by machines in Arkansas, while California cotton growers had almost fully mechanized[80]—the number of man-hours needed per acre of cotton fell by half to under 50 man-hours in the early 1960s, and by 1970, it had fallen by half again to 24 man-hours. While there were no similar developments in wheat production, it too saw productivity gains, with the man-hours needed to produce an acre falling to less than 3 by 1970.[81] The productivity gains reduced employment in agriculture from 6 percent of the population in 1950 to 2.6 percent in 1960 and less than 0.5 percent today, allowing those who once worked in agriculture, or whose parents worked in agriculture, to work in other industries.[82]

Industry too has seen large gains in productivity over the last 65 years. The median value added per production worker per year (in real, 1982–84 dollars) was a little less than $33,000 in 1950 but had risen to almost $112,000 by 2008. These gains should also lead to less support for open immigration, as firms need fewer workers today than they did in the past.[83]

Testing the Effects of Postwar Globalization on Support for Immigration

Table 5.2 examines how these increases in trade openness, firm mobility, and productivity affected senators' voting behavior on immigration. As before, each model regresses the proportion of votes for openness in a given

---

[78] E.g., Irwin (1998).

[79] Census Bureau (1975).

[80] Holley (2000, 131).

[81] Census Bureau (1975).

[82] Holley (2000) and White (2008).

[83] They also likely need more high-skill labor today. Helpman, Itskhoki, and Redding (2009).

TABLE 5.2
Effect of International Free Trade and Firm Mobility on Senators' Preference for Immigration.

DV: proportion of votes for open immigration	(1) 1950–2008	(2) 1963–2008	(3) 1970–2000	(4) 1970–2008	(5) 1970–1996	(6) 1970–2008
1-tariff rate	−3.98*	−11.78***	−21.70***	−15.99***	−3.43***	−0.17***
	(1.62)	(1.80)	(5.35)	(2.70)	(0.79)	(0.04)
Weighted low-wage import penetration (1-year lag)		0.11**	0.02	0.08*	0.08+	0.13***
		(0.04)	(0.04)	(0.03)	(0.04)	(0.03)
Agriculture sector						
FDI restrictions abroad			−1.05**		−0.18	
			(0.28)		(0.35)	
Average world capital openness				−0.06		−0.11**
				(0.03)		(0.04)
Value added	−0.01	−0.02***	−0.02***	−0.02***	−0.01**	−0.01*
	(0.01)	(0.00)	(0.00)	(0.00)	(0.00)	(0.00)
Value of agricultural equipment			−0.04*	−0.01	0.00	0.01
			(0.02)	(0.01)	(0.01)	(0.01)
% Foreign-born	1.15***	−1.56**	−1.45***	−1.33**	−0.29	−1.76***
	(0.18)	(0.43)	(0.35)	(0.37)	(1.25)	(0.43)
% Union	0.00	0.01***	0.01***	0.01***	0.00	0.01***
	(0.00)	(0.00)	(0.00)	(0.00)	(0.01)	(0.00)
Welfare per capita		0.01	−0.05*	0.00	−0.03	−0.02*
		(0.03)	(0.02)	(0.03)	(0.02)	(0.01)

TABLE 5.2
Continued

DV: proportion of votes for open immigration	(1) 1950–2008	(2) 1963–2008	(3) 1970–2000	(4) 1970–2008	(5) 1970–1996	(6) 1970–2008
GDP growth	0.00	0.54+	−0.03	0.32	0.32	
	(0.00)	(0.28)	(0.29)	(0.24)	(0.46)	
Linear time trend		0.02***	0.03***	0.02***	0.01	0.01***
		(0.00)	(0.01)	(0.00)	(0.00)	(0.00)
Constant	3.61**	5.72***	15.96***	9.80***	−2.17*	−4.27***
	(1.16)	(1.44)	(4.79)	(2.26)	(0.81)	(0.72)
Observations	4804	3690	2704	3414	2042	3054
R^2	0.013	0.057	0.111	0.074	0.009	0.028

Notes: All models include senator fixed effects. Robust standard errors clustered by Congress in parentheses. $^+ p < 0.10$, $^* p < 0.05$, $^{**} p < 0.01$, $^{***} p < 0.001$. *1-tariff rate* is 1 minus the average tariff on all goods entering the United States from Clemens and Williamson (2004). *Weighted low-wage import penetration (1-year lag)* is the import penetration in each industry from low-wage countries (from Bernard, Jensen, and Schott (2006)) weighted by the percent employed in that industry in the senators' state (from Ruggles et al. (2010)). *Agricultural sector* is the real value of agriculture in the state (logged) from Bureau of Economic Analysis (2009). *FDI restrictions* is 1 minus the average level of FDI restrictions in English-speaking countries from Pandya (2014). *Average world capital openness* is from Chinn and Ito (2008). *Value added* is the real value added per worker (logged) from Census Bureau (Various Yearsb). *Value of agricultural equipment* is in real terms (logged) from Haines, Fishback, and Rhode (2014). *% foreign-born* is the percentage of foreign-born in the state from Adler (2009) and Ruggles et al. (2010). Squared percent foreign-born was not included as it was not statistically significant and did not improve model fit. *% union* is the percent of workers represented by a union from Adler (2009) and Census Bureau (Various Yearsc). *Welfare per capita* is the real cash welfare spending per capita by state (logged) from Census Bureau (Various Yearsa). *GDP growth* is from Bureau of Economic Analysis (2009). Agricultural sector, value added, value of agricultural equipment, state employment by industry, % union, and foreign-born are from the last census year.

year on variables that capture changes in the trade openness of the United States, firm mobility, and technology/productivity gains using ordinary least squares.[84] Additionally, I include variables to examine our other theories of what affects immigration policymaking, including the number of foreign-born, the size of welfare programs, and the size of unions, all at the state level. I also include GDP growth at the state level to see whether the economic climate has an effect. I again include senator fixed effects to capture each senator's ideology, as immigration during this time period also often created divides within the parties rather than dividing the two parties. Additionally, the senator fixed effects mean that we are estimating how the changes that occur in a state during the senator's tenure affects her voting. I include a linear time trend, but I cannot include year fixed effects, as they are collinear with the US tariff level and the FDI entry restrictions variables.[85] Robust standard errors are clustered by Congress as voting is likely not independent within a single Congress. As not all variables are available for all years, model 1 is the most basic model and examines all the years of data (1950–2008); model 2 adds in the size of the agricultural sector, the welfare state, and GDP growth and examines the 1960s onward; and models 3 through 6 add in measures of firm mobility and weighted low-wage import penetration, examining the 1970s onward. For variables that are not available for all years, I use data from the last census year. This means, however, that I often cannot use the lagged variable, even though we may think that the effects are not instantaneous.

THE EFFECT OF TRADE OPENNESS ON SUPPORT FOR IMMIGRATION

Trade openness leads to the closure of low-skill-intensive firms, which decreases support for open immigration and should make senators more likely to vote for restrictions. The data bear this out: trade openness—measured either as the average tariff rate on all goods for the entire United States or as the level of import penetration from low-wage countries weighted by employment in the state—has a statistically and substantively significant negative effect on senators' votes on immigration. In models 1 through 4, opening trade from the 25th percentile of openness to the 75th percentile of openness leads to a change of between -0.11 and -0.26 ($p < 0.001$), which is one-third to two-thirds of a standard deviation on the voting behavior variable. Although the effect is smaller, increasing low-wage import penetration in industries in the state also leads to less support for open immigration.

---

[84] Since most of the observations lie between 0 and 1, OLS produces very similar results to tobit (see Peters (2014*b*)).

[85] Peters (2014*b*) examines these changes in a first difference model and finds similar results.

THE EFFECT OF FIRM MOBILITY ON SUPPORT FOR IMMIGRATION

While the effect of firm mobility is not as consistent as that of trade openness, it does appear that increasing firm mobility leads to less support for open immigration. We can examine the effects of firm mobility by focusing on a sector that is relatively immobile—agriculture. Throughout much of this time period, agriculture has been immobile owing to the inability to ship produce over long distances. In models 2, 4, 5, and 6, the larger the agricultural sector (in real terms, logged), the more support there is for open immigration.[86] In model 6, for example, if the size of the agricultural sector expanded from the mean (about $2 billion in 2013 dollars) to the size of California's agricultural sector in 2008 (about $26.6 billion in 2013 dollars), support for open immigration would increase by 0.34 ($p < 0.001$). FDI restrictions and the average world level of capital openness have similar, if not as large, effects. In model 3, if FDI restrictions are reduced from the 75th percentile to the 25th percentile, support for open immigration would drop by 0.07 ($p < 0.001$).[87] Changes in the average world capital openness have similarly sized effects; in model 6, a change from the 25th to the 75th percentile leads to about a 0.06 ($p < 0.05$) drop in support for open immigration.

THE EFFECT OF PRODUCTIVITY ON SUPPORT FOR IMMIGRATION

Increases in productivity should also lead to more support for restrictions by senators as firms need fewer workers and so are less likely to support immigration. The data show that productivity increases have had this effect: the coefficient on value added per worker (in real terms, logged) is statistically significant in all but model 1.[88] There is also an effect of increasing use of technology in agriculture, measured as the total value of equipment (in real terms, logged) in model 3.[89]

SUPPORT FOR ALTERNATIVE EXPLANATIONS

What else helps explain voting on immigration during this time period? The effect of the foreign-born—which may capture nativism or the power of immigrants themselves—on Senate voting has different effects

---

[86] Data are from Bureau of Economic Analysis (2009).

[87] As in chapter 3, FDI restrictions are rescaled so that higher values signal fewer restrictions.

[88] Data are from Census Bureau (Various Years*b*).

[89] Data are from Haines, Fishback, and Rhode (2014).

depending on time period.[90] There appears to be a structural break in the relationship between the percent of foreign-born in the state and voting in the mid-1960s. Prior to the mid-1960s, the relationship between the percent of foreign-born and voting is positive; after this time period it becomes negative.[91] In the 1950s, there were still some states with very high levels of foreign-born from Europe, who likely had some clout, in the Northeast. As migration shifted to less-powerful and more marginalized groups after the Immigration and Nationality Act of 1965, the effect of increasing foreign-born populations became negative. There is also some support for the fiscal argument. Increasing the size of welfare programs also affects voting on immigration as we would expect.[92]

There is less support for the power of labor argument. In contrast to those who argue that unions have had an important effect on immigration policy, increasing unionization leads to greater support for open immigration.[93] This effect may be a result of the rise of public sector unions and the change in the composition of union membership. Public sector employees often do not compete with immigrants and may serve immigrants; increased immigration, therefore, may lead to increased work in the public sector. Additionally, unions in the private sector have increasingly organized immigrant workers; therefore, these unions, like the Service Employees International Union, may act as immigrant rights organizations. There is also less support for arguments based on the state of the economy; GDP growth in each state is significant only in model 2 at the 10 percent level, suggesting—similar to the cross-national data—that senators oppose immigration in good times and bad.

The Link between Lobbying and Senate Voting

Given the results that increases in trade openness, firm mobility, and productivity and technology adoption lead senators to increasingly vote for restrictions, I examine whether the mechanism linking these changes is lobbying. To do this, I use the sector lobbying data from chapter 4 and allocate the amount of lobbying each sector does on immigration

[90] Data are from Adler (2009) and Ruggles et al. (2010), and data from the last census or American Community Survey are used. Goldin (1994) and Timmer and Williamson (1998) also use the percent foreign-born as a measure of nativism.
[91] A Chow test for a break at 1964 is statistically significant at $p < 0.001$; breaks at 1963, 1966, and 1967 are also statistically significant at $p < 0.05$.
[92] Data are from Census Bureau (Various Years$a$).
[93] Briggs (1984, 2001). Union data are from Adler (2009) and Census Bureau (Various Years$c$). Milner and Tingley find a positive and significant effect of labor PAC contributions on House votes on immigration. Milner and Tingley (2012). This result is also in the opposite direction from what scholars have predicted.

(the proportion of all issues listed on their disclosure form represented by immigration) to each state by the share of employment in that sector. I then use a structural equations model to first examine how trade, firm mobility, and productivity affect lobbying and then how lobbying affects voting behavior, essentially reestimating models 5 and 6 from table 5.3 but including lobbying as the mechanism. In the model, I use trade, firm mobility, and productivity changes to predict lobbying and then use the lobbying to predict voting behavior in a second equation. The model I use assumes that trade, firm mobility, and productivity have an effect on voting behavior *only* through their effect on the disclosed lobbying. Given all the limitations of the lobbying data discussed in chapter 4, this may not be the case.

Lobbying does appear to play a role as a mechanism between trade, firm mobility, and productivity and voting behavior (table 5.3). The first column for each model reports the results for the equation determining voting behavior; the second column reports the results for the equation for lobbying; and the third reports the total effect of trade, firm mobility, and productivity on voting behavior through lobbying. When trade is more open, there is less lobbying. States with larger agriculture sectors have more lobbying, but when that agriculture is more capital intensive, lobbying drops. The results on capital openness and value added run counter to my predictions. Average capital openness is associated with more lobbying. This result may be due to the temporal dimension; both lobbying and capital openness are increasing over this time period. Increased value added is also associated with greater lobbying; this may reflect the fact that larger firms both do more lobbying and typically have greater value added.

When firms' lobbying on immigration increases, so too does the senator's support for immigration, although not always at statistically significant levels. This may be a result of the noise in the lobbying measure. The lobbying measure does not represent how much the senators from the state are lobbied—there are not good data on lobbying of individuals. It also does not measure how much lobbying is done by firms in the senator's state—the lobbying data do list addresses, but those are only for firm headquarters and not where production takes place—but instead is the amount of lobbying done by sectors weighted by the employment in the sector in the senator's state.

Finally, we see that in model 1, all of our total effect of variables of interest for trade, firm mobility, and productivity are generally in line with their effects in table 5.3, model 5. In model 2, the results are similar, but not as statistically significant as in model 1. It thus appears, even when noisy lobbying data are used, that trade, firm mobility, and productivity are having their effects through lobbying by firms.

TABLE 5.3
Effect of Free Trade and Firm Mobility on Senators' Preference for Immigration through the Mechanism of Lobbying, 1998–2008.

Dependent variable:	(1)			(2)		
	Senate voting	% of lobbying on Immigration	Total effect: senate voting	Senate voting	% of lobbying on immigration	Total effect: senate voting
% Lobbying on immigration (weighted)	0.01			0.01		
	(0.01)			(0.01)		
1-tariff rate		−81.99*	−0.94***			
		(35.64)	(0.23)			
Weighted low-wage import penetration (1-year lag)					−0.58**	−0.003
					(0.22)	(0.004)
Average world capital openness		9.09*	0.10***		5.16**	0.029
		(3.99)	(0.03)		(1.97)	(0.032)
Value added		0.02***	0.00		0.01**	0.00
		(0.01)	(0.00)		(0.00)	(0.00)
Agriculture sector		0.14***	0.002+		0.16**	0.001
		(0.04)	(0.001)		(0.05)	(0.001)
Value of agricultural equipment		−0.16*	−0.002*		−0.19*	−0.001
		(0.07)	(0.001)		(0.08)	(0.001)
% Foreign-born	0.49***			0.40***		
	(0.11)			(0.09)		
% Union	0.00***			0.00***		
	(0.00)			(0.00)		
Welfare per capita	0.02*			0.02*		
	(0.01)			(0.01)		
GDP growth	0.62*			0.70*		
	(0.26)			(0.32)		

TABLE 5.3
Continued

Dependent variable:	(1)			(2)		
	Senate voting	% of lobbying on Immigration	Total effect: senate voting	Senate voting	% of lobbying on immigration	Total effect: senate voting
Linear time trend	−0.00			0.00		
	(0.00)			(0.00)		
Republican	−0.03			−0.03		
	(0.02)			(0.02)		
Constant	0.93***	64.84*		0.47*	−9.14**	
	(0.20)	(29.25)		(0.23)	(3.14)	
Observations	5150	5150	5150	5150	5150	5150

Notes: Robust standard errors clustered by Congress in parentheses. $^{+} p < 0.10$, $^{*} p < 0.05$, $^{**} p < 0.01$, $^{***} p < 0.001$. *% lobbying on immigration (weighted)* is the proportion of all issues immigration represents in each sector (from chapter 4) weighted by the percent employed in that industry in the senators' state (from Ruggles et al. (2010)). *1-tariff Rate* is 1 minus the average tariff on all goods entering the United States from Clemens and Williamson (2004). *Weighted low-wage import penetration (1-year lag)* is the import penetration in each industry from low-wage countries (from Bernard, Jensen, and Schott (2006)) weighted by the percent employed in that industry in the senators' state (from Ruggles et al. (2010)). *Agricultural sector* is the real value of agriculture in the state (logged) from Bureau of Economic Analysis (2009). *FDI restrictions* is 1 minus the average level of FDI restrictions in English-speaking countries from Pandya (2014). *Average world capital openness* is from Chinn and Ito (2008). *Value added* is the real value added per worker (logged) from Census Bureau (Various Yearsb). *Value of agricultural equipment* is in real terms (logged) from Haines, Fishback, and Rhode (2014). *% foreign-born* is the percentage of foreign-born in the state from Adler (2009) and Ruggles et al. (2010). Squared percent foreign-born was not included, as it was not statistically significant and did not improve model fit. *% union* is the percent of workers represented by a union from Adler (2009) and Census Bureau (Various Yearsc). *Welfare per capita* is the real cash welfare spending per capita by state (logged) from Census Bureau (Various Yearsa). *GDP growth* is from Bureau of Economic Analysis (2009). Agricultural sector, value added, value of agricultural equipment, state employment by industry, % union, and % foreign-born are from the last census year.

Agriculture and Support for Immigration

In the results above, it is clear that the size of the agricultural sector in the state has a large, positive effect on the way senators from that state vote on immigration, but not all agriculture needs the same amount of labor. In particular, grains and soy do not need nearly as much labor as other crops. In table 5.4, I examine how different types of crops that need less labor, and the mechanization of one type of crop—cotton—affect senator's voting on immigration. I expect that senators from states with less labor-intensive agriculture should be less likely to support open immigration. As before, I include senator fixed effects to control for ideology and to examine how changes in the state affect the senator's voting behavior, and a time trend to control for time dependence. As in table 5.2, I include the percentage of foreign-born and the percent in a union. Since we do not have good state-level GDP data for the entire time period, I include the unemployment rate to control for the state of the economy.

In model 1, I examine the effect of larger grain and soy production. These crops were easily amenable to advances in technology, such as the tractor, and manufactured inputs, like chemical fertilizers and high-yield seeds, freeing agricultural labor to work in industry. Model 1 shows that senators from states that produce a greater percentage of the United States' soy and grain crop are less likely to support open immigration, consistent with the argument. In model 2, I examine how a change in technology in the production of cotton affects the way senators from cotton-producing states vote. As the percent of cotton harvested mechanically increased, cotton farmers needed much less labor and senators voted for open immigration less frequently.[94] Mechanization of cotton released workers from agriculture, leading to the second wave of the Great Migration of African Americans from the South to the factories of the North.[95]

The mechanization of farming may be a reason that the United States did not have a large-scale guest worker program as did the states of Western Europe. The United States and Western Europe both had large postwar booms and low rates of unemployment, which should have led to employer demand for more immigration, given that firm mobility was relatively low and there were still relatively high trade barriers.[96] Yet the United States did not have a large-scale program or really any discussion of one. Because crops like grains and soy further mechanized in the 1950s and early 1960s, there was a new, domestic source of labor —former farmers and their families— that firms could draw upon instead of seeking new immigration.

[94] Data on cotton harvesting from Census Bureau (1975).
[95] Alston and Ferrie (1999) and Holley (2000).
[96] The United States also had more open borders for goods during this time period, which also likely explains its lack of a guest worker program.

TABLE 5.4
Effect of Mechanization of Agriculture on Senators' Preference for Immigration.

DV: proportion of votes for open immigration	(1) 1950–2008	(2) 1950–1970
% Soy and grains	−0.79***	
	(0.18)	
% Cotton mechanized		−0.67***
		(0.13)
Agriculture sector	0.12*	
	(0.05)	
% Foreign-born	−2.53**	0.77***
	(0.75)	(0.08)
% Union	0.01*	−0.00
	(0.00)	(0.01)
Unemployment rate	2.64**	0.13
	(0.77)	(2.21)
Linear time trend	0.00	0.03**
	(0.00)	(0.01)
Constant	−2.66*	−4.52**
	(1.00)	(1.26)
Observations	2821	537
R^2	0.026	0.048

Notes: All models include senator fixed effects. Robust standard errors clustered by Congress in parentheses. [+] $p < 0.10$, * $p < 0.05$, ** $p < 0.01$, *** $p < 0.001$. *% soy and grains* is the amount of all soy and grains grown in the state as a percent of total production in the United States from Haines, Fishback, and Rhode (2014). *% cotton mechanized* is the amount of cotton harvested with a mechanical harvester as a percent of total cotton produced in the state from Census Bureau (1975). *Agricultural sector* is the real value of agriculture in the state (logged) from Bureau of Economic Analysis (2009). *% foreign-born* is the percentage of foreign-born in the state from Adler (2009) and Ruggles et al. (2010). Squared percent foreign-born was not included, as it was not statistically significant and did not improve model fit. *% union* is the percent of workers represented by a union from Adler (2009) and Census Bureau (Various Yearsc). *Unemployment rate* is from from Adler (2009) and Census Bureau (Various Yearsc).

Further, the mechanization of agriculture, especially of cotton grown in the western United States, may have helped lead to the end of the guest worker program the country did have, the Bracero Program, in 1964. An explanation for its end was the high number of labor abuses associated with the program, which raised the ire of organized labor.[97] Yet the program

[97] Calavita (2010).

had been cited for labor abuses since at least the early 1950s. What had changed by the early 1960s was the need for labor, especially on the cotton farms of the West. By 1964, about 85 percent of total US production of cotton had been mechanized, but the percent of cotton mechanized in western states was much higher, ranging from 90 percent in Texas to 98 percent in California and Arizona. Even cotton farmers in the South, who had not used the Bracero Program to a great degree, also became more supportive of immigration restrictions as mechanization increased. The Bracero Program had ensured that Southwestern farmers would not recruit farm laborers from the South, which protected Southern farmers' labor supply. As mechanization proceeded throughout the South, Southern farmers no longer needed this protection and became less supportive of low-skill immigration.[98] With the loss of the cotton lobby, senators may have felt less pressure to maintain the Bracero Program.

CHANGE IN PARTISAN SUPPORT FOR IMMIGRATION

Thus far, I have accounted for senators' ideology and partisanship through the use of senator fixed effects. These fixed effects allowed us to see how changes in the senator's state while she was in office affected her voting on immigration, but tell us little about the change in parties' positions on immigration.

Figure 5.5 shows support for immigration by the mean Republican and mean Democratic senator in each year. These data confirm the conventional wisdom about support for immigration by the two parties. In the 1850s through the 1880s, Republicans opposed immigration to a greater degree than did Democrats. In the early days of the Republican Party, the party gained support from smaller parties, like the Know-Nothings, which were anti-Catholic and anti-immigrant. After the Civil War, Northeast producers, who favored open immigration to keep labor costs down, came to dominate the Republican Party; at the same time the Democratic Party increasingly represented labor, which tended to be anti-immigration. In the 1970s, the parties again changed positions, with the Democrats more in favor of immigration than were the Republicans.

To explain the change in positions between the two parties in the 1970s, table 5.5 repeats the analysis of table 5.2 but removes the fixed effects and instead includes an indicator for affiliation with the Republican Party and interacts that with all the key variables. Democrats increasingly support open immigration during this time period. This seems to be driven by

---

[98] See Alston and Ferrie for a similar analysis of the effects of mechanization on Southern support for the Bracero Program. Alston and Ferrie (1999). See also Grove (1996).

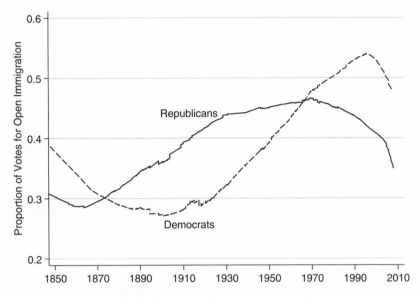

Figure 5.5: Support for Immigration by the Two Parties, 1850–2008.
Note: Voting behavior smoothed with a loess smoother, bandwidth of 0.5. Voting data from Poole (2009), Poole and Lewis (2009), and Poole and McCarty (2009) and coded by the author.

two factors: the percent of foreign-born in their state and the size of the welfare state. Democrats have long been the party of immigrants; therefore, it is not surprising that as the percentage of foreign-born increased after the change to nondiscriminatory quotas in 1965, Democrats became more pro-immigration. Further, the effect of the foreign-born is strongest in the 1970–96 period, when we see a great increase in support for open immigration from Democrats. The size of the welfare state also seems to positively affect Democrats during this time period. This is consistent with the embedded liberalism hypothesis: in return for greater openness to the world economy, states increased the size of the welfare state to protect those hurt by openness.[99]

Yet even with increases in the foreign-born and the welfare state, Democrats still have not universally favored immigration. The increased support for open immigration from Democrats seems to be attenuated by increased trade openness, firm mobility, and productivity. In models 2 through 4, there is a negative and statistically significant coefficient on

[99] Ruggie (1982).

TABLE 5.5
Partisan Shifts on Immigration.

DV: proportion of votes for open immigration	(1) 1950–2008	(2) 1963–2008	(3) 1970–2000	(4) 1970–2008	(5) 1970–1996	(6) 1970–2008
		Democrats				
1-tariff rate	−1.91 (1.82)	−8.03*** (1.25)	−19.14*** (5.00)	−16.66*** (1.45)		−0.12 (0.09)
Weighted low-wage import penetration (1-year lag)					−0.42 (1.39)	
Agriculture sector		0.01 (0.00)	0.01 (0.02)	0.00 (0.01)	−0.03 (0.03)	−0.01 (0.01)
FDI restrictions abroad			−0.99** (0.35)		−0.16 (0.39)	
Average world capital openness				0.12*** (0.03)		0.01 (0.02)
Value added	−0.00 (0.01)	−0.02* (0.01)	−0.02*** (0.01)	−0.02* (0.01)	−0.01** (0.00)	−0.01 (0.01)
Value of agricultural equipment			−0.02 (0.02)	0.00 (0.01)	0.03* (0.01)	0.02*** (0.01)
% Foreign-born	0.50** (0.15)	0.05 (0.19)	0.14 (0.34)	0.04 (0.14)	1.15*** (0.31)	0.04 (0.17)
% Union	0.00* (0.00)	0.00+ (0.00)	0.00+ (0.00)	0.00* (0.00)	0.00 (0.00)	0.00 (0.00)
Welfare per capita		0.04* (0.02)	0.01 (0.03)	0.04** (0.01)	−0.01 (0.05)	0.05+ (0.02)

TABLE 5.5
Continued

DV: proportion of votes for open immigration	(1) 1950–2008	(2) 1963–2008	(3) 1970–2000	(4) 1970–2008	(5) 1970–1996	(6) 1970–2008
GDP growth		0.68* (0.31)	−0.32 (0.33)	0.32 (0.24)	0.49+ (0.28)	
			Republicans			
Republican	1.29+ (0.76)	−0.90 (0.85)	1.13 (2.37)	−4.24 (3.01)	−0.45 (0.69)	−1.15*** (0.17)
1-tariff rate	−1.25+ (0.73)	0.25 (0.89)	−2.65 (2.19)	3.44 (3.21)		
Weighted low-wage import penetration (1-year lag)					−5.83* (2.66)	0.04 (0.07)
Agriculture sector		0.01 (0.01)	0.06*** (0.01)	0.05*** (0.01)	0.08*** (0.01)	0.05*** (0.01)
FDI restrictions abroad			−0.09 (0.24)		−0.01 (0.26)	
Average world capital openness				−0.24*** (0.06)		−0.10*** (0.03)
Value added	−0.02+ (0.01)	−0.00 (0.01)	−0.00 (0.00)	0.01 (0.01)	−0.00 (0.00)	0.01 (0.01)
Value of agricultural equipment			−0.04*** (0.01)	−0.04*** (0.01)	−0.06*** (0.01)	−0.05*** (0.01)
% Foreign-born	−0.02 (0.17)	−0.60+ (0.35)	−0.11 (0.74)	−0.31 (0.23)	−0.91* (0.45)	−0.19 (0.34)

TABLE 5.5
Continued

DV: proportion of votes for open immigration	(1) 1950–2008	(2) 1963–2008	(3) 1970–2000	(4) 1970–2008	(5) 1970–1996	(6) 1970–2008
% Union	0.00	0.01***	0.01***	0.00+	0.00+	0.01*
	(0.00)	(0.00)	(0.00)	(0.00)	(0.00)	(0.00)
Welfare per capita		−0.03	−0.07	−0.06**	0.04	−0.06*
		(0.03)	(0.08)	(0.02)	(0.06)	(0.03)
GDP growth		−0.30	0.41	−0.06	−0.46*	
		(0.27)	(0.31)	(0.27)	(0.22)	(0.03)
Linear time trend	0.00	0.01***	0.03***	0.02***	0.01	0.00
	(0.00)	(0.00)	(0.01)	(0.00)	(0.00)	(0.00)
Constant	1.60	5.84***	14.12***	13.08***	−0.49	0.12
	(1.43)	(0.98)	(3.21)	(1.20)	(1.47)	(0.71)
Observations	4790	3676	2699	3400	2039	3042
R^2	0.028	0.064	0.138	0.112	0.110	0.060

Notes: All models include senator fixed effects. Robust standard errors clustered by Congress in parentheses. $+\ p < 0.10$, $*\ p < 0.05$, $**\ p < 0.01$, $***\ p < 0.001$. Coefficients in the top half of the table are for Democrats and in the bottom half is the interaction with Republicans. Total effect for Republicans is the sum of two coefficients. All variables the same as in table 5.2.

the average trade openness variable; in model 3 there is a negative and statistically significant coefficient on FDI restrictions; and in models 2 through 5 there is a negative coefficient on value added per worker.

Republicans have become less supportive of open immigration during this time period owing to decreased firm support for open immigration. In all models, the total effect of trade openness, measured as the linear combination of the base term for 1 minus the national tariff rate or as the weighted low-wage import penetration and the interaction with the indicator for Republican, is negative and statistically significant at least at the 10 percent level. Similarly, increased firm mobility has led to decreased support for open immigration for Republicans: in all models, states with Republican senators that have large agricultural sectors are more likely to support open immigration (the linear combination of the two coefficients on the agriculture sector is positive and statistically significant); increased average world capital mobility has a negative effect on all Republican senators (the linear combination is negative and significant); and the effect of FDI restrictions abroad is negative as well (the linear combination of the two coefficients is negative and statistically significant in model 3). Additionally, increased productivity in industry and agriculture also led to decreased support by Republicans for open immigration: in most models, the linear combinations of the coefficients on value added and value of agricultural equipment are negative and statistically significant.

Nativism, and perhaps the fiscal effects of immigrants, also had some effect on how Republicans voted on immigration. In model 2, the effect of more foreign-born in the state has a negative effect on Republicans; in models 3 through 6, the effect of the foreign-born is attenuated to zero. In contrast to Democrats, increasing the size of the welfare state did not lead to increased support for open immigration from Republicans; the linear combination of the two coefficients on welfare per capita is not statistically different from zero in all models.

Thus it appears that Republican senators became less supportive toward open immigration largely because of changing firm demand for immigration as a result of greater trade openness, increased ability to move production abroad, and increased productivity. There is also some evidence that Republicans responded more and more to nativism from their constituents as a result of the growth of the foreign-born population or an expansion of the welfare state. These results are consistent with the history of the shifting bases of support for the two parties. Through the mid-twentieth century, Republicans still represented Northern industrial interests, and Democrats still were split between Northern labor and Southern whites. With the realignment of the parties after the civil rights movement and the deindustrialization of the North, Republicans lost their constituencies among Northern industrial interests but gained Southern whites, and Democrats picked up the North and minority voters, including immigrants, and lost Southern whites. Although Republicans are still thought of as representing business interests, those interests have changed their position on immigration and have become a less important voice on this issue.

CONCLUSION

In this chapter, I used Senate voting on immigration as a complement to the results from the cross-national data in chapter 3 and the lobbying data in chapter 4. In chapter 3, I showed that trade openness and firm mobility have a robustly negative effect on immigration policy in many different countries and over two hundred years. In chapter 4, I showed that trade openness, increases in firm mobility, and technology adoption all led firms to lobby less on low-skill immigration. This chapter and the next bridge these results by showing that increases in both intra-US and international trade openness, firm mobility, and technology that are out of the control of US senators led to restrictions in immigration policy, and not the other way around. The subnational study also allowed the testing of productivity variables that are simply not available on the international level.

The data show that the increasing integration of US regional markets before World War II and the integration of world markets after World War II have had the hypothesized effect on support for open immigration. Prior to World War II, as US markets integrated, firms in the Northeast and Midwest—the firms that employed the most immigrants—faced increasing competition from goods produced elsewhere in the United States, especially the South, which had lower labor costs, in part owing to fewer labor laws and limits on unions. Firms in the Northeast and Midwest either closed, increased productivity, or moved to the South in response to this threat. These changes in intra-US trade openness and firm mobility, and increases in productivity in both industry and agriculture, help explain Senate voting during this time period. Senators were also affected by the size of the foreign-born population in their states as well as the change to direct elections.

Increased intra-US trade may also help explain one of the most xenophobic immigration laws of the time period, the Chinese Exclusion Act. Although there had been anti-Chinese episodes prior to the completion of the transcontinental railroad, senators' support for immigration increased as the size of the Chinese population in their states increased. After the completion of the railroad, this relationship changed, as I argue that firms were no longer as supportive of open immigration. Many firms in the western United States closed, and those that did not could take advantage of the white and Chinese labor that was laid off by the railroads and firms that had closed. Thus, in the face of rising xenophobia, these firms decided to change production strategies or close rather than lobby for continued immigration.

This pattern of increasing restrictions in response to trade openness, firm mobility, and productivity repeated itself in the post–World War II era. The United States opened somewhat to immigration after World War II, replacing its racist national origins policy with a policy that was still based on national origins but that treated each country equally. Increasing trade openness, firm mobility, and productivity, however, have wiped away much of the support for open immigration in the Senate and in the United States in general. Instead, as firm support for open immigration has decreased, there has been more space for anti-immigrant groups to influence policy, leading to more and more restrictions on immigration over time. Changes in the global economy may also help to explain the changing partisan support for immigration. Republicans have become less supportive of open immigration than Democrats (on average) since the 1970s; changes in trade openness, firm mobility, and productivity in agriculture help explain this shift. Thus we can have greater confidence in the argument, as it holds in two different contexts where the changes in trade openness, firm mobility, and productivity were largely outside the control of the policymaker.

CHAPTER 6

Immigration Policy in Small Countries:
The Cases of Singapore and the Netherlands

IN THIS CHAPTER, I EXAMINE THE EVOLUTION OF IMMIGRATION POLICY in two small economies—Singapore and the Netherlands after World War II—to help establish that it is increases in trade openness, firm mobility, and productivity that cause the restrictions in immigration policy, and not the other way around, addressing the *reverse causality* problem. As small countries, neither Singapore nor the Netherlands has had much control over the global economy, and many of these states' firms produce for the export markets rather than for the home market. In this chapter, I focus on how other states' actions affect the ability of Singaporean and Dutch firms to compete in the export markets.

In addition to addressing the reverse causality problem, the Singapore and Netherlands case studies show that the argument applies to very different countries. In both countries, the relationship between firms and the government differs from that in the United States. In the Netherlands, firms' interests are represented through the Social and Economic Council (SER), which provides an institutionalized forum for employers organizations, unions, and third-party experts to have a voice in crafting policy. Because of their representation on the SER, firms do not need to lobby the government in the same manner as do firms in the United States, where a similar institutional link does not exist.

Singapore represents yet another form of business-government relationship. Nominally, Singapore has a corporatist structure similar to that of the Netherlands, and indeed there are institutionalized forums for firms to comment on draft legislation. Yet the informal connections between firms and the government may be more important. The Singaporean government has investments in large swaths of the economy, and there is a revolving door between government and private business. These connections give firms the ability to help shape policy, as any profit-maximizing firm would like.

In addition to having different relationships between firms and the government, both states' relationships with the rest of society differ markedly from that of the United States. As an electoral autocracy, the People's Action Party (PAP) in Singapore has less accountability to the public than do officials in a democracy. Yet policy in Singapore cannot stray too far from the will of the people, or else the PAP is likely to suffer a loss of legitimacy and support. The Netherlands is a proportional representation (PR), parliamentary democracy based on a corporatist system of government. PR systems allow for more, smaller parties, which give greater voice to more extreme elements. Furthermore, unions get one-third of the seats in the SER, which gives labor increased influence over policy. Thus, in Singapore, we might expect that the rest of society has relatively less influence over policy than it does in the United States; in the Netherlands, the rest of society, especially unions, should have relatively more influence over policy. If the argument holds in both places, then, we should have greater confidence in its ability to apply to many different countries.

METHODOLOGY AND EXPECTATIONS

In this chapter, I use process tracing to establish that my argument is causally identified (it does not suffer from either the reverse causality problem or the omitted variables problem) and applies generally. As Bennett explains, process tracing evaluates competing arguments by examining the intervening steps in a hypothesized causal process.[1] As with the US case studies, Singapore and the Netherlands are what Seawright and Gerring call *typical cases*, ones in which the hypothesized relationship holds.[2] As we saw in chapter 3, trade openness, especially as measured by the value of the exchange rate, and firm mobility are negatively correlated with immigration policy. The goal of this chapter, then, is to show that the relationship is causal; namely, that business support for immigration in these two countries decreased with greater trade openness and firm mobility, and that policymakers reacted to these changes by restricting immigration policy. As I will show, the change in business support was not the only factor that affected immigration policy, but it is a major factor and it is the only one that can explain the entire post–World War II immigration history of these states.

I support my argument with evidence from interviews and primary and secondary sources. For both cases, interviews were conducted in the summer of 2013. In Singapore, I conducted interviews with high-level civil servants in the agencies responsible for immigration policy: the Ministry of Manpower (MOM), the Ministry of Trade and Industry (MTI), and the National Population and Talent Division (NPTD). I also met with a high-level official at SPRING, an agency under MTI, responsible for helping small and medium-size enterprises (SMEs) grow, and that

[1] Bennett (2010).
[2] Seawright and Gerring (2008).

generally represents the interests of SMEs. This official has also served on numerous corporate boards and discussed his views on immigration from that perspective as well. Additionally, I met with one of the leaders of the Singapore Democratic Party (SDP), one of the larger opposition parties.

The interviews nevertheless provide an incomplete picture. I was unable to meet with officials from two of the major opposition parties, the Workers' Party and the National Solidarity Party, and with nonaligned members of Parliament. For these groups, I rely on their public campaign materials to gauge their opinions on immigration. I was also unable to meet with officials from the major government holding companies that own shares in large swaths of the economy. Ideally, these interviews would have given me greater insight into firms' preferences over immigration and how firms influence government policy; instead, I rely on primary and secondary source material.

The main source of bias from the data is the lack of direct information on firm preferences and on their ability to lobby the government. As I discuss below, the government has a stake in a large swath of the economy. Yet it is unclear how large of a stake it has, and how the government influences corporate behavior and vice versa. In large part, this is due to the government's desire to downplay its role in the economy. This bias in reporting should make it less likely that a link will be discovered between firms' preferences and government policy.

For the Dutch case study, I contacted all major political parties, all the employers organizations, all the unions, the ministries that oversee immigration policy and enforcement, and several academics. I received positive responses from one member of Parliament, two of the large employers organizations, one of the large unions, the Ministry of Security and Justice, which oversees enforcement, and several academics. As in the Singapore case, these interviews provide an incomplete picture; I complete the picture with primary and secondary sources.

My argument leads to the following causal chain in these two states. Changes in the global economy, outside the control of Singaporean or Dutch policymakers, led to an erosion of competitiveness of domestic low-skill-labor-intensive firms in export markets and, potentially, in the domestic market. The erosion of competitiveness for these firms leads them to increase their productivity or the skill level of their production process, move production to another country with lower costs, or close. All of these lead to less support for open immigration for low-skill immigrants and restriction on low-skill immigration. The argument, then, predicts a specific sequencing of events: changes in the global economy should lead to changes in the composition of firms, which then should lead to changes in policy.

As I show below, the Singapore case does not always follow this sequence exactly but is an exception that proves the rule. Low-skill-intensive Singaporean firms have lost competitiveness with changes in the global economy, most notably the rise of China. Yet instead of decreasing firm lobbying always preceding immigration restrictions, the government at times has restricted immigration in hopes of forcing low-skill-intensive firms to increase productivity, change to a more capital/skill-intensive product line, or move production overseas, while retaining headquarters in Singapore. The government is even willing to tolerate firms' closing as the cost of increasing the skill intensity of production in Singapore (what they term *upskilling*). In Singapore, then, changes in the global economy lead directly to both less firm support for open immigration and less *government* support for open immigration.

The main alternative explanations for immigration policy have different causal chains. If immigration policy is driven by the role of labor, we expect that increases in the power of labor should precede greater restrictions, and that decreases in the power of labor should precede greater openness. If the fiscal argument drives immigration policy, we expect that welfare-spending increases and/or a budgetary crisis should precede immigration restrictions. For the nativism hypothesis, we expect that increased nativist sentiment should precede more restrictions. As discussed in earlier chapters, these hypotheses are not mutually exclusive. Trade and capital openness will lead to restrictions only if there are groups that dislike immigrants in the polity. Otherwise, immigration policy may stay the same after openness. Similarly, a lack of nativism, weak labor, and a small social welfare system will produce immigration openness only if there is a group—firms—that wants immigrants.

Following Van Evera, I examine data that lend themselves to four different types of tests.[3] The least demanding test, the *straw in the wind test*, provides suggestive evidence that a hypotheses is correct, but is neither necessary nor sufficient.[4] *Hoop tests* provide necessary but not sufficient evidence; these types of data can rule out but not rule in a hypothesis.[5] Much of the evidence presented is in the form of hoop tests: they show that the conditions each hypothesis argues should precede a change in immigration policy did, or importantly did not, occur. A third type of test is the *smoking gun test*; passing this test confirms the hypothesis, but failing does not eliminate it.[6] Some of the evidence presented here—especially statements of officials—falls in this category. These statements

[3] Van Evera (1997).
[4] Bennett (2010).
[5] Bennett (2010).
[6] Bennett (2010).

confirm the argument, but if an official had not given the statement, the argument would not have been eliminated. The final type of test is a *doubly decisive test* that confirms a single hypothesis and eliminates the others.[7] Van Evera notes that doubly decisive tests are rare in social science, but that a combination of hoop tests and smoking gun tests accomplish the same goal.[8] Below, most of the evidence falls into one of the first three categories, but it cumulatively supports my argument.

SINGAPORE

In 2011, voters in Singapore sent a resounding rebuke to the People's Action Party (PAP) largely because of its immigration policy, garnering the PAP its worst performance since independence.[9] The next year, a wildcat strike by Chinese-immigrant bus drivers over pay disparities with Malaysian-immigrant bus drivers sparked widespread hostility against immigrant workers.[10] Opposition to the PAP's immigration policy further increased in 2013, when it was announced that the draft population target for 2030 would be 6.9 million, of which only 55 percent would be native-born Singaporeans. The announced target led to an unprecedented four-thousand-person protest against the policy.[11] After a five-day debate in Parliament, one of the longest debates in Singapore's history, the government was forced to walk back its policy.[12] Since then, the government has enacted a new set of restrictions on both low- and high-skill immigration.

The fact that popular opposition to immigration has forced the government to restrict low-skill immigration is somewhat surprising given existing theories of immigration policy. Organized labor is extremely weak; the government controls the labor unions. Arguments based on immigrants' use of the social welfare system cannot explain the restrictions either; low-skill immigrants (referred to as foreign workers rather than immigrants) are not eligible to use the social welfare system. Finally, if employers should have a voice in immigration policy anywhere, it should be in Singapore, where the government controls a large stake in many corporations.

How, then, did Singapore get to this point? I will argue in this chapter that the PAP's immigration policy has been a balancing act between

---

[7] Bennett (2010).
[8] Van Evera (1997, 32).
[9] Brown (2011).
[10] Barr (2014).
[11] Barr (2014).
[12] Chen (2013).

keeping Singaporean companies competitive in an increasingly competitive international marketplace and keeping opposition to the PAP low. The PAP has been able to keep its hold on power in large part because it has been able to deliver export-led economic growth. Yet its ability to provide this growth has been challenged as other Asian countries have developed. At first, it responded to the loss of competitiveness by increasing openness to foreign workers. However, openness has sparked fears that natives would be overrun and the traditional ethnic balance would be lost. In response to the fears that Singapore was losing its competitive edge and that immigration would lead to a backlash, the government has encouraged firms to increase productivity and/or move low-skill production overseas, while maintaining research and development and headquarters functions in Singapore. The focus on increasing competitiveness has decreased firms' demand for low-skill workers, especially in the manufacturing sector, and pushed the government to restrict low-skill immigration to force firms to be more productive.

The Structure of Immigration Policy in Singapore

Immigration policy in Singapore is divided into separate policies for low- and high-skill immigrants to a much greater degree than is the case in most countries. Currently there are three major categories for immigrants, not including family reunification immigration, which is limited to family members of natives and high-skill immigrants. Low-skill immigrants come under the Work Permit category; middle-skill immigrants come under the S Pass category; and high-skill immigrants come under the Employment Pass category.

Within the Work Permit category, the number of immigrants who are allowed to enter each year is based on nationality restrictions that allow low-skill immigrants from only some Asian countries to apply for a work permit; a dependency ratio ceiling that determines the proportion of foreign workers (including S Pass holders) to native workers in a company; and a monthly levy (tax) on firms for each immigrant they want to employ. When the government wants to change the number of low-skill immigrants entering the country, it uses any or all of these different policy tools. It has changed which nationalities can apply for work permits; adjusted the dependency ratio and created separate dependency ratios for different sectors; and increased the monthly levy and tied it to the dependency ratio.[13]

Permanent residence and citizenship are also based in part on skill level. Singapore takes a "holistic approach" in granting permanent residence and

---

[13] National Population and Talent Division (2012, 34).

citizenship, which includes family ties to Singapore, economic contribution, qualifications, and age, along with the applicant's ability to integrate into Singapore and willingness to maintain ties to the country.[14] Except for spouses and children of citizens and permanent residents, these criteria make it impossible for low-skill immigrants to gain permanent residence or citizenship.

Firm Lobbying in Singapore

Firms' lobbying "looks" different in a nondemocracy like Singapore from how it appears in the United States. First, there is an official channel for businesses and other groups to influence policy, somewhat similar to notice-and-comment rule making in the United States. To get an understanding of public opinion on issues, the Singaporean government seeks comments from stakeholders through structured dialogue.[15] For example, before publishing the 2013 White Paper on Population, the government published an issue paper on population that sought comments from the public.[16] According to a civil servant at the National Population and Talent Division, the government constantly seeks feedback before developing a new policy:

> We met the unions, the business leaders, social media, the youth, students, ... voluntary organizations, community leaders ... We also held some larger facilitated discussions and met lots with the public. Together with the launch of the issues paper in July, we also launched a publishing microsite on the Internet. People could use that microsite to submit their views and feedback on specific issues related to population. We took all this into account in drafting the population policies that eventually went into the White Paper [on Population]. It was almost a full year of engagement ... That was generally the approach that we were taking.[17]

Firms, then, through their official meetings on immigration policy (and other issues) can make their preferences known to the government, and these preferences are taken into account when the final policy is drafted.

Second, firms in Singapore likely have influence over policy through their political connections. The Singaporean government is linked to firms through two main types of organizations: statutory boards and government-linked corporations (GLCs). Most of the statutory boards are

[14] National Population and Talent Division (2012, 33).

[15] Chong (2007, 954).

[16] National Population and Talent Division (2012).

[17] Civil servant at the National Population and Talent Division. Personal interview. June 4, 2013.

advisory or charity organizations, but they are also responsible for key infrastructure in the state including much of the housing, development of industrial parks, and airports.[18] Examples of statutory boards include the Economic Development Board, which helps to attract and subsidizes foreign direct investment in Singapore, and Jurong Town Corporation, which is the principal developer and manager of industrial parks. The boards of directors of these organizations are appointed by the minister to whom they report, and they usually include civil servants from the relevant ministry. Further, Parliament approves their budget, and the Ministry of Finance approves any additional funding requirements.[19]

In the second type of organization, GLCs, the government owns a share of companies. Most shares in the GLCs are held by one of the government's holding companies, the largest being Temasek Holding Company. Temasek is wholly owned by the Ministry of Finance, which had been the main agency responsible for investing in domestic firms.[20] There are additional companies that are not held through Temasek, and there are further investments made by the Central Provident Fund and through fiscal surpluses as well.[21] In 1996, the government created the Standards, Productivity and Innovation Board (SPRING Singapore) to invest in small and medium enterprises. Other holding companies include Sheng-Li Holdings, owned by the Ministry of Defense, which invests in defense industries, and holding companies associated with the National Trade Union Council, which owns taxi companies, supermarkets, and real estate development firms.[22]

It is not known how large a stake the Singaporean government has in its economy, but it is clear that the government has had a financial interest in most sectors of the economy.[23] In 1993, the US Embassy estimated that GLCs accounted for about 60 percent of GDP, although the Singaporean government disputed that claim.[24] In 1998, listed companies held by Temasek had a market capitalization of S$88.2 billion, 25 percent of the total capitalization in the Singaporean stock market.[25] The Department

---

[18] Gómez and Bok (2005).

[19] Gómez and Bok (2005).

[20] Low (2003, 135).

[21] Low (2003, 136).

[22] Gómez and Bok (2005).

[23] The government argues that publishing exact amounts of their investments both at home and abroad would lead to speculative attacks on the Singapore dollar. Former prime minister Lee Kuan Yew said, while serving as the head of the Government Investment Corporation, "We are a special investment fund. The ultimate shareholders are the electorate. It is not in the people's interest, in the nation's interest, to detail our assets and their yearly returns." Rodan (2004, 483).

[24] Low (2003, 140).

[25] Low (2002, 287).

of Statistics reported in 2001 that first-tier GLCs, those in which the government had a 20 percent share or greater, constituted 13 percent of Singapore's GDP in 1998.[26] More recently (2008–13), GLCs made up 37 percent of the listed firms on the Singapore stock exchange, and government-linked firms made up 54 percent of the real estate investment trusts sector.[27]

GLCs have also been active in most sectors of the economy. In the past, Temasek held shares in firms involved in food processing, electronics, chemicals, textiles, and tourism.[28] Temasek has since divested itself from more low-skill-labor-intensive sectors, such as food processing and textiles, as these sectors have shrunk. As I argue in greater detail below, this shows that the government is more than willing to allow uncompetitive, low-skill-labor-intensive sectors to fold, rather than prop them up through subsidies from Temasek or through low-skill immigration. As of 2014, Temasek held 30 percent of its portfolio in the financial sector, 23 percent in telecommunications, 20 percent in transportation and industry, 14 percent in life sciences, consumer products, and real estate, 6 percent in energy and resources, and the remainder in other industries.[29] GLCs, then, seem to be a large part of the Singaporean economy and are in most sectors.

A major difference between GLCs in Singapore and much of the rest of the world has been their reputation as well-managed firms. In the 2002 Budget Speech, the government stated that it would "not favour GLCs with special privileges or hidden subsidies" or "burden them with uneconomic 'national service' responsibilities"; instead, GLCs were "expected to compete on a level playing field" with other firms of the private sector.[30] Temasek allows GLCs to hire their own professional managers at market rates and rarely meddles in the day-to-day operations of the firms.[31] However, it does meet with them regularly "to make its feelings known."[32]

Even though many observers believe that the GLCs are well managed, there is a revolving door between business, especially in the GLC sector, and the government. Rodan has argued that GLCs provide channels for political reward and retribution.[33] Officials and their relatives cycle on and off lucrative board of director positions, which pay internationally competitive rates and offer stock options.[34] According to a 2002 report, written

---

[26] Low (2003, 141).
[27] Sim, Thomsen, and Yeong (2014, 6).
[28] Low (2003, 142–43).
[29] *Major Investments* (2015).
[30] Quoted in Sim, Thomsen, and Yeong (2014, 27).
[31] *From SOE to GLC: China's Rulers Look to Singapore for Tips on Portfolio Management* (2013).
[32] *From SOE to GLC: China's Rulers Look to Singapore for Tips on Portfolio Management* (2013).
[33] Rodan (2004).
[34] See also Shih (2009) on the revolving door between business and the government.

under the pseudonym of Tan Boon Seng and circulated to international journalists and on the Internet, these positions can serve as rewards to loyal party members. For example, the wife of Prime Minister Lee Hsien Loong (who at the time was deputy prime minister) was chairwoman of Chartered Semiconductor, ST Engineering, ST Capital, and StarHub; deputy chairwoman of Singapore Technologies; and director of Temasek Holdings and SembCorp. His brother and several of his uncles, cousins, and in-laws have had similar high-level positions.[35] Current and former government officials and members of Parliament are also given plush positions: for example, the former minister of defense, Lim Kim San, was the chairman of Singapore Press Holdings; in 2003, Cedric Foo, the MP for West Coast GRC, was a senior vice president of Singapore Airlines; and Wang Kai Yuen, the MP from Bukit Timah, was a director of Comfort Group, Comfort Transportation, and Comfort Automotive Services.[36]

Current and former civil servants and members of Parliament are also represented on the corporate boards of *non*-GLCs. In 2012, 19.54 percent of the boards of directors of non-GLCs that are publicly traded on the Singaporean Exchange (SGX) were politically connected.[37] This is lower than the percentage of politically connected board members of GLCs (42.26 percent) but still represents a significant connection between non-GLCs and the government.[38]

In addition to providing loyal civil servants and party members with a source of income, GLCs have also been a recruiting ground for potential members of Parliament and ministers. Those who prove themselves successful in business, whether at a GLC or a private corporation, are often asked to join the PAP and run for Parliament and/or are given a position in a ministry.[39] Goh Chok Tong, the second prime minister of Singapore, previously was the managing director of Neptune Orient Lines, a container shipping and logistics company. Similarly, Lee Boon Yang, who served as minister of manpower, was a senior manager of Primary Industries Enterprise, which manufactures veterinarian equipment and supplies.[40]

Thus the government-linked sector seems both to cover a large swath of the Singaporean economy and to have deep connections to the government. Because of the revolving door between government and the private sector, Hamilton-Hart argues that it is hard to distinguish a government official from a private sector actor, and that these actors tend to have similar

[35] Tan (2002).
[36] Tan (2002).
[37] Sim, Thomsen, and Yeong (2014).
[38] Sim, Thomsen, and Yeong (2014).
[39] Hamilton-Hart (2000).
[40] Tan (2002).

interests.[41] While the government may argue that it does not interfere with the operations of these firms, it is highly likely that these firms easily influence government policy. According to an official in the Singapore Democratic Party (an opposition party): "[the leaders of government] are the employers, they are not only the biggest employer... I'm not even talking about [the civil service]; I'm talking about the private sector."[42] As such, the government makes policies that favor firms' interests.[43]

How Other Groups Lobby

While protests are more or less illegal and, therefore, rare in Singapore, Singaporeans have a few channels to affect government policy. First, the average Singaporean can use elections to hold the PAP accountable to some extent. The latest example was the loss of a seat in Parliament to the Workers' Party in a 2013 by-election, spurred in part by concerns over immigration.[44] Second, as discussed above, the government conducts hearings on major policy issues with stakeholders, including unions and other groups that represent the average Singaporean. Third, the PAP wants to retain its grip on power and therefore is unwilling to push too hard against public opinion for fear of losing power. Thus, through these channels, anti-immigrant sentiment can be expressed and taken into account by the government.

The Transformation of the Singaporean Economy and Immigration Policy, 1965–2014

Figure 6.1 shows Singapore's immigration, trade, and capital policy and a measure of the over- (under-)valuation of its currency for the period since independence. As a small, open economy, Singapore has maintained very low tariffs throughout its history as an independent nation. It has also had relatively open capital policies since the late 1970s. Nonetheless, as Singapore produces mostly for foreign markets, its competitiveness is affected to a greater extent by its exchange rate and the trade policies of its main export markets in the United States, Japan, and Europe. As can be seen in the graph, the Singaporean dollar was undervalued (values less than zero) until about 1990 and has largely been overvalued since then. Immigration policy has largely tracked the exchange rate, opening as the Singaporean dollar dropped in value and becoming more restricted as

[41] Hamilton-Hart (2000).
[42] SDP official. Personal interview. June 7, 2013.
[43] SDP official. Personal interview. June 7, 2013.
[44] Lim (2013).

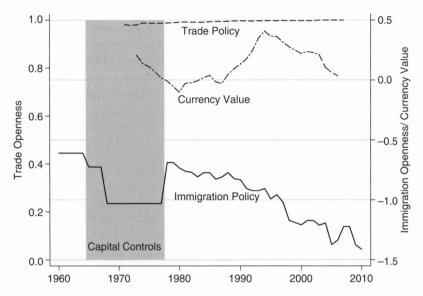

Figure 6.1: Immigration, Trade, and Capital Policy and Value of the Currency in Singapore, 1965–2010.

Note: Shaded region denotes period of capital controls; data are from Bordo et al. (2001). Trade policy is the percent of imports entering without duties (or 1 minus the tariff rate); higher values signify greater openness. Trade data are from Clemens and Williamson (2004). Immigration policy is described in greater detail in chapter 3; higher values signify greater openness. Currency valuation is from Steinberg and Malhotra (2014) and is the difference between the actual real exchange rate and a predicted exchange rate.

the dollar has gained value (correlation of -0.43, $p < 0.05$). For analytical traction, I split the time period into three eras: immediate postcolonial era (1965–71), the labor-intensive economy era (1972–78), and the upskilling and offshoring era (1979–2014).

THE IMMEDIATE POSTCOLONIAL ERA (1965–71)

Throughout the colonial period, Singapore had a very open immigration policy. Local Malay workers were brought to work in the ports, as were immigrants from the East India colonies. Chinese immigrants came via older trading networks as well to work both as merchants and as laborers. By the 1830s, the Chinese had become the dominant ethnic group in Singapore.[45]

[45] Nasir and Turner (2014, 17).

Throughout the colonial period, the economy of Singapore was mostly based on entrepôt trade and military spending by the British. Both of these industries relied on relatively low-skill labor and provided little in the way of economic development, although the ports would become a major driver of development once Singapore gained its independence. There was one key development, however: the creation of a civil service. It was the development of the civil service that helped create the PAP and its technocratic government.

Independence and the federation with Malaysia ushered in a new era in economic development and immigration policy. The Malay Federation government undertook a policy of import-substitution industrialization (ISI) to develop the economy, which Singapore took part in. Migration between the members of the federation was completely open. There were, however, problems with the federation from the start owing to the ethnic composition of the members. Singapore was dominated by ethnic Chinese, whereas the Alliance Party that ruled Malaysia was composed of ethnic Malays. As ethnic tensions between Chinese and Malays flared, especially the riots between ethnic Chinese and Malays in 1963, the PAP decided to leave Malaysia.

Concerns over ethnic tensions have always affected Singapore's immigration policy and are likely a major source of anti-immigration pressure from both within and outside the PAP. Lee Kuan Yew, the first and longtime prime minister, was very concerned over ethnic tensions within Singapore. Riots between ethnic groups had frequently occurred during the 1950s and early 1960s and threatened the country's survival. In a 1985 speech, Lee said of these riots: "Communal riots. We again fought for our lives. That's why the generation that's alive and can remember '65 must know how fragile, how delicate this whole creation is."[46] Immigration policy, therefore, has been crafted with an eye to maintaining the ethnic balance.

The exit of Singapore from the Malay Federation had an immediate effect on its economy. As a small city-state, Singapore could not develop using ISI; Singapore simply did not have a large enough domestic market. Instead, it adopted a strategy of export-led growth, driven in part by multinational corporations (MNCs), as recommended by the United Nations Development Program (also known as the Winsemius plan).[47] The UNDP plan called on the government to create a board to finance local industrialization as well as foster investment from MNCs.[48] In 1961, the government created the Economic Development Board (EDB), and in

---

[46] Quoted in Kuhn (2015).
[47] Soon and Stoever (1996, 319).
[48] Low (1998).

1968 it spun off the financing of investments to the Development Bank of Singapore and industrial development to the Jurong Town Corporation.[49]

MNCs and inward foreign direct investment have always played a large role in Singapore's economy. In the 1960s, most MNCs were attracted by Singapore's strategic location and cheap labor. The EDB was able to attract foreign firms in low-skill-intensive sectors like garments, textiles, and toys but also a few investments in higher-skill sectors such as petrochemicals, iron, and steel. As we will see below, as Singapore has lost competitiveness to other Asian nations, the government has sought more inward FDI in more highly skilled sectors, starting in the 1970s with the semiconductor industry.

Independence also had an immediate effect on immigration into Singapore. Malaysians could no longer freely enter Singapore; instead, immigration was tightly controlled. Economic growth during this first period relied on native unemployed and underemployed labor and labor repression, leading to low firm demand for immigration. In 1966, the PAP had passed the Trade Unions (Amendment) Act, which made it mandatory that unions hold a secret ballot before striking; later amendments made strikes in essential services and sympathy strikes illegal. The Employment Act in 1968 sought to increase productivity and decrease labor costs by increasing the length of the workday and reducing fringe benefits.[50] The Industrial Relations Act, also in 1968, shifted the balance of power to management to hire and fire workers and kept unions from using their labor power to negotiate contracts that were better than those offered in "pioneer industries," industries that the government was trying to develop.[51] While there is no smoking gun evidence that low firm demand for immigration led to the restrictions, my argument does pass the hoop test, as labor repression lowered firm demand.

Can our other theories help explain this time period? The power of labor and fiscal arguments do not pass the hoop test, making it unlikely that either played a large role in the formation of immigration policy: labor was particularly weak during this time period, as in 1969 the main labor union, the NTUC, formalized its role as part of the government, and the social welfare state was not large. In contrast, nativism likely played some role in the immigration restrictions; while lacking a smoking gun, it does pass the hoop test. The Singaporean government has sought to maintain the ethnic balance of the state, especially the dominance of the Chinese; allowing many Malays to immigrate would have upset this balance.

[49] Low (1998, 38).
[50] Loh (2011, 205).
[51] Loh (2011, 206).

THE LABOR-INTENSIVE ECONOMY (1972–78)

Singapore began to lose its economic edge in the immediate post–Bretton Woods era as domestic labor became relatively scarce and other Asian countries, like Taiwan, Hong Kong, and South Korea, developed. The government used three policies to improve its competitive position, which all led to a large low-skill-intensive sector. First, it devalued its currency in the early 1970s. The devaluation led to increased production in low-skill industries; however, there was no longer a native unemployed/underemployed workforce to supply these industries, leading to calls for immigration. It also subsidized threatened industries.[52] This too increased the demand for labor. Finally, in 1972, it enacted wage suppression policies, keeping wages artificially low to help firms compete in global markets.[53] As wages were capped at artificially low rates, employers had an incentive to maintain labor-intensive production or even shift from more capital-intensive production to more labor-intensive production, increasing the demand for labor further.

In response to this increased demand for labor, the government allowed greater migration of low-skill workers. In 1975, it allowed low-skill workers to work in the country for longer than one year.[54] In 1978, it allowed for the recruitment of workers from outside Malaysia, including India, Bangladesh, Sri Lanka, the Philippines, and Thailand, even though this would threaten the ethnic balance. The government also created a daily pass for workers from Malaysia so that they could live in Malaysia but work in Singapore, which also increased the relative share of Malaysians working, if not living, in Singapore.[55]

At the time, it appeared that increased immigration and wage restraint would allow Singapore to remain competitive; but an unintended consequence of these policies was that they led firms to maintain and even develop less efficient production methods, reducing productivity by 6 percent and further eroding Singapore's competitiveness.[56] Later, Singapore's leaders would use this period as an example of why increasing immigration to remain competitive is a poor strategy. Again in this time period, my argument passes the hoop test—an undervalued currency led to the expansion of the low-skill sector and then to increased openness of immigration—but there is no smoking gun.

[52] Low (1998, 45).
[53] As discussed below, the Netherlands also engaged in wage suppression in the late 1940s and early 1950s.
[54] Kaur (2006) and Wong (1996).
[55] Hui (1998).
[56] Low (1998, 45).

Do our other explanations of immigration policy help account for the changing policies in this era? Native labor was relatively weak throughout this time period, consistent with the increased openness. Low-skill immigrants could not access the small social welfare state, which also is consistent with the increased openness. Finally, it appears that nativism was low during this time period; there were few protests or outbreaks of communal violence. Thus all three alternatives pass the hoop test, and openness is overdetermined in this era.

UPSKILLING AND OFFSHORING (1979–2014)

The worldwide recession of the late 1970s and early 1980s clearly showed the cracks in Singapore's strategy for development. Singapore was dependent on external markets and therefore was subjected to intense competition from other Asian countries. Other developing nations in Southeast Asia, especially Thailand, Malaysia, and the Philippines, were beginning to industrialize and compete with Singapore in its export markets.[57] Its currency was also strengthening, in part driven by the government's desire to have Singapore become a financial center, eroding its competitiveness further.

In response, instead of opening immigration, the PAP chose to encourage companies to upskill their production in Singapore, through increasing their productivity and/or offshoring low-skill production. Singapore began its upskilling policy in 1979 with a "corrective" wage policy that greatly increased wages in order to discourage the use of labor and encourage greater use of capital.[58] The PAP limited immigration in hopes of forcing firms to increase productivity or relocate low-skill production.[59] In 1982, the PAP told firms that "work permit holders from non-traditional countries have been allowed into Singapore only as a temporary measure" and would be phased out by 1984.[60] Therefore, in what can be considered as smoking gun evidence for my argument, "[manufacturers] must further mechanize, automate, computerize, and improve management to cut down on workers or they will have to relocate their factories."[61] In order to reduce the reliance on low-skill foreign workers, the government introduced the foreign worker levy.

In addition to the corrective wage policy and the foreign worker levy, the EDB subsidized investment in more high-skill manufacturing, including

[57] Rigg (1988, 342–43) and Toh (1989, 300).
[58] Lim (1983, 757).
[59] Toh (1989, 300).
[60] Fong and Lim (1982).
[61] Fong and Lim (1982).

computer parts, peripherals, software, and silicon wafers.[62] The EDB also pushed upskilling and automation by offering low-cost financing and technical assistance for firms that wanted to automate production through the Robot Leasing Scheme.[63]

The Singapore government's policies to increase productivity and up-skill industry were relatively successful. During the 1980s, value added per worker grew on average 4.7 percent.[64] Low-skill-intensive industries, like food and beverages, textiles and apparel, and wood-based industries declined from 45 percent of manufacturing output in the early 1960s to 15 percent in the 1980s to just 5 percent in 1990.[65]

Regional competition between firms for market share only increased in the 1990s and 2000s. The opening of China fundamentally altered the pattern of global foreign direct investment, leading Singapore to fall in the ranking of global competitiveness.[66] The concern over losing ground to other Asian economies, especially China, is prevalent throughout government documents. For example, in a Ministry of Trade and Industry report, the government noted that "Singapore is located in a fast growing region—this brings us more economic opportunities but also increased competition. We need to calibrate our politics carefully in order to maintain our competitiveness, and yet grow at a sustainable rate so that all Singaporeans can enjoy an improving quality of life."[67] The concern that Singapore is losing competitiveness is also evident in the infamous 2013 White Paper on Population that sparked the controversy on immigration: "Many Asian cities are modernising rapidly, and catching up on us. Singapore must continue to develop and upgrade to remain a key node in the network of global cities, a vibrant place where jobs and opportunities are created."[68] Given that the PAP's survival in large part depends on continued economic growth, it is not surprising that they take threats to the economy seriously.

Increasing competition in the region led the Singaporean government to continue the upskilling trend, with a focus on developing a "knowledge economy." Private businesses are encouraged to increase productivity or move out of low-skill-labor-intensive activities. The government also directed state-owned enterprises to move into more high-skill industries, including defense and semiconductor wafer fabrication.[69] As in the 1980s,

[62] Economic Development Board of Singapore (2015).

[63] Economic Development Board of Singapore (2015).

[64] From Department of Statistics and Economic Development Board, Singapore (N.d.), cited in Wong (1998, 117).

[65] Wong (1998, 116).

[66] Low (2003, 137).

[67] Ministry of Trade and Industry (2012, 2).

[68] National Population and Talent Division (2013, 2).

[69] Wong (1998, 121).

upskilling focused not only on the activities of Singaporean firms but also on the types of inward FDI that Singapore wanted to attract. The Economic Development Board again shifted focus in the 1990s from manufacturing to even more high-skill and capital-intensive sectors, such as chemicals, electronics, engineering, and biomedical.[70] In addition to increasing the productivity of existing firms in Singapore and those seeking to invest in Singapore, the late 1980s and 1990s saw the beginning of Singapore's policy of regionalization. The goal of regionalization is for companies to place their regional (or international) headquarters along with research and development and other high-skill-intensive production activities in Singapore, and to distribute their manufacturing and low-skill-intensive production throughout the region.[71] As discussed in a 2010 government report: "Business must *expand abroad and capture new growth opportunities in order to grow high-value activities in Singapore.* Expanding abroad will often mean relocating lower cost activities overseas. But it creates and retains more good jobs in Singapore—in higher value production, regional management and marketing operations, product development and design, and in trade, finance and business services."[72]

As part of this strategy, the Singaporean government has helped to create offshoring centers across the Singapore Strait in Batam, Indonesia, and across the causeway in Johor, Malaysia, including negotiating the Indonesia-Malaysia-Singapore Growth Triangle free trade area. Regionalization has also led to outward foreign direct investment from Singapore into China by the Economic Development Board and GLCs. Singaporean firms that used to manufacture low-skill-intensive products for MNCs in Singapore now produce the same goods for the same MNCs (and for others) in these regional manufacturing centers.[73] What remains in Singapore are the more high-skill headquarters positions and research and development.

The government's push for greater productivity in the 1990s was relatively successful. From 1990 to 1995, value added per worker grew on average 5.7 percent.[74] Because of the upskilling and regionalization strategy, the Singaporean economy also shed many of the remaining low-skill-intensive manufacturing industries: in 1995 the share of output from the food and beverages, textiles and apparel, timber and furniture, and paper and printing industries had declined to 8 percent combined.[75]

---

[70] Economic Development Board of Singapore (2015).
[71] Low (2003, 137).
[72] Economic Strategies Committee (2010, 6). Emphasis in original.
[73] Wong (1998, 120).
[74] From Department of Statistics and Economic Development Board, Singapore (N.d.), cited in Wong (1998, 117).
[75] Wong (1998, 116, 118).

The focus on upskilling has continued even though it threatens low-skill-intensive firms. In fact, the government has not been shy in telling these firms that they must reduce their reliance on foreign workers or get out of the economy. According to the minister of finance, "The structure of some of our industries will inevitably have to change, given our tight labor market. Consolidation is part and parcel of restructuring. While efficient enterprises and those who develop stronger brands will grow, others may eventually downsize, switch to new business lines, or move parts of their operations abroad. This is indeed how productivity has advanced in most developed economies—not just by individual firms innovating and upgrading, but also through the freeing up of space in the industry for more dynamic enterprises to obtain workers and grow."[76] Additionally, according to a civil servant at the Ministry of Trade and Industry: "I think in Singapore we do recognize that we need to constantly move up the value chain, and given that we have very limited land, so as we progress, right, there's some industries that need to move out of Singapore because you need to make way for higher value added production. So I think the resistance to industries moving out, of course it's not en masse, it's part of the restructuring process that goes on. So the resistance to industries moving out isn't that—isn't as strong as the Western countries."[77] Further, "There's always this process of when the product starts to be manufactured, there's a learning curve and as the learning curve matures, right, it becomes less valuable, and that's when you need to—Singapore becomes too expensive for these processes, and we need to move it out. So I think it's true for probably most of the products, and when a product matures, you just have to recognize that you're probably not the best place to manufacture it, and you just move on to other products that are more high value added. I think ... that has been the development history of Singapore."[78]

In addition to upskilling manufacturing, the government has sought to increase productivity in nontradable sectors, such as construction and food service. Construction in Singapore has been highly dependent on low-skill workers, including a large number of foreign workers.[79] In the mid-1990s, the Construction Industry Development Board established a ten-year plan to increase productivity that included more screening of foreign workers to allow only those with greater skills to enter, having private firms develop training centers to train foreign workers before they immigrate to Singapore, and training more domestic workers and

[76] Shanmugaratnam (2013, 19).
[77] Civil servant, Ministry of Trade and Industry. Personal interview. June 4, 2013.
[78] Civil servant, Ministry of Trade and Industry. Personal interview. June 4, 2013.
[79] Toh (1998, 143, 161).

supervisors.[80] The government also passed a law that forces construction firms to use more prefabricated building components, in order to cut down on the labor needed to complete projects.[81] Finally, the government changed immigration policy to force firms to become more productive. It increased the tax paid by businesses for unskilled foreign workers while decreasing the tax for skilled foreign workers.[82] Recently, the government has set aside S$2 billion to help small and medium firms in the nontradable sector increase their productivity;[83] created the National Productivity and Continuing Education Council in 2010 to research ways to increase productivity; and provided grants for businesses, primarily small and medium enterprises, to increase their productivity as well.

Given that low-skill industry has mostly moved out of Singapore and that nontradable sectors have been forced to be more productive, it is not surprising that firm demand for low-skill immigrant labor has decreased as well, leading the government to restrict low-skill immigration. However, where Singapore differs from many other states is that the government has explicitly increased low-skill immigration restrictions in order to force firms to become more competitive, providing smoking gun evidence for my argument. In 2010, the Economic Strategies Committee argued, "If access to labour is too easy, companies will have little incentive to invest in productivity improvements, which will affect our efforts to upgrade the skills and wages of lower-income Singaporeans."[84] In his 2013 Budget Speech, the minister of finance argued that "the basic reality is that these *sectors which are most dependent on foreign workers* are also the ones *furthest behind in international standards of productivity*, and which account for the lag in productivity in our overall economy."[85] These concerns were echoed by the civil servants I interviewed:

> Then on the other side of the picture, I think the easy access to foreign labor may also present less pressure for companies to improve their processes to be more manpower-efficient, so if they have relatively easy access, the temptation would be to [use] our foreign workers to fuel the growth in their business rather than changes in the processes ... So as part of the efforts to get firms to improve productivity, what we've been doing is ... to increase the cost to employers of foreign workers, so that there is [an] incentive for them to upgrade their processes.[86]

[80] Toh (1998, 164).
[81] Toh (1998, 165).
[82] Toh (1998, 165).
[83] Civil servant, Ministry of Trade and Industry. Personal interview. June 4, 2013.
[84] Economic Strategies Committee (2010, 6).
[85] Shanmugaratnam (2013, 18). Emphasis in original.
[86] Civil servant. Personal interview. June 12, 2013.

Most recently, to prod firms into increasing productivity and reducing their use of foreign workers, the 2014–15 increases on foreign worker levies will be the highest on those industries with the lowest level of productivity.[87]

In many ways, the government's latest immigration policy is simply a continuation of its policy over the last thirty years. "On the economic front, [we are] significantly slowing [the growth of] our workforce, so not growth at all costs. We talked about uplifting Singapore workers into higher new jobs, for training, creating a conducive environment for more Singaporeans to join the workforce, increase our employment rates, our labor force participation. Complementing the workforce with some foreigners, and also helping businesses restructure through this, so move them to a higher-productivity kind of business models."[88] For now, the Singaporean government will still allow high-skill immigrants to enter and become permanent residents and citizens. In addition, it will allow low-skill workers to enter temporarily to work in the low-skill service industry, such as health-care aides and domestic workers, and construction, which will provide "flexibility to businesses during upswings, while buffering Singaporean workers from job losses during downturns."[89]

My argument that firm demand for low-skill workers is driving immigration policy passes the hoop test—increased trade competition, firm mobility, and productivity increases have led to less firm demand for immigration; it also passes the smoking gun test—policymakers have explicitly said they are reducing immigration to make firms increase productivity, and that those firms which cannot compete without immigrant labor should close, move, or become more productive. In contrast, both the power of labor argument and the fiscal argument fail the hoop test. As noted above, the labor unions are controlled by the government and therefore are unlikely to be a source of the restrictions. Low-skill immigrants are not eligible for social welfare benefits either, as they cannot be granted citizenship. Instead, these immigrants are classified as nonresident populations and are easily deported if they become indigent.

Nativism, however, does help explain the immigration restrictions. The PAP has become increasingly worried about popular backlash from too many immigrants. The backlash has taken two forms: concerns about congestion and how large a population the island can support, and concerns about Singapore's national character.

One often-cited reason for concerns about immigration is that the island of Singapore simply does not have the space for more immigrants.

---

[87] Shanmugaratnam (2013, 20).

[88] Civil servant at the National Population and Talent Division. Personal interview. June 4, 2013.

[89] National Population and Talent Division (2013, 40).

This is often seen as a complaint about the amount of congestion on the roads, trains, and buses as well as a lack of adequate housing and other infrastructure.[90] "On the one hand there's a need to make sure that the employers have access to the people that they need so that this generates sufficient growth in the economy, because that growth, then, also provides jobs for Singaporeans. Then on the other hand the physical constraints that we face in Singapore, so infrastructure, space constraints, so in order to balance those two objectives we've got a number of tools."[91] Opposition parties have pointed to congestion and depressed living standards due to immigration as a failure of the PAP's policy. For example, the Singapore Democratic Party (SDP) policy manifesto argues that "overcrowding on public transport, longer waiting times for flats, rigging prices of public goods, heightened competition for school places, and the additional space demands on leisure and consumer facilities have decreased the quality of life for all residents on our island."[92] The PAP has acknowledged these concerns as well: "There are concerns arising from the fast pace of population growth. We are experiencing congestion on our transport systems and a high housing market. The development of supporting infrastructure did not keep pace with population growth."[93] As noted by civil servants: "In a sense, a lot of infrastructure is coming our way, and some of this crowding will ease [in] time. But immediately, we're playing catch-up; therefore there's a lot of crowding on the ground and some unhappiness from the ground on this."[94]

Since its exit from the Malay Federation, the PAP has also sought to maintain the ethnic balance of the population in response to concerns about ethnic riots that might destabilize the country. For example, a minister in the prime minister's office said: "We recognize the need to maintain the racial balance in Singapore's population in order to preserve social stability. The pace and profile of our immigration intake have been calibrated to preserve this racial balance."[95] Yet there have still been concerns about social cohesion and the new immigrants. According to civil servants at the National Population and Talent Division, "Some of these social constraints have come up [in discussions of population policy]— people have talked about changing the social fabric, changing the level of cohesion, changing the level of identity with more and more foreigners

---

[90] Nasir and Turner (2014, 105).

[91] Civil servant. Personal interview. June 12, 2013.

[92] Singapore Democratic Party (2013, 8).

[93] National Population and Talent Division (2012, 6).

[94] Civil servant at the National Population and Talent Division. Personal interview. June 4, 2013.

[95] Grace Fu, minister in the prime minister's office, February 6, 2013, *New Paper*, quoted in Nasir and Turner (2014, 25).

coming into Singapore."[96] Opposition parties have argued that "many of these immigrants and migrant workers congregate among themselves and form their own enclaves, raising barriers to social integration"[97] and that immigration is "precipitating a crisis of national identity."[98] The PAP further acknowledged these fears in its 2012 draft policy paper on population: "There have also been pockets of friction between Singaporeans and some foreigners and new immigrants, partly arising from cultural differences ... [Singaporeans] are concerned about the weakening of our social cohesion."[99] In response to these concerns, the government has argued that "we have already taken steps to manage the flow of immigrants. We maintain strict immigration criteria to ensure that we take in new immigrants who are more likely to fit in here, and adapt to our customs and culture."[100]

In many ways, the PAP is the rational policymaker from our models. The PAP does not have (many) ideological goals but seeks to maintain power; to stay in power, the PAP has had to provide economic growth and keep opposition to its regime low. As the governing party of an extremely small, open economy, the PAP had to follow an export-led growth strategy. As its neighbors, especially China, have developed, this has increased competition in Singapore's key markets. When faced with this increased competition, as an autocracy, Singapore could have opened immigration to keep labor costs low and suppressed any opposition that arose. In the 1970s, Singapore in fact followed this strategy. Yet open low-skill immigration is unsustainable in Singapore, as it generates too much opposition—threatening the ethnic balance along with increasing overcrowding—something the government found out in 2011 and again in 2013. Instead, the government has sought to upskill manufacturing: increase productivity and offshore low-skill-intensive activities while maintaining headquarters and research and development in Singapore. As the skill intensity of production has increased, demand for low-skill labor has decreased, allowing the government to restrict low-skill immigration. The government has also restricted low-skill immigration in hopes of forcing firms to restructure. While Singapore still has a relatively high number of low-skill immigrants, this number is likely much lower than it would be had Singapore not restricted immigration.

---

[96] Civil servant at the National Population and Talent Division. Personal interview. June 4, 2013.

[97] Singapore Democratic Party (2013, 27).

[98] Singapore Democratic Party (2013, 11).

[99] National Population and Talent Division (2012, 6).

[100] National Population and Talent Division (2012, 21).

THE NETHERLANDS

In the 2002 Dutch parliamentary elections, List Pim Fortuyn (LPF), a far-right anti-immigrant party, shocked Dutch political society by winning twenty-six seats and entering the government as the second-largest party. This was the largest gain for a new party in the history of the Dutch Lower House; the previous record was set in 1967 by the party Democraten 66 (D66). While LPF quickly collapsed as a party once in power—the assassination of its leader Pim Fortuyn prior to the election left it leaderless—it nonetheless opened the door for other far-right parties, including Geert Wilders's Freedom Party (PVV), and forced other Dutch political parties, including the Liberal Party (VVD) and the Christian Democrats (CDA), to move to the right on immigration.

Why did the Netherlands, which had been welcoming of guest workers in the 1950s and 1960s and a major proponent of multiculturalism in the 1980s, finally succumb to the anti-immigration wave sweeping Europe? I show in this chapter that changes in firm preferences over immigration help explain the change. In the immediate postwar period, the Netherlands used a relatively undervalued currency and capital controls to become the low-wage producer in increasingly open European markets. The protection provided by the undervalued currency and the inability to move production because of capital controls led to an increase in low-skill production and support for immigration. In the 1970s, overvaluation of the currency as well as inflation decreased the competitive position of Dutch firms, leading many firms to close, become more productive (or move into high-skill product lines), or move production overseas. This process continues today and has led to ever lower support for open immigration from firms. This change has allowed nativist groups more say over immigration policy and led to greater restrictions.

How Firms Lobby in the Netherlands

As in the Singaporean case, firms in the Netherlands do not lobby the government in the same way as do firms in the United States. Instead, firms have a much more formal channel through which to influence policy, the Social and Economic Council (Sociaal-Economische Raad, or SER). The SER was established in 1950 and has the mandate to advise the government on socioeconomic issues, providing advice to promote a balanced economic growth, sustainable development, the highest possible level of employment, and a fair distribution of income. The SER comments on policy on all major socioeconomic issues, including medium-term social and economic developments, regulatory issues, social security, labor and industrial law, agricultural policy, and European policy, among other policy issues.[101]

The SER has 33 members, 11 from employers organizations, 11 from unions, and 11 Crown members, who are independent experts on social and economic policy. Of the 11 members from employers organizations, 7 are representatives from the large employers organization (VNO-NCW), 3 are from MKB Nederlands, which represents small and medium enterprises, and the last representative is from Landen Tuinbouw Organisatie (LTO), which represents agriculture and horticulture employers. Most employers (about 80 percent) are represented by one of these sector-based organizations, and the firms represented by VNO-NCW employ 90 percent of workers in the private sector.[102]

The SER provides advice either upon the request of the government or on its own initiative. Usually, a minister, deputy minister, or member of Parliament will initiate a request for advice. A draft report is circulated to all the member organizations for feedback and the council issues its advice. The government, while not obliged to follow the SER's advice, must respond to it within three months and must provide a reason for not following it.

In addition to the SER, the Labour Foundation, a private organization founded in 1945, primarily brings employers organizations together with the unions, but twice a year it also consults with the government. Firms, then, have two official channels—the SER and the Labour Foundation—through which to influence policy. In both organizations, their views are balanced by those of labor; in the SER, they are also balanced by the Crown representatives. Nonetheless, the fact that recommendations are often unanimous means that the firms are able to shift policy closer to their ideal point than would be the case without their representation. Firms may do little formal lobbying of policymakers but instead make their preferences known through these organizations.

Firms have also had long-standing ties to several political parties. As noted by Lijphart, traditionally Dutch politics has been characterized by pillarization.[103] Each social group had its own political party and other organizations tied to its pillar. Catholics and Protestants had their own unions, employers associations, and political parties (the KVP/CDA and the ARP, and CHU/CDA, respectively). Secular workers had their own unions and voted for the secular Labor Party (PvdA); secular employers had their own associations and, with the secular middle class, voted for the secular

[101] Sociaal-Economische Raad (2013, 12).
[102] Sociaal-Economische Raad (2013). The average percent of employers represented in the EU is 55 percent; only Austria has a higher percent of firms represented.
[103] Lijphart (1975).

Liberal Party (VVD). While the pillars have been in decline since the 1960s, they nonetheless have affected the ways in which firms influence politics.[104] Because of the tight ties within the pillars, employers associations have been tied to the parties within their pillar. These parties, then, internalize the preferences of firms.

In addition to these more official channels, firms also have informal channels through which to influence policy. The formal consultative process has also led to more informal meetings between top officials and the employers associations (and the unions), and employers associations and unions have relatively easy access to cabinet ministers, civil servants, and members of Parliament.[105]

The History of Immigration Policy in Postwar Netherlands

Figure 6.2 shows Dutch immigration, trade, and capital policy for the postwar period. The time period can be split into three: the immediate postwar period through the early 1970s; the mid-1980s through today; and the transition period from one to the other. In the first period—termed the modern golden age of the Dutch economy owing to the high levels of employment and economic growth—capital movements were restricted; while there were few impediments to the entry of goods de jure, the Dutch government in exile rejoined the gold standard in 1944 with a guilder devalued by 30 percent against the dollar and devalued by another 30 percent against the dollar in 1949, leading to a de facto tariff and export subsidy. Immigration policy was relatively open and opened further with the signing of several guest worker treaties.[106] The second time period—what I will refer to as the transition period—reversed these policy trends with the opening of capital markets; increased international trade competition with a revaluation of the guilder first by 5 percent in 1961 and then by a de facto revaluation with the end of Bretton Woods in 1971; and implemented a much more restricted immigration policy beginning with the abrogation of the guest worker programs in 1973. The third time period—what I refer to as the service economy owing to the increasing importance of services in the economy—consolidated the trends that began with the end of Bretton Woods, with increased openness to trade and capital mobility both within and outside the EU and increasing immigration restrictions on low-skill immigrants from outside the European Union.

---

[104] See Van Kessel (2011) on depillarization.

[105] Visser and Hemerijck (1997, 90).

[106] Nonetheless Dutch immigration policy did not become as open as it had been in the nineteenth century. See chapter 3.

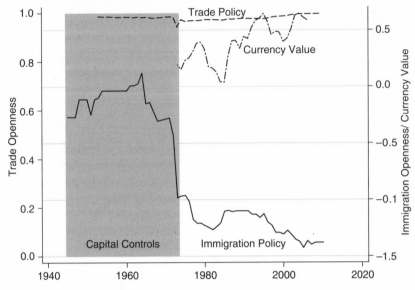

Figure 6.2: Immigration, Trade, and Capital Policy in the Netherlands, 1945–2010.
   Note: Shaded region denotes period of capital controls; data are from
   Bordo et al. (2001). Trade policy is the percent of imports entering
   without duties (or 1 minus the tariff rate); higher values signify greater
   openness. Trade data are from Clemens and Williamson (2004). Immigration policy is described in greater detail in chapter 3; higher values
   signify greater openness. Currency valuation is from Steinberg and
   Malhotra (2014) and is the difference between the actual real exchange
   rate and a predicted exchange rate.

The Modern Golden Age: 1945–71

The immediate postwar period until 1971 has been referred to as a golden
period in modern Dutch economic history. The Netherlands began the
postwar period with some of the worst destruction from the war in all
of Europe. Toward the end of the war, and especially after the Allies
invaded France, the Nazis stole the capital stock—machines, rolling stock,
vehicles—that they could and destroyed what they could not. Additionally
the Nazi government forced thousands of Dutch to migrate to Germany to
work in the fields and factories, and killed thousands of Dutch Jews and
others. The fighting between the Nazis and Allies led to further destruction
of infrastructure and to a higher death toll. Moreover, German monetary
policy had introduced a relatively high level of inflation, leading to much
higher costs than before the war. After the war ended, the Dutch economy
was in shambles, in need of millions of dollars of aid; industrial capacity

was low owing to the theft of industrial capital by the Nazis; productivity was also low owing to the high level of population growth in the previous decades; and the costs of labor and inputs were relatively high owing to the German inflation.[107]

The Dutch government took four major actions to restore economic growth and international competitiveness. First, it implemented currency reform and devalued the guilder to pay to rebuild the country and regain economic competitiveness. As part of the currency reform, all Dutch had to put their money into blocked bank accounts, which would be taxed to pay for rebuilding the country; in return, they would receive the new, devalued currency. Altogether, the government cut the money supply by about two-thirds.[108] To ensure that the taxes were paid and that the devaluation was successful, the government put strict capital controls in place.[109] Second, the Dutch government received a great deal of assistance from the Marshall Plan, allowing it to purchase capital equipment from abroad and undertake large-scale infrastructure projects. Third, Dutch employers, unions, and the government enacted an agreement on a guided wage policy. This policy, which grew out of prewar collective bargaining agreements, allowed the government to intervene in wage bargaining and approve all wage agreements.[110] In 1945 the employers, the unions, and the government agreed to relatively low wages with yearly cost-of-living increases, but no real wage increases, to keep wages low and increase international competitiveness. Finally, the Dutch government entered into greater cooperation with other European countries, first with the creation of the Benelux area before the war ended, with a new trade agreement with West Germany in 1949, and with the creation of the European Coal and Steel Community (ECSC) in 1951. Together, these actions made the Netherlands a relatively low-cost producer in an increasingly open Europe, with labor costs at about 80 percent of those of its principal European competitors.[111]

The economic policies put into place immediately after the war—especially the protection afforded by the devalued guilder—quickly led to high levels of export-led economic growth. Between 1948 and 1973, economic growth averaged almost 5 percent per year.[112] Growth in exports was a major source of economic growth: exports grew on average 8.3 percent in 1951–63 and 10.4 percent in 1964–73.[113] The increasing

---

[107] van Zanden (1998, 124).

[108] Eichengreen (2007, 97).

[109] van Zanden (1998, 126).

[110] van Zanden (1998, 79).

[111] Eichengreen (2007, 98). See also van Rijckeghem (1982).

[112] van Zanden (1998, 134).

[113] Calculated from Centraal Bureau voor de Statistiek (Statistics Netherlands) (1958–95) by van Zanden (1998, 135).

economic growth led to increased employment in all sectors of the economy except for agriculture and energy through 1963; after 1963, employment began to decrease in most sectors.[114] Nonetheless, unemployment soon dipped below 2 percent, leading to an almost constant demand for labor throughout the 1960s.[115]

If the argument of this book is correct, the increasing demand for labor as a result of trade protection through a devalued currency and capital controls should have led to increased demand for immigrant labor. Part of the demand for labor was satiated by the return migration of about 300,000 former emigrants to the Dutch East Indies between the end of World War II and the independence of Indonesia in 1949.[116] Yet as early as 1948 employers began to demand more labor, resulting in the first guest worker treaty signed with Italy for mine workers.[117] That the treaty was signed for workers in an immobile and declining industry is in line with the argument of the book. Dutch mines had to compete for labor with other, growing sectors of the Dutch economy, which increased pressure for higher wages. Further, they faced increased competition as French and German coal mines began producing again after the war, leading to lower revenues. The options for Dutch mines were to cut costs, especially labor costs; obtain subsidies; or close, as they could not move production overseas.[118] Faced with this declining industry, the government chose to help them cut labor costs by allowing the recruitment of immigrant workers. Nonetheless, the further decline of competitiveness of the mining industry in the early 1960s led the government to create a plan in 1965 to gradually close all the mines and transform the national mining company (DSM) into a chemical company.[119]

Throughout the 1950s, the labor market continued to be tight, prompting additional openness toward immigrants, especially immigrants from the colonies. Citizenship and free movement rights were granted to subjects in Suriname, Aruba, and the Antilles.[120] There was also some increased mobility from other European countries owing to the the Benelux agreement and ECSC, but not much. Although Article 69 of the Treaty of Paris, which created the ECSC, was supposed to allow for freedom of

---

[114] Calculated from Centraal Bureau voor de Statistiek (Statistics Netherlands) (1986) by van Zanden (1998, 136).

[115] van Zanden (1998, 134).

[116] Eichengreen (2007, 87).

[117] *Agreement concerning the Employment of Italian Workers for Underground Work in the Netherlands Mines* (1948).

[118] While it is possible to move mining technology, it is impossible to move the actual mine.

[119] van Zanden (1998, 144).

[120] Indonesia had gained independence in 1949 and was thus unaffected by these changes. Most former emigrants to Indonesia had returned by this point.

movement for nationals in the coal and steel industries, the labor mobility agreement—ratified in 1957, six years after the Treaty of Paris was signed— covered only 20 percent to 25 percent of labor.[121]

The tightness of the labor market also led to increased pressure on wages and the erosion of Dutch international competitiveness, as I argued in chapter 2, could happen. In 1959, the guided wage policy fell apart. Employers in expanding industries—especially metals and construction— complained that they were unable to obtain the workers they needed, and asked to increase their wages in line with productivity increases.[122] The government agreed to allow wages in the metals industry to increase by 5 percent, a relatively large increase at the time.[123] Workers in other industries clamored for wage increases as well, which led to increased wages in most other industries as these industries sought to keep their workforce. Rising wages led to the beginning of a decline in the competitiveness of labor-intensive Dutch goods on the international market. Nonetheless, wages in 1960 were about 20 percent lower in the Netherlands than in Belgium and Germany.[124]

The competitiveness of Dutch goods was further eroded following the revaluation of the Deutschmark and the guilder in 1961. Both Germany and the Netherlands had been facing inflationary pressure as well as balance of payments surpluses. In order to address its balance of payments surplus, Germany revalued. Because of the close links between the German and the Dutch economy, the Dutch central bank went along with the revaluation.

At first, the Dutch government used subsidies and other policies to increase the competitiveness of Dutch firms, especially in shipbuilding, textiles, leather, and mining, directly lowering these industries' costs. The government also sought to help these industries lower their costs through immigration. It continued to sign treaties for guest workers throughout the 1960s, signing treaties with Spain in 1961, Portugal in 1963, Morocco in 1964, Turkey in 1965, Greece in 1966, Yugoslavia in 1970, and Tunisia in 1971. Like the Italian mine workers, many guest workers also tended to go into industries that were in decline, providing a cheaper labor force and lowering labor costs.[125] There was some additional labor from the European Economic Community as well. The Treaty of Rome (signed in 1957) gave freedom of movement to all workers except those employed in public services, with seasonal and frontier workers obtaining labor

[121] Geddes and Money (2011, 33).

[122] van Zanden (1998, 82–83).

[123] van Zanden (1998, 83).

[124] Eichengreen (2007, 98).

[125] Tesseltje de Lange, assistant professor, administrative and migration law, the Law Faculty of the University of Amsterdam and member of the Advisory Committee on Migration Affairs. Personal interview. July 1, 2013.

market access earlier.[126] Additionally, the government pushed for, and helped fund, mergers in these declining industries in hopes of lowering overhead costs and taking advantage of economies of scale. Finally, the government pushed some companies—as in the example of the Dutch mines—to diversify out of the declining industries.

Thus the evidence from the first period of Dutch postwar economic history passes the hoop test. Trade restrictions—in the form of a devalued currency—along with capital restrictions led to economic growth and increased demands for workers. In response to this demand, the government allowed for more open immigration. As the economy expanded further, wage pressure increased further. The wage increases along with the 1961 revaluation of the guilder led to somewhat decreased competitiveness in the increasingly globalized economy. In response, the government increased subsidies, helped firms restructure, and increased immigration.

The major theories have less explanatory power during this period. If the power of labor drove immigration policy during this time period, then we would expect that, since immigration policy was relatively open, labor must have been relatively weak. However, the immediate postwar period through 1971 was a period of extremely strong labor unions, as evidenced by the wage bargains. Further, the Labor Party (the PvdA) was a coalition partner in government from 1946 to 1958. Similarly, if immigration policy was driven by taxpayer concerns over the impact of immigrants on the social welfare system, we would expect that the welfare state must have been relatively small and/or contracting during this time period. Welfare spending, however, was exploding in the Netherlands during this time period; social transfers increased from 6.6 percent of GDP in 1950 to 11.7 percent of GDP in 1960 and 22.5 percent of GDP in 1970.[127] Finally, the nativism hypothesis would suggest that nativism must have been at a low point for immigration to be opened, and indeed it was. After World War II, the Far Right was discredited owing to their association with the Nazis, and support remained low; for example, the most important party of the Far Right, the Boerenpartij (Farmers' Party), won its highest vote share in 1966 with 6 percent of the vote.[128] Thus, given that both the power of labor and the fiscal argument fail the hoop test, it appears that openness to immigration during this time period was driven by an increase in firm demand for low-skill labor owing to trade protection and the inability to move production overseas, combined with little opposition from far-right anti-immigrant groups.

---

[126] Geddes and Money (2011, 34–35).
[127] van Zanden (1998, 57).
[128] Voerman and Lucardie (1992, 37).

The Transition from the Golden Age to the Service Economy: 1971–85

Beginning in the late 1960s, the Dutch economy began to suffer from increased international competition, which led to deindustrialization and the rise of the service economy. There were two exogenous shocks that decreased the competitiveness of Dutch firms, especially labor-intensive firms. The first shock was the disintegration of the Bretton Woods system in 1971. The Dutch guilder immediately appreciated against the dollar, hurting the competitiveness of Dutch firms. In place of the gold standard, the Dutch and the other governments of the European Community in 1972 created the "snake," in which currencies were to float against one another within a narrow band. While the Netherlands, Germany, and Belgium were able to stay on the snake, several others were not, including Great Britain, France, and Italy, all major trading partners of the Netherlands. The devaluation of the pound, franc, and lira pushed the value of the guilder higher and competitiveness lower. By 1979, the effective exchange rate of the guilder had increased by 30–40 percent.[129] After a final devaluation in 1983, the guilder remained at parity with the Deutschmark, and relatively overvalued, until the creation of the euro in 1999.[130]

The second major shock to hit the Dutch economy comprised the two oil crises in 1973 and 1979. While the Netherlands was a net oil and gas exporter, Dutch firms and consumers still paid higher prices for imported goods. As most collective agreements on wages tied them to inflation, wages also quickly rose, resulting in an inflationary spiral, further reducing the competitiveness of Dutch firms.

The increase in oil and gas prices also had a secondary effect of supporting an overvalued currency. As Dutch industry became less competitive, manufacturing exports fell, which should have led to downward pressure on the guilder and, eventually, a greater competitive position for Dutch firms. However, the exports of oil and gas led to a positive balance of payments and supported the value of the guilder. The overvalued guilder, then, reduced the competitiveness of Dutch firms even more, resulting in what is now famously called *Dutch disease*.

Together, these shocks led to end of the modern Dutch golden age and industrial production in several industries. Many labor-intensive industries such as shipbuilding, textiles, leather, and mining all but disappeared. As discussed above, the Dutch coal mines were closed, and the national mining company was turned into a chemicals firm. Employment in textiles, clothing, and shoemaking fell by about 70 percent between 1970

[129] van Zanden (1998, 164).
[130] Watson et al. (1999, 16).

and 1984.[131] Unemployment reached double-digit levels by the early 1980s.[132]

In contrast to the 1960s, when increasing wage costs combined with relatively protected trade and closed capital led the government to open immigration to keep wage costs low, in this later period the government, under declining trade protection, greatly restricted immigration. In 1973, the Dutch government prohibited the employment of immigrants from outside the European Economic Area (*third-country nationals*, or *TCNs*) unless employers could prove that an employee could not be found within the EEA, which effectively prevented the immigration of all TCNs.[133] Migration from within the EEA was unlikely to provide much low-skill labor, as the EEA consisted of mostly wealthy, highly educated populations at this point.[134] Family reunification was still allowed, but only for minor children under the age of fifteen and spouses who had employment.[135] In 1975, Suriname gained independence and, with it, Surinamese lost their Dutch citizenship, although a transitional program was put into place that allowed Surinamese to freely migrate to the Netherlands until 1980. In 1979, in an effort to crack down on illegal immigration, the Dutch government began to require visas for those who wished to visit the Netherlands from "high immigration countries," such as Turkey, Morocco, and Suriname.

Instead of increasing immigration, the government used subsidies to try to keep uncompetitive firms in business. However, by the early 1980s, the Dutch government could no longer afford to subsidize these firms owing to increasingly large budget deficits. The withdrawal of the subsidies led to a wave of bankruptcies in the early 1980s: 27,000 firms went bankrupt and 150,000 workers lost jobs.[136]

The government's use of subsidies, rather than immigration, was likely driven by the lower demand for low-skill labor in the economy. Decreasing demand for labor was in part caused by the closure of labor-intensive firms in textiles, mining, and shipbuilding, among other industries, and in part by increasing productivity. Between 1960 and 1973, productivity increased by 7.8 percent in agriculture and 7.1 percent in industry on average per year.[137] During this time period, output was increasing in both sectors,

---

[131] van Zanden (1998, 162).

[132] Eichengreen (2007, 293).

[133] Roodenburg, Euwals, and Rele (2003, 34–35).

[134] Irish and Greek migrants were the exceptions; however, there was a transition period for migration from Greece. Geddes and Money (2011).

[135] Zorlu and Hartog (2002, 124).

[136] van Zanden (1998, 171).

[137] Calculated from Centraal Bureau voor de Statistiek (Statistics Netherlands) (1986) by van Zanden (1998, 136).

while employment was falling.[138] Firms, therefore, were producing more with less, decreasing their demand for labor. Moreover, they demanded more highly skilled workers, as is often the case when firms increase productivity, either because the technology they use in their production process demands a higher level of skill or because they simply use education as a signaling device.[139] This too led to a lowering of demand for immigrant workers.

Agriculture, a traditional employer of much immigrant labor, became a prominent example of firms producing more with fewer workers. During the Great Depression, agriculture was one of the few industries to receive government assistance in the form of price supports.[140] The price supports, along with increased exports after the devaluation of the guilder in 1936, led to an increase in incomes in agriculture, an increase in employment, and a decrease in labor productivity. On average, labor productivity in agriculture increased only 2 percent per year from 1900 to 1950.[141] After the war, the government sought to modernize agriculture and increase labor productivity. In part, labor was drawn out of agriculture and into industry through the higher wages offered in industry; but also, the government subsidized the consolidation of small farms and subsidized mechanization through the Marshall Plan. Further, the government subsidized research, education, and extension services, which helped increase labor productivity as well.[142] Labor productivity increased on average by 6 percent between 1950 and 1973, and has further increased at a rate of about 5 percent per year since then.[143] Concomitantly, employment in agriculture fell by on average 2.9 percent per year in 1953–63 and 3.3 percent per year in 1963–73.[144]

My argument passes the hoop test in this period as well; the transition from relative openness of immigration to relative closure in the 1970s and early 1980s was, in part, driven by the decline of firms in labor-intensive industries. The revaluation of the guilder in 1971 removed the de facto trade protection, exposing many previously protected firms to greater international competition. In response, some of these firms closed, especially after subsidies were removed in the early 1980s; some of these firms—like the mining industry—moved into other lines of business that

---

[138] Data from Centraal Bureau voor de Statistiek (Statistics Netherlands) (1986) cited by van Zanden (1998, 136).

[139] Helpman, Itskhoki, and Redding (2009).

[140] van Zanden (1998, 116).

[141] Berend (2006, 245).

[142] van Zanden (1998, 141).

[143] Berend (2006, 245).

[144] Calculated from Centraal Bureau voor de Statistiek (Statistics Netherlands) (1986) by van Zanden (1998, 136).

did not need as many workers, or increased productivity; and some, with the end of capital controls in the early 1970s, moved their production overseas. In all, the exogenous shocks of the end of Bretton Woods and the oil crises of 1973 and 1979 led to increased international competition and decreased support for immigration openness.

Again we can ask whether the alternative explanations for immigration policy can help explain the decline of immigration during this time period. If the power of labor argument is correct, we would expect that labor was relatively strong at this time. However, union density was falling during this period from 42.1 percent of the population in 1963 to 38.0 percent in 1975 to 24.0 percent in 1990.[145] The decline of unionism especially affected the FNV, the most "radical" union, which lost almost 200,000 members between 1980 and 1985.[146] The weakened position of labor can also be seen in the unions' acceptance of wage restraint in the 1982 Wassenaar Accord. The unions, however, may still have had outsized influence in politics in 1973–77, as the PvdA (the Labor Party) held the prime minister position in a coalition government. Thus there is at least some straw in the wind evidence for the power of labor argument.

As discussed above, the size of the welfare state likely had at least an indirect effect on immigration policy through its effects on firms. In the early 1980s, the government was forced to cut its budget and chose to cut subsidies for firms hurt by increased competition, which led to their closure, relocation overseas, or increased productivity, weakening demand for immigrant labor. It is less clear whether the welfare state had a direct effect. Most immigrants were still employed prior to the end of the guest worker program in 1973 and thus did not use social services much. After 1973, however, a significant number of immigrants ended up using the social welfare system.[147] With increasing budget deficits, the use of the welfare state by immigrants became a flash point for those who opposed immigration. Thus the fiscal argument likely passes the hoop test.

Finally, there is little evidence that nativism affected policy during this time period. While anti-immigrant sentiment may have increased, it did not yet translate into electoral success for far-right, anti-immigrant parties. The Boerenpartij remained one of the most important far-right parties during this period and continued to have a few seats in Parliament until 1981. Yet it never achieved as much electoral success as it had in 1966.[148]

[145] Crouch (1993).

[146] van Zanden (1998, 88).

[147] van Amersfoort and Penninx (1994). Tesseltje de Lange, assistant professor, administrative and migration law, the Law Faculty of the University of Amsterdam and member of the Advisory Committee on Migration Affairs. Personal interview. July 1, 2013.

[148] Voerman and Lucardie (1992, 37).

The Netherlands People's Union (NVU) came into existence in 1971 with a clear anti-immigrant message, but at its height, in 1977, it gained only 0.4 percent of the vote.[149] Similarly, the other new far-right party of this era, the Center Party, garnered small shares of the vote: 0.1 percent in 1981, 0.8 percent in 1982, and 2.5 percent in the 1985 elections for the European Parliament.[150] It is less likely, therefore, that nativist sentiment contributed to the increasing immigration restrictions during this period.

The Service Economy: 1985–Today

After the recession of 1979–85, the Dutch economy began to expand again at an average rate of almost 3 percent a year.[151] Many observers point to the 1982 Wassenaar Accord as the source of increased growth. The Wassenaar Accord was a new wage-moderation agreement brokered by the government between employers association and unions. Since the postwar wage-moderation agreement fell apart in the late 1950s and early 1960s, wages had been indexed to inflation, exacerbating the underlying conditions. The Wassenaar Accord stopped the practice of indexing wages to inflation, while decreasing taxes on labor to make up for the lost wages. Welfare spending was later reduced in line with the government's lower tax income. The effect of the Wassenaar Accord was that unit labor costs did not rise in the Netherlands between 1983 and 1995, whereas they increased by 2 percent in France and 2.6 percent in Germany.[152]

With increased economic growth in comparison to the 1970s and 1980s, we might have expected a greater demand for immigration. As we saw in the Singapore case in the 1970s, the wage moderation put into place with the Wassenaar Accord might have led to more demand for immigration as firms moved to more labor-intensive production processes. Instead, the Dutch government has sought to crack down on immigration. At this time, most low-skill TCNs entered as asylum seekers or under family reunification. As in the rest of Western Europe, there were increased fears that asylum seekers were economic migrants in disguise, leading to greater restrictions on who can enter the country to seek asylum and increasing regulations on who may claim asylum. Family reunification was also made more difficult. In 1998, spouses had to wait outside the country for a permit; starting in 2000, the Dutch government required sponsors to have a minimum income and employment before their spouse could enter the country. In addition to cracking down on the two main channels of entry

---

[149] Voerman and Lucardie (1992, 39).

[150] Voerman and Lucardie (1992, 39). The larger vote share in the European Parliament elections is typical for extreme parties owing to relatively low turnout.

[151] GDP growth calculated from Maddison (2011).

[152] Visser and Hemerijck (1997, 27).

for low-skill TCNs, the Dutch government also increased enforcement both within the Netherlands, with increased employer sanctions and other regulations, and within the EU, with increased border enforcement. When possible, the Dutch government also sought to restrict the entry of low(er)-skill Europeans, waiting until 2007 to allow nationals from the Accession Eight (A8) countries to enter the Netherlands, and until 2014 to allow Romanians and Bulgarians to enter. Thus throughout this time period the Dutch government has continued to restrict low-skill immigration from outside the EU and has sought to minimize migration from the poorer countries of the EU.

The integration of EU labor markets, especially with the A8 countries, Romania, and Bulgaria, has had an effect on the demand for third-country national immigrant labor similar to that brought about by the creation of a national market in the United States. As discussed in chapter 5, technological advancements in transportation and communication in the late nineteenth and early twentieth centuries allowed firms in the United States to produce for and in all US markets, rather than just in their region. It also allowed for even greater intra-US migration. As producers in any one region of the United States could not get "trade protection" from any other region, they were subject to greater competition from low-wage areas, such as the South. Because they could move to lower-wage regions, such as the South, they "offshored" their production to these low-wage areas. Finally, those firms that were immobile—primarily agriculture and services—relied on intra-US migrants. The integration of the EU is having a similar effect: Dutch firms can receive only a small amount of trade protection from firms within the EU; they can easily move production to areas within the EU with lower costs; and those that cannot can use EU migrant labor. The integration of the EU, then, has led to "migrant diversion," as immobile industries can rely on intra-EU migrants instead of TCNs.

The expanding economy did not lead to increased openness toward immigrants because, owing to increased international competition and increased opportunities to offshore production, Dutch firms have a much lesser need for immigrant labor than they did in the 1950s and 1960s. Further, Dutch firms have increased their productivity, increasing their need for high-skill labor, as they have decreased their overall need for low-skill labor.

The interviews with members of Parliament, leaders of employers organizations, and unions about immigration provide additional evidence for my argument. According to a member of Parliament who has worked on immigration issues, employers associations are still one of the major pressure groups on immigration, but their demands have changed.[153] Whereas employers groups had once wanted low-skill immigrants, they now mostly

---

[153] Member of parliament. Telephone interview. June 19, 2013.

seek high-skill immigrants, although there are a few industries, like agriculture and some services, that want low-skill immigrants.[154] In large part, the decreased demand for low-skill immigrants has been driven by the offshoring of low-skill-intensive industries. According to this MP, low-skill-intensive industries, such as textiles, have mostly moved to Asia.[155] In other low-skill-intensive industries, such as agriculture and construction, the use of migrants from the A8 countries and Bulgaria and Romania has increased.[156] The evidence from this member of Parliament provides a smoking gun that firms' demands for immigration have decreased, leading to reduced pressure for open immigration.

Employers association and union spokespeople echoed these themes. For example, the secretariat director of BZW, the employers organization for Brabant and Zeeland, also reported that the demand for immigrants tended to be bifurcated: "For example [demand is increasing] at the high tech companies who are at the moment looking for highly skilled workers, ... and the other part of it, [is] the agricultural sector where we need people from Poland, from Bulgaria here to actually do the work in the fields which is, to put it a bit bluntly, low-skilled work."[157] Demand for low-skill immigrants has decreased in mobile industries, providing additional smoking gun evidence; he argues that "more and more companies are replacing their production units towards other countries, to have their factories [in] other countries, which means that you don't need your workers here anymore."[158] In immobile industries, the demand for immigrant labor had been filled in part by those coming from Eastern Europe.[159]

The head of the International Unit at one of the other large employers organizations expressed similar sentiments. He too mentioned the need for high-skill immigrant labor in the IT sector as well as low-skill labor in immobile industries, such as agriculture and health care.[160] Additionally, he noted that the firms that had previously used immigrant labor during the guest worker era had disappeared: "For example we had a great shipping industry... they disappeared saying [it would] be impossible to have construction of ships in the Netherlands... We had the mining industry at the time [of the guest workers programs], but it nearly closed down at that moment, and industrialization of the agriculture sector also had a part in it."[161] Firms that survived the downturn of the 1970s and 1980s increasingly

---

[154] Member of parliament. Telephone interview. June 19, 2013.
[155] Member of parliament. Telephone interview. June 19, 2013.
[156] Member of parliament. Telephone interview. June 19, 2013.
[157] BZW secretariat director. Telephone interview. June 25, 2013.
[158] BZW secretariat director. Telephone interview. June 25, 2013.
[159] BZW secretariat director. Telephone interview. June 25, 2013.
[160] Head of the International Unit. Employers association. Personal interview. June 26, 2013.
[161] Head of the International Unit. Employers association. Personal interview. June 26, 2013.

offshored production: "I don't think besides some small companies that companies in the Netherlands don't have foreign subsidiaries."[162] Union officials also have seen a decreased demand for immigration from many industries, with demand now concentrated in immobile industries like agriculture and construction as well as high-skill industries. According to union officials, "The most pro-immigration are agriculture and the greenhouses."[163]

This third time period, too, conforms to the expectations of the argument, passing both the hoop test and the smoking gun test. International competition and opportunities to move production overseas have increased within Europe as the EU has expanded eastward. Further, technological advancements in trade and communications, along with the opening of economies in Asia, especially China, have led to even greater competition from states with much lower labor costs. Thus much of the low-skill manufacturing that used to be done in the Netherlands is now done overseas. The few remaining industries that use low-skill workers are in relatively immobile industries, such as construction, services, and agriculture. The demand for low-skill workers in these industries, however, has not increased enough to create a large demand for immigrant labor; instead, much of the demand for immigrant labor can be met by EU nationals. Thus throughout this time period Dutch immigration policy toward TNCs, especially asylum policy, has become more restrictive.

It is also not the case that low-skill-intensive industries have simply replaced legal migrant workers with illegal ones, as the conventional wisdom on illegal immigration might suggest. Instead, both employer groups and unions today want migrants to be organized, and the rules regarding employment of migrant workers to be transparent and fair.[164] As discussed in chapter 2, large employers prefer immigration restrictions to be enforced to level the playing field. According to the head of the International Unit at a major employers association, "Of course illegal workers shouldn't be allowed because it's unfair competition."[165] Union officials similarly have seen how the use of illegal workers by some firms has led to unfair competition: "[Employers with legal workers] also lose money because of [illegal workers]."[166]

In order to compete with firms that use immigrant subcontractors unfairly, employers groups joined with unions in the Social and Economic Council to push for new regulations on subcontractors. Under EU rules,

---

[162] Head of the International Unit. Employers association. Personal interview. June 26, 2013.

[163] Dutch union official. Personal interview. June 28, 2013.

[164] Member of parliament. Telephone interview. June 19, 2013.

[165] Head of the International Unit. Employers association. Personal interview. June 26, 2013.

[166] Dutch union official. Personal interview. June 28, 2013.

firms from outside the state can employ what are termed *seconded* workers from their own country. Essentially, a foreign firm (including temporary employment firms) can hire workers from their home country and employ them in the host country. Prior to the passage of the Terms of Employments (Cross-border Work) Act or WAGA, seconded workers were not subject to the collective bargaining agreements in an industry. Instead, seconded workers were often paid at the prevailing wage in their home country. This had meant that firms could hire seconded workers through a subcontractor at much lower wage rates. WAGA subjects the employment of seconded workers to the collective bargaining agreements, making their wage costs equivalent to that of a Dutch worker. Nonetheless, social security payments for seconded workers are still made at the home rate, not at the Dutch rate, making them cheaper to use.[167]

The use of seconded workers, then, provides a competitive advantage for the firms that use them. Larger firms that use fewer of these workers, though, would prefer that no firms gain an advantage through the use of seconded workers. According to a union official in the Netherlands:

> The employer organizations are trying to stop [the use of illegal workers] because it undermines the collective agreement and the system that we have, because the companies that adhere to the collective agreement are becoming too—they cannot compete anymore with these shady companies. So it's really especially in the construction sector and in the transport sector that there's a common approach to stop this.[168]

In this case, the employers organizations teamed up with the labor unions to advocate for new regulations that would crack down on the use of these semilegal workers, because the employers could not compete with firms that used seconded labor. Because employers organizations and unions together are relatively powerful in the Netherlands, they were able to obtain the regulations (an amendment to WAGA) that they were seeking. Thus there is smoking gun evidence that large firms want increased enforcement of immigration laws to prevent smaller firms that use illegal labor from gaining a competitive advantage by doing so.

The other explanations for immigration policy again receive mixed support during this time period. The power of labor argument does not pass the hoop test during this period. As noted above, unionism began to decline with the decline of industry in the 1970s and has only further declined today. Instead, unions, as in the American case, have sought to integrate foreign workers, which has led them to have a bifurcated view of immigration in which they want more rights for foreign workers but fewer

---

[167] Kremer and Schrijvars (2014, 9).
[168] Dutch union official. Personal interview. June 28, 2013.

foreign workers in total and restrictions on intra-EU migration.[169] Further, the PvdA (the Labor Party) held the prime ministership for only seven years (1994–2002) of this period, making it less likely that the power of labor can explain this era's immigration policy. Moreover, after the success of the List Pim Fortuyn (LPF) in 2002, the PvdA moved its platform on multiculturalism sharply to the right to counter the success that LPF, and later the Freedom Party (PVV), have had with working-class voters.[170]

Similarly, the fiscal argument has less explanatory power, failing the hoop test as well. Throughout much of this period, the Netherlands was ruled by the CDA, which favors a smaller social welfare system as part of its ideology of "shared responsibility." As such, the CDA has sought to rein in the welfare state. In 1986–87, the Netherlands reformed its unemployment insurance system, cutting income replacement rates and reducing the duration of benefits for younger workers from thirty to six months. Disability insurance was also scaled back, reducing the maximum benefit and tightening requirements; further, partially disabled workers were required to find employment.[171] In the early 1990s, there was further reform of the disability system.

In contrast, the rise of nativism in the Netherlands helps explain this time period. Nativism had been on the rise in the Netherlands since at least the mid-1990s, when opposition to the multiculturalism policies put into place in the 1980s grew to more than 60 percent.[172] Immigration has increased in salience as well.[173]

Electoral nativism reached its zenith in 2002 when List Pim Fortuyn won 17 percent of the votes and twenty-six seats in parliament.[174] Even though electoral support for anti-immigrant parties has faded somewhat— in 2006 the Freedom Party (PVV) won 5.9 percent of the vote and nine seats—nativism is still a palpable sentiment in the Netherlands today. According to the secretariat director of BZW, one of the most important issues about immigration policy today is nativism: "First of all there's a general tendency that we are, and this started about a decade ago I think, that we are rather hesitant to accept people today who are coming here as

[169] Member of parliament. Telephone interview. June 19, 2013. Dutch union official. Personal interview. June 28, 2013.
[170] Van Kessel (2011, 78).
[171] Eichengreen (2007, 389–90).
[172] Koopmans and Muis (2009, 646).
[173] Van Kessel (2011, 79).
[174] There is debate over what led to the breakout of a far-right party in 2002. The depillarization of Dutch society likely had an effect, leading to a decrease in support for the major parties and opening space for new appeals based on issues, like immigration, that the major parties did not address. Pellikaan, de Lange, and Van der Meer (2007), Van Kersbergen and Krouwel (2008), and Van Kessel (2011).

a refugee or are here from a perspective of family reunions ... the general culture in the Netherlands at this moment, it's far too defensive towards other cultures, people from other cultures."[175] Thus nativism passes the hoop test during this period.

In addition to creating an opening for far-right parties, increases in nativism have led established parties to move to the right on immigration as well. As noted above, the Labor Party (PvdA) shifted their stance on multiculturalism to the right after the success of List Pim Fortuyn (LPF). The Christian Democrats (the CDA), one of the major center-right parties, also shifted to the right.[176] The Liberal Party (VVD) had already become a critic of multiculturalism (and, by extension, immigration) in the 1990s.[177]

The VVD's rightward shift is in some ways more surprising than that of the PvdA or the CDA. The PvdA has always represented unions, as well as the secular Left, which tend to oppose immigration on economic grounds even if they are in favor of integration. The CDA has historically represented practicing Christians—in 2002, the CDA still garnered 66 percent of the vote of practicing Catholics, 53 percent of practicing Dutch Reformed Church members, and 43 percent of practicing Calvinists—who typically are more conservative on social issues, including migration of religious minorities. The VVD historically has represented the liberal bourgeoisie and employers, taking laissez-faire positions on economic policy, including on immigration, and historically has been constrained in how far it can move to the right on immigration without angering its base.[178]

My argument suggests that since at least the 1990s the VVD did not have to fear a large-scale defection from employers if the party moved rightward on immigration. Because employers already avail themselves of outside options, such as moving to a low-wage country or increasing productivity, they no longer care as much about an open immigration policy. In a counterfactual world where employers were more pro-immigration, the VVD might not have moved as far to the right or might have suffered a large-scale defection for the move.

Thus it is likely that nativism has made greater openness to immigration politically impossible. Yet the lack of employer support for open immigration has meant that nativism has gained a larger foothold in politics than it might have otherwise. Anti-immigrant sentiment has transformed from being a fringe, marginalized viewpoint to one that respectable parties like the VVD, the PvdA, and the CDA can articulate to a greater or lesser

---

[175] BZW secretariat director. Telephone interview. June 25, 2013.

[176] Van Kessel (2011, 78).

[177] Van Kessel (2011, 78).

[178] Van Kersbergen and Krouwel (2008, 402).

extent.[179] As a result, even though the Netherlands can do little about the expansion of labor market rights to Eastern European EU citizens, the government has cracked down on TCNs, restricting family reunification, asylum, and work for those from outside the EU.

CONCLUSION

The postwar histories of Singapore and the Netherlands provide additional evidence in favor of my argument. Singapore is, in many ways, the exception that proves the rule. Since the mid-1980s, the PAP has decided that low-skill immigration hurts its chances to stay in power, as it keeps firms from moving up the value chain and providing increasingly high-skill and high-paying jobs for natives, and as it can lead to nativist backlash. It has been proactive in encouraging firms to increase productivity or move low-skill-intensive production overseas and, at times, has even told firms to close rather than support them with increased immigration.

The Dutch government, in contrast, has been much more reactive to firms' changing demands. During the modern golden age, Dutch industry was protected from foreign competition both at home and abroad through the undervalued guilder. The trade protection led to greater production in the industrial sector, which in turn led to economic growth throughout the economy and a tight labor market. As wages increased, firms, especially in low-skill-intensive industries like shipbuilding and textiles, sought to maintain their competitiveness. The government opened immigration through guest worker treaties and provided subsidies for these firms. As Dutch competitiveness began to fade with the revaluation of the guilder and the oil shocks of the 1970s, firms that had used much immigrant labor became more productive or closed. Some took advantage of newly opened capital markets and moved production, as well. These changes in the economy led to reduced demand for immigrant labor, and immigration was restricted. Even though the economy recovered, support for immigration from firms has been weak, and immigration has been restricted further.

Both case studies show some support for the main alternative hypotheses, but neither of them supports all three. The case of Singapore provides little support for the power of labor and fiscal arguments—labor has no power in the state, and low-skill immigrants cannot use the small social welfare state—but does show how nativism makes openness to low-skill

---

[179] As late as 1997, Hans Janmaat, the leader of the Center Democrats, was convicted of inciting racial discrimination for saying that he planned to abolish multiculturalism as soon as his party gained power. Van Kersbergen and Krouwel (2008, 404).

immigration a very difficult policy to impose even in a stable autocracy. The Dutch case provides more evidence for the other arguments. During the transition from the golden age to the service economy, unions still had some power in Dutch politics, in part owing to the powerful position of the Labor Party, and their opposition to immigration likely helped to put restrictions into place. Similarly, during the same time period, the Dutch government had to decrease the size of government, which led indirectly to more immigration restrictions through the end of subsidies for firms and their subsequent closure, and directly through opposition to immigrants' use of the social welfare system. Finally, the lack of nativism in the 1950s and 1960s helps explain why it was relatively easy for firms to get their preferred policy of open immigration, and increased nativism in the 1990s and 2000s made it harder for firms to get immigration openness, leading them to choose another strategy—increasing productivity or moving—when faced with greater international competition. Yet nativism was relatively weak in the transitional period when the major immigration restrictions were put into place.

CHAPTER 7

The Rise of Anti-Immigration Sentiment and Undocumented Immigration as Explanations for Immigration Policy

IN THE PREVIOUS CHAPTERS, I articulated and tested a theory of a political dilemma between open low-skill immigration, on the one hand, and open trade and firm mobility, on the other. I argue that trade, firm mobility, and productivity have been the major drivers of low-skill immigration policy by means of their effect on firms. Firms are not one interest group among many, but the most important interest group. The data have shown that trade openness, firm mobility, and productivity gains have led to reduced support from firms for open immigration, which has allowed policymakers to place more weight on other interest groups, leading to restrictions on low-skill immigration.

But what of alternative explanations that have focused on antipathy toward immigrants as the source of immigration restrictions? In chapters 4 through 6, I examined how these other explanations affected the crafting of immigration policy in the United States, Singapore, and the Netherlands. In those cases, these alternative explanations helped complete the picture of a process of immigration policymaking driven by firms but did not provide the complete picture on their own. Perhaps the United States, Singapore, and the Netherlands are special cases. In this chapter, I return to the cross-national data on low-skill immigration policy and examine whether the alternative explanations do a better job of explaining differences in policy across states.

I begin by examining the evidence for theories based on the macropolitical and macroeconomic conditions of the state. Next, I examine other interest group explanations. Finally, I return to the evidence for the common belief that borders are increasingly restricted while enforcement lags in order to create an undocumented workforce that can easily be exploited.

MACROPOLITICAL AND MACROECONOMIC EXPLANATIONS: DEMOCRATIZATION, GROWTH, WAR, AND STATE IDENTITIES

One major political change that has been hypothesized to affect immigration policy is democratization. Scholars since Polanyi have argued that the enfranchisement of the masses led policymakers to choose policies that benefit the average citizen.[1] Democratization and the extension of the franchise may lead to greater immigration restrictions through shifting the identity of the median voter.[2] As the median voter becomes poorer, she is more likely to compete with immigrants in the labor market and thus more likely to oppose immigration. If this is correct, we should expect that when the state democratizes or when the franchise is extended to poorer citizenry, immigration should be restricted.

In chapter 5, I found that the direct election of senators, which increased the power of the median voter, led to greater restrictions on immigration. But does this hypothesis hold more generally? Table 3.2, reprinted here as table 7.1, examined this hypothesis using the Polity IV democracy score. As we see in that table, there is no statistically significant effect of regime type as measured by Polity. This suggests that democratization does not have the same effect everywhere as it did in the United States.

The lack of a statistically significant result may be due to the way Polity codes democracy, focusing on procedural democracy rather than the franchise. To further examine this argument, I reran the models in table 3.2 using a measure of the franchise from Przeworski and colleagues (table 7.2).[3] I recoded the Przeworski data to include two indicators of the franchise. The first indicator measures whether the franchise is limited based on property ownership, income, education, or profession, which captures whether the franchise is limited to relatively high-skill and/or high-income natives. The second indicator measures whether there are no limitations on the franchise. The excluded category involves states that have no voting; I include in this category states that are very autocratic (Polity score of less than −3 on the −10 to 10 scale) but that have legislatures, since these legislatures have little effect on policy. Trade openness, as measured by the absence of tariffs, still has a negative and statistically significant effect in most of the models. The effect of increasing the franchise, however, is in the opposite direction from what the argument about democratization would predict. Over all the years, the coefficients on either limited or unlimited franchise are positive, and the difference between a limited and an unlimited franchise is statistically indistinguishable from zero. Importantly, this effect holds in the nineteenth-century globalization era and the interwar period, when the franchise was extended in most of the settler states and the European liberal democracies. In sum, it does not appear that extending the franchise or democratizing has led to more immigration restrictions across countries.

[1] Polanyi (1944).
[2] Hatton and Williamson (1998).
[3] Przeworski et al. (2013).

TABLE 7.1
Immigration Policy Regressed on Trade Policy by Era.

DV: immigration policy	All years	Preglobalization	19th-century globalization	Interwar	Bretton Woods	Post–Bretton Woods	Post–Bretton Woods, no Argentina
Trade openness	−3.04**	−1.81*	−1.68*	−3.27+	−1.25*	−1.33	−3.61**
	(0.89)	(0.67)	(0.58)	(1.66)	(0.55)	(1.21)	(1.13)
Linear time trend	−0.02***	−0.00	−0.02***	−0.03**	0.01	−0.01***	−0.01**
	(0.00)	(0.01)	(0.00)	(0.01)	(0.01)	(0.00)	(0.00)
Polity	0.01	0.06*	0.15	0.02	0.02+	0.01+	0.01
	(0.01)	(0.02)	(0.09)	(0.02)	(0.01)	(0.00)	(0.01)
GDP growth	0.17	0.18	0.19	−0.15	0.05	0.16	0.01
	(0.16)	(0.16)	(0.12)	(0.33)	(0.34)	(0.18)	(0.16)
War	0.17	0.96	0.00	0.20	−0.00	−0.03	−0.03
	(0.12)	(0.52)	(0.05)	(0.21)	(0.10)	(0.04)	(0.04)
Constant	4.32***	2.07*	2.79***	6.04*	−1.98	1.78	3.75***
	(0.89)	(0.81)	(0.52)	(1.95)	(1.45)	(1.21)	(0.92)
Observations	1577	77	297	298	325	580	548
R^2	0.77	0.64	0.53	0.56	0.30	0.36	0.48

Notes: Also included: country and year fixed effects. Robust standard errors in parentheses. $^+$ $p < 0.10$, * $p < 0.05$, ** $p < 0.01$, *** $p < 0.001$. *Trade openness* is 1 minus the tariff rate from Clemens and Williamson (2004) and updated by the author. *GDP growth* is from Maddison (2011). *Polity* is the measure of regime type from Marshall, Gurr, and Jaggers (2011). *War* is an indicator variable for war from Sarkees and Wayman (2010). *Linear time trend* is a time trend for each country. Originally published in Peters (2015) and reprinted with permission.

TABLE 7.2
Immigration Policy Regressed on Trade Policy and Changes in the Franchise by Era.

DV: immigration policy	All years	Pre-globalization	19th-century globalization	Interwar	Bretton Woods	Post-Bretton Woods	Post-Bretton Woods, no Argentina
Trade openness	-3.05*	-1.15	-1.67*	-3.35*	-0.95	-2.14*	-4.02**
	(1.17)	(1.99)	(0.68)	(1.21)	(0.67)	(0.99)	(1.21)
Limited franchise	0.50**		0.76	0.93	0.48***	0.09	0.19+
	(0.15)		(0.51)	(0.55)	(0.09)	(0.08)	(0.10)
Unlimited franchise	0.38*	0.41	0.76	0.66+	-0.03	0.06	0.08
	(0.15)	(0.33)	(0.51)	(0.32)	(0.05)	(0.07)	(0.09)
Linear time trend	-0.01***	-0.01	-0.02***	-0.02**	0.01	-0.01***	-0.01**
	(0.00)	(0.01)	(0.00)	(0.01)	(0.01)	(0.00)	(0.00)
GDP growth	-0.01	0.33	0.25*	-0.45	0.09	0.11	0.07
	(0.23)	(0.49)	(0.10)	(0.35)	(0.31)	(0.14)	(0.13)
War	0.14	0.51	0.03	0.06	0.03	-0.06	-0.09
	(0.11)	(0.60)	(0.02)	(0.13)	(0.09)	(0.07)	(0.06)
Constant	3.74**	1.98	2.38***	4.50*	-1.14	2.32*	3.96**
	(1.05)	(1.37)	(0.64)	(1.43)	(1.04)	(1.04)	(1.13)
Observations	1380	57	249	300	316	458	433
R^2	0.73	0.41	0.53	0.65	0.23	0.36	0.44

Notes: Also included: country and year fixed effects. Robust standard errors in parentheses. $+ p < 0.10$, $* p < 0.05$, $** p < 0.01$, $*** p < 0.001$. Trade openness is 1 minus the tariff rate from Clemens and Williamson (2004) and updated by the author. Limited franchise is an indicator denoting that at least some of the population can vote, and unlimited franchise is an indicator that all adults in the state can vote; both are from Przeworski et al. (2013). The excluded category, no franchise, indicates states in which no one can vote or states that, although they have elections, are very autocratic (Polity score less than −3). GDP growth is from Maddison (2011). War is an indicator variable for war from Sarkees and Wayman (2010). Linear time trend is a time trend for each country.

Next, I examine the effect of GDP growth on immigration. In the previous chapters and in the analysis here, I find little evidence that GDP growth affects immigration policy. Nonetheless, there are many cases in which economic hard times led to immigration restrictions. Two notable ones are the Great Depression, which led to restrictions throughout the settler states and the European liberal democracies, and the end of Bretton Woods and the first oil crisis, which led many European states to restrict immigration, in part by ending guest worker programs. However, immigration is also often restricted in good economic times. In the United States, the 1924 Quota Act was passed during a boom period, as were the 1986 Immigration Reform and Control Act and the 1996 Illegal Immigration Reform and Immigrant Responsibility Act. Thus while economic hard times are often a catalyst for restrictions, such restrictions are passed in good times as well, leading to a null effect.

There is also no effect of engaging in a war. War is theorized to have two effects on immigration policy. On the one hand, war could lead to more immigration restrictions; many states have restricted the immigration of so-called enemy aliens during wartime for fear that these immigrants will aid the enemy in some way. On the other hand, wars, especially large wars, may increase the need for labor. For example, the United States started the Bracero Program in 1942 in response to the tight labor market caused by World War II. The combination of these two effects may lead to the null effect of war on immigration policy.

As I discussed in chapter 2, there are additional societal-based explanations arguing that societies see themselves as either immigrant or nonimmigrant states, and these identities affect the political discussion around border controls.[4] One way to examine these identities is through the country fixed effects included in the regressions for table 3.2 (reestimated without a constant). The fixed effects on their own have relatively little meaning; instead, what is important is their relative size. All of the fixed effects are positive and statistically significant and have similar magnitudes; however, they vary in their size and rank order (table 7.3). For interpretation, Singapore can be used as the reference category; Taiwan's baseline preference for immigration is similar to Singapore's, and all other states have a baseline preference for greater openness. These patterns do not directly conform to the previous hypotheses about why these different identities exist: the East Asian and Persian Gulf states have lower baseline preferences than do the settler states, but there is little pattern to the size of the fixed effects in European countries. Thus while it is clear that states have baseline preferences for immigration, we do not have a good understanding of what causes these baselines.

---

[4] See Freeman (1995), Hansen (2002), and Zolberg (1989).

TABLE 7.3
Fixed Effects by Country in Order of Size.

Country	Coefficient	Standard error
Singapore	2.63***	(0.21)
Taiwan	2.64***	(0.19)
South Korea	2.79***	(0.20)
Kuwait	2.99***	(0.21)
Germany	3.00***	(0.19)
Japan	3.24***	(0.20)
Switzerland	3.58***	(0.19)
US	3.65***	(0.20)
South Africa	4.13***	(0.20)
Brazil	4.15***	(0.18)
New Zealand	4.20***	(0.19)
Netherlands	4.35***	(0.20)
Argentina	4.40***	(0.20)
Canada	4.45***	(0.20)
France	4.59***	(0.21)
Australia	4.72***	(0.19)
UK	4.85***	(0.20)

Notes: Lines denote whether coefficients are statistically different from each other. $^+$ $p < 0.10$, * $p < 0.05$, ** $p < 0.01$, *** $p < 0.001$. Model was run without a constant so that all fixed effects could be reported. Saudi Arabia and Hong Kong are dropped owing to lack of trade data. Originally published in Peters (2015) and reprinted with permission.

ALTERNATIVE INTEREST GROUP EXPLANATIONS FOR IMMIGRATION POLICY

There are four additional explanations for mass public support for immigration and/or other interest group activity on immigration: the role of workers, the effect of immigrants on the welfare state, nativism, and the impact of immigrants themselves. Most explanations invoking the role of workers and their interest group (i.e., unions) argue that because more low-skill immigration leads to lower wages, workers should oppose immigration.[5] If this argument is correct, we expect that as unions increase in size, they increase in political power and immigration should be restricted. Nonetheless, there are some unions—the International Workers of the World, the Congress of Industrial Organizations, and the Service

[5] Briggs (2001).

Employees International Union, for example—that have been supportive of immigration to organize immigrant workers instead of antagonizing them. It is, therefore, an open empirical question whether unions generally have a positive or a negative effect on the openness to immigration. To test this argument, I regress my immigration policy measure on a measure of net union density from Golden and colleagues.[6]

A second form of the workers' role explanation focuses on inequality. Hatton and Williamson argue that voters do not like inequality and are likely to push for immigration restrictions when inequality increases. I examine whether inequality has the predicted effect using the Gini coefficient, which measures how disperse incomes are. If this argument is correct, increases in inequality (a larger Gini coefficient) should be associated with more restrictive immigration policy.

Scholars have also argued that the fiscal effects of immigrants should affect immigration policy. Fiscal burden arguments suggest that citizens oppose immigration because immigrants (are thought to) use more resources, in the form of government services, than they provide in tax revenue.[7] As the size of the welfare state increases, we would expect immigration to become more restrictive to cut down on the cost of immigrants. I use Cusack's measure of taxation for social spending to examine this hypothesis.[8]

Immigration also changes the national culture, which is threatening to nativists. While arguments on nativism seek to explain when and why nativism arises, there has not been a clear articulation of the conditions that allow nativists to affect policy, or how to measure nativism.[9] As a proxy, I examine the ideology of the party in power, because nativists tend to join right parties. Therefore, if the nativist hypothesis is correct, immigration should be more restrictive under right parties.[10]

Not only do immigrants change the national culture, but in many states they also become voters. Because immigrants usually favor a more open immigration policy—it allows their friends and family to immigrate and makes them feel more secure about their place in society—we should expect that greater immigration should lead to a more open immigration policy. If, on the other hand, more immigration leads to a nativist backlash, we should expect that more immigration should lead to more restrictions

---

[6] Golden, Lange, and Wallerstein (2009). I use the net union density measure because it is comparable across countries and covers a greater number of years and countries.

[7] Hanson, Scheve, and Slaughter (2007), Hatton and Williamson (2008), Money (1999), and Neuman (1993).

[8] Cusack (2000*b*).

[9] E.g., Castro (1999) and Olzak (1989).

[10] The data on parties are from Cusack (2000*a*).

on immigration. To measure immigration, I use the total flow of immigrants lagged five years from Fitzgerald and colleagues.[11]

Table 7.4 examines these hypotheses for OECD countries from 1972 to 1995 by regressing immigration policy on these measures, as well as trade policy and our measure of firm mobility using OLS. The time span and set of countries were determined by the data availability for these additional explanations. Models 1 and 2 include only trade policy; models 3 and 4 include the firm mobility measures but do not included fixed effects to examine the entire sample of countries (standard errors are clustered by country); and models 5 and 6 include fixed effects. The even-numbered models include the immigrant flows measure; even lagged five years, immigrant flows are endogenous to immigration policy. Immigration policy does not change very often, so the policy that created the flows five years ago may still be in place today, and the flows measure may be a proxy for immigration policy.

First, we see that the effects of trade openness and firm mobility are relatively unchanged even with the inclusion of these additional variables. The exception is the inclusion of immigrant flows. Trade policy is almost statistically significant at the 10 percent level in model 4 and model 6, which suggests that countries with more open trade also have more open immigration policies, but that within countries, greater trade openness leads to more immigration restrictions.

Next, we see that the unions measure has a negative effect on immigration policy in the models with fixed effects (models 1, 2, 5, and 6) but a positive effect in the models without fixed effects (models 3 and 4). This suggests that as unions gain power, they fight for immigration restrictions, but that states with high union density typically have more open immigration policy. Further, the result that left parties are more likely to restrict immigration suggests that they do so to appease labor, giving more credence to the argument that unions fight for immigration restrictions. While the coefficient on Gini is negatively signed in models with fixed effects, it is not consistently statistically significant, giving less support for arguments based on the effects of income inequality on immigration policy. There also seems to be little support for the fiscal burden argument; the coefficient on welfare taxes is negative but not statistically significant. Finally, there is some support for the nativism argument: greater flows of immigrants five years ago are correlated with more immigration restrictions today. The effect of immigrant flows suggests that large flows of immigrants lead to a backlash against immigration. However, center and right parties, which often represent nativist groups, tend to be more likely to open immigration, suggesting a smaller role for nativism.

---

[11] Fitzgerald, Leblang, and Teets (2014).

TABLE 7.4
Immigration Policy Regressed on Trade and Capital Policy and Additional Explanations, 1972–1995.

DV: immigration policy	(1)	(2)	(3)	(4)	(5)	(6)
Trade openness	−6.64*	−4.46*	−4.91[+]	3.58	−5.08*	−2.26
	(2.08)	(1.59)	(2.65)	(2.98)	(1.93)	(1.20)
Capital openness			0.27*	−0.04	0.67***	0.45**
			(0.11)	(0.20)	(0.07)	(0.09)
Nonrestricted entry			−0.04	0.27	0.45	0.38
			(0.63)	(0.92)	(0.32)	(0.33)
Capital openness* nonrestricted entry			−0.30*	−0.07	−0.76***	−0.57***
			(0.12)	(0.20)	(0.08)	(0.08)
Union density (Golden et al.)	−2.04[+]	−2.15[+]	4.92***	3.61*	−2.67*	−1.77[+]
	(0.93)	(1.03)	(1.46)	(1.48)	(0.89)	(0.73)
Gini coefficient	−0.00	−0.00	0.01	0.02	−0.01*	−0.00
	(0.00)	(0.00)	(0.02)	(0.02)	(0.00)	(0.00)
Welfare taxes	−0.02	−0.02	0.03	−0.05	−0.01	−0.04
	(0.01)	(0.02)	(0.04)	(0.04)	(0.03)	(0.04)
Center party in power	0.05[+]	0.06*	0.15	0.22[+]	0.05	0.09*
	(0.03)	(0.03)	(0.11)	(0.13)	(0.04)	(0.03)
Right party in power	0.08*	0.07*	0.12	0.12	0.04	0.06[+]
	(0.03)	(0.03)	(0.10)	(0.08)	(0.04)	(0.03)
Lagged total immigrant flow (100,000s)	−0.03***	−0.03***		−0.05**		−0.02**
	(0.01)	(0.01)		(0.02)		(0.00)
Linear time trend	−0.01	−0.03***	0.00	−0.01	−0.02[+]	−0.02
	(0.01)	(0.00)	(0.00)	(0.01)	(0.01)	(0.01)

TABLE 7.4
Continued

DV: immigration policy	(1)	(2)	(3)	(4)	(5)	(6)
Polity	-0.21***		-0.23+	-0.86+	-0.31***	
	(0.04)		(0.13)	(0.45)	(0.03)	
GDP growth	1.47	1.22	1.98	-0.31	1.62**	0.92
	(0.85)	(0.72)	(1.55)	(1.62)	(0.36)	(0.66)
War	0.06	0.01	0.07	-0.12	0.06	-0.04
	(0.06)	(0.09)	(0.13)	(0.16)	(0.06)	(0.11)
Constant	10.32**	8.56**	3.34	4.37	10.64**	4.79
	(2.18)	(2.43)	(2.55)	(7.30)	(2.27)	(2.58)
Observations	154	122	117	99	117	99
R-squared	0.62	0.80	0.86	0.92	0.81	0.88

Notes: Also included: year fixed effects. Standard errors in parentheses. $+ p < 0.10$, $* p < 0.05$, $** p < 0.01$, $*** p < 0.001$. *Trade openness* is 1 minus the tariff rate from Clemens and Williamson (2004) and updated by the author. *Capital openness* measures how freely capital can flow in and out of a country from Chinn and Ito (2008). *Nonrestricted entry* is the average percent of all manufacturing and service industries that foreigners can invest in directly in developing states that share the same language from Pandya (2014). *Union density* is net union density from Golden, Lange, and Wallerstein (2009). *Gini coefficient* is the Gini coefficient from World Bank Group (2012). *Welfare taxes* is the percent of taxation for social spending from Cusack (2000b). *Center parties* is an indicator for a center party in power, and *right parties* is an indicator for a right party in power (left parties are the excluded category) from Cusack (2000a). *Lagged total immigrant flow (100,000s)* is the number of immigrants who entered the state five years ago from Fitzgerald, Leblang, and Teets (2014). *Linear time trend* is a time trend for each country. *Polity* is the measure of regime type from Marshall, Gurr, and Jaggers (2011). *GDP growth* is from Maddison (2011). *War* is an indicator variable for war from Sarkees and Wayman (2010).

Immigration Policy and the Conventional Wisdom on Firms and Undocumented Immigration

Finally, I examine some observable implications from the conventional wisdom on firms and undocumented immigration. In chapter 2, I discussed how some scholars have argued that firms benefit from having a more restrictive border entry policy with lax enforcement.[12] These scholars argue that firms can pay undocumented immigrants less than legal workers and can break labor laws because they have little fear that their undocumented immigrant employees will report them. The firms gain a competitive advantage, then, by using undocumented immigrants.

In contrast, I argued in chapter 2 that firms may have different preferences over using undocumented immigrants based on their need for a stable workforce and on their size. These different preferences may lead some firms to lobby for greater enforcement, and lead others to lobby for more open legal immigration; in the case studies in chapters 4 and 6, I examine the support for these mechanisms. Here, I examine whether three observable implications of the conventional wisdom are correct. First, if firms prefer a system of undocumented immigration, then they should prefer more border restrictions combined with relatively lax enforcement, and we expect a negative relationship between these two variables. Instead, we find that border entry and enforcement regulations are positively correlated ($\rho = 0.54$, $p < 0.001$). States that have more open borders tend to have less enforcement of their borders, and states that have greater restrictions on the admission of immigration tend to have more enforcement of these laws.

A second implication of the conventional wisdom is that states would increase border entry restrictions and place the onus of enforcement on the undocumented immigrants by increasing deportation regulations. Increased deportation regulations make it more likely that, if caught, an undocumented immigrant will be deported. Regulations that make deportation easier would make undocumented immigrants less likely to complain when exploited by their employer. Thus we should expect that increased border entry restrictions should be coupled with increased deportation regulations.

Figure 7.1 shows the relationship between border entry and deportation restrictions for all nineteen countries and all years. The two policies are plotted against each other, and there is a loess-smoothed line to show the relationship between the two. Again, we do not see the relationship that we would expect if employers were driving policy with an eye toward exploiting undocumented immigrant labor. States that have very open borders tend to have lax deportation restrictions. States that have restricted

---

[12] See, for example, Joppke (1998) and Motomura (2014).

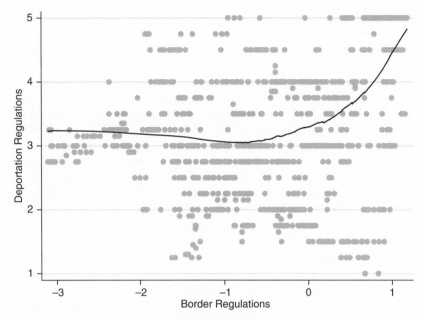

Figure 7.1: Border Entry and Deportation Regulations.
Note: Lower values of both border entry and deportation regulation signify greater restrictions and greater ease of deportation, respectively. The loess-smoothed line shows the relationship between the two variables. Data coded by author; see appendix A for details.

the border, on the other hand, tend to have moderately strong deportation restrictions, not the strong deportation laws that we would expect if firms wanted to exploit undocumented workers. These states have some judicial process overseeing deportation that acts as a check, limiting employers' ability to exploit undocumented immigrant workers.

Finally, if the argument that firms prefer to use undocumented immigration is correct, there should be a stronger relationship in states with more labor laws. In countries like Saudi Arabia and Kuwait, where there are few laws on the minimum wage or the treatment of workers, firms should not prefer to use undocumented immigrants because there is no advantage to using them. Firms in these countries can pay documented and undocumented immigrants the same (low) pay and treat them the same. In contrast, in states with more labor laws, there is a greater advantage to using undocumented immigrants. I operationalize labor laws in two ways: first, I examine the relationship in democracies versus autocracies and, second, among democracies, I examine those with stronger or weaker unions (measured as the net union density). Democracies typically have more labor laws, since workers can vote, and democracies with stronger unions have greater protections, since unions fight for these protections. I further restrict the sample to post-1945, since many worker protections were implemented in the interwar period.

Figure 7.2 examines the relationships between border entry regulations and enforcement and border entry and deportation in autocracies and democracies. Again, we find little evidence supporting the conventional wisdom. In democracies, which have more worker protections and thus more employers who would benefit from using illegal workers, there is no relationship between the border restrictions and the level of enforcement or deportation. There is also little relationship between border regulations and enforcement among the autocracies, and on deportation we find the opposite of what we would expect if employers lobbied for the ability to use illegal workers: the strongest deportation laws are in the autocracies with the most open entry criteria.

Next, we examine the relationship within democracies by examining whether the strength of their unions affects the relationship between border entry regulations and enforcement and deportation (figure 7.3). We expect that, if the conventional wisdom is true, states with stronger unions (measured as union density) should have more worker protections and higher wages, and therefore firms should be more likely to want to exploit undocumented immigrants. Again, the evidence does not seem to support the conventional wisdom: there is little relationship between border regulations and enforcement or deportation in either the low- or high-union-density states. The high-union-density states do not have much less enforcement, nor is deportation markedly easier. Thus it is unlikely that firms' preferences to use undocumented immigrants are driving immigration policy.

CONCLUSION

In the previous three chapters, I found mixed support for the alternative explanations for immigration policy. In this chapter, I systematically analyzed the support for these arguments across countries. Explanations based on macropolitical or macroeconomic phenomena seem to explain little variation in immigration policy. There is little support for arguments based on democratization or extension of the franchise, at least outside the United States. Nor do economic conditions seem to explain immigration policy; countries restrict immigration in good times and bad. States do seem to have different baseline preferences for immigration, but what explains these baselines is unclear.

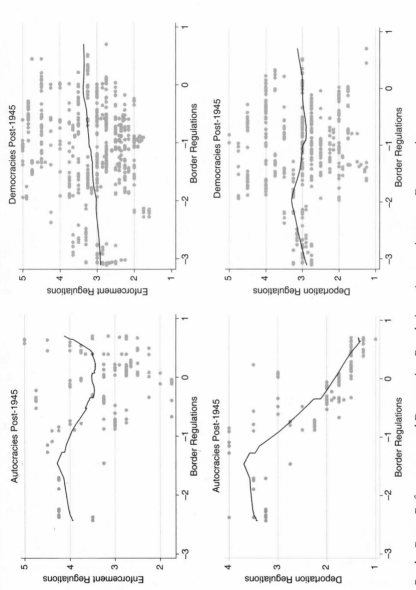

Figure 7.2: Border Entry, Enforcement, and Deportation Regulations: Autocracies versus Democracies.
Note: Democracies are defined as states scoring at least a 7 on the Polity score from −10 to 10. Lower values of border entry, enforcement, and deportation regulation signify greater restrictions, greater enforcement, and greater ease of deportation, respectively. The loess-smoothed line shows the relationship between the two variables. Data coded by author; see appendix A for details.

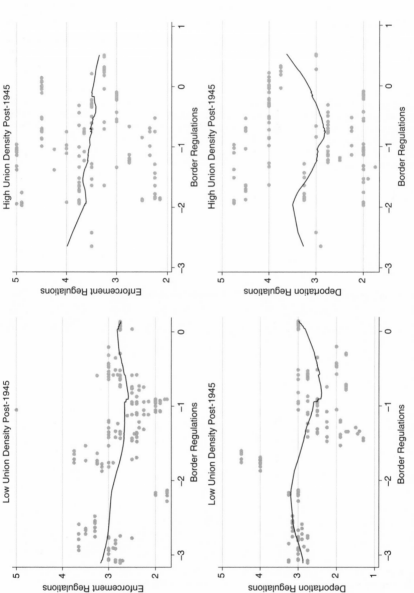

Figure 7.3: Border Entry, Enforcement, and Deportation Regulations: Low- versus High-Union-Density Democracies.
Note: High-union-density states have at least the median level of union density (31.6 percent). Lower values of border entry, enforcement, and deportation regulation signify greater restrictions, greater enforcement, and greater ease of deportation, respectively. The loess-smoothed line shows the relationship between the two variables. Data coded by author; see appendix A for details.

It does not appear to be the case that firms have somehow gamed the immigration system, either. Although clearly there are cases of unscrupulous employers that exploit undocumented immigrants, it does not appear that firms in general are actively lobbying for increased restrictions on the entry of immigrants combined with lax enforcement. Instead of being a conspiracy driven by businesses, undocumented immigration is a product of the great demand to move to the developed world; fewer legal ways to enter these states; and governments' reluctance to pay the exorbitant costs to reduce these flows to zero.

Together, then, the data support an interest-group-based argument for immigration policy. Firms are the most important interest group; they are not one among equals but one above the rest. When firms' support for open immigration drops, either because low-skill-intensive firms have closed as a result of trade competition or because they can move production overseas, immigration restrictions increase. Immigration restrictions also increase when unions gain more power, or when there is a backlash against immigration resulting from high numbers of immigrants.

CHAPTER 8

Immigration in an Increasingly Globalized World

WHENEVER IMMIGRATION COMES UP AS A POLITICAL ISSUE, the same arguments get brought up to oppose it. It is claimed that immigrants take the jobs of natives, even though there is little evidence of that.[1] Immigrants are believed to end up on welfare, a concern that in the nineteenth century sparked laws (many of which remain on the books to this day) restricting the entry of those likely to become a public charge.[2] In 2015, Republican presidential candidate Donald Trump claimed that Mexican immigrants were criminals,[3] an argument used since the colonial era when Great Britain *did* transport criminals to what is now the United States. Politicians in Europe worry that terrorists might be hiding among the ranks of the Syrian refugees, a common argument since the 1790s when fears of radical Jacobites led to one of the most draconian deportation laws in US history. Finally concerns about the cultural integration of Syrian refugees in Europe would have resonated with Benjamin Franklin, who argued that "swarthy" Germans could not be integrated in the American colonies in the 1750s.[4]

While these arguments about the problems that immigration poses have been ubiquitous throughout modern history, movements based on them have not always been successful in restricting immigration. In the nineteenth and early twentieth centuries, migrants were relatively free to legally move to any other country in the world so long as they could afford it; even those who could not afford it were often offered subsidized transportation to many countries. Today, most wealthy countries restrict low-skill immigration to a greater or lesser degree. Why have anti-immigration movements had more success in shaping policy today?

A further difference between the nineteenth-century economy and today's economy has been the difference in mobility for firms and for people. In the nineteenth and early twentieth centuries, people could move relatively easily, but a lack of communications and transportation technology in combination with the relatively high trade barriers made moving production from one country to another very difficult.

---

[1] Ottaviano and Peri (2012).
[2] Neuman (1993) and Zolberg (2006).
[3] Ye Hee Lee (2015).
[4] Franklin (1755).

Today, firms are increasingly seen as footloose, moving to whichever country will offer them the best deal.

I have argued in this book that these questions are interrelated. Policymakers face a dilemma when they choose to open their borders to the outside world: they can either open low-skill immigration but keep trade and firm mobility restricted, or they can open trade and/or firm mobility but restrict low-skill immigration. They face this dilemma because of the effects of trade and firm mobility on the firms that produce within their borders. Firms that use much low-skill labor have been the major proponent of greater openness to immigrants. Immigration helps lower their costs, making them more competitive at home and abroad. However, increased international competition due to low trade barriers and greater economic development in the developing world led many of these firms in wealthy countries to close. The ability to move overseas gave these firms another option when faced with international competition: if they could not beat the competition, they would join them. Finally, productivity increases allowed those firms that remained behind to do more with fewer workers. Together, these changes in the international economy sapped the support of firms for immigration at home, allowed anti-immigrant groups to have more voice, and led to greater restrictions on immigration.

Modern globalization did not have to take the form it did, with mobility for goods and firms but not people. When states sought to rebuild the global economy after the Great Depression and World War II, they could have reinstated free mobility of people as they reinstated the gold standard. Instead, trade openness and, later, capital mobility were privileged. States' political choices to open their borders to goods and to allow firms to move freely led to increased restrictions on low-skill immigration. While these prior choices were often made for reasons far removed from immigration policy, they have had profound effects on the ability of people to move across borders and for both domestic and international politics. I explore some of these effects below, examining implications for the study of international political economy, for migration around the world, and for the shape of the international system and foreign policy.

IMPLICATIONS FOR THE STUDY OF INTERNATIONAL POLITICAL ECONOMY

Taking the "Open" Part of Open Economy Politics Seriously

Open economy politics (OEP) has become the dominant mode of scholarship on international political economy in the United States. Lake describes

OEP as including three parts: the derivation of preferences over some policy of individuals, firms, or groups (usually) based on material self-interest; the study of how institutions aggregate those preferences; and an examination of international bargaining over the policy issue.[5] Scholars usually assume that preferences are constructed in a small, open economy.

This book follows the paradigm of OEP: firms' interests on immigration were derived from their material interests and then aggregated through institutions.[6] Where I differ, however, is in taking openness seriously by examining how different forms of economic openness affect one another. Too often, scholars who study OEP examine only one flow—trade flows, capital flows, or, more rarely, migrant flows—rather than studying how they interact.[7] But, as this book as shown, openness in one area can have important effects on other areas. Thus scholars of trade and capital mobility should take migration policy into account.

Firm Heterogeneity

Since Melitz's groundbreaking work on intraindustry trade, firm heterogeneity has become a more and more important way of thinking about trade and firms in general.[8] In the Melitz model and those derived from it, differences in firms' productivity levels affect their ability to trade and to invest overseas. This book extends this line of thinking in two ways. First, these models, as models of trade, necessarily focus on firms in the tradable sector. Yet we can extend the logic to the nontradable sector to think about other issue areas in which firms with different levels of productivity may have differing preferences. Second, even among the tradable sector, there are industries in which the inputs are such that even the largest, most productive firms may not choose to engage in FDI and therefore are relatively nonmobile. Here, the example of agriculture stands out. Although large producers of wine in California or France could easily move production abroad, many choose not to, so as not to lose access to a specific input—the soil (or terroir). Other industries may likewise be unwilling to move if their inputs are highly specific, and if they can gain a rent from using that input. Scholars should consider whether other dimensions that firms differ on are important to their preferences as well.

---

[5] Lake (2009).

[6] I did not include any study of international bargaining on immigration as there has been very little of it. Peters (2014*a*).

[7] Copelovitch and Pevehouse (2013), Leblang (2010), and Singer (2010) are notable exceptions.

[8] Melitz (2003).

Domestic Policy and the Race to the Bottom

Examining how changes in firms' production strategies—what they produce, where they produce, and how they produce—affect their preferences over policy may help explain more than just low-skill immigration policy. Firms' changing production strategies are also likely to affect other policy areas. In the nineteenth- and early twentieth-century era of globalization, firms were much less likely to face international competition or be able to move overseas than in the modern era of globalization. This has meant that the industrial mix in the nineteenth and early twentieth centuries was different from that today. One policy area where this has likely had an impact is environmental policy. As we saw in chapter 6, in the 1950s and 1960s there were coal and other mining operations within the Netherlands. As the Dutch economy opened, these mines became unprofitable and were closed. The loss of these environmentally damaging mining operations likely meant that the Dutch could more easily implement environmental legislation: the "dirty" firms no longer existed to lobby against this legislation. Similarly, greater international competition has meant that many polluting industries in developed states have closed, moved production overseas, or cleaned up as they have adopted more productive technologies, likely making it easier to pass environmental legislation in developed states. Yet it has likely made it harder to pass environmental legislation in the developing states where these industries moved. Another area with similar dynamics is labor and health and safety regulations; it has likely become easier to pass labor and health and safety laws once the firms that relied on having cheap labor closed, moved, or became more productive.

The argument of this book, then, could help explain why scholars have gotten conflicting results when they test the *race to the bottom* argument. Proponents of the race to the bottom argue that states will do anything to keep footloose firms at home, including cutting corporate taxes and gutting social and environmental policy. Other scholars argue that this has not occurred. The evidence, so far, has been mixed. As in the case of immigration, this may be because when these firms first face international competition and the ability to move, they increase lobbying for lower taxes and fewer regulations, and sometimes governments grant them these subsidies. Yet as the international economy opens further and there are increased opportunities to move overseas, further subsidies become politically unsustainable, which leads these firms to close, move, or become more productive. Together, these trends lessen the pressure to cut taxes and/or regulations and even allow politicians to increase them.

Furthermore, the evidence of this book shows that governments are not beholden to corporations. The race to the bottom literature assumes that governments will do whatever they can to keep firms. Yet, at least in the case of low-skill immigration, governments—even autocratic governments, like the People's Action Party in Singapore, that hold shares in many corporations—are willing to let firms close or move rather than promote an unpopular policy. As many firms have moved production overseas or closed as a result of increased trade and capital openness, it is clear that governments often refuse to grant subsidies or change policy to keep firms. One question for future research is why policymakers are willing to give in to corporate demands on some issues but not others.

IMPLICATIONS FOR MIGRATION

Immigration Policy Going Forward

For advocates of more open immigration, the fact that globalization decreases firms' support for open immigration does not bode well. In wealthy countries, like the United States, there are few firms and industries today willing to put their money and political capital on the line for immigration. As the business coalition has decreased its support for open immigration, the anti-immigration coalition has gained greater voice. It is not surprising, then, that comprehensive immigration reform has failed to pass as of 2016. Given these trends, it is likely that any comprehensive immigration reform bill that allows greater low-skill immigration will be very difficult to pass.

Furthermore, the anti-immigration coalition throughout the West has been given new ammunition with the securitization of immigration. Securitization of immigration is not new; witness the laws against German immigrants in the United States during both world wars and the internment of Japanese citizens in the United States during World War II. Yet fears of immigrants as terrorists have taken on new life since 9/11. The terrorists who executed the attacks on the United States were in the country on student visas, and first- and second-generation immigrants have been implicated in the Paris attacks in 2015 and the Brussels attack in 2016. These attacks are yet another reason why we are unlikely to see developed states open their borders to immigration.

Even if trade barriers in wealthy states increase or politicians find incentives to keep firms producing at home, low-skill immigration is unlikely to become as open as it was in the nineteenth century owing to technological developments. As we saw in chapter 4, production of what were once low-skill-intensive products like textiles has now gotten much more high-tech. If, for example, all textiles had to be produced in the United States to be sold in the United States, the textile sector would expand but would do so using laborsaving technology. On the flip side, if an anti-immigration politician, like Donald Trump in the United States,

Marine Le Pen in France, or Geert Wilders in the Netherlands, were able to restrict low-skill immigration to a greater extent, we would expect that even more firms would move overseas, adopt laborsaving technology, or close, furthering deindustrialization in the OECD.

This trend is likely to continue in states that are just now receiving large flows of immigrants as well. These tend to be middle-income states that still protect their economies to a greater degree than do most developed states. As these states develop further, it is likely that they too will be under pressure from the WTO and developed countries to open their economies. Their low-skill-intensive industries will come under greater pressure from international competition as the least developed countries develop. In all likelihood, middle-income countries will also find that their low-skill-intensive industries are forced to increase productivity, close, or move to the least developed countries, leading to reduced support for immigration in these states as well.

It is unlikely that other interest groups will make up for the loss of business support. As I have argued, business is not one interest group among many but an interest group without equal. Although some in the media and other scholars have noted that immigrants can be an important part of an electorate, immigrants' votes are unlikely to shift low-skill immigration policy to greater openness for two reasons. First, immigrants tend to care much more about the *rights* they receive than the openness of the border. In the United States, for example, immigrants' interest groups are pushing for the right of undocumented immigrants to stay, not for more low-skill immigrants to be admitted. This may be because new immigrants tend to compete with earlier immigrants rather than with natives—thus the immigrants in the country are acting in their material self-interest—or because rights are simply a more salient issue to immigrants in the country. But increasing rights often leads to more restrictive border policies.[9] Second, left political parties, the parties that most often integrate immigrants, need to balance their pursuit of the immigrant vote with maintaining the support of longtime constituents.[10]

It is likely, then, that the only way wealthy states will open their borders to increased low-skill immigration is if there is a fundamental change in how the mass public and the elites, who often drive public opinion, view low-skill immigration. In this, trade may serve as a good example. Elites in the United States were much more divided on open trade throughout the late nineteenth and early twentieth centuries with the Republicans implementing high tariff barriers and the Democrats taking them down. Today, the majority of elites in both parties are pro–free trade.

[9] Ruhs (2013).
[10] Dancygier (2013).

Scholars have argued that greater education on the benefits of trade has led to greater support for free trade.[11] Perhaps if more economists, political scientists, and others taught about the benefits of low-skill immigration for wealthy states and developing countries, there would be more elite support for immigration, and perhaps this elite support would trickle down to the mass public, as has appeared to happen for trade.[12]

International Cooperation on Migration

In comparison to the cooperation of trade and firm mobility, there has been relatively little cooperation on migration. International trade is now regulated through the World Trade Organization and a host of other preferential trading agreements. It has also been legalized to an extent that is not seen elsewhere in international relations. Firm mobility in the form of foreign direct investment has been regulated at the international level as well, with the signing of many bilateral investment treaties that also include provisions for international legal adjudication. In contrast, there are only a handful of free trade zones that also allow free migration (the European Union and MERCOSUR being two), and a relatively small number of bilateral treaties on migration that cover labor migration, repatriation of undocumented migrants, and joint enforcement.

As I have argued in this book, it was in part the creation of legalization in trade and FDI that have led to immigration restrictions and hence to a lack of cooperation on migration. Immigrant-receiving countries want to restrict immigration, whereas developing countries would like to open migration, leaving them little to negotiate on. Even those states that want migration find little reason to sign a treaty on immigration given that migrants will move on their own. Only in special circumstances, when the receiving state needs a particular type of migrant or needs help repatriating migrants, will states be willing to cooperate on migration.[13]

Perhaps an organization could emerge from these negotiations that would help prevent labor abuses in autocratic states, like the countries of the Gulf Cooperative Council, that could help legitimize their temporary worker programs. Or an organization could help repatriate workers when their contract is over to prevent overstaying, which has led to large numbers of undocumented immigrants in the United States and Europe. In general, though, as wealthy countries close their doors to immigrants, there will

---

[11] Hainmueller and Hiscox (2006).

[12] See Goldstein and Peters (2014) for evidence that the mass public is largely supportive of free trade, even during the Great Recession.

[13] Peters (2014a).

likely be an increasing number of people who are willing to move almost anywhere, negating the need for much cooperation on labor migration.

Climate Change Migration

In addition to helping to explain the rise of environmental protection policies in the developed world, my argument may also speak to the increasing problem of climate change migration. The effects of climate change on migration thus far have been small in comparison to what many scientists think will happen. Nonetheless, climate change has led to more severe weather events that have created droughts, flooding, and storm damage. These events have tended to produce short-term displacement rather than creating refugees who cannot return home, but this is likely to change with rising sea levels and desertification that will make some areas, including entire countries, uninhabitable. Most of these countries are in the developing world, and the migrants they are likely to produce will be low-skill migrants.

If this book is any guide, climate migration will become a major political problem. Between the lack of a pro-immigration coalition in developed states (and perhaps middle-income states as well) and the lack of international cooperation, it is likely that these migrants will not be allowed to move to the developed nations that are responsible for much of the change in the climate. Instead, these migrants, in all probability, will be shunted to developing nations, where they may place a large burden on these governments.

Yet perhaps the threat of migration will create incentives for developed country governments to invest in technology and foreign aid that will mitigate the effects of climate change. One could imagine that the threat of tens of millions of Bangladeshi migrants might lead the European Union to send Dutch engineers to build better dikes there. Flows of climate migrants fleeing desertification in Africa might be stopped with drought-tolerant food crops and better irrigation systems developed in California.

The Politics of Internal Migration

This book addresses international migration but has implications for the politics of internal migration as well. Internal migration poses a similar dilemma for policymakers. Internal migration allows labor to move from where returns to labor are low to where returns are high, improving economic efficiency and leading to growth. Further, capital owners (firm and land owners) in areas where labor is scarce support increased internal migration, while labor and others in these areas may oppose it. Internal migration also often causes cultural concerns similar to those caused by international migration, especially if the migrants do not share the same ethnicity, language, or religion as the locals. An extreme example was the Great Migration of African Americans from the US South to Northern cities after World War II, which caused locals, who were overwhelmingly white, to abandon the cities, in what is known as *white flight*. Although this is an extreme example, internal migration has often caused political conflict over resources, even when the migration is rural to urban migration among coethnics.

Internal migration may also pose two additional problems for policy-makers. First, capital owners in areas of labor abundance may oppose out-migration. Chapter 5 provided an example of this: Southern rural elites were concerned about out-migration of African Americans and poor whites during World War II and took steps to prevent their out-migration to areas where they could make more money, including preventing their conscription by the army, preventing recruitment by employment agents from the North, and supporting Mexican immigration into the Southwest.[14] Second, rural-to-urban migration may be especially problematic for autocratic leaders. In-migration of rural citizens may increase the grievances of urban residents, who may lose jobs or access to public goods, or become victims of crime.[15] Additionally, it is much easier for those disaffected by the regime to organize in urban centers than it is in rural areas. The growth of cities, then, is problematic, even more so for capital cities in which protests may turn into revolution.[16]

Given the downside of internal migration for urban residents, some elites, and the regime, we should see policies that encourage internal migration only when low-skill production is expanding and/or to areas with more low-skill production. When low-skill production is stagnating, we should see leaders try to prevent internal migration to cities either through formal restrictions, like the *hukou* system in China, or through clearing urban slums.[17]

My argument, then, may explain some of the variation in the use of controls on internal migration over time. For example, many scholars have noted that the decline of cities, and especially of the Hanse cities, preceded the rise of serfdom in Eastern Europe in the late Middle Ages and early modern period.[18] Anderson and Fukuyama argue that their decline meant that the cities did not have the ability to act as a counterweight to the

[14] Alston and Ferrie (1999).

[15] Wallace (2014).

[16] Wallace (2014).

[17] See Wallace (2014) on policies that authoritarian leaders have used to control internal migration.

[18] Anderson (1974) and Fukuyama (2011).

demands by rural elites (the nobles) to limit peasant mobility.[19] It may also have been the case that, even if the cities had relatively more power with the king, they would not have fought restrictions on peasant mobility. The opening of the Baltic Sea to trade with the areas that would become the Netherlands and Belgium was one of the major reasons for the decline of these towns. Proto-factories in the Netherlands and Flanders could produce goods much more cheaply than could be done in the towns in Eastern Europe, leading to a decline in the production of these goods and fewer jobs for rural migrants.[20] As such, these towns would have had to deal with the costs of in-migrants without the benefits of cheaper labor for proto-industrial production. The lack of demand for rural migrants, then, may have doomed the peasants to serfdom.

The demand for low-skill labor has also affected migration policy in China. Starting in the late 1990s, the Chinese Communist Party (CCP) allowed some areas to experiment with reforms to the *hukou* system. Local leaders appear to have used these reforms to increase migration to outlying industrial towns and small cities to develop manufacturing, while keeping migrants out of the county seats.[21] In this way, the CCP has provided labor to growing areas while preventing the spread of dangerous cities.[22] As China develops further and loses its competitive edge in the production of low-skill-intensive goods to countries like Vietnam, we might see greater enforcement of the *hukou* system as the demand for low-skill urban labor recedes, raising the costs of urban growth without the benefits.

IMPLICATIONS FOR THE SHAPE OF THE INTERNATIONAL SYSTEM AND FOREIGN POLICY

The Integration of the European Union

The European Union has faced three major crises in the past ten years: the euro crisis, especially the possibility of Greece's exit from the Eurozone (the Grexit); the Syrian refugee crisis; and the (currently ongoing) Brexit, the referendum of the United Kingdom to leave the EU. All three have shown the limits of Europe's integration thus far: the euro crisis has highlighted the lack of fiscal integration; the Syrian refugee crisis has highlighted the lack of political integration, especially on foreign policy issues like immigration and defense; and Brexit has shown the lack of social integration and the democratic deficit within the EU. Yet all three

[19] Anderson (1974) and Fukuyama (2011).
[20] Horlings (2001).
[21] Wallace (2014).
[22] Wallace (2014).

crises were, to some degree, baked into the European Union by how policymakers have chosen to open their borders.

The European Union has almost always integrated markets for goods and capital markets before it integrated labor markets. When it first began as the European Coal and Steel Community, it created a common market for coal and steel products but implemented provisions on labor mobility only five years after the treaty began, and even then, the labor mobility provisions covered only about 20 to 25 percent of workers in the industry.[23] This meant that the less productive mines and factories faced competition long before they could use immigrant labor. Later, as the European Community widened to new member states, the entrance of new members, except for the Scandinavian countries, led to a reduction of trade barriers and barriers to capital mobility *before* barriers to migration were lifted.[24]

The sequencing of the policies in the European Union, then, has had an effect on the immigration policies of the member states as well as on the migrant networks that have formed *within* the Union. This sequencing meant that companies within the old EU faced trade competition from the new member states and could move to these new states before migrants from those states could move into the old EU. Thus these firms faced competitive pressure and incentives to move before they received the benefit of lower wages at home from new migrants. These firms became less supportive of open immigration at home, which again gave greater voice to anti-immigrant forces. It is less surprising that older EU members of late have sought to restrict not just immigration from outside the EU but also immigration within it.

Effects of the restrictionist bent in immigration policy toward third-country nationals—those who are not citizens of an EU member state—can be felt clearly in the Syrian refugee crisis. Because there is less demand in general for low-skill immigrants, there is a smaller coalition to support refugee resettlement, leading to little generosity on the part of most member states toward the refugees. What is perhaps more surprising has been the unwillingness of states like Hungary to allow refugees to *transit* through their country. Much of Hungary's anti-refugee politics is blamed on the fascist ideology of the Jobbik party, the second-largest party in Parliament.[25] But Hungary and the other poorer transit countries are right to fear increased immigration into the rest of the European Union. As of now, poorer countries in the European Union can use their low-cost advantage to lure firms away from the rest of the European Union

[23] Geddes and Money (2011, 33).
[24] Geddes and Money (2011).
[25] Frayer (2015).

much as the US South used its low-cost advantage to lure firms from the US North in the early twentieth century. EU firms can also "second" their workers to projects in other EU countries; these workers are paid according to the wage and social welfare standards of the home country while working in the other country. This gives Eastern European firms an advantage when competing against Western European firms, which cannot profit from seconded labor owing to the high labor costs in their countries. This advantage might be lost if large numbers of Syrians were resettled in Western Europe. Thus the periphery has a reason to oppose more openness to outsiders, making it more difficult for the European Union to respond to refugee crises.

The effects of the sequencing may have also hurt migrant networks. As many manufacturing firms closed because of competition with firms from the poorer members of the European Union or relocated to new member countries (or, for that matter, to developing countries outside the European Union), they did not need to recruit low(er)-skill labor from the poorer members within the Union. Without these firms, there have been fewer opportunities for labor to move from the poorer countries to the wealthy countries in the European Union than might have occurred if the policy sequencing had been reversed. This has resulted in less migration within the European Union than there has been in other large free-migration areas.

The lack of migrant networks has become problematic owing to the adoption of the euro. As many economists have noted, the countries that adopted the euro lack the conditions needed for an *optimal currency area* (*OCA*), an area that should have a single currency to lower transaction costs. To maintain an OCA in the face of asymmetric economic shocks, the area should have either fiscal transfers from areas that are doing well to areas that are suffering, or migration from the areas in crisis to the areas that have growing economies. For example, in the United States, there are both automatic fiscal stabilizers (through unemployment, welfare, social security, and other programs) that help states in recession, and migration from areas that are stagnating (e.g., Detroit) to areas that are growing (e.g., Dallas). The low levels of migration within the Eurozone, then, are problematic for the stability of the currency. Without more low-skill job opportunities for those from the poorer countries, people are unwilling to move, leaving the 2015 unemployment rate in Greece at about 25 percent instead of closer to Germany's 6 percent. Additionally, had there been more migrants, remittances to the countries in crisis could have acted as fiscal transfers, making the currency union easier to maintain.[26]

Increased migration within the European Union might have helped increase fiscal transfers between states as well. Bernhard and Leblang argue

[26] Singer (2010).

that migration increased support in Germany for the bailout of Greece, such as it was, because the Germans wanted to prevent future migration.[27] Without a bailout from the rest of the European Union, Greece and the other countries in trouble (Ireland, Italy, Portugal, and Spain) might have defaulted on their sovereign debt, leading to an even more severe crisis (at least in the short run). With open borders, this might have led to increased migration from these countries into Germany and other wealthy countries. Given the lack of a large pro-immigration business coalition, this migration would have been problematic for the leaders of the wealthy member states. The possibility of increased immigration may have been a factor in Germany's willingness to bail out these countries. Had there already been larger migrant networks, the fear about more intra-EU migration might have been greater and might have led to a larger bailout.

Yet fear of immigration in an environment without a strong pro-immigration stance from the business community in Europe may, paradoxically, bring the Union closer together. Wealthier members may be more willing to support fiscal transfers to help the poorer members in hopes of slowing the flow of immigrants.[28] The poorer member states could strategically use migration to increase fiscal transfers, as suggested by the Greek defense minister, Panos Kamenos, who threatened to "unleash a wave of millions of economic migrants" unless the creditor nations backed down on the terms of austerity they wanted.[29]

The increased power of anti-immigration forces may also have made the European Union's procedures stronger. To come to an agreement over the resettlement of Syrian refugees, Germany and other powerful members forced through an agreement without consensus, unlike what is usually done on this type of issue. With many divergent preferences on key issues, the European Union may need to use majority rule more often to overcome differences that threaten the Union. Thus this procedural change may set something of a precedent that could lead to a more effective European Union.

Nonetheless, migration within the European Union may be more destabilizing than stabilizing for the Union. This can be seen most clearly in Brexit, the United Kingdom's referendum to leave the EU. Brexit was largely the result of the rise of the anti-immigration UK Independence Party (UKIP): UKIP advocates not only for less immigration from countries outside of the European Union but also for less immigration from

---

[27] Bernhard and Leblang (2014)

[28] Similarly, one reason for extending trade and capital mobility to new member states before extending migrant rights was to help these states develop before they could send migrants, in hopes of reducing the incentives to migrate.

[29] Waterfield (2015). As yet, Greece has not made good on this threat.

within it. UKIP's success led to the renegotiation of Britain's role in the EU and, then, a referendum on membership. While few commentators believed that voters in the United Kingdom would support leaving the EU, the Leave campaign won the day, largely on anti-immigrant sentiment. In this case, the decline of business support for open immigration likely created the conditions for the Brexit vote. The Tory (conservative) Party, usually the party of business, was threatened on the right by UKIP and split on whether to leave or remain in the EU. With greater business support for immigration, the Tories might never have moved so far right on immigration, for fear of damaging their relations with a key constituency, and might not have held the referendum.

As business support for open low-skill immigration shrinks further, far-right parties will gain more legitimacy on the issue of immigration, making intra-EU migration seem like more of a threat. In combination with increased migratory pressure from outside the European Union, the demand to control borders may make the temporary controls put in place during the refugee crisis in 2015 within the Schengen Zone, in which there had been no internal passport control, permanent. What would be more harmful is if this demand to stop intra-EU migration leads (more) states to exit the European Union.[30]

The Size of States

My argument also speaks to the question of what is the "right" size of a state or federation of states. States, or federations of states, need to be large enough to defend themselves against aggressors but not so large as to be ungovernable. The "right" size of states has changed over time. Historically, there have been periods when political organizations ranging from city-states to large empires have existed side by side. Although there are few, if any, empires today, there are still a few surviving city-states—for example, Singapore and Luxembourg. Nonetheless, since the Middle Ages, European states have tended to increase in size, becoming what Tilly calls "national states."[31] This model of a state was then transported to the rest of the world.

The size of the national state was a product of its time. States in Europe needed large populations to fund the state, serve in the army, and produce the goods needed to defend it.[32] Global supply chains and productivity

---

[30] As this book went to press, the United Kingdom had not yet invoked Article 50 to begin the process of exiting the EU and there has been some uncertainty as to whether it will indeed do so.

[31] Tilly (1992).

[32] Tilly (1992, 58).

gains in both industry and warfare have decreased the need for states to have large populations, at least for developed states. In addition to transforming most developed states' economies from industrial to service economies, productivity gains and technology in warfare have made mass armies unnecessary.[33] Now, having a poor periphery may be a liability instead of a necessity for developed countries.

Singapore may be an example of future states. As chapter 6 described, the Singaporean government has sought productivity gains in industry to decrease the need for labor. When productivity gains have been impossible to achieve, it has pushed companies to offshore production to Indonesia, Malaysia, and now China, allowing Singapore to produce a large number of goods and services with relatively few people. Singapore does not need a large population for defense, either. The Singaporean government has invested in technology—ships, airplanes, and the like—and human capital through training that makes its military more effective than larger forces.[34]

Catalonia's demand for independence may be a sign of the changing size required to be an effective state. Catalonia was its own state before it was brought into the Spanish Empire in the late Middle Ages. At that time, Catalonia was bound to become part of a larger state, as it was likely too small to survive the advances in warfare on its own. Today, Catalonia no longer needs the rest of Spain for survival: it can import the food and goods that it does not produce; it can create wealth through capital- and skill-intensive industries, which do not require a large labor force; and, if need be, it could create a military like Singapore's, which relies on technology and training to beat larger opponents.

The dynamics that led to reduced support for low-skill immigration may also have led to the end of empire. Colonial empires benefited the metropole by allowing them to ensure access to important commodities, providing a larger labor force, and, in some cases, to project power over long distances. Nonetheless, maintaining colonial empires was costly, necessitating manpower and treasure that could be spent at home. The benefits of empire have declined over time with advances in technology, the ability to trade, and the ability to move firms.[35] As noted, the armed forces of major powers are much more efficient than they once were in terms of manpower, and these states no longer need colonies to project power; aircraft carriers, intercontinental ballistic missiles, and long-range aircraft

---

[33] Onorato, Scheve, and Stasavage (2014). Even China recently announced that it was cutting the size of its army as it no longer needed as large a fighting force.

[34] Israel is the example par excellence of this type of armed forces with its small military that relies on training and technology to beat much larger opponents.

[35] Colgan (2014).

provide much of the power projection needed. The ease of trade means that no one country controls trade in any given commodity.[36] Finally, laborsaving technology and firm mobility have meant that developed powers no longer need as large a labor force under their control in order to produce and consume the goods they need.

Together, then, the ability to trade and to move low-skill-labor-intensive production overseas, and technology adoption may have shrunk the size of states—in terms of people and territory—that can survive in the world system. With the greater ability of small states to survive, the disagreements within countries that once seemed small may loom larger. For some countries, and especially those in a relatively benign security environment such as Belgium, Canada, or Spain, these dynamics may lead to the breakup of what were once thought to be stable states. Even countries like China that have built their power in part on being large states may find that the cost of keeping restive provinces, like Xinjiang, now outweighs the benefits they receive from them.

Democratization and the Quality of Democracy

This book speaks to the debate on democratization and on the quality of democracy as well. Scholars such as Acemoglu and Robinson have focused on the amount of redistribution that would occur under democracy as an important factor in whether states democratize.[37] Increased restrictions on low-skill immigration mean that there will be fewer low-skill people to redistribute to. These restrictions may make democratization in the developed autocracies easier.[38] On the other hand, the increased restrictions decrease emigration, leading to greater populations in less developed autocracies and making democratization less likely in these states.[39]

For debates on the quality of democracy, this book may be more hopeful. Corporate interests do not always lead to policy changes; when the public cares enough about an issue, the policymaker cannot grant corporations the policy they want without jeopardizing her position. Thus although the powerful interest groups usually win, this book shows that on issues that are of great importance to the population, powerful interests can be appeased through other means.

---

[36] It looked as if the Chinese were going to gain control over rare earth minerals, but their projected monopoly created the incentive for other countries to continue to mine these minerals.

[37] Acemoglu and Robinson (2006).

[38] Bearce and Hutnick (2011).

[39] See Miller and Peters (2014) for more on how emigration may lead to democratization.

Immigration Externalities and Foreign Intervention

Failed and weak states create many externalities for the developed world. One of the clearest externalities is the large flows of refugees that emerge from these areas. Two of the recent refugee crises—the wave of Central American children entering the United States and the Syrian refugee crisis—have been a product of failed and weak states that cannot control the security environment in their countries.

In both these cases, refugees flows have been caused by states' failures to protect their citizens from gross human rights violations, including, in the case of some Syrian and Iraqi ethnic minorities, ethnic cleansing and genocide. These human rights violations should invoke the norm of *Responsibility to Protect (R2P)*. R2P grew out of the Rwandan genocide and the Srebrenica massacre in the mid-1990s. Proponents of R2P argue that the international community has the obligation to intervene when gross violations of human rights occur, even if that intervention violates sovereignty. R2P has become United Nations policy and was used as a reason for military intervention in Libya in 2011.

Yet for all the rhetoric around R2P, most proponents do not suggest the most effective, most cost-efficient solution to protect civilians: resettling refugees from these countries. Instead, most proponents suggest diplomatic pressure, economic sanctions, or military intervention to protect civilians and end conflicts. Diplomacy may be relatively cheap but is usually ineffective on its own. To be effective, economic sanctions need the cooperation of many states and nonstate actors over long periods of time.[40] While peacekeeping may be effective, military intervention prior to the creation of peace, when most of the gross human rights violations happen, is less effective.[41] Furthermore, rebuilding of states after war, especially failed states, is unlikely to produce functioning states that are able to protect their citizens' human rights.[42] For example, Libya, where the international community intervened under the rationale of R2P in the middle of the fighting, is now a failed state, and Iraq, where the United States spent hundreds of billions of dollars and eight years trying to create a democracy, quickly fell back into civil war once US troops left.

In contrast, resettling refugees is much less expensive and much more effective at keeping people out of harm's way, especially over the long term. Like economic immigration, refugee resettlement would, for the most part, shift people out of labor-abundant countries to labor-scarce countries, increasing their incomes while creating an economic surplus that

---

[40] Drezner (1999).
[41] Doyle and Sambanis (2006).
[42] Lake and Fariss (2014).

could be used to pay for their social and welfare costs. Refugee resettlement would provide protection for those who need it while, unlike military intervention, not creating failed states.[43]

Why isn't refugee resettlement on the R2P agenda? As this book shows, the constituency for more open immigration does not exist in most wealthy countries. Firms have been the supporters not only of economic immigration but also of refugee resettlement as a way to increase immigration; employers do not·care why an immigrant was allowed to enter the country, just that she did. As discussed in chapter 1, the American Farm Bureau and other employers groups lobbied for the Displaced Persons Act in the United States in 1948 in order to increase the number of immigrants entering the country at a time when the immigration policy was relatively restrictive. Since firms do not need as many low-skill workers and since most refugees are relatively low-skill (in comparison to workers in the developed world, not necessarily in comparison to those left behind), there has been less support for refugee policies than there might otherwise have been.

The recent refugee crises, especially the Syrian refugee crisis, may also make states rethink their support for dictators and military interventions in civil conflicts. The civil war in Syria was not a sudden conflagration; protests against the Assad regime began in March 2011, but the conflict did not turn into a civil war until sometime in the summer of 2011 after members of the Syrian military defected, creating the Free Syrian Army. It is possible that intervention either on the side for or against the Assad regime might have resulted in a more peaceful resolution, as the protests in Egypt did. However, the international community was divided, with the Russians, Iranians, and Chinese supporting al-Assad and the West opposing his regime. Perhaps if Russia, Iran, and China had pushed al-Assad to step down or if the West had turned a blind eye to his repression (as they have to the el-Sisi regime in Egypt), the war could have been prevented. Gaining international cooperation to punish a dictator is more difficult than turning a blind eye; in the future, the West may be more willing to turn a blind eye or even support dictators if they think doing so will prevent refugee flows.

In contrast, anti-immigration sentiment may make intervention in failed states more likely. When there is no central authority, however repugnant, to keep order, developed states may choose to intervene in hopes of creating a stable environment. Thus the threat of a new refugee crisis in an environment where anti-immigrant forces have greater influence over

---

[43] It is possible that refugee resettlement may cause a moral hazard problem, in which dictators push out refugees to get rid of opposition instead of addressing the concerns of that opposition. However, dictators are unlikely to address these concerns and instead are likely to intimidate, jail, or kill opposition members regardless of other states' refugee policies.

policy may lead to the entrenchment of powerful dictators who can keep order, and to costly intervention in failed states rather than the resettlement of refugees.

CONCLUSION: THE IMPORTANCE OF OPEN BORDERS

Too often when discussing immigration policy, scholars and policymakers alike treat it like a domestic policy, affected only by domestic politics and affecting only those within the country. As I have shown in this book, immigration policy is not solely domestic; it is part of foreign economic policy and is affected by the other elements of foreign policy, including trade and capital policy. Importantly, we should also remember that immigration policy does not primarily affect those within wealthy countries. Immigrants make up a relatively small minority of most countries, and their effect on societies is usually positive. Immigration leads to increased economic growth, innovation, and increased opportunities for even the lowest-skill native. Even the cultural changes they make to the host societies are usually positive; where would American cuisine be without pizza and tacos; British cuisine without curry; or German cuisine without kebabs?

While immigration has meant stronger economic growth (and better food) for citizens of wealthy countries, it has been the most effective antipoverty tool for citizens of poor countries. Migration has given millions a chance to flee crushing poverty, famine, political violence, and war. Migrants, in return, have often made their home countries stronger, sending back remittances; increasing trade networks,[44] investment,[45] and foreign aid;[46] and spreading democratic norms.[47] Migration is the most effective development tool,[48] and it is not even on the development agenda.

This book helps explain why greater migration is not on the development agenda by focusing on the shrinking business-based pro-immigration coalition. Advocates for more open borders need to forge a new coalition, based on mass political support rather than narrow economic interests. Right now, anti-immigration forces have won popular support against low-skill immigration by appealing to the mass public's fears: fear of economic insecurity, fear of increased tax burdens, fear of crime, and, perhaps most important, fear of change. The pro-immigration camp has shot back with

---

[44] Gould (1994).
[45] Leblang (2010)
[46] Bermeo and Leblang (2015).
[47] Miller and Peters (2014).
[48] Clemens (2009).

facts and figures focused on the economic benefits of immigration for natives.

Yet this rational, material-based approach is unlikely to win the hearts of the citizens of the wealthy nations of the world even if it does appeal to their minds. Instead, the pro-immigration camp should take a page from the civil rights, women's rights, and LGBTQ rights campaigns. While discrimination against African Americans, women, and the LGBTQ community are all a drain on the economy, greater rights and changes in norms were not granted on economic appeals; the right of homosexuals to marry may be a boon to the wedding industry, but Justice Kennedy did not vote to legalize gay marriage to increase economic growth. Instead, these groups appealed to notions of fairness and human rights. Instead of tilting at windmills—promoting the economic benefits of immigration— advocates for open borders need to make the case that migration is the fair solution to a world in which where you are born determines so much of your success in life.

APPENDIX A

Collection and Coding of the Immigration Policy Variable

ONE OF THE MAJOR OBSTACLES TO RESEARCH on immigration has been the lack of longitudinal cross-national data. In response to this lacuna, this book creates a new dataset on the de jure immigration policy of nineteen countries over the last 225 years. This appendix describes how the dataset was compiled.

I define "immigration policy," as the laws that policymakers pass to regulate the number of low-skill immigrants entering (and potentially leaving) the country in a given year. Of course, there are many factors outside policymakers' control that will affect these numbers. The policy measure, then, captures their intent: do they want to encourage, or at least not discourage, more low-skill immigration, or do they want to discourage low-skill immigration.

We want a low-skill immigration policy variable that is comparable across both time and countries, so I focus on what immigration policy targeting low-skill immigrants means to policymakers. Who counts as high- or low-skill has changed over time: in the late twentieth and early twenty-first centuries, those with a high school education or less can be classified as low-skill. But in the late nineteenth century, there was even less educational attainment, and those with several years of school or an apprenticeship were considered high-skill. I define low-skill immigrants as those who have few formal skills: for example, skills attained through schooling or previous technical training. By "low-skill immigration," I identify policies that either specifically target low-skill immigrants, such as agricultural workers programs, or that target all immigrant groups and do not exclude low-skill immigrants.

I assume that the policymakers are sincere when they craft laws. As chapter 2 notes, scholars have argued that firms want a more restrictive policy coupled with lax enforcement so that they can exploit undocumented immigrant workers. I include measures of de jure enforcement to ensure that a de jure restrictive policy is de facto restrictive as well. In an ideal world, we would have a de facto measure of enforcement because even strict enforcement laws often have an element of prosecutorial discretion. Unfortunately, because the thing we would like to measure—undocumented immigration—is an illegal activity, we do not have good cross-country estimates of it.

CASE SELECTION

There are two overlapping universes of cases to which the theory could apply. First, the theory applies to relatively (low-skill) labor-scarce states. These are states that have relatively high wages in comparison to the rest of the world or in comparison to their major trading partners. Second, we want to ensure that the countries studied are countries that migrants want to move to. If migrants are not interested in moving to the state, the state can set any immigration policy because migrants would not move there regardless of the policy. Previous research on migration suggests that migrants choose locations where wages are high relative to the transaction costs of moving.[1]

This criterion was operationalized as states with GDP per capita above 200 percent of the world average GDP per capita, or above 200 percent of the average GDP per capita for the geographic region in which the state is located, for at least ten years. GDP data were taken from both Maddison's dataset and the World Bank's World Development Indicators.[2] The absolute criterion captures states that are attractive to immigrants from all countries, whereas the regional criterion captures states that are attractive to immigrants because of relatively high wages combined with proximity. These two criteria lead to the inclusion of seventy-seven states (or state-like entities) over at least some part of the period between 1800 and 2008.

Collecting data on immigration policies is a time-intensive endeavor, and so from this universe of cases a subset of nineteen was chosen. I chose states to ensure that there would be variation in the explanatory variables for both my argument as well as arguments from the literature in both the cross-section and within countries over time. Table A1 lists the states included in the dataset along with the years of coverage for each state.

Every state was coded through 2010, but they vary by when they enter the dataset. In the cases of Australia, New Zealand, South Africa, and Hong Kong, immigration policy was coded from the date that the colony began and obtained responsible government through a governor-general. Canada obtained a level of control over its immigration policy after the thirteen American colonies revolted. Singapore and Kuwait were granted the same level of control over their immigration policy only when the first legislature was elected, in the case of Singapore, and when independence was attained, in the case of Kuwait. Similarly, Argentina, Brazil, South Korea, Taiwan, and the United States did not gain control of immigration until they

---

[1] See Massey et al. (1993) for a review.
[2] Maddison (2011) and World Bank (2014).

TABLE A1
Countries Included in the Dataset and the Dates of Inclusion.

Region	Country
Settler states/ New World	US (1790–2010) Australia (1787–2010) Canada (1783–2010) New Zealand (1840–2010) South Africa (1806–2010) Argentina (1810–2010) Brazil (1808–2010)
Europe	UK (1792–2010) France (1793–2010) Germany (1871–2010) Netherlands (1815–2010) Switzerland (1848–2010)
East Asia	Japan (1868–2010) Hong Kong (1843–2010) Singapore (1955–2010) South Korea (1948–2010) Taiwan (1949–2010)
Persian Gulf	Saudi Arabia (1950–2010) Kuwait (1961–2010)

Originally published in Peters (2015) and reprinted with permission.

gained independence.[3] Germany, the Netherlands, and Switzerland are coded from when the modern state came into existence; for the years 1945–90, the policy coded for Germany is that of West Germany. The United Kingdom, France, and Japan are coded from the year they passed their first modern immigration policy. Finally, Saudi Arabia is coded from 1950 for two reasons: GDP data do not exist prior to 1950, and major oil production did not begin until after World War II, making it likely that Saudi Arabia was not wealthy enough until about 1950 to attract immigrants.

As noted, there were states that could have been included but were not. For example, most other indexes include many more European states. Owing to limited resources, I chose not to code additional European states to focus attention on non-European states, especially including more autocracies, to increase the external validity of the study.

---

[3] In the case of the United States, immigration policy is not coded until 1790, when the federal government was granted sole responsibility for immigration policy.

The exclusion of additional European states may bias this study's results if there are values of explanatory variables that would affect both the key independent variables—trade policy, firm mobility, and technology adoption—and the dependent variable, immigration policy. One set of states that are often included in the literature are the Nordic countries. The Nordic countries are often thought to be "kinder" to immigrants than other states in Western Europe because of their communitarian values. These values likely affect the size of their welfare state—they tend to have more generous welfare states than even other states in Western Europe—but this does not seem to affect their openness to trade or their willingness to allow firms to move. Nonetheless, the exclusion of these states might bias the results on the welfare state. Another set of European states that are often included are the new states of immigration—states like Portugal, Spain, Italy, Greece, and to some extent Ireland—that were once major senders of emigrants and are now receivers of immigrants. It is unlikely that being a new state of immigration affects both immigration policy and policies that affect trade, firm mobility, and technology adoption. Nonetheless, if this is an important characteristic, South Korea and Taiwan are both new states of immigration that, like Portugal, Spain, and Greece, became states of immigration after transitioning to democracy.

As part of the case selection, I wanted to ensure that I had states in the Global South—Argentina, Brazil, South Africa, and to some extent South Korea, Singapore, and Taiwan—to examine whether the process of immigration policymaking is different there. These states are still the relatively wealthy states of the region. There are also large flows of immigrants between developing states that do not reach the 200 percent GDP per capita threshold, for example flows from Nepal to India. The argument of this book may apply to these states as well; however, I cannot test whether it extends to poorer immigrant-receiving states with this dataset.

A final coding decision to make about case selection was how to handle federal states. All federal states are coded according to the policy of the most open member of the state until the time when the federal government takes sole responsibility for immigration policy, at which point the federal policy is coded. This coding scheme is used because most federal states allow the free movement of people among the members of the federation. Therefore, an immigrant who can come to one of the members can then have access to all the members of the federation. Because of this coding, only US federal, and not state, immigration policy is coded. Prior to the 1849 *Passenger Cases* decision of the Supreme Court, many states enacted their own immigration policies. However, not all states enacted them, so immigration was relatively unrestricted through at least some ports of entry into the United States. The policies that states did enact—provisions against criminals and those likely to become public charges—were similar to the 1875 Federal Immigration Act.[4] If we coded the United States using these state policies, the US immigration policy would be restricted to the level it was in 1875, regardless of the lack of action at the federal level beginning in 1789 until 1875. The results of this study, however, do not change with this coding. Switzerland is not included in the dataset prior to 1848 because citizens of the different cantons did not have the right to live in another canton. Therefore, for natives and immigrants alike each canton was like a separate country. Among EU members, the immigration policies of the most liberal country are not coded because these countries' freedom-of-movement policies do not extend to third-country nationals. When EU policy does affect some or all of the nations, the EU policy is coded as the policy for each nation it affects.

FINDING DATA ON IMMIGRATION POLICY

Search Procedure

I relied on both primary and secondary sources to find data on immigration policy. With the help of undergraduate research assistants, I used a snowball search approach to find sources on immigration policy. I began my search by entering the term "immigration policy" and the country name into both Google Scholar and WorldCat. For countries like the United States or Canada, this procedure led to hundreds of thousands of articles and books. I prioritized the search using the relevance data given by Google and WorldCat: that is, I examined the first entries first. For all articles, I quickly examined their abstracts and excluded all articles that were clearly on public opinion about immigration or about immigrant characteristics rather than immigration policy. Once a source was found, it was read by my research assistants or me, and the relevant data were entered into the database (details follow). After examining each source, we then examined the sources that it listed.

As a next step, we searched the websites of the relevant agencies in charge of immigration to see if they listed information on the immigration laws. We examined all documents that we could find on their websites about immigration policy. Most of these documents were about recent (post-2000) law changes, but occasionally these agencies had documents that discussed the history of immigration policy in the country as well.

We found that this search procedure easily provided data on countries that are often studied in the immigration literature, such as the United States or France, and periods that are often studied, such as immigration

[4] Neuman (1993).

to Argentina, Brazil, and South Africa during the nineteenth century, but it did not turn up as much information on lesser-studied countries like Taiwan, or lesser-studied periods, such as those of Argentina, Brazil, and South Africa post–World War II. To obtain data on these states and eras, we used broader search criteria, including the search terms "immigrant," "migration," "foreigners," and "foreign-born," as well as including search terms on the time period. We also searched Google in addition to Google Scholar and WorldCat to find news articles as well.

We found that for some countries, some areas of immigration policy, such as skill criteria or regulations based on nationality, were discussed more often than others, such as citizenship policy or refugee and asylum policy. For issue areas where we had found little information, we would add issue-area-specific search criteria, such as "refugee" and the country name.

The collection of data was complete for each country once we had coverage of the whole time period, coverage of all dimensions of the immigration policy (details follow), and discussion of major laws by multiple (at least three but often five or more) sources. If we later found information about that country's immigration laws from a source about another country, that information was also included.

In total over five hundred sources were examined with, on average, sixty-one sources per country. Online appendix B lists the sources for each country. Most of the sources examined were in English; my research assistants also examined sources in Spanish, French, and German and provided translations.

For the majority of laws, we found at least two discussions of each law; on average we found discussions of the law in four sources (the median number of sources was two). For the major changes in the law in highly studied countries, we frequently had over ten different discussions of the law. We had information on a law from only one source in fewer than half the cases; usually these were more minor changes in the law. I erred on the side of inclusiveness and incorporated these law changes as well because I was concerned about the bias against minor laws.

Potential Sources of Bias

The use of both primary and secondary source documents might introduce bias into the dataset. As scholars like Thies note, "facts" from both primary and secondary sources are biased.[5] Primary documents are not written by unbiased government officials or reporters, but instead reflect their agendas. Historians and other scholars have implicit or explicit theoretical

---

[5] Thies (2002).

approaches that affect what sources they use and what they report. Even though I used these sources to get basic information about immigration policy, such as the year of passage, the contents of the law, and the body passing the law, the use of primary and secondary sources may have introduced bias into the data.

The primary sources used to construct the dataset consist of both government documents and newspaper articles. Government documents are rarely propaganda free; they tend to highlight aspects of law changes that are likely to play well with the public in general, or with important constituencies for the party or regime in power, and downplay those aspects of the law that would be less popular. From public opinion data, we know that most of the time the public is against open immigration. We might expect that governments will be more likely to tout their ability to control migration so that only the "most desirable" immigrants enter the state. Most government documents and statements about immigration are likely, therefore, to be biased in the restrictionist direction. Press accounts at the time of these laws' passage are likely to report the government's restrictionist bias as well. Since historians also use these primary sources to construct their work, they too likely have a restrictionist bias.

This bias, then, can be thought of as an intercept shift in the data. The real immigration policy is probably more open than it is reported to be, although it's unclear how much more open. This bias would be problematic if the argument of this book or those in the literature were about absolute levels of immigration policy. Instead, because we are interested in how changes in the explanatory variables lead to changes to immigration policy, the existence of an intercept shift is not a problem. In fact, because most of the analysis relies on within-country changes in immigration policy, rather than changes across countries, the different intercept shifts by country will not affect the results (instead, these will be reflected in the fixed effects). However, scholars who are interested in using these data to examine changes across countries should be aware that this bias might exist.

Another source of bias comes from the use of secondary sources. Historians and scholars in other fields whose work we use may be biased. Most important, these scholars present the facts based on some implicit or explicit theory. The selective presentation of facts by scholars is mitigated through the use of multiple sources from different traditions and fields. Because we usually rely upon multiple sources for each policy change, we are likely to get a more complete picture of what was contained in the law.

Finally, even when multiple sources are used, there is likely to be a selection effect in which changes in law get reported. Small changes in immigration policy are less likely to be reported in newspapers or government reports and therefore are less likely to appear in secondary sources as well. It is likely, then, that the dataset more accurately codes major changes in immigration policy and misses more minor changes. It is unclear, a priori, how the limited reporting of these small changes might affect the resulting coding. Nonetheless, the lack of reporting for smaller changes in immigration policy will introduce bias into the results only if this lack of reporting is also correlated with one of the explanatory variables. It is unlikely that this is the case.

DATA COLLECTED AND ENTERED INTO MASTER DATASET

Several undergraduate research assistants and I collected the data. For each source, we marked references to any laws on immigration. This included laws on the number of immigrants allowed in a country, the type of immigrants allowed in or excluded, and the recruitment of immigrants; citizenship laws; laws on the rights immigrants have to own land, gain employment, have their own schools/teach children in their own language, have their own ministers paid for by the state, have access to the welfare state, and the like; laws on asylum seekers and refugees; laws on deportation and on other types of enforcement actions such as border patrols, fences, carrier sanctions, amnesties, and so forth. Details of administrative action in democracies—rather than laws passed through a legislature—were not included, as they are not consistently reported. My research assistants and I collected data on both low-skill and high-skill immigration policies, but only policies for low-skill immigrants have been coded for this dataset.

We then entered the data into the master dataset. We erred on the side of inclusiveness: even if a source did not list all the data we wanted on a law, we entered the information that it did include. These entries served as a check for sources with more detail. We also copied and scanned all the pages that were marked from each source to keep a record. Each country had its own sheet within the master dataset.

Fields and Entry Protocol for Master Dataset

Year What year did the law change take place? If exact year is noted, enter that year. If a range was given (e.g., the 1930s or 1850–60), enter the earliest year of the range and enter the range given in the *year range* field.

Year Range If the source did not give an exact year for the change in law, but did give a range, enter the range. The purpose of the year range field is to capture the approximate date of a law change. Often other sources we consulted through our snowball search listed the exact date. When we were still missing the exact date, we used the year range and any other data about law change to search for more information about it using Google.

Number of Bill Occasionally, the source would mention the number of the bill as it was introduced in the legislature (e.g., HR2020), the statute of the bill (e.g., 1 stat 1950), or a common name for the bill (McCarren-Walter or Asian Exclusion Act); enter this name or number.

Details of the Legislation Enter any details about the legislation that the source mentioned. In some cases, this consisted of only a sentence or two, and in other cases this consisted of several pages of text.

Body Passing Law This field relates to federal states and to colonies that eventually became one state (i.e., the colonies that became Australia and Canada). Enter if the law was passed by the federal legislature or by state legislatures.

Quota Numbers If the bill enacts a quota, how many immigrants are allowed in?

Source Author name (year) of source of the data.

Page Number Page on which the data were found.

CODING SCHEME

Policymakers have used many different tools to control immigration. These tools can be used separately or in combination to allow the policymaker to design her preferred policy. Policymakers have used three broad categories of policies to regulate the number of immigrants that they want: border regulations, immigrant rights, and enforcement. Border regulations determine who gains entry to the country; immigrant rights affect the demand to immigrate to one country versus another (or to migrate at all); and enforcement ensures that a restrictive immigration policy is not a de facto open policy. To create a valid measure, then, we need to account for these different tools.

As a first attempt at coding the data, my research assistants tried using the coding scheme developed by Timmer and Williamson.[6] Their coding scheme is a −5 to 5 coding based on many different aspects of immigration policy, including entry regulations, citizenship, rights, and enforcement. For example, a 5 on their scheme is "Active worker recruitment abroad with advertising and labor offices, free land or subsidized land purchase, subsidized or assisted passage, temporary lodging, free transport inland

[6] Timmer and Williamson (1996, xiv).

from port of arrival, easy naturalization, legal property ownership."[7] A −5 on their scheme is "Closed (or only slightly ajar) doors, enforced."[8] My research assistants and I found that replicating this coding scheme was nearly impossible because too many different aspects of immigration policy were coded together.

Instead, I developed a coding scheme based on twelve different categories that put laws based on similar criteria together (see below). The twelve categories were chosen after we examined many, but not all, sources in the dataset. This is not the only way to disaggregate these policies; for example, the rights category could be broken down into more categories, as could the other enforcement category. Restrictions based on nationality could be disaggregated into country-based restrictions passed domestically and those created by a treaty, and so on.

For each country, I took the data collected in the master dataset and entered them into a new dataset. Each country dataset had the following fields: the year and, for each of the twelve dimensions, both a field for the law and one for coding the law. (A more detailed explanation of the dimensions and their coding is listed below.) Each country dataset included observations for all the years that were included in the dataset. For years in which there were no laws passed, "No change" was entered into the *law* field, and the code from the year before was entered into the *code* field.

I created a draft of the coding scheme and had my research assistants use it to code a subset of the data. I used their feedback to revise the coding scheme in an iterative process. Once the final scheme was created, I coded all the data and had a second coder code eight of the countries as a check on my coding. Our codings correlated at 0.9.

Based on the detailed explanation of the law, I categorized each law change. Some law changes affected only one dimension. For example, in 1902 the US Congress passed a law that extended the Chinese Exclusion Act until a new treaty with China could be negotiated. Since that act affected the universality by only nationality, it was coded for that category only. When other changes affected several categories, the information for each category was entered. For example, the 1952 McCarren-Walter Act in the United States changed the quota formula for different nationalities (universality by nationality); changed the skill criteria (universality by skill); affected the rights of immigrants (other rights); allowed those who were convicted of a purely political crime to gain asylum (asylum); repealed the Contract Labor Law (recruitment); afforded greater procedural safeguards to aliens subject to deportation (deportation); created the attorney general's parole authority (other enforcement); and changed the quota (quota).

---

[7] Timmer and Williamson (1996, xiv).
[8] Timmer and Williamson (1996, xiv).

Each dimension was coded from 1 to 5, with greater restrictions taking lower values and more openness taking greater value. Theoretically, immigration policy has no bounds; states could always pay people more money to come to their country; for example, in the 1960s, South Africa not only paid the cost of passage for European workers, but also established them with bonuses and other monetary goods. At the other end of the spectrum, states could also denaturalize part of their population and force them to leave, as the Germans did to the Jews under the Nazi regime or the South Africans did to Africans under apartheid. These examples, however, are very rare. Most states fall in between these two extremes. The changes in coding could range in size from 0.1 for minor changes to 4 for major changes, although states rarely changed law that much.

For family reunification, refugee, and asylum laws a third variable was coded, *provisions*, as a 0 for all years before the state had laws that specifically targeted these groups, and as a 1 once a law that affected these groups was put into place. Prior to the twentieth century, few states had any laws on family migration, refugees, and asylum seekers. Immigrants in these categories, however, could easily enter the state because there were few restrictions on migration. Once states restricted immigration in the interwar period, these laws began to emerge. Prior to this point, it is an open question whether we should code states' policies as restrictive because they had no special provisions for these groups, or as open because these groups could enter the state. This variable allows us to code the overall immigration policy variable both ways and see how it affects the results.

DIMENSIONS AND THEIR CODING

Here I list all twelve dimensions in more detail. I list the questions that led a law or part of a law to be coded in each dimension. If any of those questions were answered "yes," the law (or section of the law) was coded in that category. If all questions were answered "no," the law was not coded in that category.

Nationality Restrictions

One frequently used method of control has been regulations based on nationality. Such regulations tend to take one of two forms: prohibitions based on nationality or special access based on nationality. With prohibitions, states often grant entry to immigrants from all states except those prohibited; with special access, states often prohibit or limit entry of immigrants from all states except those granted special access. Examples of prohibitions based on nationality include the Chinese Exclusion Act in the

United States and laws against Polish immigration in Germany in the late nineteenth century. Examples of special access include the free migration areas (FMAs) in which migrants from within the area are granted free or preferred access, whereas those from outside the area are restricted.

Regardless of whether the laws take the form of prohibitions or of special access, nationality-based laws are often used to restrict immigration from countries that send many low-skill migrants and grant access to states that send higher-skill migrants. For example, the 1921 and 1924 Quota Acts in the United States explicitly restricted immigration from Southern and Eastern Europe as well as from Asia, while allowing greater access to immigrants from Northern and Western Europe. At the time, immigrants from Southern and Eastern Europe and Asia tended to have lower levels of education than those from Northern and Western Europe.

Where special access ends and prohibition begins can be hard to gauge; therefore, these criteria are operationalized through the examination of how many nationalities can enter a state. If only a few or no nationalities are restricted, the state is relatively open on this measure; if many or most nationalities are restricted, the state is relatively closed on this measure. By coding how many nationalities are restricted, we can account for any "migration diversion" that might occur when states sign a bilateral labor migration treaty (BLMT) or join a free migration area (FMA). Similar to free trade areas, BLMTs and FMAs can lead to "migration diversion" when states open their borders to migrants from within the FMA while restricting migration from outside the FMA. For example, as most EU members have opened their borders to migrants from within the EU, they have restricted access from outside of the EU. For this study, what matters is the overall openness to low-skill immigration; thus joining an FMA or signing a BLMT leads to greater openness only if it does not lead to migration diversion.

When the main part of a state's immigration policy does not discriminate based on national origin, but the state enacts a special category that allows in additional immigration from one or more states, this law is coded as a skill restriction based on the average skill level of the immigrants. For example, New Zealand today does not discriminate in the major part of its immigration law, but it does offer special visas for citizens of the Pacific Islands, who are generally low-skill. I could have coded the law as discriminatory against all other nationalities. However, in cases like these, I chose to code these programs as skill-based programs for two reasons. First, these are typically relatively small in scope and do not affect the majority of those who can enter the state. Second, coding these programs as nationality restrictions would lead us to code the policy as more restrictive. Given that most of these programs have been enacted in more recent years when trade is relatively open and firms can easily move, coding these policies as nationality restrictions would lead to bias in favor of my hypotheses.

CODING CRITERIA FOR THE NATIONALITY CATEGORY

Does the law pertain to specific nationalities? Are exclusions based on national origin? Did the state sign a bilateral labor migration treaty or another international agreement on immigration?

1 Only descendants of natives allowed in.
2 A few nationalities allowed entrance but not many. Example: if a European country allowed immigrants from other EU countries only.
3 Many nationalities allowed in but not all, or migrants from some regions excluded. Example: Between 1921 and 1924, the US quota system allowed in many Northern Europeans, some Southern and Eastern Europeans, anyone from the Western Hemisphere, and no one from Asia.
4 Almost all nationalities allowed in. Example: In the late nineteenth century, only Chinese were excluded from the United States.
5 No exclusions based on nationality.

EXAMPLE OF CODING FOR THE NATIONALITY CATEGORY

Table A2 shows examples of how nationality restrictions were coded for the United States. The table lists the nationality component of the major changes in US law but does not include all the changes in immigration policy. In 1790, when the federal government officially took responsibility for immigration policy, it did little to regulate immigration (although there were state regulations that affected immigrants through some ports of entry). It was not until 1870 that Congress passed its first regulation on immigration based on nationality, which restricted the entry of women from China unless it could be shown that they were voluntary migrants. Because this regulation affected only women from one nationality and did not completely restrict the flow, the nationality category was coded as a 4.5. In 1882, when Congress passed the Chinese Exclusion Act, the nationality coding drops to a 4. Additional restrictions on Chinese immigration and further prohibitions on Asian immigrants during the late nineteenth and early twentieth centuries lead to a decrease in the nationality score to 3.5. The 1921 Quota Act is scored as a 3; it prohibited all Asian and African immigrants from entering and greatly restricted immigration from Southern and Eastern Europe. When the 1924 Quota Act increased the 1921 quota's restrictiveness, the nationality coding falls to 2.75. With the 1952 McCarren-Walter Act, Congress allowed Asian immigrants to enter the United States again and reduced the quota's restrictions for Europeans, raising the score back to 3.5. Finally, in 1965 when the country got rid of the discriminatory quotas and enacted equal quotas, the score returns to a 5.

TABLE A2
Examples of Coding of US Nationality and Skill Restrictions.

	Nationality		Skill	
Year	Restrictions	Coding	Restrictions	Coding
1790	No restrictions	5	No restrictions	5
1819	No change	5	Safety restrictions on boats increase cost of passage	4.85
1862	No change	5	Ban on indentured labor	4.5
1870	Restrictions on the entry of Chinese women	4.5	No change	4.5
1875	No change	4.5	Creation of excludable classes	4.25
1882	Chinese Exclusion Act	4	Additional excludable classes, including those likely to become a public charge	4
1917	No change	3.5	Literacy Act	2.75
1921	First national origins quota based on the 1910 census	3	Preference system based on skill; repeal of Literacy Act	3.5
1924	Second national origins quota based on the 1890 census	2.75	Preference system based on skill	3.5
1952	McCarren-Walter Act: national origin quota based on 1920 census; 100-person quota allocated to Asian countries	3.5	Revision of preference system to put greater emphasis on skill	3.4
1965	Abolishment of discriminatory quotas; all states from Eastern Hemisphere given the same cap	5	Preference scheme established based on family reunification and skill; no country cap for Western Hemisphere countries	4
1976	No change	5	The 20,000 per-country limit is applied to the Western Hemisphere	4
1986	No change	5	Creation of Seasonal Agricultural Workers program; creation of diversity visas	4.25

The 1965 Immigration and Nationality Act is an example of a law in which the majority of the policy does not discriminate by national origin, but parts of it give preferential access to some nationalities. In this case, the law gave a country cap to every country in the Eastern Hemisphere, but while there was an overall cap on immigration from the Western Hemisphere, those countries were not given a cap. In practice, this meant that immigrants from Mexico got most of the Western Hemisphere quota. I code this part of the law in the skill category because it allowed more immigrants with a lower level of skill to enter (skill coding increases from a 3.4 to a 4). If I had coded this under the nationality category, the nationality category score would be lower (there would be discrimination), and the skill code would be lower, because this is no longer coded as greater openness to low-skill immigrants. Similarly, when Congress created the diversity visa program in 1986, this change in the law is also coded in the skill category because it did not affect the majority of the entry criteria.

Skill Restrictions

Another frequently used criterion for regulating low-skill immigration has been to directly use skill or wealth requirements. Some of the first skill requirements were used by the British dominions—Australia, Canada, New Zealand, and South Africa. Although these states wanted to explicitly restrict low-skill Asian immigration, Great Britain did not want the dominions passing prohibitions against Indian immigrants, owing to protests from elites in colonial India. The British government made it clear that it would not sanction obviously anti-Indian legislation. Instead, the Natal colony in South Africa required a literacy test to be given in "any European language." This was copied by Australia, Canada, and New Zealand. Immigration officers would simply give the test in a language that the undesirable, low-skill immigrant would not know, failing him automatically.[9] Once the dominions gained independence, they all enacted explicit prohibitions against Asian immigrants.

After World War II, when nationality as a basis for prohibitions against immigrants was delegitimized, skill requirements often replaced nationality requirements in many states as a way to keep out the same people. This substitution of skill requirements for nationality requirements can be seen most clearly in the case of Australia and Canada, where nationality-based criteria were replaced by points systems designed to keep Asian immigrants out.[10] While the points systems have not been effective in

[9] This test was different from the literacy test enacted in the United States, which allowed immigrants to choose the language of the test they would take.

[10] Jupp (2002) and Kelley and Trebilcock (1998).

keeping Asian immigrants out of these countries because these immigrants have gained more education and skills, they have been effective in keeping newer groups of low-skill immigrants out.

States have also taxed migrants directly, as in the head tax enacted in the United States in the early twentieth century, or indirectly by taxing employers for each immigrant, costs that then get passed on to immigrants directly through recruitment fees or indirectly through lower salaries. Either way, these taxes increase the costs and reduce the benefits of migrating, which restricts low-skill migrants' ability to move.

States often enact special programs for high-skill workers at the same time that they restrict low-skill migration, either within the same regulations, as in points systems, or as part of omnibus legislation. For coding purposes, what matters is whether these programs are used in place of openness for low-skill workers. If the establishment of these programs does not affect the immigration of low-skill workers, then they are not coded as restrictions.

CODING CRITERIA FOR THE SKILL CATEGORY

Does the law restrict by the skills or income an immigrant possesses? Does it use a points system with points given for education or special skills? Are people excluded based on profession (i.e., no prostitutes), illness (e.g., no epileptics), or likelihood of becoming a public charge?

1 Only highly educated, high-income earners allowed in; many excludable classes.
2 Mostly highly educated, high earners, but some allowances for low-skill workers; some excludable classes.
3 Preference for high-skill workers, but many opportunities for low-skill workers; some excludable classes.
4 Few slots reserved for high-skill/high-income workers (i.e., like the H1B visa in the United States); most visas open for anyone; few excludable classes (e.g., only criminals or those likely to become a public charge).
5 No skill restrictions for any visas; no excludable classes.

EXAMPLE OF CODING FOR THE SKILL CATEGORY

Table A2 gives examples of how the skill criterion is coded for the United States. The first law to affect the skill level of immigrants was the 1819 law regulating passage to the country. The restrictions put in place under this law increased the cost of passage and thereby ensured that poorer, low-skill immigrants could not afford to migrate. The next law to greatly affect the skill level of immigrants was the 1862 ban on indentured labor, which meant that poor immigrants had to find the money to move on their own—something that was out of reach for many Asian migrants. In 1875, Congress created the first set of excludable classes, which largely targeted the poor and low-skill migrants; in 1882, they included those likely to become a public charge as an excluded class, which again targeted the poor and low-skill. The 1917 Literacy Act created an explicit skill requirement, lowering the coding of US policy to a 2.75. With its repeal, and later the 1965 Immigration and Nationality Act, the United States has largely relied on family reunification and a quota to control immigration and has only occasionally focused on skill as a requirement. While there have been tweaks to the skill requirements since 1986, the skill restrictions have largely stayed the same since 1965.

As a contrast to the United States, table A3 shows how Canada has used nationality and skill criteria to affect who can enter the state. Like the United States, Canada began to limit Asian immigration, beginning with immigration from India in 1863, and created excludable classes of immigrants, including those likely to become a public charge, in the middle of the nineteenth century. Unlike the United States, Canada adopted a head tax for all immigrants much earlier, with a general head tax imposed in 1851.[11] In 1926, Canada passed a major immigration law that used both nationality and skill restrictions. Similar to the US 1921 and 1924 Quota Acts, this law restricted immigration from all areas except the United States, Great Britain, and Northern Europe. Additionally, Canada used a literacy test as well as many excludable classes. At the height of the Great Depression, in 1931 Canada further limited immigration to white British subjects and American citizens. After World War II, Canada began to reopen immigration, and in 1962 it removed most of the national origin basis from its law. In 1967, Canada removed the final discriminatory aspects of its immigration law but enacted a points system that explicitly restricted the entry of low-skill immigrants. From 1967 to 2001, the Canadian government made some modifications to the points system and created other temporary worker programs. In 2001, it undertook a major policy revision that further restricted the entry of low-skill immigrants.

Quotas

Numeric quotas are another tool that states have used to regulate the flow of either all immigrants or specifically low-skill immigrants; however, this tool is used infrequently (in 8.4 percent of the country-years). Typically, the quota is allocated by some type of preference ordering. The coding of

---

[11] Zolberg (1978, 261).

TABLE A3
Examples of Coding of Canada's Nationality and Skill Restrictions.

Year	Nationality		Skill	
	Restrictions	Coding	Restrictions	Coding
1926	Four-tiered immigration-admissions system: white British and American citizens were permitted to enter Canada relatively freely; immigrants from Northern Europe and Scandinavia could enter Canada if they were sponsored by Canadian relatives, or had a needed occupation. Immigrants from Eastern and Southern Europe were admitted through special permits, and those from Asia and Africa were virtually excluded	2.5	Literacy test; large numbers of excluded classes	3
1931	Restricts classes of immigrants who were admissible to (1) British subjects defined as "British by reason of birth, or naturalization in Great Britain or Ireland, Newfoundland, New Zealand, Australia, and the Union of South Africa"; (2) US citizens	1.5	Agriculturalists with sufficient means allowed from countries other than Britain and dominions and the US	2
1947	Dutch and Maltese immigrants are allowed entry into Canada. Removal of Italians from enemy alien list. Polish ex-servicemen allowed entrance provided they would work for a farmer for 1 year	1.75	Admissible classes are widened to include farm workers, miners, and loggers as long as they had secured employment in Canada. Additionally any agriculturalist could come if he had a Canadian relative or was assured employment on a farm	2.5

| Year | Nationality | | Skill | |
	Restrictions	Coding	Restrictions	Coding
1962	Removal of racial discrimination in the independent immigrant category	4	Removes most of the racial discrimination, except still allows Europeans to sponsor a wider range of relatives. Independent immigration: a person who by reason of his education, training, skills, or other special qualifications is likely to be able to establish himself successfully in Canada	3.85
1967	No more racial requirements	5	Creation of a points system. Assigned points for arranged employment or designated occupation (0–10), knowledge in English or French (0–10), relative in Canada (0–5), area of destination (0–5), education and training (0–20), personal qualities (0–15), occupational demand (0–15), occupational skill (1–10), and age (0–10). Created three immigrant categories: independent, sponsored, and nominated	3.15
2001	No change	5	New points system: greater reward for education, language, and experience. There are four separate migrant worker programs: skilled occupations, the Seasonal Agricultural Worker, the Live-In Caregiver Program, and the Temporary Foreign Worker Program, which admits workers to fill vacant jobs that require a high school diploma or less	2.35

quotas is based on what percentage of the population (total quota divided by population) the country is willing to allow in each year. Because most of these states rarely update their quotas, the measure can become more restrictive over time without a law change by the policymaker. Nonetheless, this restrictiveness is built into quotas; as the population and economy grow, there would likely be a demand for more immigrant workers. Policymakers can update the quotas to account for the increased demand but often choose not to. For example, Congress last updated the US quota in 1990. Since that time US population has increased by almost 70 million, and the US economy has almost doubled in size, yet the quota has remained the same. Thus by neglecting immigration policy, Congress has made it more restrictive.

CODING CRITERIA FOR THE QUOTA CATEGORY

Is there a quota and how restrictive is it?

Quotas are coded only when the quota is a numerical limit on a large portion of immigrants, not when it is a target for the number of immigrants. Targets, like policy statements or development plans, are not coded because they are not changes in legislation but usually administrative policies. The quota does not need to be binding on all immigrants. This is because it is rare to have a quota that binds on all immigrants. Usually at least wives and minor children of citizens are allowed in above the quota; this policy is denoted in the family immigration policy coding. Sometimes, the quota is on only one class of immigrants, such as the Hong Kong quota on Chinese immigrants, but this class makes up the majority of immigrants entering the country. Again, high-skill workers from other countries could enter above the quota, although wives and minor children of Hong Kong belongers (equivalent to citizens) cannot. This is denoted in the other categories.

1 Less than 0.25% of population can enter annually.
2 0.25–0.5% of population can enter annually.
3 0.5–1% of the population can enter annually.
4 Over 1% of population can enter annually.
5 No quota.

EXAMPLE OF CODING FOR THE QUOTA CATEGORY

The United States has been one of the few states to use a quota as a major part of its immigration policy. The quota was first introduced in 1921; for 1921–23 the quota was set at 350,000, or about 0.32 percent of the population (coded as a 2). In 1924, the quota was lowered to 150,000, or about 0.13 percent of the population (coded as 1). Since then, the quota, in comparison to the US population, has been quite low, always less than 0.3 percent and often less than 0.25 percent of the population. In comparison, since 1978 Hong Kong has placed a quota on immigration from mainland China, but this quota has been much larger proportionately. For much of its history, mainland Chinese have been the major immigrant group to Hong Kong; a quota on them, then, limits the majority of immigration to Hong Kong. In 1978, the quota was for 113,150 mainland Chinese residents, or about 2.4 percent of Hong Kong's population at the time. In 1989, Hong Kong added a quota for all foreign workers as well as immigrants from mainland China. Since then, most years the quota has allowed in slightly more than 1 percent of the population.

Recruitment

States have at times recruited immigrants as a way to increase the number of immigrants coming to their country. In this case, the policymaker has decided that the "natural rate" of immigration is too low and wants to increase it. Governments have sometimes paid to recruit immigrants through their own budget and at other times have allowed employers to pay to recruit immigrants. States that fund recruitment out of their own budget are given the highest score, states that allow employers to recruit are given scores between 2 and 4 depending on how easy it is for firms to recruit, and states that do not allow recruitment are given the lowest score.

CODING CRITERIA FOR THE RECRUITMENT CATEGORY

Are there special visas or procedures to recruit labor or settlers? To recruit workers, do employers have to advertise first or otherwise seek approval from a government ministry? Can all industries recruit? Do firms have to pay levies or other taxes for foreign workers? Does the government pay for passage or give settlers or workers other benefits to induce them to come?

1 No special procedure or visa, come in under the same system of regulation as everyone else; labor recruitment prohibited.
2 Small set of visas for special groups of workers (e.g., agricultural workers); trigger to reduce numbers based on employment data; employers are not allowed to pay for moving expenses; many restrictions including no unemployed natives in the industry.
3 Moderate number of visas for all groups, or many groups obtain visas; employers allowed to pay for moving expenses; some procedures for recruiting workers.
4 Few or no restrictions on visas for any type of worker; employers are allowed to pay moving expenses; few restrictions or procedures for obtaining work visas.

TABLE A4
Examples of Coding of Australia's Recruitment Policies.

	Recruitment	
Year	Restrictions	Coding
1792	First settlers are given free passage, land grants, provisions for two years, tools and implements, and the services of a convict for two years	4.5
1807	Creation of a graduated scale by which the amount of land and other assistance granted to settlers would depend on the amount of capital they brought to the colony	4.4
1818	Only emigrants with capital of at least £500 can receive land	4.15
1831	New South Wales begins scheme of assisted female emigration, along with skilled workmen	4.5
1835	Loan program for skilled workers in New South Wales becomes a free bounty. All passages become entirely free and paid out of the colonial funds. Creation of two systems: the bounty and government systems	4.75
1847	Assistance to immigrants from outside the UK first granted	4.8
1893	All Australian colonies stop offering assisted passage	4
1896	Queensland revives financial aid for immigrants	4.25
1906	Resumption of assisted immigration for all parts of Australia	4.25
1922	Beginning of Empire Settlement Act	4.65
1926	Development and Migration Act of 1926 to assist the emigration of British implements the 34-million-pound agreement	4.7
1930	Australia virtually ceases assisted migration	4.05
1937	Assisted migration resumes under the Empire Settlement Act	4.25
1948	Scope of free and assisted passage schemes with Britain is widened; new program for assisted passage from Ireland	4.75
1954	Assisted passage is provided for people from the US, Switzerland, Denmark, Norway, Sweden, and Finland	4.9
1957	Bring out a Briton Campaign	4.8
1982	Abolishment of assisted passages, except for refugees	3.5

5 Government program to recruit workers or settlers; government pays for the workers' transportation cost and helps pay for firms or government officials to recruit workers.

EXAMPLE OF CODING FOR THE RECRUITMENT CATEGORY

Table A4 uses Australia's policies on recruitment as an example of how this category is coded. It also provides an example of how federal states are coded before the federal government takes sole responsibility for the policy; prior to Australia's becoming a commonwealth in 1901, I code the policy of the most open state. New South Wales first began recruitment of settlers in 1792 with free passage, land, provisions, and the use of convict labor given to settlers. All Australian colonies ended free passage by 1893, but it was resumed in 1896 by Queensland and in 1906 for all of Australia. During the Great Depression, in 1930 Australia again ended recruitment of immigrants. After World War II, Australia began recruitment again, first from Britain and later from other Western European countries (and the United States and Canada), and then finally opened up recruitment to Southern Europe and Turkey in the 1960s. All assisted passage schemes, except assistance for refugees, were ended in 1982.

Labor Prohibitions

Another way to regulate immigration is to deter people from migrating by prohibiting them from working in certain industries or limiting the number of immigrant workers that employers can use. When coding labor regulations, we gave states with few regulations the highest score; we gave the lowest score to states that excluded immigrants from many positions or let them be only a small part of the labor force. In the interwar period, work prohibitions were used throughout Europe and in the settler countries as a way of reducing unemployment pressures, or at least the political pressure from unemployment. Most of these states have since relaxed these laws and allowed immigrants to work in most industries. South Africa continued many of these prohibitions through the Colour Bar—the laws that prevented both foreigners and natives of Asian and African descent from holding higher-skill positions. These laws were repealed at the end of apartheid, though other restrictions remained in place. While many of the other Western democracies do not explicitly limit access to the labor market, they do use occupational licensing criteria. These criteria frequently affect high-skill workers, such as doctors, rather than low-skill workers. Only the French, and to some extent the New Zealanders and Swiss, have continued to use these prohibitions for low-skill workers to a great degree.

CODING CRITERIA FOR THE LABOR PROHIBITIONS CATEGORY

Can immigrants work in all occupations? Are there requirements to have a certain number of native workers in an occupation/firm, or that foreign workers can make up only a certain percentage of workers? Do the rules cover all occupations? Just certain industries? Are there racially based policies?

1 Immigrants completely blocked from the labor market.
2 Immigrants restricted from many occupations; less than 30% of the workers in a given occupation/firm can be immigrants (covering most or all occupations).

3 Immigrants restricted from some occupations; 30–50% of workers in a given occupation/firm can be immigrants (covers some occupations).
4 Immigrants cannot hold public sector positions; 50% or more of the workers in a given occupation/firm can be immigrants (covers some occupations).
5 Immigrants can hold any position (except for highly sensitive national security positions); no restrictions on the number of immigrant workers in a given occupation/firm.

EXAMPLE OF CODING FOR THE LABOR PROHIBITIONS CATEGORY

Table A5 gives examples of how Singapore has used labor prohibitions, and how these restrictions have been coded. In 1987, Singapore began using "dependency ratios," which outline what percentage of workers in a given firm can be foreign (temporary) workers. The dependency ratio was first set at 50 percent for all sectors except domestic workers and workers in the marine sector. In 1988, the dependency ratio was decreased to 40 percent. In 1992, the government began to distinguish between sectors, targeting the service sector, which as we saw in chapter 6 was extremely reliant on foreign labor, with a dependency ratio of 20 percent. Taiwan has used a similar dependency ratio since 1992, but set even lower limits on the use of foreign workers. In the Persian Gulf, states have passed "native-ization" (Saudi-zation, Kuwait-ization, etc.) laws that require employers to increase the percentage of natives that firms employ by replacing foreign workers with natives. Saudi Arabia passed its first Saudi-zation law in 1969 when it stipulated that Saudis must make up 75 percent of employees for firms with more than 100 workers, and that they must make up 51 percent of the payroll.

Family Reunification

Family reunification policies, in contrast to the policies examined thus far, regulate some forms of potentially noneconomic migrants: citizens' and permanent residents' family members. Family reunification is included in the low-skill immigration policy measure because many family migrants join the labor force sooner or later.

The coding of family migration is based on how many family members a citizen or resident can sponsor as well as how hard it is for her to sponsor her family member. States are given the highest score if citizens and residents can easily sponsor many degrees of relatives (e.g., spouses, adult children, parents, and siblings). States are scored lower if they restrict the degrees of family that can be sponsored, and if they increase the difficulty in sponsoring relatives, such as by requiring citizens or residents sponsoring

Table A5
Examples of Coding of Singapore's Labor Prohibitions.

	Labor Prohibitions	
Year	Restrictions	Coding
1987	Creation of dependency ratios. For all sectors except domestic workers and marine sectors, employers can employ only up to 50% foreign workers	3.25
1988	Firms can employ 40% foreign workers in all sectors except domestic workers	3.5
1990	Malaysians can be employed in any sector. For others, previous prohibitions apply	3.75
1992	Percent of workers in manufacturing who can be foreign is raised to 45%; service sector is now set at 20%, and construction at 80%	3.75
1994	Service sector to 25%, manufacturing to 50%	4

family members to have a certain income. States are given the lowest score if they allow only native-born and wealthy men to sponsor wives and minor children. For example, Saudi Arabia allows native-born men and wealthy, high-skill expatriate men, but not women, to sponsor their spouse and children.

One issue with family migration is that many states did not have a family reunification policy when there were few restrictions by nationality or skill. Family reunification policies came into being only once other restrictions were put in place. Given that the states have no policy on family migration during these times, these years are scored as a 1.

CODING CRITERIA FOR THE FAMILY REUNIFICATION CATEGORY

Do family members get special treatment? Can they immigrate more easily than others? Are there racial or skill distinctions?

1 No special provisions for family reunification; family members must enter under the same procedures as others.
2 Only wives and minor children of citizens or legal permanent residents can be sponsored, but they are free from other controls.
3 Increased number of relatives can be sponsored (e.g., adult children or dependent parents), but only by citizens and/or relatives (except minor children and wives); need to possess the same characteristics as nonfamily immigration (e.g., if there is a literacy test, relatives must pass the test); a relative in the country has to pay bond or otherwise be responsible.

4 Many categories of relatives can be sponsored by citizens or residents (e.g., siblings, parents not dependent on migrant) but still must possess the same characteristics as nonfamily immigrants (except minor children and wives); a relative in the country has to be responsible for the immigrant.

5 Many categories of relatives can be sponsored by citizens or residents, and they do not need to possess the characteristics of nonfamily immigrants (exemption from literacy exams, etc.); no bond or responsibility for the relative in the country required.

Family Provisions Coded 0 before first mention of special provisions for families; 1 after.

EXAMPLE OF CODING FOR THE FAMILY REUNIFICATION CATEGORY

Table A6 shows how major changes in US family reunification policy were coded, as well as an alternative coding. From 1790 until 1917, there were no special preference categories for family-based immigration. Under the coding rules, if a state in a given year does not have any family-reunification policy, family reunification in that state-year is coded as a 1. Family members, however, were free to enter during this period under the rules that governed all other migrants. As an alternative coding, I coded family reunification as 5 until there was a law that would restrict the entry of at least some family members, which was defined as the nationality or skill coding falling below a 4. Under the main coding rules, family reunification is coded as a 1 from 1790 until 1917; under the alternative coding, it is coded as a 5 from 1790 until 1884, when the nationality coding falls below 4. The 1917 Literacy Act provided the first family reunification policy by allowing wives and minor children to enter the United States without taking the literacy test. Since the advent of the quota system in 1921, several classes of relatives have been allowed visas that do not count against the quota or have been given priority under the quota. The coding, then, reflects the degree of relative that can gain entry.

Table A7 shows how family reunification is coded in a points system using Canada's family reunification as an example. Similar to the United States, Canada did not have a separate policy for family migrants until the early twentieth century. With the implementation of the points system in 1967, Canada allowed citizens to sponsor immediate relatives and created a "nominated" class of relatives who could gain entrance more easily than independent immigrants. The family-reunification system has been altered since then with greater access for family migrants given in the 1970s through the early 1990s, and greater restrictions placed on family reunification beginning in the mid-1990s. In 1996, Canada placed further requirements on the sponsoring family member to provide support for the

TABLE A6
Examples of Coding of US Family Reunification Policies.

	Family Reunification			
Year	Restrictions	Coding	Existence of Law	Alternative Coding
1790	No policy	1	0	5
1884	Nationality coding drops below 4	1	0	1
1917	Wives and minor children are allowed to enter without taking the literacy test	2	1	2
1921	The quota limitation, however, does not apply to minor children of citizens. Also grants preference to wives, parents, brothers, sisters, children under 18, and fiancees of citizens and resident aliens	3.5	1	3.5
1924	Preference quota status is established for unmarried children under 21, parents, and spouses of US citizens aged 21 and over; nonquota status is accorded to wives and unmarried minor children under 18 of US citizens	3.5	1	3.5
1952	Nonquota classes change to include children and spouses of citizens without regard to age of children or date of marriage. Revision of quota preference to visas for parents of adult citizens, spouses, and children of lawfully admitted resident aliens, and close relatives of citizens	3.5	1	3.5
1965	Immediate relatives (spouses, children, parents) of US citizens not subject to numerical restrictions	4.75	1	4.75
1990	Allocates an unlimited number of visas for immediate relatives of US citizens and 226,000 visas for other family-based immigration	4.5	1	4.5

TABLE A7
Examples of Coding of Canada's Family Reunification Policies.

| | Family Reunification | | | |
Year	Restrictions	Coding	Existence of Law	Alternative Coding
1783	No policy	1	0	5
1902	Nationality coding drops below a 4	1	0	1
1921	Entry of wives and children of Indian migrants already settled in Canada allowed	2	1	2
1926	Immigrants from the preferred countries of Northern Europe and Scandinavia can enter if they are sponsored by Canadian relatives	3	1	3
1930	All immigrants except dependents of already established heads of families are excluded from entry. Asian immigration is restricted to the wife and unmarried minor children of any Canadian citizen in a position to care for his dependents	2	1	2
1967	Immediate relatives can continue to be sponsored; more distant "nominated" relatives are subjected to the long-term criteria in points system but short-term requirements are waived	3	1	3
1976	Family class immigrants are exempted from points system and need to pass only security, criminal, and medical screening. Family class includes spouses, fiancées, unmarried minor children, aged (over 60) or disabled parents, orphaned siblings, nieces, nephews, or grandchildren under 18 and unmarried. Canadian citizens and residents must sponsor relatives	3.5	1	3.5
1992	Family class eligibility changes to all parents, regardless of age; all children under 19 and children above that age if they are dependent on the parents	4	1	4
1996	The sponsor and the family member being sponsored are now required to sign a new agreement outlining mutual obligations to support themselves for their first 10 years in Canada	3.5	1	3.5

sponsored family member, which effectively limits the entry of low-skill migrants' family members because these migrants may be unable to prove that they can provide support.

Refugee Policy

The final two dimensions of border regulations also look at potentially noneconomic migrants: refugees and asylees. Refugees are defined as people fleeing from their country who are outside the state they are trying to enter. Refugee policy, then, deals with the resettlement of refugees. An asylee is defined as someone who is at the state's borders or inside the country who claims refugee status, and asylum policy deals with whether the migrant can gain entry to or stay in the state.

Refugee and asylee policies are categorized as border regulation policies, rather than rights, because refugees and asylees are potential labor market participants. Additionally, asylees are often considered economic migrants who cannot enter in another way.[12] As noted in chapter 1, refugees and asylum seekers often join the labor force, and firms have been keenly interested in refugee and asylum policy, especially as a way to gain immigrant labor if they cannot obtain it through other channels.

States are coded depending on the ease of entry as a refugee or asylum seeker. States without a refugee or asylee status are coded as a 1. As with family reunification, most states had no refugee or asylum policies until after World War I, and still others have not adopted a refugee or asylum policy as yet. In the nineteenth century, this was not a problem for refugees, as they could immigrate to most states as general migrants. As in the family reunification case, the main coding codes refugee and asylum policy as a 1 in these states even when a refugee could come in as a general migrant. I use an alternative coding where these states are coded as having a very generous refugee and asylum program (coded as a 5) until there are nationality or skill regulations that would bar the entrance of refugees or asylum seekers (operationalized as the nationality or skill coding dropping below a 4), and then the policy was coded as a 1.

Refugee policy is coded based on the definition of who counts as a refugee, whether there is a formal resettlement process or an ad hoc process, the number of refugees that are re-settled, and whether there are preference categories for refugees. Ad hoc refugee programs for one group during the crisis are coded as relaxing refugee restrictions, and the magnitude of the change is based on the number of refugees the state was willing to allow in. The change in coding lasts only as long as the refugee program was in place; for example, when New Zealand took in Ugandan refugees in 1973,

---

[12] See, for example, Kay and Miles (1988) and Kaye (1994).

but no other years, the increase in the refugee score is calculated for 1973 only.

Does the state have a resettlement policy? Does it resettle refugees on an ad hoc basis? How selective is its refugee policy? Does it let in many refugees? Are refugees defined as only those who meet the 1951 convention or 1967 protocol, or is there a more expansive definition?

1 Almost no refugees allowed in; those that are allowed in must follow normal immigration procedures.
2 Some refugees allowed in; special refugee visas but refugees chosen by some sort of preference or must be able to pass tests that nonrefugee immigrants take; few reasons for being a refugee or ad hoc policy.
3 Special refugee visa; preference system but not overly burdensome; moderate number of refugees allowed in; must follow some of the requirements that a nonrefugee immigrant would have to pass; the UN definition of a refugee is followed.
4 Large number of refugees allowed in; no preference system or very weak system; easy to obtain refugee visa; exemption from requirements of nonrefugee immigrant; at least the UN definition of a refugee is followed.
5 Large number of refugees; no preference system or requirements; very easy to obtain refugee visa; many categories of refugees included, not just the UN definition.

Refugee Provisions Coded 0 before first mention of refugee in law; 1 after.

Table A8 again uses the United States as an example. Prior to the Displaced Persons Act (DPA) in 1948, the United States did not have a formal refugee policy. Throughout the 1950s and into the 1960s, the nation extended the DPA program and created other ad hoc programs to deal with the Hungarian and Cuban refugee crises. In the 1970s, the United States again used an ad hoc program to resettle Cambodian and Vietnamese refugees. Finally in 1980, the country created a permanent refugee program.

Asylum Policy

States are coded as having a more generous asylum policy when they make it easier for asylum seekers to obtain status. This policy is coded as more restrictive when states enact safe-country-of-origin policies that

TABLE A8
Examples of Coding of US Refugee Policies.

Year	Restrictions	Coding	Existence of Law	Alternative Coding
		Refugee Policy		
1790	No policy	1	0	5
1884	Nationality score below 4	1	0	1
1948	Displaced Persons Act	4	1	4
1958	Bill grants admission for permanent residence to Hungarian parolees	4.25	1	4.25
1960	Authorizes the AG to parole refugees. Decrease in quota for refugees.	3.5	1	3.5
1975	Establishes a program of domestic resettlement for Cambodian and Vietnamese refugees	4	1	4
1980	Refugee Act passes. Creates resettlement program	4.5	1	4.5

make it impossible for citizens of that state to claim refugee status; safe-third-country policies that force asylum seekers to make a claim in that third country; policies that allow border agents to decide that a claim is manifestly unfounded; and the like.

CODING CRITERIA FOR THE ASYLUM CATEGORY

Does the law discuss asylum seekers, that is, migrants who are at the border or in the state claiming refugee status? How easy is it to gain asylum? What rights do asylum seekers and asylees have? Are they kept in detention centers? Are they repatriated? Is there only one asylum status or is there temporary protected status as well? What are the procedures, and are there legal safeguards?

1 No asylum.
2 Extremely difficult process; asylum granted in only a few cases; little ability to work or access welfare state while awaiting determination; little recourse if not granted asylum; no temporary protected status; limited access for political refugees.
3 Difficult process; asylum granted for more cases; some access to the welfare state or labor market; more recourse including ability to access courts if denied; some temporary protected status allowed.

4 Fairly easy process; asylum granted to many groups; access to labor market and welfare system; access to courts and other procedures if denied; temporary protected status given to many groups.

5 Easy process; asylum granted for most cases; access to labor markets and welfare state; constitutionally protected procedure; no need for temporary protected status because almost everyone gets asylum.

Asylum Provisions Coded 0 before first mention of asylum; 1 after.

EXAMPLES OF CODING FOR ASYLUM CATEGORY

Table A9 also uses US asylum policy as an example. The United States first allowed for asylum when Congress began regulating immigration in 1875 by allowing entry to those who had committed a political crime because they would have been denied entry as a criminal. The nation did not create a more formal asylum process until 1980. Throughout the 1990s, Congress at times made asylum more generous by allowing the attorney general to grant temporary protected status for immigrants not covered under the Refugee Act and created new classes of refugees, but at other times made asylum harder to obtain by limiting applicants' ability to work while the claim was being adjudicated.

Citizenship

Citizenship and rights are another lever that politicians can use to attract or deter migrants. Migrants want security in their position in the state to ensure that they receive the wages they were promised; that they can own businesses or land from which to make a living; that they will not be arbitrarily imprisoned or have their possessions taken from them without due process; and so on. Giving migrants rights—the right to own property, the right to join a union, the right to gain access to the social welfare state, and ultimately the right to join the political community through citizenship—increases migrants' security and their willingness to enter a state. In fact, Fitzgerald and colleagues have found that more liberal citizenship regimes attract migrants and can make up for worse economic conditions.[13]

The most important right is citizenship, which allows the immigrant to have the same rights as natives and prevents their deportation. Some colonial powers granted citizenship to those in their colonies or former colonies, allowing colonial citizens to immigrate to the metropole, even when others could not. For example, even after the United States banned immigration from Asian countries in 1921, Filipinos could still immigrate

---

[13] Fitzgerald, Leblang, and Teets (2014).

TABLE A9
Examples of Coding of US Asylum Policies.

	Asylum Policy			
Year	Restrictions	Coding	Existence of Law	Alternative Coding
1790	No policy	1	0	5
1875	Allows those who committed political crimes to enter	2	1	2
1990	The attorney general is authorized to grant temporary protected status to undocumented immigrants of designated countries subject to armed conflict or natural disasters	3.5	1	3.5
1995	New regulations to expedite the asylum cases and to limit the right to work pending resolution of the claim	3.25	1	3.25
1996	Existing INS regulations regarding asylum are recodified and provide that the attorney general's parole authority may be exercised only on a case-by-case basis for urgent humanitarian reasons or significant public health. Applications for asylum must be made within one year of entering the US, and those applying must demonstrate a "credible fear" of persecution	3	1	3
1999	Foreigners cannot be deported if they face torture at home	3.5	1	3.5
2001	Safe-third-country agreement with Canada passes	3.25	1	3.25

to the country because of their citizenship in an American colony. Algerians and other North Africans were also granted French citizenship, allowing them easier entrance into France. When this colonial citizenship was taken away, immigrants from these countries lost their easier access to the state. Similarly, some states have given citizenship to coethnics living abroad. For example, after World War II, West Germany gave citizenship to all people with German ancestry living in the Eastern Bloc countries. This citizenship allowed for easy entrance for those with German ancestry, especially after the fall of the Berlin Wall. The Germans also curtailed this practice once they believed that too many immigrants were entering the state, making immigration for these groups much more difficult.

CODING CRITERIA FOR THE CITIZENSHIP CATEGORY

Does the law mention citizenship? How easy is it to obtain citizenship? What determines citizenship for children born in the country (*jus sanguinis*, *jus soli*, *double jus soli*)? Are there racial discriminations in citizenship? How easy is it for the government to denaturalize citizens? Racial discrimination in citizenship policies leads to a lower score.

1 Only by birth from a native father or mother.
2 Only by birth through native parent and/or grandparent.
3 Very difficult process to obtain citizenship (language requirements, difficult test) and/or many years to citizenship (more than ten years) and/or children receive citizenship through either parent or grandparent.
4 Moderately difficult process (relatively easy language requirements and/or an easy test) and/or moderate time to citizenship (more than five but fewer than ten years) and/or children born in state automatically get citizenship.
5 Fairly easy process (e.g., no language requirements) and short time to citizenship (five years or fewer) and children born in state automatically get citizenship.

EXAMPLE OF CODING FOR THE CITIZENSHIP CATEGORY

Table A10 uses the UK's citizenship policies as an example of how citizenship was used to both attract and repel certain immigrants, especially immigrants from current and former colonies. In 1792, when Great Britain enters the dataset, all children who were born in Great Britain were automatically subjects (jus soli) and residency led to subjecthood. Great Britain did not address the question of subjecthood again until 1914. At this point, the country gave subjecthood to everyone born within the dominions and territories, and sought to standardize naturalization among the dominions

TABLE A10
Examples of Coding of UK Subjecthood/Citizenship Regulations.

Year	Restrictions	Coding
		Citizenship
1792	Jus soli and residency lead to subjecthood	4.5
1914	Anyone born "within His Majesty's dominions and allegiance" is automatically a subject. Children of British subjects gain subjecthood as well. New naturalization scheme (including within the dominions) with a universal five years' residence requirement	4.5
1948	When a dependent territory achieves independence, most of its natives normally lose their citizenship of the UK and colonies and become citizens of the new state. Those persons who fail to obtain citizenship of the succeeding state are allowed to retain citizenship of the UK	4.5
1968	This act introduces the concept of patriality, restricting the entry of nonpatrials with UK passports, including East African Asians, by a special voucher system	4
1971	Conditions for citizenship are 5 years' residence, good character, a sufficient knowledge of English, and an intention to reside in the UK. A Commonwealth citizen who is a patrial has an absolute right to be registered after five years' residence	3.75
1981	Defines three classes of citizens. British citizens are defined as persons born in the UK or whose parents or grandparents were born or naturalized in the UK. Citizens of dependent territories are those whose parents were born in dependent territories; these citizens have no right to enter the UK. British overseas citizens are children of British citizens born outside the UK. They have the right to enter and live in the UK but cannot pass their citizenship on to their children. Children born in the UK to permanent residents automatically obtain citizenship; all other children born to immigrants can acquire British citizenship if they live in the UK for 10 years.	3.5
1999	The British government announces that it will grant full citizenship to its 150,000 remaining inhabitants in 13 overseas territories	3.75
2002	Law requires applicants for British citizenship to take language classes and demonstrate that they understand British society	3.5
2005	Beginning November 1, 2005, foreigners naturalizing in the UK must pass a $72 test demonstrating knowledge of Britain and its culture	3.25

as well. Given the relative ease of gaining citizenship (at least for European immigrants), citizenship is given a high score. Great Britain continued to allow relatively easy naturalization as well as extending citizenship to its dominions and colonies until the late 1960s. Then, policymakers sought to limit immigration from the colonies and introduced the concept of *patriality*. Patriality granted British citizenship to only those citizens of the United Kingdom and colonies whose parent or grandparent had the right to abode in the United Kingdom or to Commonwealth citizens whose father or grandfather had been born in the United Kingdom. Essentially, the law stripped citizenship, and importantly the right to live in Great Britain, from nonwhite former and current colonial subjects. Over the next twenty years, Great Britain continued to restrict citizenship, making it more difficult for those from both former and current colonies to enter. Finally, in 1999, the United Kingdom again granted citizenship to its current colonial subjects.

Immigrant Rights

This category captures the rights states give immigrants, besides citizenship and access to the labor market, which are covered in other dimensions. All other rights are included in this category: access to the social welfare system; the ability to own land or a business; the ability to vote in local elections, have state-sponsored schools in the immigrants' native language, or have the state pay for a religious leader in the immigrants' faith, and the like. Also incorporated in this category are programs designed to help immigrants learn the native language or otherwise integrate into society. The more rights states grant, the higher the score; the fewer rights granted, the lower the score. The other rights score is also affected by whether there is discrimination in the law based on the immigrants' nationality or race.

CODING CRITERIA FOR THE IMMIGRANT RIGHTS CATEGORY

Does the law mention what rights immigrants have once in the state? Are there racial/national origin discriminations? Does the government try to integrate immigrants or does it just expect them to assimilate? How easy is it to get permanent residency? Can immigrants access the social welfare system?

1 Almost no legal rights; immigrants must leave the state if they leave their job; cannot own property; cannot access the welfare state; must register; have no freedom of religion, no permanent residency, and the like.

2 Some rights but land ownership and ownership of companies restricted; limited access to the welfare state.

3 Ability to change jobs freely; some ownership of real property or companies; some access to the welfare state; some racial discrimination in laws.

4 Access to most welfare policies; few restrictions on ownership of property or firms.

5 Total access to welfare state; voting rights without citizenship; no restrictions in property ownership; integration policies; no racial discrimination; few years to permanent residency.

EXAMPLE OF CODING FOR THE IMMIGRANT RIGHTS CATEGORY

Table A11 lists changes in the rights that Australia gives to immigrants. In the early days of the colony, immigrants had substantially the same rights as citizens of the colonies. Colonists were British subjects, and most of the immigrants were also British subjects; therefore, I have found no evidence that new arrivals did not have the same rights as those who had been in the Australian colonies longer or who were born in the colonies. Immigrants' other rights began to be curtailed in the early twentieth century when the Australian government began imposing discriminatory laws against Asian immigrants.[14] This discrimination leads to a decrease in the rights score. Policymakers wanted to deter Asian and later Southern and Eastern European immigration and, if possible, get immigrants from these regions already in Australia to return home; they used increasing restrictions on these groups' rights to try to achieve this goal. After World War II, instead of deterring immigrant groups, the government sought to further encourage British and, later, other European immigration by offering relatively easy access to social welfare benefits and educational courses for immigrants. They also began sponsoring foreign-language radio stations and other media to make immigrants feel more at home. These changes lead to an increase in the other rights score. In the 1990s, the government changed the goal of rights policies again, hoping once more to deter immigrants, especially low-skill immigrants. The government restricted access to the social welfare system and began requiring costly English training, rather than assisting immigrants. These changes lead to a decrease in the other rights score.

Deportation

The final set of policies includes enforcement and deportation. Policymakers can pass many restrictions on immigration and the rights of

---

[14] Discriminatory laws against Asian immigrants in the workplace began a bit earlier.

TABLE A11

Examples of Coding of Australia's Other Rights Regulations.

	Other Rights	
Year	Restrictions	Coding
1787	Equal rights as citizens except voting	4.75
1912	Leases to Aliens Restrictions Act: Europeans can get leases of only up to five acres unless the immigrant passes a diction test	3.5
1914	Asians cannot obtain land in irrigation areas in South Australia	3.25
1921	Indian and Sinhalese residents cannot vote and do not get pensions	3
1947	Relaxation of laws against property ownership by non-European immigrants	3.75
1958	British immigrants are granted equal rights to social welfare benefits as Australians. Non-British immigrants do not qualify for all benefits until they naturalize and satisfy certain residential requirements	3.5
1972	Foreign-language broadcasting is restricted to not more than 2.5% of a commercial radio station's weekly hours of transmission	3.65
1974	Restrictions on foreign-language broadcasting are lifted	3.85
1975	Discrimination on grounds of race, skin color, or nationality is formally abolished	4.5
1977	National Ethnic Broadcasting Advisory Council is established to provide ethnic broadcasting	4.5
1993	Immigrants cannot access unemployment and medical benefits for the first 6 months after arrival	4
1996	Waiting period for most welfare benefits is increased to 2 years	3.5
2000	The right of New Zealand citizens living in Australia to obtain welfare benefits is restricted	3

immigrants; however, if these restrictions are not enforced, the law becomes a de facto open policy. Ideally, we might want to use the number of undocumented immigrants in a state as a de facto measure of enforcement. Nonetheless, since undocumented immigrants have broken the law, it is hard to get reliable estimates of the number of undocumented people, especially in autocracies. Instead, I code deportation and other enforcement measures.

States have often used deportation as an enforcement mechanism. The coding of deportation measures how easy it is to get rid of unwanted immigrants. Increased safeguards, such as access to courts, increase the score on deportation because this ensures that legal procedures will be followed. On the other hand, increasing the number of deportable offenses to include illegal immigration, losing one's job, going on welfare, or being part of a political or social group decreases the score. Paying immigrants to leave the country also decreases the score because this is clearly a sign that the government wants to decrease immigration. Some countries allow defenses against deportation such as being in the country a certain number of years or having a native-born wife or child who is dependent on the immigrant. Increasing the number of defenses against deportation increases the score. In contrast, mass expulsions decrease the score.

CODING CRITERIA FOR THE DEPORTATION CATEGORY

How easy is it to deport an immigrant? What safeguards exist? Does the state engage in mass expulsions or pay people to leave the country?

1 No appeals process; many deportable offenses, including losing one's job.
2 Administrative process with few checks; fewer deportable offenses.
3 More checks on the process and even fewer deportable offenses.
4 Judicial checks on process including going to the highest court in the land and/or very few deportable offenses.
5 Almost no deportable offenses (conviction for a criminal offense, but not for an immigration offense) and clear judicial checks.

EXAMPLE OF CODING FOR THE DEPORTATION CATEGORY

Table A12 gives examples of how US deportation laws are coded. First, as in many other areas of immigration policy, Congress did not enact many laws on deportation until the late nineteenth century. Nonetheless, Congress did enact two relatively draconian laws in the early nineteenth century: the Alien and Sedition Acts in 1798 and then a law that allowed the deportation of enemy aliens during the War of 1812. Both of these laws were quickly repealed. Congress did not address deportation again until 1882. Over the next 130 years, Congress continued to add categories of deportable offenses and occasionally removed some groups from the list of deportees. These additional classes of deportable offenses lead to a decrease in the deportation score. In contrast to some other democracies and the other autocracies, the United States has always had at least some legal safeguards and judicial review for those being deported, keeping the deportation score higher than in states without safeguards or judicial review.

TABLE A12
Examples of Coding of US Deportation and Enforcement Policies.

Year	Deportation		Enforcement	
	Restrictions	Coding	Restrictions	Coding
1790	No policy	5	No policy	5
1798	President has the authority to deport immigrants deemed to be dangerous to the safety of the US	2	No change	5
1812	The arrest, imprisonment, and deportation of immigrant men from enemy nations is permitted	2	No change	5
1882	Allows for the deportation of foreign paupers, convicts, Chinese in the US illegally	4.5	No change	5
1891	Deportation within one year of arrival for those who enter illegally or who become public charge	4	Requires shipmasters to pay return fares for those not admitted to the US. Inspection of immigrants along the Canadian and Mexican borders	4.5
1924	No change	3.25	Those entering the US need to have a visa. Establishment of the Border Patrol	3.5
1952	Greater procedural safeguards to aliens subject to deportation are afforded	3	Parole Authority given to AG. It becomes it a felony to bring in or willfully induce an alien to enter unlawfully or to harbor an undocumented immigrant. However, employment does not constitute harboring	3.5

TABLE A12
Continued

	Deportation			Enforcement	
Year	Restrictions	Coding	Restrictions		Coding
1986	No change	3	Employer sanctions. Increased border patrols and inspections, but balanced by amnesty for undocumented immigrants		2.9
1996	Unauthorized foreigners who have lived in the US for at least 10 years and can prove that their removal would cause "exceptional and extremely unusual hardship" to a legally resident spouse, parent, or child may be granted a hardship exemption. Maximum of 4,000 hardship exemptions a year. Deportees may choose to depart voluntarily and not be barred from the US or be removed, barring them from the US for 10 years	2.75	Establishes a criminal alien identification system. Establishes certain alien smuggling-related crimes as RICO offenses. Establishes an interior repatriation program. Authorizes state and local officials to arrest and detain certain illegal aliens. Expedits process of criminal alien removal. Increases border enforcement. Improves barriers along the southwest border. Increases penalties for alien smuggling. Increases penalties for illegal entry and failure to depart. Increases worksite enforcement. Reduces the number and types of documents that may be used for eligibility to work		2.5

Enforcement

Other than deportation, states use a variety of measures to enforce their borders. These policies include placing additional penalties on illegal immigration, sanctions on transportation companies that bring illegal immigrants, sanctions on employers who hire illegal immigrants, and measures to police the border. States also often give amnesty to those in the country illegally; in some cases the illegal immigrant is allowed to stay, while in others she is forced to leave but does not have to pay any of the penalties for being in the country illegally. The dimension *other enforcement* seeks to measure these other mechanisms. Placing penalties beyond deportation on illegal immigrants (such as prison time or fines) leads to a lower score, as does stricter employer sanctions. Amnesty leads to a higher score, but the increase depends on the size of the amnesty—how many people were given amnesty—and the type of amnesty. States with fines or prison time for those immigrants in the country illegally usually give amnesty that allows undocumented immigrants to leave the country without paying a fine or serving jail time. In contrast, those states without extra penalties for illegal immigration usually allow undocumented immigrants the ability to regularize their status and stay in the countries. Clearly, the first amnesty is more restrictive than the second, in which fewer people are allowed to stay.

CODING CRITERIA FOR THE ENFORCEMENT CATEGORY

Does the state enforce its borders? How strong is the enforcement? Are there employer sanctions, fines, or prison time for illegal immigration? Are there amnesties? During an amnesty are immigrants allowed to stay or just leave without paying a fine?

1 High spending, employer raids, or hard-to-forge national work IDs, strong employer sanctions, bonds placed by employers to ensure that migrants go home, large number of enforcement officials.
2 Slightly less spending, fewer raids, or easier-to-forge national work IDs; border enforcement is strong but not impossible to overcome.
3 Even less spending, no raids, easy-to-forge IDs, some border enforcement.
4 Very little enforcement, screening at points of entry, little enforcement on employers.
5 Basically no enforcement.

EXAMPLE OF CODING FOR THE ENFORCEMENT CATEGORY

Table A12 also gives examples of how enforcement laws in the United States are coded. As with deportation, the country did relatively little to enforce its borders beyond health inspections until the late nineteenth century. In 1891, the US government enacted carrier sanctions forcing shipowners to pay for the return fare for immigrants not admitted into the country. This action forced shipowners to essentially enforce US policy in Europe. In 1924, the United States created the Border Patrol and began requiring visas for entry. In 1928, Congress made entering without authorization or by fraud a crime, thus creating the crime of illegal immigration. The McCarren-Walter Act in 1952 made it a felony to bring in or harbor an undocumented immigrant but did not construe employing an undocumented immigrant as harboring him, and it also gave the attorney general parole authority. Thus while the McCarren-Walter Act increased enforcement in some ways, it decreased it in others. Like the McCarren-Walter Act, the Immigration Reform and Control Act increased some aspects of enforcement, such as creating employer sanctions and increasing border patrols, but also allowed employers the "affirmative defense," protecting them from prosecution as long as they had checked their employees' documents, and gave legal status to undocumented immigrants who had been in the country since 1982. In 1996, the Illegal Immigration Reform and Immigrant Responsibility Act added many more penalties for smuggling and for entering the country illegally, as well as increasing worksite enforcement and reducing the number of documents that could be used to prove that legal status. Since then, Congress has concentrated on increasing enforcement.

Combining the Data into a Single Index

The goal of a state's immigration policy is to attract a certain number of immigrants. One way to combine these dimensions would be to use an average of all the dimensions. By using an average, however, we would be assuming that all the dimensions are equally effective. While there is no consensus on how these different dimensions affect the flow of migrants, it is clear that not all dimensions affect migration equally.[15] For example, rules for refugees and asylum seekers target a smaller proportion of likely migrants, and citizenship and rights are likely to be less important if border restrictions are high.

If we assume that not all of these dimensions are equally important in attracting (or repelling) a certain number of immigrants, we have to decide how to weigh the different factors. I use the data to generate the weights for the different dimensions via principal component analysis rather than

---

[15] Fitzgerald, Leblang, and Teets (2014) examined how policies attract immigrants, but they used only citizenship policy and a simple coding of immigration policy.

choosing the weights myself. This removes my bias from the combination process.

Principal component analysis (PCA) seeks to recover a latent variable—one not observed directly but expressed by several observable variables—from the data. In this case, the latent variable can be thought of as the policymaker's intent to open or restrict low-skill immigration. This intent manifests itself in the twelve different dimensions of immigration policy. Principal component analysis has long been used in psychology and in the scoring of standardized tests. For example, a student's quantitative reasoning is measured through many different math questions on a standardized test. Since the questions vary in difficulty, an average of all the questions may not be appropriate. Instead, principal component analysis allows the data to weight the questions; in this example, a question that all students answered correctly would get less weight than questions that only a few students answered correctly.

The analysis reveals that these dimensions combine to create two different factors: immigration policy and immigrants' rights. There are four eigenvalues above 1, but the third and fourth eigenvalues do not describe much of the variation (less than 10 percent each). Table A13 shows the eigenvalues over the different factors. I do not use a rotation of the factor loadings. Rotation is primarily used to make interpretation of the variable easier. Varimax, which is the most popular rotation, changes the weights of the variables to increase the loadings of the most important variables for each factor and shrinks the loadings of the least important ones to close to zero. For my purposes, I do not think that this is the correct loading; instead, all the variables should have some effect on the openness of immigration. Further, if the rotated model "does not accurately represent the data, then rotation will make the solution less replicable and potentially harder to interpret because the mathematical properties of PCA have been lost."[16] Given that in the data-generating process, policymakers use tools in all the twelve dimensions to control their borders, each dimension should have some effect on the final variable.

Table A14 shows how the factors load on the variables. The first factor, immigration policy, places more weight on nationality, skill, recruitment, quotas, enforcement, and deportation policies than the second, rights of immigrants, which places more weight on family reunification, refugee, asylee, citizenship, rights, and work prohibition policies; hence the names for the two factors. The first factor correlates highly (at 0.95) with a standardized average of nationality, skill, quota, recruitment, work prohibitions, deportation, and enforcement. Henceforth, I focus on the immigration policy factor. The immigration policy variable now takes

[16] Abdi and Williams (2010).

TABLE A13
Factor Analysis.

Factor	Eigenvalue	Difference	Proportion	Cumulative
Factor1	3.66	1.44	0.30	0.30
Factor2	2.22	1.09	0.19	0.49
Factor3	1.14	0.09	0.09	0.58
Factor4	1.05	0.08	0.09	0.67
Factor5	0.97	0.31	0.08	0.75
Factor6	0.66	0.11	0.06	0.81
Factor7	0.56	0.08	0.05	0.85
Factor8	0.48	0.06	0.04	0.89
Factor9	0.41	0.02	0.03	0.93
Factor10	0.39	0.16	0.03	0.96
Factor11	0.24	0.01	0.02	0.98
Factor12	0.23	.	0.02	1.00

LR test: $chi^2(66) = 1.3e + 04$ $p < 0.000$

TABLE A14
Factor Loadings.

Variable	Factor loading immigration policy	Factor loading rights of immigrants	Uniqueness
Nationality	0.39	0.15	0.83
Skill	0.74	−0.04	0.45
Quota	0.43	−0.43	0.63
Recruitment	0.55	0.07	0.69
Work prohibitions	0.43	0.55	0.52
Family reunification	−0.69	0.44	0.33
Refugees	−0.48	0.62	0.38
Asylum	−0.45	0.44	0.60
Citizenship	0.24	0.61	0.58
Other rights	0.46	0.64	0.39
Deportation	0.74	0.41	0.28
Enforcement	0.75	−0.08	0.44

Originally published in Peters (2015) and reprinted with permission.

values between −2.25 and 1.6, with higher values signaling a more open policy. By construction, the mean of the index is 0, and the standard deviation is 1. There is no intrinsic meaning to the numbers; instead, higher numbers signal a more open policy, and lower numbers signal a more restrictive policy.

Is the Measure Reliable?

In addition to creating a valid measure—one that appropriately operationalizes the concept—we want to ensure that the variable is reliable: one that actually measures what we think we are measuring. One way to check reliability is to examine alternative coding and weighting schemes for the different dimensions.[17] As discussed earlier, not all policy dimensions have been used over the last 225 years. Most important, refugee, asylum, and family policies have been used only more recently. In the main coding of the variable, these dimensions are coded as a 1 until a policy is put into place. However, during the nineteenth century when there were few regulations on immigrants, refugees, asylum seekers, and family members could simply migrate as regular migrants. No special policy was needed for these groups because there were few restrictions keeping them from entering most countries. As an alternative coding, I coded these policies as a 5 for years with no policy, and as a 1 once there was another policy in place that would exclude a refugee, asylee, or family reunification immigrant until a policy addressing these groups was put into place.[18] I use principal component analysis to combine the new coding of these dimensions. There are four eigenvalues that have a value greater than 1, but, as in the case of the main coding, only two describe the majority of the variation and the first variable seems to describe immigration policy (henceforth, the *alternative coding*). As a third way of coding the data, we could, somewhat naively, weigh each dimension equally instead of using principal component analysis, using a standardized average (henceforth, the *standardized average*).

The three different codings correlate highly in the nineteenth century through World War II, but after World War II there is greater divergence.[19] The divergence is driven by the relative weights placed on the dimensions. The main policy measure places relatively more weight on the skill, recruitment, quotas, enforcement, and deportation dimensions; about the same weight on nationality, labor prohibition, and family dimensions; and less weight on refugee, asylum, citizenship, and rights than the alternative coding. It places much more weight on the skill, deportation, and enforcement dimensions; much less weight on citizenship; and about the same weight on the other dimensions than the standardized average.

---

[17] Additionally, the data for eight countries were recoded by a second coder; the two codings correlate at 0.9.

[18] These categories of immigrants were coded as excluded if the nationality or skill coding fell below a 4.

[19] Correlation between the main measure and the alternative coding is 0.86; between the main measure and the standardized average, 0.64.

I use the main measure because of the greater weight it places on skill, quotas, and the two enforcement dimensions. Since we are interested in low-skill immigrants, the skill criteria are likely to be the most important regulation. Additionally, given the issue of undocumented immigrants, placing more weight on enforcement is important.

As a second check on the reliability of the measure, we can see how the measure correlates with other scholars' coding of immigration policy. First, I examine the immigration policy variable created by Timmer and Williamson.[20] They include similar dimensions in their coding: border regulations, especially recruitment; rights, especially the right to own land; citizenship; and enforcement. They use an eleven-point coding scheme from −5 to 5. A zero in their coding is a laissez-faire policy with neither encouragement nor discouragement of immigration or a balance between pro- and anti-immigration policies; the policy is coded as a 5 if the government takes a very active role in recruiting immigrants, including free or assisted transportation along with free land; and a −5 is a very restrictive policy.[21] Overall, my measure correlates with their measure at 0.63 ($p < 0.000$), but some countries correlate more highly than others. The codings of US policy correlate at 0.99, whereas the codings of Brazil correlate at −0.3.

The differences in coding seem to be driven largely by differences in how Timmer and Williamson and I code recruitment, especially recruitment done by the provinces versus that done at the federal level. For example, the major differences in the two codings for Brazil occur in the period between 1860 and 1885. During this period, Timmer and Williamson code Brazil as having a laissez-faire immigration policy starting in 1860 and a pro-immigration policy starting in 1871. In their list of Brazilian immigration policies, they note, "Nothing of substance was accomplished in the 1860s";[22] however, according to my data collection, the government passed a law in 1858 that reduced anchorage fees for immigrant ships, offered inexpensive land, reimbursed the cost of the voyage to Brazil for those who purchased the land in cash, paid for the cost of transportation from the coast to the interior, built temporary housing for immigrants, and provided seed and animals for the first year. Using the Timmer and Williamson coding, I would have coded policy in 1860 as a 3 and increased it to a 4 in 1867 when the Brazilian government contracted with agents in Britain for five thousand immigrants per year. Recoding their variable this way until 1889, when they code Brazil's immigration policy as dropping

---

[20] Timmer and Williamson (1998). I thank Ashley Timmer and Jeffrey Williamson for sharing their data.

[21] Timmer and Williamson (1998, 741).

[22] Timmer and Williamson (1996, appendix C, xxii).

owing to changes in the budget for immigration, increases the correlation between the two measures for Brazil to 0.46.

We can also examine how well the data correlate with indexes that cover more recent periods. Ortega and Peri have a simple index that examines entry laws.[23] They include laws on quotas, the requirements, fees, or documents for entry, and the requirements or wait time for a residence or work permit.[24] In 1980, all countries are coded as 0; if the policy becomes more restrictive in a given year, the coding increases by a value of 1, and if the policy liberalizes, the coding decreases by 1. To make the comparison easier, I recoded their policy so that liberalization gets a value of 1 and restrictions a value of −1. Because they measure only some aspects of immigration, I compared their measure to the components of my measure that are most similar—skill requirements and labor prohibitions—by averaging these two measures.[25] The average of skill and labor prohibitions correlates with the Ortega and Peri measure at 0.66 ($p < 0.000$). Again, some countries correlate the two measures more highly than others; for example, Australia correlates at 0.74 ($p < 0.000$) but Japan correlates at −0.75 ($p < 0.000$). The difference in coding appears to be caused by the inclusion of policies that affect only more highly skilled immigrants in the Ortega and Peri dataset. For example, for both Canada and the United States they code the Canada-US Free Trade Agreement as leading to greater openness since it allowed easier entry for highly skilled immigrants. But since this law did not affect the entrance of low-skill immigrants, I did not include it.

Ruhs also has coded the openness of immigration policies for several countries for 2008 and 2009.[26] Instead of coding the overall policy, he codes the openness of different immigration programs and codes programs for high-skill, medium-skill, and low-skill immigrants, along with seasonal migrants. To ease comparability, I examine only the medium-skill, low-skill, and seasonal programs (which are often for low-skill agricultural immigrants). I took an average of his openness index for each program over the country-year and compared it to my skill code variable, which is the most comparable variable in my index. Figure A1 shows how my coding of skill (recoded to run between 0 and 1) corresponds to the average of Ruhs's codings of different programs for 2008 and 2009, respectively. While there are some outliers, there is a fairly good correspondence: countries that have

[23] Ortega and Peri (2013).

[24] Ortega and Peri (2013, 52).

[25] I do not include quotas since Ortega and Peri include only whether there is a quota and whether it is increasing or decreasing, and not whether it is increasing or decreasing in comparison to the population.

[26] Ruhs (2013).

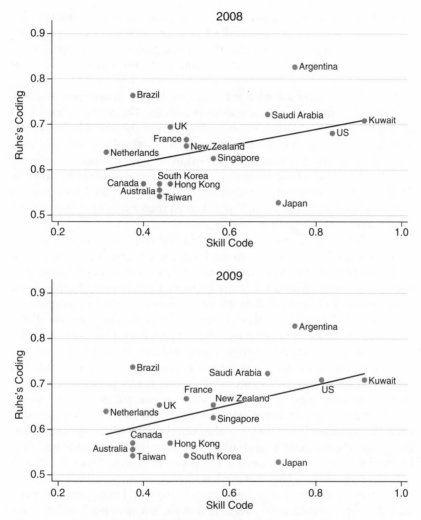

Figure A1: Comparison of the Skill Code to the Average Openness of Each State's Immigration Programs by Ruhs.

Note: Skill coding is the author's coding of skill restrictions recoded to run between 0 and 1. Ruhs's coding (Ruhs 2013) is the average of his openness score for low-skill, medium-skill, and seasonal programs for each country and year.

lower (higher) average scores on Ruhs's coding also have lower (higher) scores on average on my skill coding.

A final test to check the reliability of the measure is to examine how well it correlates with migrant flows. The policy coding may seem, at first glance, to be at odds with immigrant flows. By measures of stocks, Saudi Arabia and Kuwait, with 25 percent and 62 percent foreign-born, respectively, should be very open.[27] Similarly, the United States looks as open today as it did one hundred years ago if we examine the flows as a percentage of population.[28]

However, we must ask what is the proper counterfactual level of immigration in the absence of these restrictive policies. The counterfactual level of immigration would likely be much higher than the actual level if policy were less restrictive. Transportation costs have dropped precipitously with the rise of air travel; rising incomes worldwide have released the poverty trap that kept many from migrating; globalization has increased flows by disrupting the traditional economies of sending states; and decolonization and later the end of the Cold War led to an increase in civil wars, which should have led to large flows of refugees.

Nonetheless, we expect that the policy correlates with flows once we control for the demand to immigrate. To examine the effect of immigration policy on migrant flows, I include my immigration policy variable in a gravity model to control for many of these push-and-pull factors. I use Fitzgerald and colleagues' data on yearly flows to OECD countries for 1960 to 2000.[29] From these data, I create a directed dyad panel for all the countries in my immigration policy dataset paired with all other countries in the world. In a departure from a standard gravity model, I examined a first-differenced model. In general, the total number of migrants has been increasing over this time, while immigration policy has become more restrictive; naively regressing flows on the policy variable would lead to a negative correlation between these two variables. Additionally, I lag the immigration policy variable one year for three reasons. Most important, there are concerns about reverse causality; an increase (decrease) in immigration may lead immigration policy to change. Second, I do not have data on when in the year the law change occurred, which would be problematic if the law change occurs later in the year. Finally, many laws do not take effect immediately, meaning that the law may not have an effect until the following year. I also include several control variables: change in domestic violence, urbanization, population, and GDP per capita in both the receiving and the sending state, the imports into the receiving state from the sending state, the exports from the receiving state to the sending state, whether the states have an alliance, and whether the states are fighting a war against each other. I do not include geographic variables, such as the distance between the two states, because distance does not change.

[27] Ratha and Xu (2008).
[28] Office of Immigration Statistics (2010).
[29] Fitzgerald, Leblang, and Teets (2014).

TABLE A15
Gravity Model of the Change in Immigration Flows Regressed on the Change in Policy.

DV: Δ *bilateral immigrant flows*	Fitzgerald et al. 2014 data	
Δ immigration policy (lagged 1 year)	982.40*	(421.34)
Δ domestic violence (RC)	−777.99***	(230.36)
Δ domestic violence (SC)	16.38	(27.80)
Δ urbanization (RC)	26.02*	(13.09)
Δ urbanization (SC)	−3.06	(20.98)
Δ population (RC)	7694.11[+]	(4325.36)
Δ population (SC)	381.71	(534.93)
Δ GDP/capita (RC)	3204.32[+]	(1656.24)
Δ GDP/capita (SC)	−597.74*	(279.64)
Δ imports	−511.48	(433.19)
Δ exports	630.53	(551.17)
Δ alliance	238.12	(192.60)
Δ war	−39.34	(144.23)
Constant	−102.45[+]	(59.27)
Observations	30264	
R^2	0.01	

Notes: RC stands for receiving country and SC stands for sending country. Robust standard errors clustered by dyad in parentheses. $^{+}p < 0.10$, $^{*}p < 0.05$, $^{**}p < 0.01$, $^{***}p < 0.001$. *Immigration policy* is the measure discussed in chapter 3, coded by the author. *Population* (logged) is from Heston, Summers, and Aten (2011); *GDP/capita* (logged, in real 2000 dollars) is from Haber and Menaldo (2011) and World Bank Group (2012); *urbanization* (as a percentage of population) is from World Bank Group (2012); a 10-point rating of *domestic violence* (tracking civil and ethnic violence) is from Marshall (2010); *imports* and *exports* (in billions of US dollars) are from Barbieri and Keshk (2012); *alliance* indicates whether the two countries share a formal military alliance from Correlates of War Project (2013), and *war* indicates involvement on opposite sides of an interstate war from Sarkees and Wayman (2010).

I find that a change in the immigration policy is positively correlated with a change in the immigrant flows (table A15). The coefficient on immigration policy is positive and statistically significant at conventional levels. It is also substantively significant: the mean change (−0.013) in immigration policy during this time period leads to about 12.6 fewer immigrants per dyad year, or about 2, 500 fewer immigrants in total per year. These data suggest that changes in immigration policy as measured in the immigration policy variable have real effects on the number of immigrants who enter a country.

Bibliography

Abdi, Hervé, and Lynne J. Williams. 2010. "Principal Component Analysis." *Wiley Interdisciplinary Reviews: Computational Statistics* 2(4):433–59.

Acemoglu, Daron, and James A. Robinson. 2006. *Economic Origins of Dictatorship and Democracy*. Cambridge: Cambridge University Press.

Adler, E. Scott. 2009. "Congressional District Data File (All Years)." https://sites.google.com/a/colorado.edu/adler-scott/data/congressional-district-data. Accessed August 21, 2013.

Agreement concerning the Employment of Italian Workers for Underground Work in the Netherlands Mines. 1948. Number I-716. Geneva: United Nations Treaty Series.

Alberdi, Juan Bautista. 1952. *Bases y puntos de partida para la organización política de la Republica Argentina*. Buenos Aires, Estrada.

Alston, Lee J., and Joseph Ferrie. 1999. *Southern Paternalism and the Rise of the Welfare State: Economics, Politics, and Institutions in the US South, 1865–1965*. Cambridge: Cambridge University Press.

American Iron and Steel Institute. 2014*a*. "History of the American Iron and Steel Institute." http://www.steel.org/about-aisi/History.aspx. Accessed August 26, 2014.

American Iron and Steel Institute. 2014*b*. "Our Members." http://www.steel.org/about-aisi/Members.aspx. Accessed August 26, 2014.

Anderson, Perry. 1974. *Passages from Antiquity to Feudalism*. Vol. 2. London: NLB.

Andrews, Mildred Gwin. 1987. *The Men and the Mills: A History of the Southern Textile Industry*. Macon, GA: Mercer University Press.

Atack, Jeremy, Fred Bateman, and William N. Parker. 2000. "The Farm, the Farmer, and the Market." *The Cambridge Economic History of the United States* 2:245–84.

Atkinson, Edward. 1891. "Food and Feeding Considered as a Factor in Making the Rate of Wages or Earning." *Transactions of the New England Cotton Manufacturers' Association* 50.

Bailey, Michael A., Judith Goldstein, and Barry R. Weingast. 1997. "The Institutional Roots of American Trade Policy: Politics, Coalitions, and International Trade." *World Politics* 49(3):309–38.

Barbieri, Katherine, and Omar Keshk. 2012. "Correlates of War Project Trade Data Set Codebook, Version 3.0." www.correlatesofwar.org. Accessed September 22, 2014.

Barr, Michael D. 2014. "Singapore's Impotent Immigration Policy." *Asia Sentinel*. http://www.asiasentinel.com/society/singapore-impotent-immigration-policy/. Accessed March 24, 2015.

Bartelsman, E., and W. Gray. 2013. The NBER Manufacturing Productivity Database, 2013 Revision. Technical Working Paper 205. National Bureau of Economic Research.

Barton, John H., Judith L. Goldstein, Timothy E. Josling, and Richard H. Steinberg. 2006. *The Evolution of the Trade Regime: Politics, Law, and Economics of the GATT and the WTO*. Princeton, NJ: Princeton University Press.

Basinger, Scott J., and Mark Hallerberg. 2004. "Remodeling the Competition for Capital: How Domestic Politics Erases the Race to the Bottom." *American Political Science Review* 98(2):261–76.

Baumgartner, Frank R., Jeffrey M. Berry, Marie Hojnacki, Beth L. Leech, and David C. Kimball. 2009. *Lobbying and Policy Change: Who Wins, Who Loses, and Why*. Chicago: University of Chicago Press.

Baumgartner, F. R., and B. D. Jones. 2009. "Policy Agendas Project: Roll Call Votes." http://www.policyagendas.org. Accessed May 21, 2009.

Baumgartner, Frank R., and Bryan D. Jones. 2013. "Policy Agendas Project: Congressional Hearings." http://www.policyagendas.org/page/datasets-codebooks# congressional_hearings. Accessed December 26, 2013.

Bearce, David H., and Jennifer A. Laks Hutnick. 2011. "Toward an Alternative Explanation for the Resource Curse: Natural Resources, Immigration, and Democratization." *Comparative Political Studies* 44(6):689–718.

Bennett, Andrew. 2010. "Process Tracing and Causal Inference." In *Rethinking Social Inquiry: Diverse Tools, Shared Standards*, ed. Henry Brady and David Collier, 207–20. 2nd ed. Lanham, MD: Rowman & Littlefield.

Berend, Ivan T. 2006. *An Economic History of Twentieth-Century Europe: Economic Regimes from Laissez-Faire to Globalization*. Cambridge: Cambridge University Press.

Bermeo, Sarah Blodgett, and David Leblang. 2015. "Migration and Foreign Aid." *International Organization* 69(3):1–31.

Bernard, Andrew B., J. Bradford Jensen, and Peter K. Schott. 2006. "Survival of the Best Fit: Exposure to Low-Wage Countries and the (Uneven) Growth of US Manufacturing Plants." *Journal of International Economics* 68(1):219–37.

Bernhard, W., and B. R. Sala. 2008. "The Remaking of an American Senate: The 17th Amendment and Ideological Responsiveness." *Journal of Politics* 68(2): 345–57.

Bernhard, William, and David Leblang. 2014. "Sovereign Debt, Migration Pressure, and Government Survival." In *International Political Economy Society Annual Conference*. Washington, DC.

Bernhofen, Daniel M., Zouheir El-Sahli, and Richard Kneller. 2013. "Estimating the Effects of the Container Revolution on World Trade." Technical report. CESifo Working Paper: Trade Policy.

Bjerre, Liv, Marc Helbling, Friederike Romer, and Malisa Zobel. 2014. "Conceptualizing and Measuring Immigration Policies: A Comparative Perspective." *International Migration Review* 49(2):555–600.

Blinder, Alan S. 2007. "How Many US Jobs Might Be Offshorable." Unpublished manuscript. Princeton University.

Bordo, Michael, Barry Eichengreen, Daniela Klingebiel, and Maria Soledad Martinez-Peria. 2001. "Is the Crisis Problem Growing More Severe?" *Economic Policy* 16(32):52–82.

Borjas, George J., Jeffrey Grogger, and Gordon H., Hanson. 2008. "Imperfect Substitution between Immigrants and Natives: A Reappraisal." Working Paper

13887 National Bureau of Economic Research. http://www.nber.org/papers/w13887. Accessed May 20, 2015.

Boswell, Terry E. 1986. "A Split Labor Market Analysis of Discrimination against Chinese Immigrants, 1850–1882." *American Sociological Review* 51(3):352–71.

Briggs, Vernon M. 1984. *Immigration Policy and the American Labor Force*. Baltimore: Johns Hopkins University Press.

Briggs, Vernon M. 2001. *Immigration and American Unionism*. Ithaca, NY: Cornell University Press.

Brown, Kevin. 2011. "Singapore Opposition Makes Historic Gains." *Financial Times*. http://www.ft.com/intl/cms/s/0/ac59d4aa-7924-11e0-b655-00144feabdc0.html#axzz3888gF3nS. Accessed July 21, 2014.

Bureau of Economic Analysis. 2009. "GDP by State." http://www.bea.gov/regional/index.htm. Accessed January 9, 2010.

Bureau of Economic Analysis. 2012. *U.S. Direct Investment Abroad: Industry Detail*. Washington, DC: US Government Printing Office. http://www.bea.gov/international/index.htm#omc. Accessed November 15, 2012.

Calavita, Kitty. 2010. *Inside the State: The Bracero Program, Immigration, and the INS*. New Orleans: Quid Pro Books.

Caldwell, Alicia A. 2011. "Agriculture Industry Fears Disaster If Illegal Immigration Enforcement Program E-Verify Is Implemented." http://www.huffingtonpost.com/2011/06/04/agriculture-industry-e-verify-illegal-immigration_n_871391.html. Accessed April 28, 2014.

California Department of Food and Agriculture. 2012. "Agricultural Statistics Overview." In *California Agricultural Statistics Review 2011–2012*, 2–16. Sacramento: State of California.

Canes-Wrone, B., D. W. Brady, and J. F. Cogan. 2002. "Out of Step, Out of Office: Electoral Accountability and House Members' Voting." *American Political Science Review* 96(1):127–40.

Carr, Thomas P. 2006. "Hearings in the House of Representatives: A Guide for Preparation and Procedure." Congressional Research Service, the Library of Congress.

Carter, Susan B., Scott Sigmund Gartner, Michael R. Haines, Alan L. Olmstead, Richard Sutch, and Gavin Wright. 2006. *Historical Statistics of the United States Millennial Edition Online*. Number Table Cf8-64: Land area, by state and territory: 1790–1990. New York: Cambridge University Press. http://hsus.cambridge.org/. Accessed October 12, 2015.

Castro, Max J. 1999. "Toward a New Nativism? The Immigration Debate in the United States and Its Implications for Latin America and the Caribbean." In *Free Markets, Open Societies, Closed Borders? Trends in International Migration and Immigration Policy in the Americas*, ed. Max J. Castro. Miami: North-South Center Press.

Census Bureau. 1975. Series K 445–47, 449, 450–52, 454. In *Historical Statistics of the United States, Colonial Times to 1970*. Number 93. US Department of Commerce, Bureau of the Census.

Census Bureau. 2011. *US—All Industries—by Employment Size of Enterprise*. US Department of Commerce, Bureau of the Census. http://www.census.gov/data/tables/2011/econ/susb/2011-susb-annual.html. Accessed May 28, 2015.

Census Bureau. Various Years*a*. *Census of Governments*. Washington, DC: US Government Printing Office.

Census Bureau. Various Years*b*. *Census of Manufactures*. Washington, DC: US Government Printing Office.

Census Bureau. Various Years*c*. *Statistical Abstract of the United States*. Washington, DC: US Government Printing Office.

Census Bureau. Various Years*d*. "Number of Miles of Railroads in Operation in Each State and Territory of the United States." In *Statistical Abstract of the United States: 1881, 1885, 1888, 1891, 1897, 1900, 1904, 1907, 1910, 1911, 1914, 1916, 1919, 1921, 1922, 1924, 1926, 1929, 1931, 1934, 1936, 1938, and 1942*. Washington, DC: US Government Printing Office.

Census Bureau. Various Years*e*. "Values of, and Amounts of Duty Collected on, the Principal Commodities and Classes of Commodities Entered for Consumption." In *Statistical Abstract of the United States*: 1889, 1900, 1911, 1937, and 1948. Washington, DC: US Government Printing Office.

Center for Responsive Politics. N.d. "Opensecrets.org: Lobbying Database." http://www.opensecrets.org/lobby/index.php. Accessed June 14, 2012.

Centraal Bureau voor de Statistiek (Statistics Netherlands). 1958–95. *Nationale Rekeningen*. The Hague.

Centraal Bureau voor de Statistiek (Statistics Netherlands). 1986. *Statistical Yearbook of the Netherlands*. The Hague.

Chen, Sharon. 2013. "Singapore Population to Be Below 6.9 Million in 2030, Lee Says." *Bloomberg News*. http://www.bloomberg.com/news/2013-02-08/singapore-population-to-be-below-6-9-million-in-2030-lee-says.html. Accessed July 21, 2014.

Chinn, M. D., and H. Ito. 2008. "A New Measure of Financial Openness." *Journal of Comparative Policy Analysis: Research and Practice* 10(3):309–22.

Chong, Alan. 2007. "Singapore's Political Economy, 1997–2007: Strategizing Economic Assurance for Globalization." *Asian Survey* 47(6):952–76.

Clemens, Michael A. 2009. "Migrants Count: Five Steps to Better Migration Data." Washington, DC: Center for Global Development.

Clemens, Michael A., and Jeffrey G. Williamson. 2004. "Why Did the Tariff-Growth Correlation Change after 1950?" *Journal of Economic Growth* 9(1):5–46.

Clews, Henry. 1908. "The Financial and Trade Situation and Prospects." *Transactions of the New England Cotton Manufacturers' Association* 84:244–61.

Clifford, Stephen. 2013. "U.S. Textile Plants Return, with Floors Largely Empty of People." *New York Times*. http://www.nytimes.com/2013/09/20/business/us-textile-factories-return.html?hp&_r=1. Accessed June 12, 2015.

Clinton, J. D. 2006. "Representation in Congress: Constituents and Roll Calls in the 106th House." *Journal of Politics* 68(2):397–409.

Colgan, Jeff D. 2014. "The Political Economy of the End of Empire." In *International Political Economy Society Annual Conference*. Washington, DC.

Collard-Wexler, Allan, and Jan De Loecker. 2013. "Reallocation and Technology: Evidence from the US Steel Industry." Working Paper 18739. National Bureau of Economic Research.

Collins, W. J. 2003. "The Labor Market Impact of State-Level Anti-Discrimination Laws, 1940–1960." *Industrial and Labor Relations Review* 56(2):244–72.

Comin, Diego A., and Bart Hobijn. 2009. "The CHAT Dataset." National Bureau of Economic Research Working Paper No. 15319.

Congressional Quarterly. 2003. "Immigration and Naturalization Service (INS) Abolished, with Border Security, Immigration Services Divided at Department of Homeland Security (DHS)." *CQ Almanac 2002.* http://library.cqpress.com/cqalmanac/. Accessed July 12, 2010.

Congressional Quarterly. 2005. "Details of the Intelligence Overhaul Law." *CQ Almanac 2004.* http://library.cqpress.com/cqalmanac/. Accessed July 12, 2010.

Congressional Quarterly. 2006a. "Immigration, 2001–2002 Legislative Chronology." In *Congress and the Nation 2001–2004.* Vol. 11. Washington, DC: CQ Press.

Congressional Quarterly. 2006b. "War Supplemental Has Strings Attached." *CQ Almanac 2005.* http://library.cqpress.com/cqalmanac/. Accessed July 12, 2010.

Copeland, Melvin T. 1922. "The Economic Story." *Transactions of the National Association of Cotton Manufacturers* 113:66–74.

Copelovitch, Mark, and Jon C. Pevehouse. 2013. "Ties That Bind? Preferential Trade Aggreements and Exchange Rate Policy Choice." *International Studies Quarterly* 57:385–99.

Correlates of War Project. 2013. "Formal Interstate Alliance Dataset, Version 4.1." www.correlatesofwar.org. Accessed September 22, 2014.

Crook, S. B., and J. R. Hibbing. 1997. "A Not-So-Distant Mirror: The 17th Amendment and Congressional Change." *American Political Science Review* 91(4):845–53.

Crouch, Colin. 1993. *Industrial Relations and European State Traditions.* Oxford: Oxford University Press.

Cusack, Thomas R. 2000a. "Center of Political Gravity Dataset." http://www.edac.eu/indicators_desc.cfm?v_id=193. Accessed August 15, 2013.

Cusack, Thomas R. 2000b. "Public Finance Data for 20 OECD Countries" http://www.edac.eu/indicators_desc.cfm?v_id=192. Accessed August 15, 2013.

Dancygier, Rafaela. 2013. "The Left and Minority Representation: The Labour Party, Muslim Candidates, and Inclusion Tradeoffs." *Comparative Politics* 46(1): 1–21.

David, Paul A. 1975. *Technical Choice Innovation and Economic Growth: Essays on American and British Experience in the Nineteenth Century.* Cambridge: Cambridge University Press.

Davis, L. E. 1965. "The Investment Market, 1870–1914: The Evolution of a National Market." *Journal of Economic History* 25(3):355–99.

Donaldson, Dave, and Richard Hornbeck. 2013. "Railroads and American Economic Growth: A 'Market Access' Approach." Technical report. National Bureau of Economic Research.

Doyle, Michael W., and Nicholas Sambanis. 2006. *Making War and Building Peace: United Nations Peace Operations.* Princeton, NJ: Princeton University Press.

Drezner, Daniel W. 1999. *The Sanctions Paradox: Economic Statecraft and International Relations.* Cambridge Studies in International Relations, no. 65. Cambridge: Cambridge University Press.

Drutman, Lee. 2015. *The Business of America Is Lobbying: How Corporations Became Politicized and Politics Became More Corporate.* New York: Oxford University Press.

Dustmann, Christian, Tommaso Frattini, and Caroline Halls. 2010. "Assessing the Fiscal Costs and Benefits of A8 Migration to the UK." *Fiscal Studies* 31(1):1–41.

Economic Development Board of Singapore. 2015. "Our History." Technical report. https://www.edb.gov.sg/content/edb/en/why-singapore/about-singapore/our-history/1960s.html. Accessed March 25, 2015.

Economic Strategies Committee. 2010. "Report of the Economic Strategies Committee." https://www.mti.gov.sg/ResearchRoom/Documents/app.mti.gov.sg/data/pages/885/doc/ESC%20Full%20Report.pdf. Accessed May 24, 2013.

Eichengreen, Barry. 1995. "Financing Infrastructure in Developing Countries: Lessons from the Railway Age." *World Bank Research Observer* 10(1):75–91.

Eichengreen, Barry. 2007. *The European Economy since 1945: Coordinated Capitalism and Beyond*. Princeton, NJ: Princeton University Press.

Engerman, Stanley L., and Kenneth L. Sokoloff. 2000. "Technology and Industrialization, 1790–1914." *The Cambridge Economic History of the United States* 2:367–401.

Eurostat. 2016. http://ec.europa.eu/eurostat/statistics-explained/index.php/Asylum_statistics. Accessed March 10, 2016.

Faist, Thomas. 1994. "How to Define a Foreigner? The Symbolic Politics of Immigration in German Partisan Discourse, 1978–1992." *West European Politics* 17(2):50–71.

Feenstra, Robert C., and Gordon H. Hanson. 1996. "Globalization, Outsourcing, and Wage Inequality." *American Economic Review* 86(2):240–45.

Feller, Irwin. 1974. "The Diffusion and Location of Technological Change in the American Cotton-Textile Industry, 1890–1970." *Technology and Culture* 15:569–93.

Ferenczi, Imre, and Walter Francis Willcox. 1929. *International Migrations: Statistics.* Vol. 1. New York: National Bureau of Economic Research.

Fitzgerald, Jennifer, David A. Leblang, and Jessica Teets. 2014. "Defying the Law of Gravity: The Political Economy of International Migration." *World Politics* 66(3):406–45.

Fogel, Robert William. 1994. *Railroads and American Economic Growth*. New York: Cambridge University Press.

Fong, Pang Eng, and Linda Lim. 1982. "Foreign Labor and Economic Development in Singapore." *International Migration Review* 16(3):548–76.

Foreman-Peck, James. 1992. "A Political Economy of International Migration, 1815–1914." *The Manchester School* 60(4):359–76.

Franklin, Benjamin. 1755. *Observations on the late and present Conduct of the French, with Regard to their Encroachments upon the British Colonies in North America....To which is added, wrote by another Hand; Observations concerning the Increase of Mankind, Peopling of Countries, &c.* Boston: Printed by William Clarke and Sold by S. Kneeland in Queen-Street.

Frayer, Lauren. 2015. "Hungary's Catholics Are Largely Absent from Refugee Drama." *Morning Edition*. http://www.npr.org/2015/09/30/444660127/despite-popes-urging-hungarys-catholics-are-largely-absent-from-refugee-drama. Accessed September 30, 2015.

Freeman, Gary P. 1995. "Modes of Immigration Politics in Liberal Democratic States." *International Migration Review* 29(4):881–902.

Frieden, Jeffry A. 2014. *Currency Politics: The Political Economy of Exchange Rate Policy*. Princeton, NJ: Princeton University Press.

Friedman, G. 2000. "The Political Economy of Early Southern Unionism: Race, Politics, and Labor in the South, 1880–1953." *Journal of Economic History* 60(2):384–413.

From SOE to GLC: China's Rulers Look to Singapore for Tips on Portfolio Management. 2013. *Economist.* http://www.economist.com/news/finance-and-economics/2159 0562-chinas-rulers-look-singapore-tips-portfolio-management-soe-glc. Accessed March 25, 2015.

Fukuyama, Francis. 2011. *The Origins of Political Order: From Prehuman Times to the French Revolution.* London: Profile Books.

Gailmard, Sean, and Jeffery A. Jenkins. 2009. "Agency Problems, the 17th Amendment, and Representation in the Senate." *American Journal of Political Science* 53(2):324–42.

Galenson, Alice. 1985. *The Migration of the Cotton Textile Industry from New England to the South, 1880–1930.* New York: Garland.

Garrett, Geoffrey. 1995. "Capital Mobility, Trade, and the Domestic Politics of Economic Policy." *International Organization* 49(1):657–87.

Gary, Elbert H. 1923. "Address of the President." *Yearbook of the American Iron and Steel Institute,* 11–15.

Geddes, Andrew, and Jeannette Money. 2011. "Mobility within the European Union." In *Migration, Nation States, and International Cooperation,* ed. Randall Hansen, Jobst Koehler, and Jeannette Money, 31–43. New York: Routledge.

Gerber, Alan S., Gregory A. Huber, Daniel R. Biggers, and David J. Hendry. 2014. "Self Interest, Beliefs, and Policy Opinions: Understanding the Economic Source of Immigration Policy Preferences." huber.research.yale.edu/materials/46_paper.pdf. Accessed November 18, 2014.

Glaeser, Edward L., and Andrei Shleifer. 2005. "The Curley Effect: The Economics of Shaping the Electorate." *Journal of Law, Economics, & Organization* 21(1):1–19.

Golden, Miriam, Peter Lange, and Michael Wallerstein. 2009. "Union Centralization among Advanced Industrial Societies: An Empirical Study." https://dataverse.harvard.edu/dataset.xhtml?persistentId=hdl:1902.1/10193. Accessed June 12, 2011.

Goldin, Claudia. 1994. "The Political Economy of Immigration Restrictions in the United States, 1890 to 1921." In *The Regulated Economy: A Historical Approach to Political Economy,* ed. Claudia Goldin and Gary Libecap. Chicago: University of Chicago Press.

Goldin, Claudia, and Lawrence F. Katz. 1998. "The Origins of Technology-Skill Complementarity." *Quarterly Journal of Economics* 113(3): 693–732.

Goldstein, Judith L., and Margaret E. Peters. 2014. "Nativism or Economic Threat: Attitudes toward Immigrants during the Great Recession." *International Interactions* 40(3):376–401.

Gómez, José A., and Derek C. Bok. 2005. *Singapore's Public Enterprises.* Cambridge, MA: Kennedy School of Government.

Gould, David M. 1994. "Immigrant Links to the Home Country: Empirical Implications for US Bilateral Trade Flows." *Review of Economics and Statistics* 76(2):302–16.

Grove, Wayne A. 1996. "The Mexican Farm Labor Program, 1942–1964: Government-Administered Labor Market Insurance for Farmers." *Agricultural History* 70(2):302–20.

Ha, E. and G. Tsebelis. 2010. "Globalization and Welfare: Which Causes Which?" University of Michigan. www.academia.edu/18730950/Globalization_and_ Welfare_Which_Causes_Which. Accessed August 21, 2013.

Haber, Stephen, and Victor Menaldo. 2011. "Do Natural Resources Fuel Authoritarianism? A Reappraisal of the Resource Curse." *American Political Science Review* 105(1):1–26.

Haines, Michael, Price Fishback, and Paul Rhode. 2014. "United States Agriculture Data, 1840–2010." Technical Report ICPSR35206-v1. Inter-university Consortium for Political and Social Research [distributor]. http://doi.org/10.3886/ICPSR35206.v1. Accessed January 21, 2015.

Hainmueller, Jens, and Michael J. Hiscox. 2006. "Learning to Love Globalization: Education and Individual Attitudes Toward International Trade." *International Organization* 60(2):469–98.

Hainmueller, Jens, and Michael J. Hiscox. 2007. "Educated Preferences: Explaining Attitudes toward Immigration in Europe." *International Organization* 61(2): 399–442.

Hainmueller, Jens, and Michael J. Hiscox. 2010. "Attitudes toward Highly Skilled and Low-Skilled Immigration: Evidence from a Survey Experiment." *American Political Science Review* 104(1):1–24.

Hall, Christopher G. L. 1997. *Steel Phoenix: The Fall and Rise of the US Steel Industry*. New York: Palgrave Macmillan.

Hamilton-Hart, Natasha. 2000. "The Singapore State Revisited." *Pacific Review* 13(2):195–216.

Hansen, Randall. 2002. "Globalization, Embedded Realism, and Path Dependence: The Other Immigrants to Europe." *Comparative Political Studies* 35(3):259–83.

Hanson, Gordon H., Kenneth Scheve, and Matthew J. Slaughter. 2007. "Public Finance and Individual Preferences over Globalization Strategies." *Economics & Politics* 19(1):1–33.

Hartog, Chris Den, and Nathan W. Monroe. 2011. *Agenda Setting in the U.S. Senate*. Cambridge: Cambridge University Press.

Hatton, Timothy J., and Jeffrey G. Williamson. 1998. *The Age of Mass Migration: Causes and Economic Impact*. New York: Oxford University Press.

Hatton, Timothy J., and Jeffrey G. Williamson. 2005a. "A Dual Policy Paradox: Why Have Trade and Immigration Policies Always Differed in Labor-Scarce Economies?" Unpublished manuscript. National Bureau of Economic Research, Boston, MA.

Hatton, Timothy J., and Jeffrey G. Williamson. 2005b. *Global Migration and the World Economy*. Cambridge, MA: MIT Press.

Hatton, Timothy J., and Jeffrey G. Williamson. 2008. "The Impact of Immigration: Comparing Two Global Eras." *World Development* 36(3):345–61.

Helpman, Elhanan. 2006. "Trade, FDI, and the Organization of Firms." *Journal of Economic Literature* 44(3):589–630.

Helpman, Elhanan, Oleg Itskhoki, and Stephen Redding. 2009. "Inequality and Unemployment in a Global Economy." Unpublished manuscript. CEPR Discussion Paper No. 7353.

Heston, Alan, Robert Summers, and Bettina Aten. 2011. "Penn World Table Version 7.0." *Center for International Comparisons of Production, Income and Prices, University of Pennsylvania* . https://knoema.com/PWT2011JUN/penn-world-table-7-0. Accessed September 22, 2014.

Hiscox, Michael J. 2002. *International Trade and Political Conflict: Commerce, Coalitions, and Mobility*. Princeton, NJ: Princeton University Press.

Holborn, Louise W. 1965. "International Organizations for Migration of European Nationals and Refugees." *International Journal* 20(3):331–49.

Holley, Donald. 2000. *The Second Great Emancipation: The Mechanical Cotton Picker, Black Migration, and How They Shaped the Modern South*. Fayetteville: University of Arkansas Press.

Horlings, Edwin. 2001. "Pre-industrial Economic Growth and the Transition to an Industrial Economy." In *Early Modern Capitalism: Economic and Social Change in Europe 1400–1800*, ed. Maarten Prak, 88–104. London: Routledge.

Hui, W. T. 1998. "The Regional Economic Crisis and Singapore: Implications for Labor Migration." *Asian and Pacific Migration Journal* 7(2–3):187–218.

Hull, Cordell. 1948. *The Memoirs of Cordell Hull*. New York: Macmillan.

Hutchinson, Edward P. 1981. *Legislative History of American Immigration Policy, 1798–1965*. Philadelphia: University of Pennsylvania Press.

Ikenberry, G. John. 2001. *After Victory: Institutions, Strategic Restraint, and the Rebuilding of Order after Major Wars*. Princeton, NJ: Princeton University Press.

Irwin, Douglas A. 1998. "From Smoot-Hawley to Reciprocal Trade Agreements: Changing the Course of U.S. Trade Policy in the 1930s." In *The Defining Moment: The Great Depression and the American Economy in the Twentieth Century*, ed. Michael D. Bordo, Claudia Goldin, and Eugene N. White, 325–52. Chicago: University of Chicago Press.

Irwin, Douglas A., and Randall S. Kroszner. 1996. "Log-Rolling and Economic Interests in the Passage of the Smoot-Hawley Tariff." *Carnegie-Rochester Conference Series on Public Policy* 45:173–200.

James, J. A. 1976. "The Development of the National Money Market, 1893–1911." *Journal of Economic History* 36(4):878–97.

Joppke, Christian. 1998. "Why Liberal States Accept Unwanted Immigration." *World Politics* 50(2):266–93.

Jordan, Virgil. 1927. "Address by Virgil Jordan." Yearbook of the American Iron and Steel Institute. (May):498–512.

Jupp, James. 2002. *From White Australia to Woomera: The Story of Australian Immigration*. New York: Cambridge University Press.

Kaur, A. 2006. *International Migration in Malaysia and Singapore since the 1880s: State Policies, Migration Trends and Governance of Migration*. New England, NSW: The University of New England Asia Centre (UNEAC) for the Malaysia and Singapore Society of Australia.

Kay, Diana, and Robert Miles. 1988. "Refugees or Migrant Workers? The Case of the European Volunteer Workers in Britain (1946–1951)." *Journal of Refugee Studies* 1(3–4):214–36.

Kaye, Ronald. 1994. "Defining the Agenda: British Refugee Policy and the Role of Parties." *Journal of Refugee Studies* 7(2–3):144.

Kelley, Ninette, and M. J. Trebilcock. 1998. *The Making of the Mosaic: A History of Canadian Immigration Policy*. Toronto: University of Toronto Press.

Kenney, Martin, and Richard L. Florida. 2004. *Locating Global Advantage: Industry Dynamics in the International Economy*. Stanford, CA: Stanford University Press.

Key, Nigel, and David Runsten. 1999. "Contract Farming, Smallholders, and Rural Development in Latin America: The Organization of Agroprocessing Firms and the Scale of Outgrower Production." *World Development* 27(2):381–401.

Kim, Sukkoo. 1995. "Expansion of Markets and the Geographic Distribution of Economic Activities: The Trends in US Regional Manufacturing Structure, 1860–1987." *Quarterly Journal of Economics* 110(4):881–908.

Kollman, Ken. 1997. "Inviting Friends to Lobby: Interest Groups, Ideological Bias, and Congressional Committees." *American Journal of Political Science* 41(2):519–44.

Koopmans, Ruud, and Jasper Muis. 2009. "The Rise of Right-Wing Populist Pim Fortuyn in the Netherlands: A Discursive Opportunity Approach." *European Journal of Political Research* 48(5):642–64.

Kremer, Michael. 2006. "Globalization of Labor Markets and Inequality." *Brookings Trade Forum*, 211–28.

Kremer, Monique, and Erik Schrijvars. 2014. "Making Romanian and Bulgarian Migration Work in the Netherlands." Technical report. WRR-Policy Brief 1 Netherlands Scientific Council for Government Policy (WRR). http://www.wrr.nl/fileadmin/en/publicaties/PDF-WRR-Policy_Briefs/2014-01_WRR_Policy_Brief_1_ENGELS_05.pdf. Accessed April 7, 2015.

Kuhn, Anthony. 2015. "Founding Father of Modern Singapore, Lee Kuan Yew, Dies at 91." *National Public Radio*. http://www.npr.org/blogs/parallels/2015/03/22/393824362/founding-father-of-modern-singapore-lee-kuan-yew-dies-at-91. Accessed March 26, 2015.

Lake, David A. 2009. "Open Economy Politics: A Critical Review." *Review of International Organizations* 4(3):219–44.

Lake, David A., and Christopher J. Fariss. 2014. "Why International Trusteeship Fails: The Politics of External Authority in Areas of Limited Statehood." *Governance* 27(4):569–87.

Lamoreaux, Naomi R. 2000. "Entrepreneurship, Business Organization, and Economic Concentration." *The Cambridge Economic History of the United States* 2:403–34.

Lapinski, J. S. 2004. "Direct Election and the Emergence of the Modern Senate." Unpublished manuscript. Yale University.

Lazarus, Emma. 1883. www.poetryfoundation.org/poems-and-poets/poems/detail/46550.

Leblang, David. 2010. "Familiarity Breeds Investment: Diaspora Networks and International Investment." *American Political Science Review* 104(3):584–600.

Lee, Frances. 2009. *Beyond Ideology: Politics, Principles, and Partisanship in the U.S. Senate*. Chicago: University of Chicago Press.

Legislative Report. 2004. *Western Grower and Shipper*. (December):11–12.

Levitt, S. D. 1996. "How Do Senators Vote? Disentangling the Role of Voter Preferences, Party Affiliation, and Senator Ideology." *American Economic Review* 86(3):425–41.

Lewis, Ethan. 2011. "Immigration, Skill Mix, and Capital Skill Complementarity." *Quarterly Journal of Economics* 126(2):1029–69.

Leyden, Kevin M. 1995. "Interest Group Resources and Testimony at Congressional Hearings." *Legislative Studies Quarterly* 20(3):431–439.

Lijphart, Arend. 1975. *The Politics of Accommodation: Pluralism and Democracy in the Netherlands*. Berkely: University of California Press.

Lim, Kevin. 2013. "By-election Shines a Light on Discontented Singapore." *Reuters*. http://www.reuters.com/article/2013/01/25/us-singapore-politics-idUSBRE90O0 B020130125. Accessed July 22, 2013.

Lim, Linda Y. C. 1983. "Singapore's Success: The Myth of the Free Market Economy." *Asian Survey* 23(6):752–64.

Linden, Tom. 1997. "Labor Laws Offer Opportunities, Pitfalls." *Western Grower and Shipper*. (WGA Yearbook):47–48.

Linden, Tom. 1999. "INS Launches New Offensive." *Western Grower and Shipper*. (May):19.

Linden, Tom. 2006. "Myths and Theories; Facts and Fiction: Misinformation Frames Immigration Reform Debate." *Western Grower and Shipper*, January: 11–17.

Loh, Kah Seng. 2011. "The British Military Withdrawal from Singapore and the Anatomy of a Catalyst." In *Singapore in Global History*, ed. Derek Heng and Syed Muhd Khairudin Aljunied, 195–213. Amsterdam: Amsterdam University Press.

Longhi, Simonetta, Peter Nijkamp, and Jacques Poot. 2005. "A Meta-analytic Assessment of the Effect of Immigration on Wages." *Journal of Economic Surveys* 19(3):451–77.

Low, Linda. 1998. *The Political Economy of a City-State: Government-Made Singapore*. Singapore: Oxford University Press.

Low, Linda. 2002. "Rethinking Singapore Inc. and GLCs." *Southeast Asian Affairs*, 282–302.

Low, Linda. 2003. "Sustaining the Competitiveness of Singapore Inc in the Knowledge-Based Global Economy." In *Sustaining Competitiveness in the New Global Economy: The Experience of Singapore*, ed. Ramkishen S. Rajan, 135–50. Cheltenham, UK: Edward Elgar.

Maddison, Angus. 2011. "Statistics on World Population, GDP, and Per Capita GDP, 1–2008 AD." http://www.ggdc.net/maddison/maddison-project/home.htm. Accessed August 21, 2013.

Major Investments. 2015. Technical report. Temasek Review. http://www.temasekreview.com.sg/en/major-investments.html. Accessed March 25, 2015.

Marshall, Monty G. 2010. "Major Episodes of Political Violence (MEPV) and Conflict Regions, 1946–2008." *Center for Systemic Peace*. http://pdf.thepdfportal.org/?id=280391. Accessed September 22, 2014.

Marshall, Monty G., Ted Robert Gurr, and Keith Jaggers. 2011. "Polity IV Project: Political Regime Characteristics and Transitions, 1800–2009." *Center for Systemic Peace*. www.systemicpeace.org/polity/polity4.htm. Accessed January 20, 2014.

Massey, Douglas S., Joaquin Arango, Graeme Hugo, Ali Kouaouci, Adela Pellegrino, and J. Edward Taylor. 1993. "Theories of International Migration: A Review and Appraisal." *Population and Development Review* 19(3):431–66.

Meinke, S. R. 2008. "Institutional Change and the Electoral Connection in the Senate." *Political Research Quarterly* 61(3):445–47.

Melitz, Marc J. 2003. "The Impact of Trade on Intra-industry Reallocations and Aggregate Industry Productivity." *Econometrica* 71(6):1695–1725.

Messina, Anthony M. 2008. "The Logics and Politics of post-WWII Migration to Western Europe." *West European Politics* 31(5):1096–97.

Miller, Michael K., and Margaret E. Peters. 2014. "Restraining the Huddled Masses: Migration Policy and Autocratic Survival." In *International Political Economy Society Annual Conference*. Washington DC.

Milner, Helen V., and Dustin H. Tingley. 2012. "Sailing the Water's Edge: Where Domestic Politics Meets Foreign Policy." Unpublished manuscript. Princeton University, Harvard University.

Minchin, Timothy J. 2009. " 'It knocked this city to its knees': The Closure of Pillowtex Mills in Kannapolis, North Carolina, and the Decline of the US Textile Industry." *Labor History* 50(3):287–311.

Mines, Richard, and Philip Martin. 1983. "Foreign Workers in California's Produce Industry." *Western Grower and Shipper*, 10–12, 36–37.

Ministry of Trade and Industry. 2012. "MTI Occasional Paper on Population and Economy." www.mti.gov.sg/mtiinsights/pages/mti-occasional-paper-on-population-and-economy.aspx. Accessed May 25, 2014.

Mirilovic, Nikola. 2010. "The Politics of Immigration: Dictatorship, Development, and Defense." *Comparative Politics* 42(3):273–92.

Mittelhauser, Mark. 1997. "Employment Trends in Textiles and Apparel, 1973–2005." *Monthly Labor Review* 120:24–35

Moch, Leslie Page. 1995. "Moving Europeans: Historical Migration Practices in Western Europe." *The Cambridge Survey of World Migration*, 126–30.

Money, Jeannette. 1999. *Fences and Neighbors: The Political Geography of Immigration Control*. Ithaca, NY: Cornell University Press.

Morris, James A. 1953. "Cotton and Wool Textiles—Case Studies in Industrial Migration." *Journal of Industrial Economics* 2(1):65–83.

Mosley, Layna. 2000. "Room to Move: International Financial Markets and National Welfare States." *International Organization* 54(4):737–73.

Motomura, Hiroshi. 2014. *Immigration outside the Law*. Oxford: Oxford University Press.

Nasir, Kamaludeen Mohamed, and Bryan S. Turner. 2014. *The Future of Singapore: Population, Society and the Nature of the State*. London: Routledge.

Nassif, Tom. 2005. "Immigration Reform: National Security Begins at Breakfast." *Western Grower and Shipper*. (March):5–6.

Nassif, Tom. 2006*a*. "Hasta La Vista, Baby." *Western Grower and Shipper*, April:4.

Nassif, Tom. 2006*b*. "The Key." *Western Grower and Shipper*, May:5–6.

Nassif Takes on Dobbs, transcript. 2005. *Western Grower and Shipper*. (May):8–9.

National Population and Talent Division. 2012. "Our Population, Our Future." Singapore: Government of Singapore.

National Population and Talent Division. 2013. *A Sustainable Population for a Dynamic Singapore: Population White Paper*. Singapore: Government of Singapore.

Neuman, Gerald L. 1993. "The Lost Century of American Immigration Law (1776–1875)." *Columbia Law Review* 93(8):1833–1901.

Nicholas, Stephen. 1983. "Agency Contracts, Institutional Modes, and the Transition to Foreign Direct Investment by British Manufacturing Multinationals before 1939." *Journal of Economic History* 43(3):675–86.

Oatley, Thomas. 2011. "The Reductionist Gamble: Open Economy Politics in the Global Economy." *International Organization* 65(2):311–41.

Obstfeld, M., and A. M. Taylor. 2004. *Global Capital Markets: Integration, Crisis, and Growth*. Cambridge: Cambridge University Press.

Office of Immigration Statistics. 2006. *2005 Yearbook of Immigration Statistics*. Washington, DC: Department of Homeland Security.

Office of Immigration Statistics. 2010. *2009 Yearbook of Immigration Statistics*. Washington, DC: Department of Homeland Security.

Officer, Lawrence H., and Samuel H., Williamson. 2015. "The Annual Consumer Price Index for the United States, 1774–2014." In *MeasuringWorth*. http://www.measuringworth.com/uscpi/. Accessed May 6, 2015.

Olson, Mancur. 1965. *The Logic of Collective Action*. Cambridge, MA: Harvard University Press.

Olzak, Susan. 1989. "Labor Unrest, Immigration, and Ethnic Conflict in Urban America, 1880–1914." *American Journal of Sociology* 94(6):1303–33.

Onorato, Massimiliano Gaetano, Kenneth Scheve, and David Stasavage. 2014. "Technology and the Era of the Mass Army." *Journal of Economic History* 74(2):449–81.

Ortega, Francesc, and Giovanni Peri. 2013. "The Effect of Income and Immigration Policies on International Migration." *Migration Studies* 1(1):47–74.

Ottaviano, Gianmarco I. P., and Giovanni Peri. 2012. "Rethinking the Effect of Immigration on Wages." *Journal of the European Economic Association* 10(1):152–97.

Pandya, Sonal S. 2014. *Trading Spaces: Foreign Direct Investment Regulation, 1970–2000*. Cambridge: Cambridge University Press.

Pellikaan, Huib, Sarah L. de Lange, and Tom Van der Meer. 2007. "Fortuyn's Legacy: Party System Change in the Netherlands." *Comparative European Politics* 5(3):282–302.

Peters, Margaret E. 2014*a*. "Immigration, Delegation and International Law." Working Paper, Yale University.

Peters, Margaret E. 2014*b*. "Trade, Foreign Direct Investment and Immigration Policy Making in the US." *International Organization* 68(4):811–44.

Peters, Margaret E. 2015. "Open Trade, Closed Borders: Immigration in the Era of Globalization." *World Politics* 67(1):114–54.

Peters, Margaret E., and Alexander M. Tahk. 2010. "Are Policy Makers Out of Touch with Their Constituencies When It Comes to Immigration?" In *International Political Economy Society Annual Conference*. Cambridge, MA.

Polanyi, Karl. 1944. *The Great Transformation: The Political and Economic Origins of Our Time*. New York: Rinehart.

Poole, Keith T. 2009. "1st–101st Senate Roll Call Data." http://voteview.com/. Accessed January 9, 2010.

Poole, Keith T., and Jeff Lewis. 2009. "109th–110th Senate Roll Call Data." http://voteview.com/. Accessed January 9, 2010.

Poole, Keith T., and Nolan McCarty. 2009. "102nd–108th Senate Roll Call Data." http://voteview.com/. Accessed January 9, 2010.

Przeworski, Adam, et al. 2013. "Political Institutions and Political Events (PIPE) Data Set." https://sites.google.com/a/nyu.edu/adam-przeworski/home/data. Accessed December 15, 2014.

Quincy, Josiah. 1896. "Address by Mayor Quincy of Boston." *Transactions of the New England Cotton Manufacturers' Association* 60:65–67.

Rajan, Raghuram G., and Luigi Zingales. 2003. "The Great Reversals: The Politics of Financial Development in the Twentieth Century." *Journal of Financial Economics* 69:5–50.

Ratha, Dilip, and Zhimei Xu. 2008. *Migration and Remittances Factbook 2008*. Washington, DC: The World Bank.

Resnick, Jason. 2006. "Labor Shortage Woes Continue." *Western Grower and Shipper* (December):31–33.

Rigg, Jonathan. 1988. "Singapore and the Recession of 1985." *Asian Survey*, 28(3):340–52.

Rodan, Gary. 2004. "International Capital, Singapore's State Companies, and Security." *Critical Asian Studies* 36(3):479–99.

Rogers, Robert P. 2009. *An Economic History of the American Steel Industry*. London: Routledge.

Roodenburg, H., R. Euwals, and H. T. Rele. 2003. *Immigration and the Dutch Economy*. The Hague: CPB Netherlands Bureau for Economic Policy Analysis.

Rosenblum, Marc R., and Idean Salehyan. 2004. "Norms and Interests in US Asylum Enforcement." *Journal of Peace Research* 41(6):677–97.

Ruggie, John Gerard. 1982. "International Regimes, Transactions, and Change: Embedded Liberalism in the Postwar Economic Order." *International Organization* 36(2):379–415.

Ruggles, Steven, J. Trent Alexander, Katie Genadek, Ronald Goeken, Matthew B. Schroeder, and Matthew Sobek. 2010. *Integrated Public Use Microdata Series: Version 5.0 [Machine-readable database]*. Minneapolis: University of Minnesota.

Ruhs, Martin. 2013. *The Price of Rights: Regulating International Labor Migration*. Princeton, NJ: Princeton University Press.

Sachs, Richard C. 2003. "Hearings in the US Senate: A Guide for Preparation and Procedure." Congressional Research Service, the Library of Congress.

Salehyan, Idean. 2008. "The Externalities of Civil Strife: Refugees as a Source of International Conflict." *American Journal of Political Science* 52(4): 787–801.

Salehyan, Idean, and Kristian Skrede Gleditsch. 2006. "Refugees and the Spread of Civil War." *International Organization* 60(2):335–66.

Sarkees, Meredith Reid, and Frank Wayman. 2010. *Resort to War: 1816–2007*. Washington DC: CQ Press.

Saxton, A. 1971. *The Indispensable Enemy: Labor and the Anti-Chinese Movement in California*. Berkeley: University of California Press.

Schott, Peter K. 2010. "U.S. Manufacturing Exports and Imports by SIC or NAICS Category and Partner Country, 1972 to 2005." Unpublished manuscript. Yale School of Management.

Seawright, Jason, and John Gerring. 2008. "Case Selection Techniques in Case Study Research: A Menu of Qualitative and Quantitative Options." *Political Research Quarterly* 61(2):294–308.

Shanmugaratnam, Tharman. 2013 "A Better Singapore: Quality Growth, an Inclusive Society, Budget Speech Delivered in Parliament 25 February 2013," transcript, *Budget 2014 Singapore*. http://www.singaporebudget.gov.sg/budget_2013/budget_speech.html. Accessed July 24, 2014.

Shih, Victor. 2009. "Tools of Survival: Sovereign Wealth Funds in Singapore and China." *Geopolitics* 14(2):328–44.

Sim, Isabel, Steen Thomsen, and Gerard Yeong. 2014. "The State as Shareholder: The Case of Singapore." Technical report. Centre for Governance, Institutions & Organisations, NUS Business School, Singapore.

Simonds, Paul. 2007. "Only in America." *Western Grower and Shipper*. (June):10–11.

Singapore. Various Years. *Report on the Census of Industrial Production*. Singapore: Dept. of Statistics.

Singapore Democratic Party. 2013. "Building a People: Sound Policies for a Secure Future." http://yoursdp.org/publ/sdp_39_s_alternateives/our_population/launch_of_sdp_39_s_quote_building_a_people_sound_polices_for_a_secure_fit ure_quot/44-1-0-1385. Accessed June 2, 2013.

Singer, David Andrew. 2010. "Migrant Remittances and Exchange Rate Regimes in the Developing World." *American Political Science Review* 104(2):307–23.

Smith, J. P., and B. Edmonston. 1997. *The New Americans: Economic, Demographic, and Fiscal Effects of Immigration*. Washington, DC: National Academies Press.

Smith, Thomas Russell. 1944. *Cotton Textile Industry of Fall River, Massachusetts*. New York: King's Crown Press.

Sociaal-Economische Raad. 2013. "The Power of Consultation: The Dutch Consultative Economy Explained." https://www.ser.nl/en/~/media/files/internet/talen/engels/brochure/informatiebrochure-power-consultation-en.ashx. Accessed March 31, 2015.

Soon, Teck-Wong, and William A. Stoever. 1996. "Foreign Investment and Economic Development in Singapore: A Policy Oriented Approach." *Journal of Developing Areas* 30(3):317–40.

Steinberg, David A., and Krishan Malhotra. 2014. "The Effect of Authoritarian Regime Type on Exchange Rate Policy." *World Politics* 66(3):491–529.

Stopford, John M. 1974. "The Origins of British-Based Multinational Manufacturing Enterprises." *Business History Review* 48(3):303–35.

Strange, Susan. 1996. *The Retreat of the State: The Diffusion of Power in the World Economy*. New York: Cambridge University Press.

Sweezy, Alan R. 1938. "The Amoskeag Manufacturing Company." *Quarterly Journal of Economics* 52(3):473–512.

Talbert, Jeffery C., Bryan D. Jones, and Frank R. Baumgartner. 1995. "Nonlegislative Hearings and Policy Change in Congress." *American Journal of Political Science* 39(2):383–405.

Tan, Boon Seng. 2002. "Why It Might Be Difficult for the Government to Withdraw from Business." Technical report. http://www.singapore-window.org/sw02/020210gl.htm. Accessed March 24, 2015.

Thies, Cameron G. 2002. "A Pragmatic Guide to Qualitative Historical Analysis in the Study of International Relations." *International Studies Perspectives* 3(4):351–72.

Tichenor, Daniel J. 1994. "The Politics of Immigration Reform in the United States, 1981–1990." *Polity* 26(3):333–62.

Tichenor, Daniel J. 2002. *Dividing Lines: The Politics of Immigration Control in America*. Princeton, NJ: Princeton University Press.

Tilly, Charles. 1992. *Coercion, Capital, and European States, AD 990–1990*. Cambridge, MA: Blackwell.

Timmer, Ashley S., and Jeffrey G. Williamson. 1996. "Racism, Xenophobia or Markets? The Political Economy of Immigration Policy Prior to the Thirties." Working Paper 5867. National Bureau of Economic Research.

Timmer, Ashley S., and Jeffrey G. Williamson. 1998. "Immigration Policy prior to the 1930s: Labor Markets, Policy Interactions, and Globalization Backlash." *Population and Development Review* 24(4):739–71.

Toh, Mun Heng. 1989. "The Post-recessionary Singapore Economy: Performance and Prospects." *Southeast Asian Affairs* 16:299–314.

Toh, Mun Heng. 1998. "The Construction Industry: Restructuring for Competitiveness." In *Competitiveness of the Singapore Economy: A Strategic Perspective*, ed. Mun Heng Toh and Kong Yam Tan, 143–77. Singapore: Singapore University Press.

UNHCR. 2016. "Syrian Regional Refugee Response." http://data.unhcr.org/syrian refugees/regional.php. Accessed March 29, 2016.

United Nations Development Program. 2009. *Human Development Report*. New York: United Nations.

US Census Bureau. 2012. "Agriculture." In *Statistical Abstract of the United States*. Washington, DC: US Census Bureau.

US Chamber of Commerce. 2015. "Board of Directors." https://www.uschamber. com/about-us/board-directors. Accessed May 29, 2015.

US Commissioner of Labor. 1899. *Thirteenth Annual Report (1898): Hand and Machine Labor*. Washington, DC: US Government Printing Office.

van Amersfoort, H., and R. Penninx. 1994. "Regulating Migration in Europe: The Dutch Experience, 1960–92." *Annals of the American Academy of Political and Social Science* 534:133–46.

van Der Slik, Jack R., and Thomas C. Stenger. 1977. "Citizen Witnesses before Congressional Committees." *Political Science Quarterly* 92(3):465–85.

van Evera, Stephen. 1997. *Guide to Methods for Students of Political Science*. Ithaca, NY: Cornell University Press.

van Kersbergen, Kees, and André Krouwel. 2008. "A Double-Edged Sword! The Dutch Centre-Right and the 'Foreigners Issue'?" *Journal of European Public Policy* 15(3):398–414.

van Kessel, Stijn. 2011. "Explaining the Electoral Performance of Populist Parties: The Netherlands as a Case Study." *Perspectives on European Politics and Society* 12(1):68–88.

van Rijckeghem, Willy. 1982. "Benelux". In *The European Economy: Growth and Crisis*, ed. Andrea Boltho, 581–609. Oxford: Oxford University Press.

van Zanden, Jan L. 1998. *The Economic History of the Netherlands 1914–1995: A Small Open Economy in the 'Long' Twentieth Century*. London: Routledge.

Visser, Jelle, and Anton Hemerijck. 1997. 'A Dutch Miracle': Job Growth, Welfare Reform and Corporatism in the Netherlands. Amsterdam: Amsterdam University Press.

Voerman, Gerrit, and Paul Lucardie. 1992. "The Extreme Right in the Netherlands: The Centrists and Their Radical Rivals." European Journal of Political Research 22:35–54.

von Stein, Jana. 2005. "Do Treaties Constrain or Screen? Selection Bias and Treaty Compliance." American Political Science Review 99(4):611–22.

Walker, Jack L. 1983. "The Origins and Maintenance of Interest Groups in America." American Political Science Review 77(2):390–406.

Wallace, Jeremy L. 2014. Cities and Stability: Urbanization, Redistribution, and Regime Survival in China. Oxford: Oxford University Press.

Walmsley, Herbert. 1904. "President's Address." Transactions of the New England Cotton Manufacturers' Association 76.

Waterfield, Bruno. 2015. "Greece's Defence Minister Threatens to Send Migrants Including Jihadists to Western Europe." Telegraph. http://www.telegraph.co.uk/news/worldnews/islamic-state/11459675/Greeces-defence-minister-threatens-to-send-migrants-including-jihadists-to-Western-Europe.html. Accessed September 30, 2015.

Watson, C. Maxwell, Bas B. Bakker, Jan Kees Martijn, and Ioannis Halikias. 1999. The Netherlands: Transforming a Market Economy. Washington, DC: International Monetary Fund.

Whatley, W. C. 1983. "Labor for the Picking: The New Deal in the South." Journal of Economic History 43(4):905–29.

White, William. 2008. "Economic History of Tractors in the United States". In EH.net Encyclopedia, ed. Robert Whaples. http://eh.net/encyclopedia/economic-history-of-tractors-in-the-united-states/. Accessed April 14, 2015.

Wilbur, Edward. 1898. "Southern Cotton Mills and Cotton Manufacturing." Transactions of the New England Cotton Manufacturers' Association 65.

Wilkins, Mira. 1970. The Emergence of Multinational Enterprise: American Business Abroad from the Colonial Era to 1914. Cambridge, MA: Harvard University Press.

Wong, D. 1996. "Foreign Domestic Workers in Singapore." Asia and Pacific Migration Journal 5(1):117–38.

Wong, Poh Kam. 1998. "Upgrading Singapore's Manufacturing Industry." In Competitiveness of the Singapore Economy: A Strategic Perspective, ed. Mun Heng Toh and Kong Yam Tan, 115–42. Singapore: Singapore University Press.

World Bank. 2014. "GDP per Capita (current US$)." http://data.worldbank.org/indicator/NY.GDP.PCAP.CD. Accessed August 10, 2014.

World Bank Group. 2012. "World Development Indicators 2012." www.worldbank.org/data. Accessed September 22, 2014.

Wright, G. 1981. "Cheap Labor and Southern Textiles, 1880–1930." Quarterly Journal of Economics 96(4):605–29.

Wright, Matthew. 2009. "'Mordacious Years': Socio-economic Aspects and Outcomes of New Zealand's Experience in the Great Depression." Reserve Bank of New Zealand: Bulletin 72(3):43.

Yates, JoAnne. 1993. *Control through Communication: The Rise of System in American Management*. Baltimore: John Hopkins University Press.

Ye Hee Lee, Michelle. 2015. "Donald Trump's False Comments Connecting Mexican Immigrants and Crime." *Washington Post*. http://www.washingtonpost.com/blogs/fact-checker/wp/2015/07/08/donald-trumps-false-comments-connecting-mexican-immigrants-and-crime/. Accessed September 21, 2015.

Zolberg, Aristide R. 1978. "International Migration Policies in a Changing World System". In *Human Migration: Patterns and Policies*, ed. William H. McNeill and Ruth S. Adams, 241–86. Bloomington: Indiana University Press.

Zolberg, Aristide R. 1989. "The Next Waves: Migration Theory for a Changing World." *International Migration Review* 23(3):403–30.

Zolberg, Aristide R. 2006. *A Nation by Design: Immigration Policy in the Fashioning of America*. Cambridge, MA: Harvard University Press.

Zorlu, A., and J. Hartog. 2002. "Migration and Immigrants: The Case of The Netherlands." *Studies and Comments*, 1:119–40.

Index